Does The Bible Support Catholic Beliefs?

First printing 2006
Printed in the United States of America
BookSurge Publishing Company

To order additional copies, please contact us.
BookSurge, LLC
www.booksurge.com
1-866-308-6235
orders@booksurge.com

DAVID P. LANG, EDITOR

DOES THE BIBLE SUPPORT CATHOLIC BELIEFS?

A Scriptural Defense of Catholic Doctrines

BookSurge Publishing Company
2006

Does The Bible Support Catholic Beliefs?

CONTENTS

Introduction. *The Purpose of this Book*   *xvii*
(David P. Lang)

Chapter 1. *The Sources of Divine Revelation*   *1*
(Michael J. Kiessling)

Chapter 2. *The Church, the Papacy, and Apostolic Succession*   *43*
(David L. Vise)

Chapter 3. *The Holy Trinity*   *57*
(Rev. David J. Mullen)

Chapter 4. *Justification and Salvation*   *79*
(Rev. Paul L. Rothermel)

Chapter 5. *The Sacraments of Baptism and Confirmation*   *119*
(David P. Lang)

Chapter 6. *The Sacrifice of the Mass and the Holy Eucharist*   *133*
(Michael J. Kiessling)

Chapter 7. *The Ordained Priesthood*   *157*
(I) The Ordained Priesthood was Instituted by Christ
(David P. Lang)
(II) The Ordained Priesthood is Restricted to Men
(David P. Lang)
(III) The Discipline of Celibacy
(Rev. David J. Mullen)

Chapter 8. *The Sacraments of Penance and Anointing of the Sick*   *191*
(David P. Lang)

Chapter 9. *The Sacrament of Matrimony*   *203*
(I) Matrimony is a Sacrament
(David P. Lang)
(II) The Attributes of Marriage
(Andrew J. Tardiff)

Chapter 10. *The Intercession of Saints and Angels*   *223*
(I) In the Light of Jewish Scripture and Tradition
(Roy H. Schoeman)
(II) An Explanation from the New Testament
(Susan R. Lloyd)

Chapter 11. *Marian Dogmas*   *245*
(Rev. Francisco J. Anzoategui Peiro)

Chapter 12. *The Last Things*   *275*
(Montague Brown)

Endnotes.   299

DEDICATION

In honor of St. Jerome and St. Francis de Sales

EDITOR'S FOREWORD

I hereby express my deep thanks to the other nine contributing authors who made this project possible. I think I can speak for all of us when I assert that, in the course of writing our respective essays, we have experienced the reality of those famous words exclaimed by the two disciples reflecting on their encounter with our Lord Jesus Christ on the road to Emmaus in Luke 24:32: "Did not our hearts burn within us while he talked to us on the road, while he opened to us the scriptures?" Enkindled with a similar fervor, we have undertaken to respond to the Prince of the Apostles' exhortation in 1 Peter 3:15 (whatever may be our shortcomings in measuring up to the demands of such a noble mission): "Always be prepared to make a defense to any one who calls you to account for the hope that is in you, yet do it with gentleness and reverence." Each writer has labored prayerfully to bring to this task the resources and insights deemed necessary for its accomplishment. Secondary sources are sometimes used, but our primary source has been, beyond comparison, the sacred text itself.

In order that our readers might gain some acquaintance with us, I am including here brief biographical sketches of all ten contributors (listed in alphabetical order).

Rev. Francisco J. Anzoategui Peiro was born in Mexico, graduated from Catholic Theological Union in Chicago, and was ordained a Xaverian Missionary Priest on the Feast of the Immaculate Heart of Mary in June of 1988. Better known as "Father Paco", he has a Charismatic gift for teaching, preaching, and healing. He has appeared a number of times on EWTN with his program "The Treasure of our Faith", and as an anchor for the Papal visits to Mexico and Latin America. He has served as host of many radio shows in the Archdiocese of Boston, where he was recently incardinated. He was the first spiritual director for the "Asociación Nuestra Señora de las Américas", an organization that promotes devotion to Our Lady among Hispanics. His love for the Blessed Mother is clearly evident in his having led many pilgrimages to Marian shrines around the world. He has translated into English the narratives of the apparitions of Our Lady of Guadalupe in order to promote her devotion among people in America. His gift of languages has helped him to bring the message of Christ and His Mother to many countries with his preaching – including Canada, Italy, Spain, the Azores in Portugal, Puerto Rico, the Dominican Republic, and his native Mexico. Currently he serves as a parish priest at Saint Rose of Lima Parish in Chelsea, Massachusetts.

Montague Brown holds a Ph.D. degree in philosophy from Boston College and an A.B. degree in English Literature from the University of California at Berkeley. For many years, he has been a professor of philosophy at Saint Anselm College in New Hampshire. He is a member of several professional philosophical societies and several honor societies. Dr. Brown is the author of the four books *The Romance of Reason: An Adventure in the Thought of Thomas Aquinas* (St. Bede's Publications, 1993), *The Quest for Moral Foundations* (Georgetown University Press, 1996), *The One-Minute Philosopher* (Sophia Institute Press, 2001), and *Half-Truths* (Sophia Institute Press, 2003). He has had numerous articles published in such philosophical journals as *International Philosophical Quarterly*, *The New Blackfriars*, *The Thomist*, *American Catholic Philosophical Quarterly*, and *The Chesterton Review*. He has also given presentations at many conferences, which have published his papers under their *Proceedings*. He is married and the father of four children.

Michael J. Kiessling was a seminarian at St. John's Seminary in the Archdiocese of Boston, having also studied theology at Washington Theological Union. He holds a master's degree in theology/pastoral ministry, and teaches the Catholic Faith at a Catholic middle school. He is now married and the father of two children.

David P. Lang holds Ph.D. degrees in both philosophy (Boston College) and mathematics (Northeastern University) – two subjects he has taught on the college level for many years. He is the author of the books *Why Matter Matters: Philosophical and Scriptural Reflections on the Sacraments* (Our Sunday Visitor Press, 2002) and *Short Circuit to God* (Francis Books, 2003), as well as articles that have appeared in journals of philosophy and theology such as *Homiletic and Pastoral Review*, *Medieval Philosophy and Theology*, *Laval théologique et philosophique*, *Faith and Reason*, *Peripatetikos*, *Lyceum*, and *Social Justice Review*.

Susan R. Lloyd was born into a large Catholic family. She was educated in public and parochial schools and in a parent-run catechetical center. For over ten years, she has contributed columns to Catholic periodicals, and in 2000 received an award from the Catholic Press Association. Her first book, titled *Please Don't Drink the Holy Water! Homeschool Days, Rosary Nights and other Near Occasions of Sin* (Sophia Institute Press, 2004), is about the humorous side of modern Catholic family life. She holds a Bachelor of Arts degree from Thomas More College of Liberal Arts in Merrimack, New Hampshire, and an M.O.M. degree from her husband Greg and six home-schooled daughters.

Rev. David J. Mullen is a priest of the Archdiocese of Boston, having been ordained in 1982. Prior to completing his Master of Divinity studies at St. John Seminary in Brighton, Massachusetts, he received his Bachelor of Arts degree from Boston College. Fr. Mullen is now pastor of St. Brendan Parish in Bellingham, Massachusetts. For many years, he has been a pro-life and pro-family activist, debater, and speaker. Fr. Mullen is a long-standing member of the Board of Directors of Massachusetts Citizens For Life. Besides his priestly work and biblical studies, he has interests in apologetics, medical ethics, history, Russian music, nutrition, swimming, weightlifting, and his nine nieces and nephews.

Rev. Paul L. Rothermel is a happy convert to the Catholic Faith, having experienced a pious Protestant upbringing in the Reformed church of the Pennsylvania Dutch. He graduated from the Moody Bible Institute of Chicago with a diploma in Pastoral Training with a Greek Emphasis. Shortly thereafter, he graduated with a Bachelor of Arts degree in history from the Anabaptist Elizabethtown College, where he was known for his zeal as an evangelical Christian, active in the Inter-Varsity Christian Fellowship. In 1982, Paul completed his preparations for Protestant ministry, graduating from Trinity Evangelical Divinity School with a Master of Arts degree ("summa cum laude") in New Testament Studies. That same year, after much study and prayer, against the ardent desires and strong advice of his friends and relatives, he officially converted to the Catholic Faith. After taking some time to find his way within the unique world of the Roman Catholic Church, he set his focus on priesthood and went on to earn two more seminary degrees: a Master of Divinity degree and a Master of Theology degree, both from St. Charles Borromeo Seminary in Philadelphia. He was ordained to the priesthood in 1994. Currently, Father Paul serves as a parish priest within the Diocese of Allentown, Pennsylvania. For some years, he has been helping to establish and guide an apologetics club (the Truth-In-Religion Group) within the Lehigh Valley.

Roy H. Schoeman was born and raised Jewish in a suburb of New York City. He received a Bachelor of Science degree from M.I.T. and an M.B.A. ("magna cum laude") from Harvard Business School, where he then joined the faculty and taught. Following an unexpected and dramatic conversion to Christ and the Catholic Church, he began to devote more of his energies to religion. He became Assistant Producer and host of a talk show on Boston Catholic Television (*Fatima Today*). He has written a number of articles on the Catholic Faith and on Judaism in the light of Catholic revelation. His book-length study of the meaning and role of Judaism in God's plan for the salvation of all mankind is titled *Salvation is from the Jews* (Ignatius Press, 2003).

Andrew J. Tardiff holds a Ph.D. degree in philosophy from the International Academy of Philosophy in Liechtenstein. He teaches moral theology at Bishop Hendricken High School in Warwick, Rhode Island. Dr. Tardiff is married and the father of seven children.

David L. Vise was born and grew up in Lima, Peru. He was baptized and made his first Holy Communion in Miraculous Medal Church in Miraflores, a suburb of Lima. He started his college education at the Pontifical Catholic University of Peru in Lima. He left Peru at the age of twenty to continue his college studies in the United States. He received his Bachelor of Science degree in Civil Engineering from Northeastern University in Boston, and completed his coursework for the Master's Degree in Construction Engineering and Project Management at M.I.T. He has been practicing his profession for many years in Massachusetts.

His writing has been published in *Social Justice Review*. He has been married to his wife Margaret for well over twenty years and is the father of five children.

Finally, I thank my good friend **Francis B. Kelly**, who prayerfully suggested that we seek the heavenly intercession of St. Jerome and St. Francis de Sales for the writing and publication of this work of scriptural apologetics.

INTRODUCTION
The Purpose of this Book

With this book, the authors hope to convince prospective readers of the solid scriptural foundations for the truths of the Catholic Faith. We are striving to persuade Protestants that Catholicism does have profound roots in Sacred Scripture and to inculcate in Catholics a deeper appreciation of the biblical basis for Catholic beliefs. Each essay constitutes a diligent effort by its author to manifest the biblical support for the Catholic doctrine discussed therein.

Of course, we do not contend that every dogma proposed by the Church for our assent can be apodictically deduced by simple recourse to the pages of Holy Writ, unmediated by any magisterial authority. Such a quasi-rationalistic view is fatally ambitious, and would itself deny the Catholic teaching that our knowledge of the truths of divine revelation derives from Sacred Tradition along with Sacred Scripture.

What we *do* claim, though, is that every doctrine taught by the Church can be defended on scriptural grounds firmer than those alleged to prove its negation. A weighty defense, after all, is not necessarily a syllogistic demonstration. In other words, we aim to show the reader that, at the very least, the Catholic Church is **not** *un*biblical, whereas the views of some adherents of "Bible churches" ironically fail to satisfy their own scriptural litmus test. If this goal were achieved, it would go a long way toward disarming the critic.

The authors must be forthright in professing from the outset that we subscribe, in accordance with the official position of the Catholic Church, to the **absolute** inerrancy of Sacred Scripture. The Church teaches that the Bible is the inspired word of God, whose principal Author is the Holy Spirit Himself. Now, on purely metaphysical grounds, any book composed under the direction of the Holy Spirit cannot contain the slightest mistake of any kind. God is omniscient, and can neither be deceived nor deceive.

It will not do to distinguish between truths of faith and morality necessary for salvation (which are admittedly infallibly expounded), as opposed to matters of science and history (about which the secondary human authors of the Bible could supposedly err). Yes, the primary purpose of Scripture is to teach us how to go to heaven, rather than to inform us "how the heavens go" – as the aphoristic cliché puts it. Nevertheless, this attempt at an end-run around the problem of inerrancy places us on a perilous slippery slope toward total skepticism. For some matters of science and history are inextricably bound up with truths of faith necessary for our salvation (e.g., the celestial marvels reported in the Gospel infancy narratives); hence, it is impossible to draw a line that clearly demarcates the two spheres.

To vindicate our thesis on this controversial issue, let us appeal to key excerpts from three popes. The following citations are taken from Denziger's *The Sources of Catholic Dogma*.

(1) Pope Leo XIII's encyclical *Providentissimus Deus* on the study of Holy Scripture (D. 1950): "It can happen, indeed, that transcribers in copying manuscripts do so incorrectly. This is to be considered carefully and is not to be admitted readily, except in those passages where it has been properly demonstrated; it can also happen that the true sense of some passage remains ambiguous; the best rules of interpretation will contribute much toward the solution of this problem; but it would be entirely wrong either to confine inspiration only to some parts of Sacred Scripture, or to concede that the sacred author himself has erred. For the method of those is not to be tolerated, who extricated themselves from these difficulties by readily granting that divine inspiration pertains to matters of faith and morals, and nothing more."

(2) Pope St. Pius X's decree *Lamentabili Sane*, which deals with the errors of the Modernists, condemns the following proposition (D. 2011): "Divine inspiration does not so extend to all Sacred Scripture that it fortifies each and every part of it against all error."

(3) Pope Pius XII's encyclical *Divino Afflante Spiritu* on Holy Scripture (D. 2294): "This same investigation has also proven this clearly, that the people of Israel were especially pre-eminent among the rest of the ancient nations of the Orient in writing history properly, both because of the antiquity and the faithful recountal of events; which indeed, is surely the effect of divine inspiration, and the result of the special purpose of biblical history which pertains to religion. Indeed, let no one who has a right

understanding of Biblical inspiration be surprised that among the Sacred Writers, as among the other ancients, certain definite ways of explaining and narrating are found; certain kinds of idioms especially appropriate to Semitic languages, so called *approximations*, and certain hyperbolic methods of speaking, yes, sometimes even paradoxes by which events are more firmly impressed upon the mind.... Therefore, let the Catholic exegete, in order to satisfy the present day needs of Biblical matters, in explaining Sacred Scripture, and in showing and proving it free of all error, prudently use this aid, to inquire how the form of expression and the kind of literature employed by the Sacred writer, contribute to a true and genuine interpretation; and let him be convinced that this part of his office cannot be neglected without great harm to Catholic exegesis. For not uncommonly – to touch upon one thing only – when some propose by way of rebuke that the Sacred Authors have strayed away from historical truth, or have not reported events accurately, it is found to be a question of nothing other than the customary natural methods of the ancients in speaking and narrating, which in the mutual intercourse among men were regularly employed, and in fact were employed in accord with a permissible and common practice. Therefore, intellectual honesty requires that when these matters are found in divine speech which is expressed for man in human words, they be not charged more with error than when they are uttered in the daily use of life. Therefore, by a knowledge and accurate appraisal of the modes and skills of speaking and writing among the ancients, many problems will be possible of solution, which are raised against the truth and historical trustworthiness of the divine Scripture; and no less fittingly will such study contribute to a fuller and clearer understanding of the mind of the Sacred Writer."

In short, the Holy Spirit, who as the principal Author of the Bible cannot make any mistakes whatsoever, communicates this divine immunity from all error to His inspired human instruments. Thus, as the learned pontiffs explain, any apparent discrepancies from modern reckonings (assuming that the latter are truly accurate) can be attributed either to copyists' flaws (rarely) or to the hyperbolic idioms of speech customary at the time.

But it does not follow that the contributors to this book are so-called "Fundamentalists". In keeping with traditional principles of Catholic hermeneutics, we accept the literal truth of everything that is meant to be taken literally in the Bible, such as the events recorded in what are evidently intended as historical books. Certain books, however, exhibit literary genres that are plainly not being presented as history or as prophecy about the future. Obviously, metaphor abounds in biblical books of prayer (the Psalms) and poetry (Song of Solomon). Moreover, much of the imagery and numerology in the Bible's apocalyptic literature (e.g., the books of Daniel and Revelation) should probably be construed symbolically. Even the parables and other sayings of our Lord display the literary devices of creative invention and exaggeration for the sake of effect, in order to impress lessons in the minds and hearts of the listeners.

In sum, we maintain with the Church that the twin extremes of hypercritical skepticism and naïve fundamentalism must be assiduously avoided. Only via a humble heart and an open mind can we reap the rich harvest of truth with which God desires to fill us through reading His inspired word.

At this juncture, the question of methodology arises. How in practice do we implement our intention to unearth the treasures of truth in the Bible for the reader of humble heart and open mind? For one thing, we eschew an excessively analytic approach, which (possibly becoming bogged down or enmeshed in the technicalities of ancient language translation and form criticism) may never rise to the contemplative heights of divine truth insofar as it is knowable to us wayfarers in this life on earth. To the maximum extent feasible, we want to let Sacred Writ, the Word of God, speak for itself to us, since we are not worthy to loosen it from its moorings in the Old and New Testaments. Thus, as faithful servants of the Word, we have the duty to *stitch together* relevant scriptural passages into a coherent whole that reveals or uncovers the magnificent tapestry of truth that is already present in the Bible, awaiting our discovery. This synthetic method, applied to the defense of a particular Catholic doctrine, often entails an excursion through many books of the Bible in a search for *types* (prefiguring persons and events) in the Old Testament that foreshadow corresponding persons and events in the New Testament. In invoking such crucial typology, we rely heavily on the so-called "spiritual sense" of Scripture. Based on the literal sense of the text's verbal surface, the spiritual sense embraces hidden meanings through its employment of living symbolism (persons and deeds) to shed anticipatory light on later fulfillments. Hence, this panoramic sweep of Scripture culminates in endowing the reader with the immediate facility to "connect the dots" – to stand back and exclaim with an insightful gasp: "I was blind but now I **see**!" (John 9:25)

CHAPTER ONE

Sources of Divine Revelation: Scripture, Tradition, and the Magisterium

Introduction

The Catholic Church has perpetually believed and taught that God has transmitted His revelation to us in two basic ways: Sacred Scripture and Sacred Tradition. These two media have been faithfully interpreted and handed down to us by the Apostles and their successors, the bishops. As the Second Vatican Council so eloquently puts it:

> Sacred Tradition and sacred Scripture, then, are bound closely together, and communicate one with the other. For both of them, flowing out from the same divine wellspring, come together in some fashion to form one thing, and move towards the same goal. Sacred Scripture is the speech of God as it is put down in writing under the breath of the Holy Spirit, and Tradition transmits in its entirety the Word of God which has been entrusted to the apostles by Christ the Lord and the Holy Spirit. It transmits it to the successors of the apostles so that, enlightened by the Spirit of truth, they may faithfully preserve, expound and spread it abroad by their preaching. Thus it comes about that the Church of God does not draw her certainty about all revealed truths from the Holy Scriptures alone. Hence, both Scripture and Tradition must be accepted and honored with equal feelings of devotion and reverence. (*Dei Verbum* 2:9)

At a time when the New Testament had not yet been written, the Apostles themselves believed and held to an understanding of the transmission of God's revelation that included reverence for what was handed down both in writing and by oral transmission. St. Paul exhorts St. Timothy (in 2

Timothy 3:14-15): "But as for you, continue in what you have learned and have firmly believed, knowing from whom you learned it and how from childhood you have been acquainted with the sacred writings which are able to instruct you for salvation through faith in Christ Jesus." And he also says to the Thessalonians: "So then, brethren, stand firm and hold to the traditions which you were taught by us, either by word of mouth or by letter" (2 Thessalonians 2:15).

St. John himself prefers oral communication in passing down Revelation, when he says in 2 John 12: "Though I have much to write to you, I would rather not use paper and ink, but I hope to come to see you and talk with you face to face, so that our joy may be complete." He reiterates this point in 3 John 13: "I had much to write to you, but I would rather not write with pen and ink; I hope to see you soon, and we will talk together face to face."

In Catholic theology, there is a distinction between material and formal sufficiency with regard to Sacred Scripture. It is a well-respected position among Catholics that the Scriptures are materially sufficient; we might formulate this thesis as they contain everything necessary for a sure theological foundation. But no orthodox Catholic maintains that the Scriptures are formally sufficient, because they need to be interpreted. The Scriptures do not interpret themselves: *that* is left to the Church with the assistance of the Holy Spirit. On this topic Mark P. Shea writes:

> What's the difference between material and formal sufficiency? Simply put, it is the difference between having a big enough pile of bricks to build a house and having a house made of bricks. Material sufficiency means that all the bricks necessary to build doctrine is there in Scripture. However, it also teaches that since the meaning of Scripture is not always clear and that sometimes a doctrine is implied rather than explicit, other things besides Scripture have been handed to us from the apostles: things like Sacred Tradition (which is the mortar that holds the bricks together in the right order and position) and Magisterium or teaching authority of the Church (which is the trowel in the hand of the Master Builder). Taken together, these things – Sacred Scripture, Sacred Tradition, and the

Magisterium – are formally sufficient for knowing the revealed truth of God. (Shea, 181)

Sacred Scripture

Divine Inspiration

It is important to remember that in Catholic theology the technical term "inspiration" refers only to the Holy Scriptures and their composition. The term does not in any way refer to the documents composed by the councils of the Church. While the documents of official Church councils hold certain authority, they do not have the position of being "inspired". They function as authoritative explanations of Sacred Scripture and Sacred Tradition so as to "maintain the unity of the Spirit," because "there is one body and one Spirit, just as you were called to the one hope that belongs to your call, one Lord, one faith, one baptism" (Ephesians 4:3-5).

The Holy Scriptures are the inspired Word of God, and have God as their principal author: "To compose the sacred books, God chose certain men who, all the while he employed them in this task, made full use of their powers and faculties so that, though he acted in them and by them, it was as true authors that they consigned to writing whatever he wanted written, and no more." (*Dei Verbum* 3:11) God has acted in and through human mediums in the composition of the sacred text, and has done so in a manner that preserves the human authors as real human authors. Any understanding of biblical inspiration in which the human authors are mere passive instruments, or whose personality, writing style, cultural influence, personal diction, etc., are suspended from the composition of the sacred text, has been rejected by the Church.

The inspiration of the Bible must, however, be seen as one aspect of that divine providence which is leading men to salvation through Jesus Christ. God's supernatural revelation took place in the history of Israel and in the life of Christ before it was recorded in the pages of Scripture. The Bible then is the record of progressive revelation, written according to the modes of writing prevalent in the ancient Near East at the time. Consequently, it is the fruit of a long oral and written tradition in which early texts were reinterpreted, glossed, and reorganized

> before reaching the state in which we read them today.... By
> His special providence God guided this entire process, whether
> it involved action, speech, or writing. Such divine guidance
> may fittingly be called inspiration, since inspiration is simply
> any impulse brought to bear upon an intelligent creature from
> without. (Forestell, 383)

At the same time, the Bible is not reducible to a set of human books containing mankind's religious desires and aspirations. The Holy Spirit guided its entire composition, while, at the same time, preserving the freedom of the human authors as true human authors. The second letter of St. Peter teaches us that the Scriptures are no ordinary work of human activity: "First of all you must understand this, that no prophecy of scripture is a matter of one's own personal interpretation, because no prophecy ever came by the impulse of man, but men moved by the Holy Spirit spoke from God" (2 Peter 1:20-21; see also 2 Peter 3:15-16).

The early fathers of the Church acknowledged the nature of the Holy Scriptures as inspired by the Holy Spirit. Pope St. Clement of Rome, writing in 96 A.D., encouraged his flock: "Look carefully into the Scriptures, which are the true utterances of the Holy Spirit" (Bercot, 601). We see in this statement the early father's belief in the Scriptures as being exposited under the direction of God. Athenagoras, in 175 A.D., placed emphasis on the action of God upon the human person who speaks God's words. He wrote: "Prophets were lifted in ecstasy above the natural operations of their minds by the impulse of the Divine Spirit, and they spoke things with which they were inspired. The Spirit operated through them just as a flute player breathes into a flute" (Bercot, 602). Theophilus (180 A.D.) spoke of the writers of Holy Scripture as operating under the influence of the Holy Spirit: "Through the Holy Spirit, Moses, the servant of God, recorded the very beginning of the creation of the world" (Bercot, 602). Referring to the Scriptures, Clement of Alexandria, writing in 195 A.D., said: "For the mouth of the Lord, the Holy Spirit, has spoken these things" and "It was God Himself who promulgated the Scriptures by His Son" (Bercot, 602). The number of citations from the fathers of the Church could be multiplied. While some of them may have differed about the manner in which God operates through the sacred writers, with virtual unanimity the Church fathers understood the Scriptures to be the work of God.

As 2 Peter 1:20-21 implies, scriptural inspiration not only includes the text of the Holy Scriptures itself, but also the human writer who operates under the influence of the Holy Spirit. In the Roman Catholic tradition, some theologians concentrated their theological study on the way in which the sacred writers endeavored to compose the inspired text. The foremost of these theologians was St. Thomas Aquinas. Aquinas taught that, in order for the Holy Spirit to provide the Church with a sacred text, He called certain men to write those texts in such a way that they are the instrumental cause of the composition of the text, while God remains the principal cause. Just as a machine tool cannot produce any sort of effect without being used by a machinist, so too the writers of Holy Writ could not produce an inspired text on their own. In the case of the instrumental cause of Holy Scripture, however, the effect produced by the instrumental cause (the inspired writer) is far greater than the instrument itself. A machine tool produces the effect in accord with its own nature when a skilled machinist operates the tool. In the case of the writers of the Scriptures, they are not producing an effect that is in accord with their own nature, but producing an effect that surpasses their own nature's capabilities.

Does inspiration also mean that the writers of the Scriptures were conscious of their role in composing inspired text? Does inspiration necessarily mean the authors of the Sacred Scriptures fully understand everything that God has intended to reveal in what they were writing? In answer to the first question, while the prophets of the Old Testament may have believed they were speaking inspired words that came from God, this does not necessarily mean the writers of the Scriptures were aware they were under the inspiration of the Holy Spirit while they wrote. Indeed, many writings of the prophets were written down long after they lived by those who desired to keep their teachings for instruction of the people of Israel. It is not necessary, however, for the writers of the Scripture to have actual knowledge of their own participation in God's inspiration in order for God to operate through them. As for the second question, it is also not necessary for the sacred writer to fully comprehend everything that God intends to reveal by the things he has written. The inspiration of the Sacred Scriptures is the Holy Spirit's action, which, in setting forth mysteries too great to be entirely grasped by the human mind, far surpasses any of the writer's personal limitations.

Absolute Inerrancy

The books of Sacred Scripture are the utterly inerrant Word of God. Absolute inerrancy is a logical outgrowth of the divinely inspired character of Scripture. Since God, who can neither deceive nor be deceived, is the principal Author of the Bible, its books must be free from all error. The inerrancy of Sacred Scripture is an important truth, because the Scriptures lead us to accurately understand the person and work of Jesus Christ (see John 20:31).

The earliest of the Fathers of the Church testify to historical Christian faith in the total inerrancy of Scripture. Clement of Rome (96 A.D.) wrote: "You have studied the Holy Scriptures, which are true and are of the Holy Spirit. You well know that nothing unjust or fraudulent is written in them" (Jurgens, 11).

When people read the Sacred Scriptures and point to discrepancies that seem to reflect errors, the supposed problem can be cleared through an analysis of the person's own interpretative hermeneutic. The lenses we use to view the Scriptures can lead us to misinterpret them. Justin Martyr, in 155 A.D., had the humility to write: "If Scripture which appears to be such a kind (self contradictory) be brought forward, and there be a pretext for regarding it as contradictory, since I am totally convinced that no Scripture is contradictory to another, I shall admit instead that I do not understand what is spoken of, and shall strive to persuade those who assume that the Scriptures are contradictory to be rather of the same opinion as myself" (Jurgens, 61).

For example, if we view the stories of creation in Genesis 1-2 as actual historical and scientific accounts, as well as theological accounts meant to tell us about God's relationship to man and the world, we might possibly find ourselves in a quandary with respect to modern scientific thought over the beginning of our planet – depending on which cosmological theories we rely. We must exercise great care and caution here in interfacing Scripture with human science. The Bible sometimes employs the language of phenomena or "how things appear" to the ordinary human observer. On the other hand, although there can be no conflict between the Bible and *true* cosmology, we must appreciate the fact that human scientific theorizing is very often provisional (subject to future revision).

Thus, it becomes necessary for the reader of the Bible, in order to come to a better grasp of the biblical text, to understand the historical context and literary forms in which the writer of the Bible wrote. The language, style of writing, use of words, symbolic references, etc., help the reader to understand more accurately what the sacred writer intended to convey:

> Seeing that, in sacred Scripture, God speaks through men in human fashion, it follows that the interpreter of sacred Scriptures, if he is to ascertain what God has wished to communicate to us, should carefully search out the meaning which the sacred writers really had in mind, that meaning which God had thought well to manifest though the medium of their words. (*Dei Verbum* 3:12)

Sacred Tradition

Sacred Scripture in Relation to Tradition

Sacred Scripture finds its true place within the Church of God. Its true meaning and proper interpretation can be found only within the Church. Hence, the fruitful interpretation of Scripture can be accomplished only through the eyes of faith. Those who endeavor to comprehend the meaning of things God has revealed in His Word will not succeed unless they themselves are people of faith. Hence, "no less attention must be devoted to the content and unity of the whole of Scripture, taking into account the Tradition of the entire Church" (*Dei Verbum* 3:12). The Sacred Tradition of the Church is absolutely necessary to fully understand the things revealed in Scripture. The writers of Sacred Scripture did not write in isolation from the faith of the Church. The things about which they wrote had their context within the Church and its oral preaching first.

Since this is the case, the Oral Tradition is the background and context for the written Word of God. Indeed, it is out of the Sacred Oral Tradition that we come to the knowledge of the books of the Bible themselves. It was in the Church that the Scriptures were written, and it is through the Church that the books of the Bible were chosen. This fact indicates the precedence that God gives the Church with regard to accurately interpreting the written Word and understanding the things that He has revealed. As St. Paul says, "that **through the Church** the manifold wisdom of God might now be made known to the principalities and powers in the heavenly places" (Ephesians 3:10, boldface emphasis added).

It seems that both fundamentalists and liberal biblical scholars alike miss the proper understanding of Scripture. Some biblical scholars, occupying prestigious positions at universities, have a tendency to jettison tradition from their biblical interpretation. For many of them, tradition is like a useless veil placed over the sacred text that must be pealed away. Sacred Tradition must not be seen as a kind of imposition upon Scripture itself; rather, its authority and merit should be carefully weighed by those who seek to understand the meaning of any particular passage.

Sacred Tradition not only helps us understand Sacred Scripture, but it is also the place from which our knowledge of what is to be considered Scripture arises. Hence, Sacred Tradition is a much larger medium of communication of God's revelation than Sacred Scripture. Sacred Scripture and Sacred Tradition form one common deposit of the word of God. The word of God, then, is not reducible to Scripture alone.

Divine Revelation, which is capable of transforming our lives if we assent to it in faith, is found not only in Sacred Scripture, but also in Sacred Tradition. Sacred Scripture and Sacred Tradition should *not* be conceived as two separate realities not connected with each other, nor should the latter be conceived as an imposition upon the former. Both of these realities have a reciprocal relationship reflecting their one source in God (see the passage from *Dei Verbum* 2:9 quoted above).

Capital "T" Tradition

It is important to understand that not all tradition is revered with equal honor, because not all tradition has the same authority. Sacred Tradition with a capital "T" is understood differently from tradition with a lower case "t". Tradition with a lower case "t" refers to the many and various devotional practices found within the Church that may change or disappear depending upon the historical circumstances in which the Church lives. These transitory traditions, which Catholics are not bidden to hold as part of the "deposit of faith", are different from Sacred Tradition.

Sacred Tradition, or Tradition with a capital "T", means "the teachings and teaching authority of Jesus and, derivatively, the apostles. These have been handed down and entrusted to the Church." (Keating, 137) On the other hand, "the term does not mean legends or mythological accounts, nor does it mean transitory customs or practices that come and go as circumstances warrant, such as styles of priestly dress, particular forms of devotion to the saints, or even liturgical rubrics." (Keating, 137).

Sacred Tradition is authoritative Tradition that we are bound to hold as constituting the deposit of the Faith of the Church:

> The word "tradition" means handing on or handing down something to another. This term emphasizes a process or means by which something happens. Thus, tradition is the means by which Revelation and grace are mediated. The term refers to the concrete, historical and personal means by which Revelation is taught, internalized and lived out. The term "sacred" refers to the content or the ultimate source of what is handed on, namely, the divine life of God.
> If Sacred Tradition carries, transmits, hands on, or mediates Divine Revelation, its content originates in the eternal and divine life of God. It expresses Revelation from on high, suitable for transforming life here below and for leading to eternal life in the hereafter. As such, the process of transmission is more than a communication of ideas: It is the means by which Divine Revelation is made available to each generation of believers. (Miletic, 603)

The Greek word *parasdidomi*, from which the word *paradosis* ("tradition") is derived, means "to hand something over" (Wells, 981). Some people believe this word carries only negative connotations. They often cite passages like Mark 7:8-13 or Colossians 2:8. But when the devout Catholic reads these verses, he or she is able to make a distinction between bad human traditions that nullify God's word, and those traditions that do not do so, but may even be said to help clarify the meaning of God's written word. In fact, there are passages in which the word "tradition" has a positive connotation. Note, for example, 1 Corinthians 11:2 (boldface emphasis added): "I commend you because you remember me in everything and

maintain the traditions even as I have delivered them to you." Here Paul is commending the Corinthians for holding on to the traditions he passed on to them. It should be noted here that the "traditions" of which Paul is speaking came from him. It is Apostolic Tradition. Apostolic Tradition is the capital "T" Tradition the Catholic Church proposes that its members cleave to. The Catholic Church further enjoins its members to hold on to the authoritative interpretations of the Apostolic Tradition given by the Church. These are also considered apostolic insofar as they are correct interpretations of what the Apostles passed on and, therefore, manifest the will and intent of the Apostles themselves.

Oral and Written Tradition

In 2 Thessalonians 2:15, St. Paul says: "So then, brethren, stand firm and **hold to the traditions** which you were taught by us, either by word of mouth or by letter" (boldface emphasis added). Paul here reveals not only another positive connotation of the word tradition, but also its different modes: written (i.e., Scripture) and oral. He then says in 2 Thessalonians 3:6 (boldface emphasis added): "Now we command you, brethren, in the name of our Lord Jesus Christ, that you keep away from any brother who is living in idleness and not in accord with **the tradition that you received from us**." Paul goes further, saying that those who do not hold to this tradition he has passed on by "word of mouth" or "by letter" (2:15) should not be held in communion with the Church. He makes no distinction with regard to the authoritative weight of the oral versus the written tradition. Both are of equal value. He lays the pattern for which the faith should be handed on to subsequent generations of Christians. He urges them: "Follow the pattern of the sound words which you have **heard** from me, in the faith and love which are in Christ Jesus; guard the truth that has been entrusted to you by the Holy Spirit who dwells within us" (2 Timothy 1:13-14, boldface emphasis added). Paul tells Timothy to guard the truth that has been received, whether it was given by word of mouth or by letter, because the Holy Spirit has entrusted to him both vehicles of truth.

How does Paul expect Timothy to perpetuate what he has received? The answer lies in 2 Timothy 2:2: "What you have heard from me before many witnesses entrust to faithful men who will be able to teach others also." Notice the oral emphasis in passing on the faith. No command is given to write and preserve texts. This is the leadership charter of the

Catholic Church, for the Church maintains that its leadership has an unbroken line of succession back to the Apostles. Through the years, the Church has handed the ministry given to it by the Apostles to men deemed faithful to pass it onto others. Hence, the way in which the Faith is properly passed down is through a leadership that has been carefully selected by those who are also leaders. If all that should be believed as having come from the Apostles is crystallized in the Old and New Testaments, then why would Paul give this injunction to Timothy? This succession of leadership is one way in which "the houschold of God, which is the church of the living God" is said to be "the pillar and bulwark of the truth" (1 Timothy 3:15). Ephesians 4:11-15 makes it abundantly clear that there are ministries within the body of Christ designed to keep the Church persevering in truth.

The Scriptures nowhere claim to be the sole source or media of God's revelation. In fact, the Scriptures testify to the historic Christian belief that *not* all of Jesus' words and deeds are confined to writing:

> This is the disciple who is bearing witness to these things, and who has written these things; and we know that his testimony is true. But there are also many other things which Jesus did; were every one of them to be written, I suppose that the world itself could not contain the books that would be written. (John 21:24-25)
>
> Now Jesus did many other signs in the presence of the disciples, which are not written in this book; but these are written that you may believe that Jesus is the Christ, the Son of God, and that believing you may have life in his name. (John 20:30-31)

Of course, these two scriptural passages alone do not necessarily justify the overarching primacy of Tradition, but merely show the historic understanding that the Church had toward anything written down about Jesus. Yet, at the same time, the Christian community is instructed by the Lord to hold on to all that He has taught: "Go therefore and make disciples of all nations, baptizing them in the name of the Father and of the Son and of the Holy Spirit, teaching them to observe **all that I have commanded** you; and lo, I am with you always, to the close of the age" (Matthew 28:19-20, boldface emphasis added). How is the Church to hold on to "all" that is taught by our Lord if not everything He has taught was written down verbatim, and in light of St. Paul's injunction to hold on to oral and written tradition? The answer for the Catholic is sacred Tradition.

At any rate, it is evident from all the foregoing passages that the Apostles never envisioned a church in which the Scriptures functioned as the sole source of faith and morals – much less that this source would not have a protector to safeguard its proper interpretation.

As we have seen, the Scriptures tell the faithful to preserve the Tradition that they have received from the Apostles. In 2 Thessalonians 2:15, the Apostle Paul explicitly commands the Christian community to hold to the Tradition or teaching that comes to them from the Apostles – whether it is written or oral. Let us consider an objection. Some have alleged that the oral Tradition retires itself once the written Tradition (Scripture) is complete. This thinking, however, is pure conjecture. In point of fact, the Scriptures do *not* testify to a self-retiring body of oral Tradition that would later crystallize into Scripture. It is a question-begging assumption built upon the edifice of a false premise: namely, that the Scriptures alone contain authoritative doctrine. This position is even more untenable when one remembers Paul's injunction in 2 Timothy 2:2 discussed earlier. In addressing this theory, Mark P. Shea writes:

> First, where in the biblical text is the basis for the Bible-only belief that Scripture swallows Tradition? Certainly it is not 2 Thessalonians... Nor is it made clear anywhere else that the *paradosis* of which Paul spoke would someday be "crystallized" in Scripture alone. On the contrary, Paul's command in 2 Thessalonians 2:15 gives no sign whatsoever that he regards the Tradition he had given them as being in any special need of "crystallization." Granted, Paul clearly regards his writings as invested with apostolic authority and therefore as the word of God (1 Thess 2:13), but he nonetheless speaks, not of some future complete New Testament, but of "the teaching you received from us" as the one and only source of revelation – a teaching which was almost entirely oral and which 1 and 2 Thessalonians are written to underscore, not replace. (Shea, 174)

We have no way of knowing whether the oral Tradition is identical with Scripture itself. As Shea puts it, "Therefore, any claim to know that the content of this oral *paradosis* is identical to the content of his written *paradosis* is just whistling in the dark" (Shea, 176). If one wishes to be biblical, one must say of apostolic Tradition, as 2 Thessalonians 2:15 does, "hold to the traditions which you were taught by us, either by word of mouth or by letter". As we saw, Paul also refers to his own teaching as "tradition" in 2 Thessalonians 3:6. And again, he says: "I commend you because you remember me in everything and **maintain the traditions** even as I have delivered them to you" (1 Corinthians 11:2, boldface emphasis added). It is clear from these passages that Paul imparts a positive connotation to the word "tradition". As we commented earlier, too often the word "tradition" has been interpreted in a solely negative light, on account of certain passages in which Jesus or an Apostle condemns human tradition that interferes with God's word (see Mark 7:1-23; Matthew 15:3-9; Acts 20:29-30; Colossians 2:8; 1 Timothy 4:1; 1 Peter 1:18). In order to avoid this erroneous understanding of the word "tradition", one must appreciate that what is condemned is not oral tradition *as such*, but rather "human tradition" that nullifies the word of God.

Who, however, is to decide which tradition actually nullifies the word of God? Is it left to individual believers to interpret the Scriptures for themselves in order to find what they believe to be the right teaching? How is an individual to be certain that his interpretation is the right one over and above another's interpretation? What complicates things even further is this: What if that person, in trying to interpret the Scriptures himself, is ignorant of the oral Tradition to which he must hold? Does our Lord really leave us to our own fallible ability in so serious a matter as the correct interpretation of Divine Revelation enunciated in Sacred Scripture?

Appeal to personal guidance of the Holy Spirit in illuminating the believer to understand the Scriptures does little good in answering these difficulties, when one considers the multiplicity of interpretations which can be found in the Christian world today. Many sincere Christians differ in their interpretation of Sacred Scripture. The severity and extent of these disagreements have resulted in thousands of denominations. It has reached the point where a new outlook on ecclesiology has arisen. This new perspective is what I call "Creedless Christianity". In this form of

Christianity, each particular community may have its own viewpoint on the Scriptures. What then occurs is a degeneration of the proper understanding of Divine Revelation into doctrinal agnosticism, or even relativism. In order to preserve a sense of ecclesial unity, members of such churches will often write off disagreements as "non-essentials". The outcome is a doctrinal minimalism in which accepting Christ as Lord and Savior is the only criterion for being Christian. This becomes even more problematic when one considers the various interpretations that can be placed on what "accepting Christ as Lord and Savior" really means. For the Catholic, of course, it has a Trinitarian connotation, but this is not the case with all other groups of people claiming a Christian identity. Besides all this, the judgment of what is essential and what is not presumes a consensus of agreement as to what is essential.

It is evident upon the reading of Scripture that great emphasis is placed on preaching: "So faith comes from what is heard, and what is heard comes by the preaching of Christ"(Romans 10:17). Luke also acknowledges the oral passing on of the faith as binding: "He who hears you hears me, and he who rejects you rejects me, and he who rejects me rejects him who sent me" (Luke 10:16). The Scriptures are laden with many texts in which Jesus and His Apostles preach and teach, but none of them make reference to writing (see, for example, Matthew 11:1; 12:41; 13:1-2; Mark 1:38; Luke 4:44; 8:4; 11:32; Acts 8:4-5; 10:42; 13:5; 17:18; 28:31; Romans 2:21; 16:25; 1 Corinthians 1:17, 21, 23; 2:4; 9:16, 18; 15:11-12; 2 Corinthians 4:5; 10:16; Galatians 5:11; Philippians 1:15; 1 Timothy 5:17). These texts bear witness to the fact the preacher spoke with an authority coming from God. Hence, the usual mode of evangelical transmission for many centuries in the Church was preaching. It was not writing so that it could be later read and re-read. In many places in the Catholic Church today, churches no longer offer missals from which a member of the congregation may follow along as the Scriptures are publicly read. The reason for this is the liturgical renewal's attempt to retrieve the apostolic Church's custom of listening to the word of God as it is proclaimed.

The oral transmission of God's word is even preferred by the Apostles over its written counterpart. For example, in 2 John 12 and 3 John 13-14 (two passages quoted earlier), St. John declares his desire to pass on to the churches his teaching via the oral form. There is no urgency in these two letters to write anything down for the churches to retain as divine writ. Whatever it was that St. John desired to say to his fellow Christians is not recorded in Scripture, but this does not thereby make it unimportant – as the tenor of his letters proves. What he wished to teach them, he did so orally, and that was to be held onto as tenaciously as one would hold onto Scripture itself. Lastly, Paul himself sometimes prefers to communicate needful things to the Christian community via word of mouth: "If any one is hungry, let him eat at home – lest you come together to be condemned. **About the other things I will give directions when I come**" (1 Corinthians 11:34, boldface emphasis added).

If oral Tradition did not have authoritative weight for the Christian community, one would expect the writers of the New Testament to admit this. Well, not only do they *not* acknowledge it, but also in practice actually utilize the oral Tradition as though it were binding in matters of faith.

The use of extra-biblical Tradition in the New Testament is found in several places. The writers of Hebrews and Acts both refer to the Tradition that the Old Testament covenants were put into effect by angels (Acts 7:53; Hebrews 2:2). But there is a problem here for those who believe the apostles did not accept authoritative oral Tradition as equal to God's word. For "there is no place in the entire Old Testament which teaches the Mosaic Covenant was given through angels" (Shea, 178). These writers are appealing to an oral Tradition, not a written one.

Another example is from St. Paul: "As Jannes and Jambres opposed Moses, so these men also oppose the truth, men of corrupt mind and counterfeit faith; but they will not get very far, for their folly will be plain to all, as was that of those two men" (2 Timothy 3:8-9). Now, the names of Jannes and Jambres do not appear in the Old Testament. How, then, does Paul know their names? In fact, "Paul is again drawing on (and assuming Timothy will draw on) a widely known extra-biblical Tradition, and treating it as authoritative" (Shea, 179).

It does not stop there. St. Jude appears to draw upon extra-biblical tradition about Moses' death when he asserts (Jude 8-9): "Yet in like manner these men in their dreamings defile the flesh, reject authority, and revile the glorious ones. But when the archangel Michael, contending with the devil, disputed about the body of Moses, he did not presume to pronounce a reviling judgment upon him, but said, 'The Lord rebuke you.'" Nowhere in the Old Testament is there a story about the archangel Michael disputing with Satan over the corpse of Moses. It comes from Jewish Sacred Tradition, and an apocryphal work known as the *Assumption of Moses*. (Note also the citation in Jude 14-15 of a prophecy attributed to Enoch.)

Another passage of interest is Matthew 2:23: "And he went and dwelt in a city called Nazareth, that what was spoken by the prophets might be fulfilled, 'He shall be called a Nazarene.'" This prophecy ("He shall be called a Nazarene") is nowhere found in the Old Testament. As an eminent New Testament scholar says, "The reference to a prophecy here poses a classic problem of interpretation since there is no exact correspondence to any known OT text" (Viviano, 636). From whence does it come? Once again, it comes from Sacred Tradition.

One last example of oral Tradition in the New Testament will suffice for the present discussion. In 1 Corinthians 10:4 St. Paul writes: "And all drank the same supernatural drink. For they drank from the supernatural Rock which followed them, and the Rock was Christ." If one reads the story from the Old Testament in which God commands Moses to strike a rock from where water would flow, one will find that the story says nothing about that rock following them anywhere. Nevertheless, rabbinic tradition holds that the rock actually followed the Israelites on their journey in the wilderness. Paul cites this tradition, thereby assuming its truth and authoritative nature. Biblical scholar Jerome Murphy-O'Connor comments, "There is no hint of movement of the rock in the OT, but a legend developed on the basis of Jewish interpretation of Numbers 21:17" (O'Connor, 807).

One can see clearly from all these examples that the writers of the New Testament had no qualms whatsoever in accepting the reliable transmission of an oral Tradition.

Far from becoming a hindrance to proper scriptural exegesis, the Oral Tradition is very helpful. By consulting the Oral Tradition, a Scripture scholar is able to gain another insight into how a biblical text is understood by the Christian community. A good example would be the perpetual virginity of Mary. It has been longstanding Catholic Tradition that has held Mary remained a virgin throughout her life. The Old and New Testaments refer to Mary as a virgin, but never specifically say that she remained so throughout her entire life. The reference to "brothers and sisters" of Jesus does not necessarily mean blood brothers and sisters, but could extend to nephews, cousins, or close friends, since the Greek word for "brothers" extended to other kinds of kinship ties. For a Scripture scholar or reader of the Bible to declare that Mary did not remain a virgin is an assumption that has no ironclad biblical basis. What we do have, however, is a longstanding and fairly early tradition about Mary's virginal state. Why should the oral Tradition, not preserved in pen and ink in the New Testament but preserved in the life of the Church, be cast aside? Does not the oral handing on of the Faith count as historical evidence for the early Church's faith and practice?

The Biblical Canon

The issue of the authority of the oral Tradition comes to its apex when one considers the authorship of different books of the Bible and the development of the canon of the Old and New Testaments. Indeed, the interplay between Sacred Scripture and Sacred Tradition can best be highlighted by considering the process by which the books of the Bible were chosen and proposed by the Church for acceptance as divinely inspired.

First, our knowledge of who wrote each book of the Bible does not come to us from the Scriptures themselves. The books of the Bible do not introduce us to their own human authors. Nevertheless, we are comfortable in saying that Matthew or his disciple wrote the Gospel of Matthew, or that Luke wrote the Gospel of Luke and Acts, etc. We are able to make statements such as these not because the books themselves tell us who wrote them, but because we rely upon the Tradition of the Church that has passed on to us this knowledge.

With respect to the canon of the Old Testament, Catholics differ from Protestants and Jews about their inspired character. The Catholic Church believes the Old Testament consists of forty-six books, while Protestants and Jews say it contains only thirty-nine. Hence, there are seven books in the Catholic Old Testament that are disputed by some non-Catholic Christians and Jews, and also by some Fathers of the Church. These seven books are as follows: 1 and 2 Maccabees, Judith, Tobit, Wisdom, Sirach, Baruch, and portions of the books of Daniel and Esther. This matter requires some examination.

The difference between the two canons has a long and complicated history. The word "canon" comes from the Greek word *"Kanon"*, which literally means a straight rod or bar, and it appears to have been used in ancient Egyptian culture to mean an instrument for measuring something else (Bunson, 70). St. Athanasisus was the first to use the word "canon" as meaning "to give official sanction" to a particular written document. The Church now uses this word to mean the list of books found in both the Old and New Testaments. Hence, the twenty-seven books of the New Testament constitute the New Testament canon and the forty-six books of the Old Testament constitute the Old Testament canon. This is the Catholic measurement or rule for the canon of the biblical books.

In the early days of Christianity, there were two major canons of Scripture recognized by the Jewish and Christian communities. While these two canons were by no means settled by anyone at the time of Jesus, their usage by Jews and Christians alike will help one understand how the current disagreement came about. The two major canons of Scripture are the *Hebrew* canon (otherwise known as the *Palestinian* canon because of its prolific use in and around Palestine) and the *Septuagint* canon (also known as the *Alexandrian* canon owing to its origins and prolific use in and around Alexandria in North Africa). The Hebrew or Palestinian canon was written in what was considered to be the sacred language of Jews – Hebrew. Its appeal to antiquity, due to its use of the ancient Hebrew language in which the Old Testament was originally written, found itself favored by more conservative Jews, who may have looked with suspicion upon their less conservative brothers who also accepted the Septuagint. The Hebrew canon was composed of only thirty-nine books. The Septuagint, having been composed in Alexandria, was a translation of the Hebrew canon into the Greek language. Other books, however, were included in this canon that may or may not have had Hebrew counterparts. Today, those books are referred to as "Deuterocanonical" by Catholics, and as "Apocryphal" by Protestants. As time elapsed, the Septuagint became the more widely used canon, because it appealed to a larger Greek-speaking audience (since the Hebrew language was not nearly as widespread as the Greek). Many Greek-speaking Jews at the time of Jesus accepted the inspiration of the Septuagint books, and there is no evidence at this time that the seven books were ever considered uninspired by the Jewish or Christian community at large. Moreover, there is even evidence to suggest that many Jews and Christians accepted both canons as inspired. For example, the Christian community used *both* canons, as evidenced by their quotations of the Hebrew *and* Septuagint canons in the New Testament. In fact, the majority of the quotations found in the New Testament are taken not from the Palestinian canon, but from the Septuagint. Furthermore, Jewish communities in Egypt have a larger canon of Scripture than Jews elsewhere.

The first concentrated shift away from the Septuagint for the Jewish community took place after the fall of Jerusalem and the destruction of the Temple in 70 AD. After the fall of Jerusalem, there was a need for the Jewish community to regroup and decide how it was going to perpetuate the Jewish Faith now that the Romans had destroyed the Temple. Somewhere between 90 and 100 A.D., there was a meeting of prominent rabbis at a town named Jamnia. It is here, in what became known as the "Council of Jamnia", that the attending rabbis made decisions to exclude from the official list of inspired books those books Catholics refer to as Deuterocanonical. Prior to this time, there was no consensus as to what would constitute the complete canon of Scripture for either Jews or Christians: "That the canon was not completed until the Christian era is recognized by most critical scholars today, and many suggest that the rivalry offered by Christian books was a spur for the closing of the Jewish canon" (Brown and Collins, *NJBC*, 1040). Scholars today even doubt whether all seven Deuterocanonical books were indeed excluded by the rabbis at Jamnia (Brown and Collins, *NJBC*, 1040). In fact, there were persistent doubts among many Jews about the inspiration of some books of the Hebrew canon. Appealing to Jamnia as historical evidence against the acceptance of the Deuterocanonical books fails in light of the preponderance of evidence suggesting a reverse conclusion. It was only by the end of the second century A.D. that the Hebrew canon as we know it today successfully gained acceptance by the majority of the Jewish people:

> The safest statement about the closing of the Jewish canon is one which recognizes that, although in the first cent. AD there was acceptance of 22 or 24 books as sacred, there was no rigidly fixed exclusive Hebrew canon until the end of the 2d cent. In this period various Jewish groups continued to read as sacred, books not included in the 22/24 count (Brown and Collins, *NJBC*, 1040).

The conclusion that there was no rigidly closed canon in Judaism in the 1ˢᵗ and early 2d cents. AD means that when the church was in its formative period and was using the sacred books of the Jews, there was no closed canon for the church to adopt. This is exactly the situation in the NT. The NT writers cited the sacred books that ultimately found their way into the Hebrew canon, especially the Law, the Prophets, and Psalms. But they also echo some of the deuterocanonical books (Brown and Collins, *NJBC*, 1041)

Suffice it to say, the concept of a fixed Jewish canon of sacred books did not exist even into the second century A.D. of the Christian Church. Even if the Jewish community had decisively closed the canon by the end of first century A.D., which it did not, this would not therefore be binding on the Christian community. The Christian community did not see itself as bound to the decisions made by rabbis and Jewish scholars who had rejected Jesus Christ as the Messiah. For early Christians, it was the Christian community that constituted the New Israel, and to this community Christ had promised the Holy Spirit who would lead it into all truth (see John 16:13).

The first real impetus for the Christian church to decide on the question of the canon of the Bible came from the Marcionite heresy. In Marcion's theology, there was a discontinuity between the God of the Old Testament and the God of the New Testament – to such an extent that the former was considered good and the latter evil (Gasque, 629). Since the god of the Old Testament was not the God that Jesus came to reveal, the Old Testament Scriptures were considered superfluous. Not only did Marcion reject the entire Old Testament, but he also accepted only an edited version of Luke's Gospel and some of Paul's letters. Hence, "Marcion's principle of exclusion gave sharp impetus for the early church's need to define which books did or did not rank as authoritative documents to which appeal could be made" (Chadwick, 31).

While it is true that St. Athanasius is the first Church father (third century) to have arrived at the complete list of twenty-seven New Testament books, the early Church councils did, shortly thereafter (in the fourth century), make decisions on the nature and extent of the canon (Brown and Collins, *NJBC*, 1036). The councils of the Church dealing with the canon of the Old and New Testaments were the councils of Laodicea in 360 A.D., of Rome in 380 A.D., of Hippo in 393 A.D., of Carthage III in 397 A.D., and Carthage IV in 419 A.D. With the exception of the council of Laodicea, all these councils decreed that the Old and New Testaments found in today's Catholic Bibles were to be considered inspired. The council of Laodicea, in listing the Old and New Testament books, left out Tobit, Judith, Wisdom, Sirach, 1 and 2 Maccabees, and Revelation, but did include Baruch, a Deuterocanonical book found in Catholic Bibles (Dupuis, 201). These councils were local, not ecumenical, and therefore their authoritative voice does not require the response of an assent of faith by the Church's faithful. It would not be until much later that the Catholic Church would actually take up the question of the Deuterocanonical books at an ecumenical council.

At this point, I urge the reader to consider the following question. Who has the right to decide the canon? The believing Catholic affirms the need for and presence of an authoritative Church whose leadership is constituted by the successors of the Apostles (the Bishops), who are guided by the Holy Spirit to make decisions in matters of faith and morals. The early Christians did not appeal to the Scriptures themselves in determining what books should be considered inspired. They appealed to the Church through its liturgy, tradition, and faith. These functioned as the litmus test in determining which books of the Bible were to be considered inspired. The early Christians did not appeal to some nebulous testimony of the Spirit within each believer, as did John Calvin, nor did they appeal to whether a book of the Bible taught justification by faith alone, as Luther did (Keating, 131). The early Church merely asked a series of questions about the books themselves, and did not appeal to biblical verses to justify their conclusions; for it was those verses that were in need of justification in order to be considered canonical.

The questions the Church weighed included the following. Does the tradition of the Church hold that a particular book is apostolic in origin? Is the particular book used extensively in the Liturgy of the Church? Does the particular book teach what the Church knows to be the Gospel; in other words, is the particular book compatible with the preaching and teaching of the Church as it has been passed on orally by the apostles and their successors? The books of the Bible were subjected to the authoritative Oral Tradition of the Church, which itself constituted the rule of faith.

When heretical Christian sects known as the "Gnostic" Christians began to write gospels and attach the names of the Apostles to them in order to give them authority, the Church Fathers did not simply assert that the Bible, as we know it, contains the only books to be considered inspired. Instead, they appealed to the authoritative Oral Tradition found preserved by the successors to the Apostles, the Bishops.

Appealing to the Fathers of the Church will also shed light upon the issue of the Deuterocanonical books, because these Church Fathers testify to what Christians believed on various doctrinal points. It is not necessary that all the Fathers of the Church should agree on a particular point, but it is sufficient to establish only the majority consensus in order to arrive at an adequate picture of Christian belief. The writings of the ante-Nicene Fathers contain over three-hundred quotations from the Deuterocanonical books, those books not found in Jewish or Protestant Bibles (Bercot, 207). Very early documents and writers of the Church used the Deuterocanonical books, and cited those books just as they would cite any other biblical book. The Didache, a document written between 70 and 130 A.D., cites the book of Sirach 4:31: "Do not be a stretcher forth of the hands to receive and a drawer back of them when it is time to give" (Bercot, 208). This document is widely understood to be a Church manual giving instruction to the presbyters on how to deal with various problems and disciplinary and liturgical issues within the community. The author of the manual is anonymous, but his writing is of great value to our insights into Church practice and belief in first and second century Christianity. Bishop Polycarp (70 to 155 A.D.), who is said to have known the Apostle John, cited the book of Tobit 4:10 when he said, "When you can do good, defer it not, because 'alms delivers from death'" (Bercot, 208). Hippolytus, who lived from the late second to the early-middle third century, repeatedly referred to the books of Wisdom, Maccabees, and Tobit (Bercot, 208). The list of reputable Church Fathers who freely quoted from the Deuterocanonical books as if they were inspired and authoritative texts could be multiplied. Their example should give pause for us to consider the inspired character of such books.

Not only do we see frequent use of the Deuterocanonical books by the Church Fathers, but we also see the Fathers of the Church explicitly testifying to the inspired nature of the those books. One such man is Origen. He was a prolific writer in the early Church who touched on many and various topics. His works are extremely diverse, ranging from philosophy and theology to scriptural commentaries. He testifies: "The Jews do not use Tobit. It is not even found in the Hebrew hidden writings, as I learned from the Jews themselves. However, since the churches use Tobit, you must know that even in captivity, some of the captives were rich and well to do" (Bercot, 210). It could be said that there are not many quotations from the early Fathers of the Church regarding the inspired character of the Deuterocanonical books. This is because it was not until the fourth century that the Christian Church really began to consider the question in more depth as a result of the proliferation of various gnostic sects who rejected the Old Testament altogether.

The Eastern Catholic Church and the Orthodox Churches are not unified on the matter. Some of the Orthodox Churches accept the Roman Catholic Old and New Testament canon while even adding a couple of additional books (Metzger, 13). Catholic biblical scholar Raymond Brown says, regarding the disparity of Old Testaments among Christians: "Another ambiguity is that the Orthodox and Eastern Churches at times have agreed with the longer canon that Catholics use or have proposed an even larger canon" (Brown, 15). The position of the Church of England or Episcopal Church is still in dispute. What they accept to be the entire Old Testament canon is not unanimous. Hence, the canon of the Old Testament is not universal in Christianity. It seems that the majority of Christians, including Roman Catholics and some Orthodox and Anglicans, accept the larger canon of the Septuagint, while there is still a minority of Christians persistent in not accepting the inspired character of those books.

There is yet another point to consider in the debate over the canonicity of the Deuterocanoncial books: the use of, or allusion to, these books in the New Testament itself. In Hebrews 11:35 we read: "Women received their dead by resurrection. Some were tortured, refusing to accept release, that they might rise again to a better life."

There are a couple of examples of women receiving back their dead by resurrection in the Protestant Old Testament. You can find Elijah raising the son of the widow of Zarepheth in 1 Kings 17, and you can find his successor Elisha raising the son of the Shunamite woman in 2 Kings 4, but one thing you can never find – anywhere in the Protestant Old Testament, from front to back, from Genesis to Malachi – is someone being tortured and refusing to accept release for the sake of a better resurrection. If you want to find that, you have to look in the Catholic Old Testament – in the Deuterocanonical books... The story is found in 2 Maccabees 7... (Akin, 2)

I remember, when I was in seminary studying at Washington Theological Union, I asked Fr. Boadt, a renowned Old Testament and Ugaritic scholar, about the use of the Deuterocanonical books in the New Testament. He informed me that many biblical scholars believe there is a strong influence of the book of Wisdom in the New Testament. As I studied further, I discovered that some passages in the book of Wisdom have a very striking counterpart to passages in the New Testament. For example, Wisdom 2:12-20 bears a remarkable resemblance to the crucifixion account in Matthew 27:41-43. Christians who read this passage from Wisdom, without first being told it is a Deuterocanonical book, will probably see this passage as referring to Jesus Christ. They may even eagerly grab their Bibles to acquire the reference in its context. We can view yet another parallel between the book of Wisdom and a New Testament text by comparing Wisdom 13:1,5 with Romans 1:19-20.

The book of Wisdom is not the only book containing passages that prompt one to wonder whether they were in the minds of New Testament writers. The book of Sirach, another Deuterocanonical and part of the wisdom literature of ancient Israel, has some passages similar in content or structure to that of New Testament passages. For example, compare the verse "Do not prattle in the assembly of the elders, nor repeat yourself in your prayer" (Sirach 7:14) with the verse "And in praying do not heap up empty phrases as the Gentiles do; for they think that they will be heard for their many words" (Matthew 6:7).

There are numerous passages from the seven Deuterocanonical books that scholars believe have counterparts with New Testament texts, and one need only pick up a good Bible and examine the footnotes and cross-references to confirm this.

The canon of the New Testament is one that is not debated at all. All Christians accept the twenty-seven books of the New Testament to be inspired. The aforementioned fourth century councils that canonized the Septuagint likewise canonized the twenty- seven books of the New Testament. But the New Testament canon was not always recognized. Many Church Fathers disagreed as to what belonged to the New Testament canon. Eusebius of Caesarea, writing in the early fourth century, notes that the books of James, 1 Peter, Jude, 3 John, Hebrews, and Revelation were considered disputable by many Christians; that is, these books were not universally held to be inspired. Some Christian communities, such as the Corinthian Christians, accepted the letters of Clement to Corinth as inspired, but these would never be included in the New Testament. The variety of New Testaments found within the Christian community in the third and fourth centuries should, again, lead one to consider how it is we can determine which books are binding on all Christians. By the end of the fourth century, the twenty-seven books of the New Testament were universally recognized as inspired. There is no question that the fourth century councils and authoritative churchmen (for example, St. Augustine, St. Athanasius, St. Jerome, Pope Damasus, and Pope Innocent I) were the major contributing figures in the acceptance of the final canon of the New Testament.

With all of this in the background, whence does the current disagreement between Catholics and Protestants originate? The answer lies in the person of Martin Luther. Luther, reacting to the abuses of his times, began to formulate a new understanding of the Christian Faith. Part of this new understanding included a new view of the canon of Scripture that had been accepted by most Christians of his time, as well as a new understanding of authority in the Church – namely, *Sola Scriptura* or "Scriptures alone". Basing some of his arguments upon the views of the Jewish rabbis at Jamnia, Luther concluded that the seven books not found in the Hebrew Bible should not be included in the Christian Old Testament. He also cited St. Jerome's own reluctance to accept the Deuterocanonical books. (Nonetheless, St. Jerome did later accept those books on the authority of the Catholic Church.)

Part of Luther's reason for rejecting the seven Deuterocanonical books had to do with the needs of his apologetics. Many of Luther's critics cited the Deuterocanonicals as evidence against some of his doctrines. For example, the belief in praying for the dead in 2 Maccabees 12:42-46 counters Luther's objection to the doctrine of purgatory. One should also know that Luther doubted the inspired character of James, Hebrews, and Revelation. Concerning the Letter of St. James, he said: "I therefore refuse him a place among the true canon of my Bible," because, according to him, James "does violence to Scripture, and so contradicts Paul and all of Scripture" (Fastiggi, p 329). This kind of conclusion, however, did not win acceptance by the majority of his co-religionists, so he toned down his rhetoric by ranking the books of the Bible in the order of importance he believed they merited:

> Therefore John's Gospel is the one, fine, true, and chief gospel, and is far, far to be preferred over the other three and placed high above them. So, too, the epistles of St. Paul and St. Peter far surpass the other three gospels Matthew, Mark, and Luke.
> In a word St. John's Gospel and his first epistles, St. Paul's epistles, especially Romans, Galatians, and Ephesians, and St. Peter's first epistle are the books that show you Christ and teach you all that is necessary and salvatory for you to know, even if you were never to see or hear any other book or doctrine. Therefore St. James' epistle is really an epistle of straw, compared to these others, for it has nothing of the nature of the gospel about it. (Lull, 117)

It is clear that Luther's construction of the canon of Scripture was determined by what books he personally thought would preach his understanding of the Gospel. This criterion is very subjective by comparison to the early Church litmus test discussed earlier. Luther was so convinced of his viewpoint that in the early editions of his bible the books were arranged in such a manner as to reflect his novel thinking. It is not surprising that in many churches today the greatest stress is placed upon Paul's epistles or letters rather than upon the Gospels. These churches, then, follow the example of Luther in practice if not also in theory. The Catholic Church in her liturgy, however, places emphasis upon the Gospels while not denying the equally inspired character of all God's written word. The scriptural passages in the liturgy of the Catholic Church have been so arranged as to highlight the importance of the Gospel. The Liturgy of the Word culminates in the proclamation of the Gospels by the priest or deacon. For Luther it was different. He not only arranged his own canon of Scripture, but also felt free to add words to scriptural verses in order for those verses to bring forth the connotations he wanted them to have. As a crucial example, in Romans 3:28 Luther added the word "alone" after the word "faith", so that the passage would read: "For we hold that a man is justified by faith *alone* apart from works of law." If the Scriptures did indeed teach this doctrine of *sola fide*, why feel the need to add words to Scripture rather than let the Scriptures speak for themselves? In fact, it would be his understanding of the book of Romans that would act as the locus for interpreting all other books and judging other books as to their gospel quality.

> Verse 28 has also become famous through Luther's translation 'by faith alone' = sola fide. The adjective 'alone' was not in the text from which Luther translated, since no MS or edition has it. He may have added it for the purpose of bringing out the sense of the passage more clearly. In fact, however, the addition has led to the false conclusion that – faith excepted – all other works both before and after justification are of no account according to St. Paul's doctrine of salvation. (A. Theisen, 1055)

The doctrine that the only authority in matters of faith and morals is Scripture alone (*Sola Scriptura*) finds its articulation in the Protestant Reformers Luther, Zwingli, and Calvin. If Scripture alone is the only authority in faith and morals, then this doctrine itself should be found in Scripture. However, the doctrine of "Scriptures alone" is nowhere found in the Bible. Texts put forward to justify this position merely assert the inspired and binding character of the Scriptures. The understanding of a particular verse needs to be seen in the context of other affirmations in Scripture, as well as the historic faith of the Christian community. Some of these texts are 2 Timothy 3:16-17; Acts 17:11; 1 Corinthians 4:6; Mark 7:5-13; Matthew 15:3-6; and 1 John 2:26-27. They do not teach that the Scriptures *alone* are authoritative. It is the emphasis upon the word "alone" with reference to Scripture that the Catholic protests. As already shown, the Scriptures speak of a binding Oral Tradition coming to us from the Apostles to which we must hold. This Tradition itself also constitutes an authority. We will explore later the reality that the Church also constitutes another authority, and these three authorities have a dynamic interrelationship. It is the Church that is the "pillar and bulwark of the truth" (1 Timothy 3:15).

Luther believed that the truths of faith must be supported by the Scriptures and that the "teachings of the fathers are useful only to lead us to Scripture ... and then we must hold to the Scriptures alone" (Fastiggi, 333). According to Luther, if a doctrine is not easily found upon the pages of Scripture, then it should either be rejected or its importance should be treated as negligible for the Christian Church. Further reading of Luther on the subject reveals that those who do not understand Scripture as he understands it are speaking against God's word. He makes his interpretation of Scripture synonymous with the Scriptures themselves, declaring that the passages in question are manifestly clear. Luther will concede that there are certain passages in Scripture difficult to understand, but these passages are hard to understand because "of our own linguistic and grammatical ignorance" (Fastiggi, 332). If people find the contents of Scripture hard to understand or nebulous, it is due "not to any lack of clarity in the Scripture, but to their own blindness and dullness, in that they make no effort to see truth which, in itself, could not be plainer" (Fastiggi, 332).

Luther asserted that the Holy Spirit guides the believer to the correct apprehension of Scripture. Erroneously interpreting Scripture would then mean that the person is devoid of the Holy Spirit's assistance. This kind of view of scriptural exegesis is problematic. It is very possible to have devout Christians disagreeing with each other over how to interpret different passages in Scripture that are vital not only to the Christian community, but also to society at large. For example, how to understand Christ's prohibition of divorce in Matthew 19:1- 9 and Mark 10:1-11 is one that is very divisive for many Christian communities. Marriage, out of which the basic social fabric (known as the family) of the Christian community arises, is without a doubt of the utmost importance to the Church and society. Since this is the case, the question of divorce cannot be a "nonessential".

Zwingli's approach to scriptural interpretation was similar to Luther's. He held that "everyone who approaches the Bible in prayer and in faith must inevitably come to the same general apprehension of (the Scripture's) truth..." (Fastiggi, 337). The problem still remains, however. Simply because a Christian approaches a Bible passage in prayer and faith does not necessarily mean that he or she will accurately understand its meaning. Consulting the Christian community at large in order to check one's personal understanding with others will not solve the problem either. Which Christian community is the one in which we are to check our interpretation, if Christianity is broken into denominations – each one making truth claims on how to interpret the Bible, but none of them claiming to have the authority from God to declare any particular interpretation as erroneous?

Calvin attacked the idea of the definitive nature of the Church's role in determining the canon of the Bible. He did not believe that the credibility of the canon of Scripture in any way depended upon the judgment of the Church (Fastiggi, 339). Instead, he grounded one's belief in the accuracy of the canon of Scripture on the inward testimony of the Spirit alive in each believer. This, of course, reduces our knowledge of the canon of Scripture to mere subjectivity. Eliminating the judgment of an official body of interpreters necessarily leads to private interpretation of Scripture. It also does not acknowledge the problem that the early Church had in determining the canon of the Bible. Devout Christians disagreed as to what constituted the biblical canon for both the Old and New Testaments. It was only the judgment of the Church that gave clarity to the issue.

The Protestant Reformation sparked the calling of a new ecumenical council that would respond to the issues of corruption in the Church, along with the theological questions raised by the Protestant reformers. The Council of Trent was convened in 1545 by Pope Paul III and ended in 1563 under Pope Pius IV, who officially confirmed its decrees (Bunson, 851). Its long duration was due to various political difficulties and the threat of war (Hughes, *A History of the General Council*, p. 348). While this was not the first ecumenical council to address the question of the canon of the Old and New Testaments, it is the one council many historians highlight as having officially closed the question of the canon of Scripture. Other Ecumenical Councils also affirmed the Catholic Canon of Scripture: Second Council of Nicea (787 A.D.), Council of Florence (1442 A.D.), Vatican I (1870 A.D.), and, most recently, the Second Vatican Council in 1965 (Akin, 3). Most of the decrees of the Council of Trent were formulated in such a manner as to condemn the various errors of the reformers. The Council condemned both the error of *Sola Scriptura* and the refusal to accept as inspired the longer Old Testament. Trent decreed:

> Following, then, the examples of the orthodox Fathers, it receives and venerates with a feeling of piety and reverence all the books both of the Old and New Testaments, since one God is the author of both; also the traditions, whether they relate to faith or to morals, as having been dictated either orally by Christ or by the Holy Ghost, and preserved in the Catholic Church in unbroken succession. It has thought it proper, moreover, to insert in this decree a list of sacred books, lest a doubt might arise in the mind of someone as to which are the books received by this council.... If anyone does not accept as sacred and canonical the aforesaid books in their entirety and with all their parts, as they have been accustomed to be read in the Catholic Church and as they are contained in the old Latin Vulgate edition, and knowingly and deliberately rejects the aforesaid traditions, let him be anathema.... Furthermore, to check unbridled spirits, it decrees that no one relying on his own judgment shall, in matters of faith and morals pertaining to the edification of Christian doctrine, distorting the Holy Scriptures in accordance with his own conceptions, presume to interpret them contrary to that sense which holy mother Church, to whom it belongs to judge of their true sense and interpretation, has held and holds. (Schroeder, *Canons and Decrees of the Council of Trent*: Fourth Session, 17-19).

In contemporary times, and in a less polemical fashion, the Catholic Church at the Second Vatican Council reasserted the inspired character of the Old and New Testaments that are found in Catholic Bibles. It also reaffirmed that the thesis of "Scriptures alone" as the authoritative guide in faith and morals is not a proper articulation of the historic Christian Faith. It is through the magisterium of the Church (that is, through the Bishops united together with the Pope, who are guided by the Holy Spirit) that we come to receive this Faith in its completeness.

The Magisterium

Apostolic Origin

Catholics refer to the official teaching authority of the Church as "the magisterium", which consists of the Pope united together with the Bishops around the world. Catholics believe that such a teaching body is not only necessary for keeping the unity of the faith, but also divinely constituted by the Lord Himself. As we have already discussed, the Church did not have a formal canon of Scripture for the first three hundred years of the Church's life and, considering the fact that the New Testament took years to write, the first Christians had considerably less Scripture from which to draw theological truth than did Christians in later ages. Nonetheless, since the early Christians did have a Church that taught and preached in Jesus' name, it could be said that those who heard the preaching of the Christian community heard the preaching of Christ: "He who hears you hears me, and he who rejects you rejects me, and he who rejects me rejects him who sent me" (Luke 10:16). In fact, it is quite clear that Jesus also gave His apostles great authority (see Mark 6:7, 10-13)

The authority Christ gave specifically to His Apostles is no small matter, for the Apostles were to be part of the foundation of the Church:

> So then you are no longer strangers and sojourners, but you are fellow citizens with the saints and members of the household of God, **built upon the foundation of the apostles and prophets**, Christ Jesus himself being the cornerstone, in whom the whole structure is joined together and grows into a holy temple in the Lord; in whom you also are built into it for a dwelling place of God in the Spirit. (Ephesians 2:19-22, boldface emphasis added)

Notice that the Apostles are mentioned as part of the very same foundation as the prophets. The prophets spoke the oracle of God in the Old Testament and the Holy Spirit infallibly guarded their words.

Speaking erroneously was the sign of a false prophet (see Deuteronomy 18:22). Apostolic preaching must, therefore, carry with it the guidance of the Holy Spirit, for no foundation of the Church would securely endure if it were composed merely of the words of men without infallible divine guidance.

The authority of the Apostles is derived from Christ, and the exercising of this authority is such that it fosters unity. Unity in the Church is achieved not by having one book, but by having one coherent structured Church. It is often said that the church is not an organization but an organism. While this analogy is correct, it also stands that every organism is properly organized in order that it may live, thrive, and endure. When Sacred Scripture is the subject of each person's own private interpretation apart from the community of the Church, and that private interpretation becomes the tool by which to judge the Church as true or false, then endless divisions inevitably follow. If one were to read the history of any particular Protestant denomination, one would find that pattern to be a recurring phenomenon.

The Scriptures, however, teach us to obey our religious leaders. St. Paul presumes the obedience of the faithful when he writes: "Confident of your obedience, I write to you, knowing that you will do even more than I say" (Philemon 1:21). The Letter to the Hebrews instructs us to obey our leaders, because this is the way to avoid the pitfall of heresy:

> Remember your leaders, those who spoke to you the word of God; consider the outcome of their life, and imitate their faith. Jesus Christ is the same yesterday and today and for ever. Do not be led away by diverse and strange teachings; for it is well that the heart be strengthened by grace, not by foods, which have not benefited their adherents.... Obey your leaders and submit to them; for they are keeping watch over your souls, as men who will have to give account. (Hebrews 13:7-9, 17)

How is one to understand this passage if one submits to no real authority other than one's own? Why would Paul want Christians to follow a leadership that had no guidance from the Holy Spirit to teach truthfully? While one may say that Protestant Christianity also believes in church authority and obedience to such authority, it seems that such authority, while existing in some way, has no real power. It has no ability to bind the believers to assent that "x" is right while "y" is not. The experience of Protestant denominations proves that, when a pastor or preacher deviates from a congregant's own personal understanding of the Scriptures, the crisis often culminates in the creation of a new denomination – or at least in the congregant's departure from that particular community for another. This endless division creates a situation of numerous competing Christian authorities within Christendom. These divisions are an affront to our Lord, who before His death prayed for unity among His disciples (see John 17:11).

St. Paul, speaking of the Church as the body of Christ, teaches the body is ordered so that "there may be no discord in the body" (1 Corinthians 12:25) – in other words, so that there may be no *schism* in the body of Christ. While there have always been some divisions within Christianity, none have been so rampant as those divisions stemming from the Reformation. Protestantism, however, holds to the principle of "Scriptures alone" as the source of infallible authority, with no authoritative teaching church having the right to bind the consciences of its believers to profess what is taught in order to avoid clinging to erroneous understandings of Scripture. Simply put, Reformation doctrine has within it the seeds of its endless divisions. This markedly contrasts with the Catholic position, which holds that there is a Church having apostolic authority to teach in Jesus' name – teaching to which the faithful are bidden to listen.

The pattern for keeping the unity of faith and the fellowship of believers we can readily see in the infant Church. Final decisions are made by the Church itself, as indicated in Matthew 18:15-18. In this passage, we are instructed to solve disputes between each other first, but if the situation warrants the matter can be brought before the Church. There is no reason to restrict the "sin" in question to exclusively moral conduct, but can also be applied to erroneous beliefs in matters of faith (i.e., heresy) – things that the Christian community have always held to be sins. Notice that, once the Church renders a decision, the decision is final, and the individual is expected to comply or be excommunicated from the community. According to Christ, the decision that has just been "bound" on earth is now "bound" in heaven. Is such a decision subject to error? Could error and untruths be "bound" in heaven? It would seem that such a statement necessarily leads one to consider whether or not such decisions are made infallibly.

In the book of Acts, we have one such decision. St. Paul entered into debates over whether or not the new Gentile converts had to undergo the rite of circumcision that had been handed on to the Jews by Patriarch Abraham. It is a sacred rite of the utmost of solemnity for the Jewish people. Was this rite now to continue in the New Testament Church? The dispute was passionate, as recorded in Acts 15:1-5. The controversy was so severe that Paul and Barnabas could not handle it alone. Instead, they were "sent on their way by the church" (v. 3) to consider the matter with the Apostles and elders in Jerusalem. Jerusalem was probably the largest Christian community at the time, and the city was probably the locus of authority in the early Church. The Christian community of Rome may not even have existed yet, for the very disputed question had everything to do with the recent Gentile entry into the Christian community. Acts 15:6-12 illustrates the importance placed upon the Apostles in Jerusalem, among whom the chief was Peter. After much argumentation, Peter took to the floor and definitively put the matter to rest. He explicitly stated that the Gentiles have received the grace of the Holy Spirit, and hence the rite of circumcision no longer prevails. This was the matter in question, and it was Peter who first declared its truth. We are told that the answer Peter gave was met with silence, and then afterwards Barnabas and Paul gave evidence of what God has done among the Gentiles – thereby backing up Peter's decision. In response James also said, "Simeon has related..." (Acts 15:13-14). The words "has related" are actually a less forceful translation. The nuance from the Greek bears the connotation "has drawn out the truth". James merely acknowledged and supported Peter's decision, and went on to stipulate some disciplinary matters. That the Council of Jerusalem carried with it the authority to bind Christians to believe what was taught there is verified in Acts 16:4: "As they went on their way through the cities, they delivered to them for observance the decisions which had been reached by the apostles and elders who were at Jerusalem." This scenario is the pattern for Church authority: a question arose, a council called, and a decision made. People did not appeal to the Scriptures alone and argue about the meaning of various passages – only to depart from each other, believing their view was the biblical one.

I have stressed above the role of Peter in the Council of Jerusalem, because it is the Catholic belief that Peter was the first pastor of the Church. His leadership will be dealt with in greater detail in Chapter 2, where full quotations will be given. Nevertheless, it is important now to mention in summary fashion a text that highlights Peter's prominence. This, of course, is Matthew 16:13-19. This passage contains the most hotly contested verses between Catholics and Protestants. For the Catholic it asserts the uniqueness of Peter's authority.

The first distinguishing characteristic of this passage is the name change. Simon, whose name means "reed" (which sways in the wind), has his name changed to "rock" (which is not easily moved). Names were significant to the Jewish people. Changes in name meant a change in the ontology of the persons and their relationship to God and His covenant. For example, the Patriarch Abraham's name was changed from Abram, and Sarah's was changed from Sarai, whereas Jacob's was changed to Israel. On each of these occasions, God was giving a new relationship to the people whom He was calling to Himself. Christ changed Simon's name to Peter (meaning "Rock"), which would thereafter be the substitute for his original name. So, right away, we see something happening to Peter in this passage for having faithfully confessed the truth about Jesus' identity.

The passage goes on to say that Peter will be given the keys to the Kingdom of Heaven. A key in those days was a symbol and hallmark of authority. He who has the keys is said to possess ultimate authority. The background for this idea is Isaiah 22:19-24. In this passage, Eliakim received the key of David, thus giving him the authority over King David's house. He was not the owner of the key, but its possessor. He exercised its use in the name and with the authority of the king. So also does Peter. He is now to be the steward of Christ the King. The allusion here is unmistakable, and many editions of the Bible cross-reference the two passages. The symbolism of the key indicates the authority to bind and loose within the kingdom: that is, the ability to make definitive judgments pertaining to that very kingdom. Matthew 16:19 concludes with the declaration: "Whatever you bind on earth shall be bound in heaven, and whatever you loose on earth shall be loosed in heaven". In Matthew 18:18, the authority of binding and loosing is given to the Church when it gathers in authoritative councils, but in Matthew 16:19

it is given to Peter individually in the context of the keys. Once again, can any untruth or falsehood be bound in heaven? If not, then what is bound on earth must, as a logical consequence, also be bound infallibly.

Some Church fathers, commenting on Matthew 16, understood "Rock" to refer to Peter and his role in the Church. St. Cyprian, writing in the mid third century in his famous work *On the Unity of the Catholic Church*, states:

> "I say to you," He says, "you are Peter, and upon this rock I will build my church, and the gates of hell shall not prevail against it. And I will give you the keys of the kingdom of heaven; and whatever you shall bind on earth shall be ground also in heaven, and whatever you shall loose on earth shall be loosed also in heaven" (Mt 16:16-18). Upon him, being one, He built His Church and although after His resurrection He bestows equal power upon all Apostles, and says: "As the Father has sent me, I also send you. Receive the Holy Spirit: if you forgive the sins of anyone, they will be forgiven him; if you retain the sins of anyone, the will be retained" (Jn 20:21f), that He might display unity, He established by His authority the origin of the same unity as beginning from one. Surely the rest of the Apostles also were that which Peter was, endowed with equal partnership of office and of power, but the beginning proceeds from unity, that the Church of Christ may be shown to be one. (Willis, 49-51)

And again, in one of his letters, he writes,

> Our Lord, whose precepts and admonitions we ought to observe, describing the honor of a bishop and the order of His Church, speaks in the Gospel, and says to Peter, "I say unto you, that you are Peter, and upon this rock will I build my Church; and the gates of hell shall not prevail against it. And I will give unto you the keys of the kingdom of heaven: and whatsoever you shall bind on earth shall be bound in heaven; and whatsoever you shall loose on earth shall be loosed in heaven" (Mt 16:16-

18). Thence, through the changes of times and successions, the ordering of bishops and the plan of the Church flow onwards; so that the Church is founded upon bishops, and every act of the Church is controlled by these same rulers. (Willis, 50)

St. Cyprian was not alone in this affirmation. St Jerome, one of the greatest biblical scholars of his own day, also viewed the office of Peter as the Rock. Jerome writes:

> As I follow no leader save Christ, so I communicate with none but your blessedness, that is with the chair of Peter. For this, I know, is the rock on which the Church is built! This is the house where alone the paschal lamb can be rightly eaten. This is the ark of Noah, and he who is not found in it shall perish when the flood prevails. (Willis, 60)

Necessary to Preserve Unity of Faith

Why does the Catholic Church place such emphasis on the outward structures of the Church? The answer is for the sake of preserving unity in matters of faith: "Whether then it was I or they, so we preach and so you believed" (1 Corinthians 15:11). As there is only one Lord, there can be only one faith (see Ephesians 4:4-6). The church is the locus of unity – *not* the Scriptures. It is the Church that is the Body of Christ joined to Christ its head, and this oneness was meant not only to be invisible, but to be visible as well. It is not the Scriptures alone that create the unity of faith, because the Scriptures are not always easy to comprehend: "So also our beloved brother Paul wrote to you according to the wisdom given him, speaking of this as he does in all his letters. There are some things in them hard to understand, which the ignorant and unstable twist to their own destruction, as they do the other scriptures" (2 Peter 3:15-16).

Could those who do not accept the oral Tradition, the very context out of which the Scriptures arose, be without knowledge of the teaching that, while materially in the Scriptures, is not set forth formally? We are reminded to be cognizant of those who passed the faith onto us. This is crucial, because the Apostles and their successors are part and parcel of the foundation of the Church. Who our leaders are, and whether or not they have the authority to act in the name of Christ, matters to the Catholic:

> And we have the prophetic word made more sure. You will do well to pay attention to this as to a lamp shining in a dark place, until the day dawns and the morning star rises in your hearts. First of all you must understand this, that no prophecy of scripture is a matter of one's own interpretation, because no prophecy ever came by the impulse of man, but men moved by the Holy Spirit spoke from God. (2 Peter 1:19-21, boldface emphasis added)

The "we" here refers to the Apostles, and, by extension, those to whom they have entrusted the sacred deposit of the Faith. Those who were commissioned by the Apostles are referred to as the "the successors to the Apostles" in the Catholic Faith. In this passage, Peter reminds Christians of their authority. If the prophecies of Scripture are not subject to private interpretation, because by their nature they come from the Holy Spirit, then to whose interpretation are they subject? The answer is: the Church with its ministry handed down from the Apostles.

The precedent for this verdict is found at the outset of the book of Acts in the selection of Matthias as one who would take the place of Judas Iscariot (see Acts 1:15-26). Here Judas Iscariot is said to have possessed an office that could be handed on to another. This is the first example, straight from the Scriptures, of evidence for the doctrine of Apostolic Succession.

Apostolic Succession refers to the reality that the Bishops have received their ministry in a line of succession straight from the Apostles through the laying on of hands. The Catholic views the Bishops as those who have succeeded the ministry of the Apostles. While they themselves are not witnesses to the Resurrection, they are able (down through Church history) to receive their ministry of teaching, preaching, and sanctifying. The Scriptures use three words designating church leaders in the Church: presbyter, elder, and overseer. The Greek word *"episkopos"*, translated as "overseer" or "guardian", is also the word from which we derive the word "bishop". The "episcopacy" of the Catholic Church refers to the Bishops. These are the men who have been "entrusted" with the

Faith in order that it may be passed on to others: "What you have heard from me before many witnesses entrust to faithful men who will be able to teach others also" (2 Timothy 2:2). Those who have been chosen as leaders for the church have themselves been chosen by men previously selected by the proper leadership. The notion that a man would go with Bible in hand, and start a new church with himself as its leader, and his own doctrine as its distinguishing feature, was unknown prior to the Protestant Reformation. Up until that time, divisions within the church were schisms, in which those who were properly selected as leaders broke faith and/or authority with the rest of the Church.

As the Apostles and their teaching were one, so should the Faith of the Church in latter ages be one. But how can this oneness be maintained without a God-given authority manifested in an outward structure? The Church is both visible and invisible. Catholics are often accused of treating the Church's outward structures with more deference than its invisible nature. This may seem the case in Catholic-Protestant dialogues that focus on disagreements, but it is in fact far from the truth. Indeed, the invisible nature of the Church is always prominent in Catholic piety. When Christ commissioned His Apostles, He told them to go forth and make disciples – not to write books. When he sent them to preach the Gospel, he gave them authority. The Apostles, imitating their Lord, did the same. It is through this simple method of transmission that the truths of the Faith have been propagated down to the present day. Protestant doctrines are in constant flux, and what they teach today may yet be contradicted tomorrow. The Faith of the Catholic Church, while developing consistently, remains substantially the same since its birth nearly two thousand years ago. Sacred Scripture itself recognizes this important truth of the Church's stability, when it says (after much discussion on the bishop and deacon): "You may know how one ought to behave in the household of God, which is the church of the living God, the pillar and bulwark of the truth" (1 Timothy 3:15).

Bibliography

Akin, James. *"Defending the Deuterocanonicals"*. http//www.cin.org/users/james/files/deuteros.him

Bercot, David W. *A Dictionary of Early Christian Beliefs*. Peabody, MA: Hendrickson Publishers Inc., 1998.

Brown, Raymond. *Response to 101 Questions on The Bible*. Mahwah, NJ: Paulist Press, 1990.

Brown, Raymond E. and Collins, Raymond F. *The New Jerome Biblical Commentary*. Englewood Cliffs, NJ: Prentice Hall, 1990.

Bunson, Matthew. *Our Sunday Visitor's Encyclopedia of Catholic History*: *"Canon"*. Huntington, Indiana: Our Sunday Visitor Publishing Division, 1995.

Chadwick, Henry. *The Oxford History of Christianity: "The Early Christian Community"*, edited John McManners. Oxford, England: Oxford University Press, 1990.

Dupuis, J. and Neuner, J. *The Christian Faith*. New York, NY: Alba House, 1996.

Fastiggi, Robert. *Not By Scripture Alone: "What Did Early Protestant Theologians Teach about Sola Scriptura?"*, edited Robert A. Sungenis. Santa Barbara, CA: Queenship Publishing Company, 1997.

Forestell, J.T. *New Catholic Encyclopedia: "Bible"*. New York, NY: McGraw Hill Book Company, 1967.

Gasque. *The New International Dictionary of the Christian Church*: *"Marcion"*, edited Douglas Cairns. Grand Rapids, MI: Zondervan Publishing House, 1978.

Keating, Karl. *Catholicism and Fundamentalism*. San Francisco, CA: Ignatius Press, 1988.

Lull, Timothy. *Martin Luther's Basic Theological Writings: "Preface to the New Testament"*. Minneapolis, MN: Fortress Press, 1989.

Metzger, Bruce. *The Bible through the Ages.* Pleasantville, NY: Reader's Digest Association, 1996.

Miletic, Stephen F. *Our Sunday Visitor's Encyclopedia of Catholic Doctrine: "Sacred Tradition".* Huntington, IN: Our Sunday Visitor Publishing Division, 1997.

O'Connor, Jerome Murphy. *The New Jerome Biblical Commentary: "The First Letter to the Corinthians",* edited Raymond E. Brown. Englewood Cliffs, NJ: Prentice Hall, 1990.

Shea, Mark P. *Not By Scripture Alone: "What is the Relation Between Scripture and Tradition?",* edited Robert A. Sungenis. Santa Barbara, CA: Queenship Publishing Company, 1997.

Theisen, A. *A Catholic Commentary on Holy Scripture: "The Epistle to the Romans".* New York, NY: Thomas Nelson & Sons, 1953.

Viviano, Benedict. *The New Jerome Biblical Commentary: "The Gospel According to Matthew",* edited Raymond E. Brown. Englewood Cliffs, NJ: Prentice Hall, 1990.

Wells, David F. *The New International Dictionary of the Christian Church: "Tradition",* edited Douglas Cairns. Grand Rapids, MI: Zondervan Publishing House, 1978.

Willis, John R. *The Teachings of the Church Fathers.* San Francisco, CA: Ignatius Press, 2002.

CHAPTER TWO
The Church, the Papacy, and Apostolic Succession

Unity as the Express Will of God

The unity of all His followers is the Will of our Lord and Savior Jesus Christ, as recorded in John 17:20-21. This prayer in anticipation of His Passion indicates His state of mind, revealing His intense desire for a unity applicable not only to those present at the Last Supper but extending in time to us (those who will believe in Him through their word). Christ's expectations are high, since this unity is to be modeled on the Most Blessed Trinity. It is to reflect the unity between the Father and the Son, and is to serve as the witness that Jesus is who He says He is — the one sent by the Father. The believability of the Gospel rests on this unity. Expressed in the negative, if the followers of Christ do not visibly manifest this unity, then the world may not believe in Him. The stakes are high, and one is compelled to wonder whether this was clearly understood by the Apostles and the early Church and whether there were provisions made by Christ to ensure this unity. This chapter will present the biblical basis that supports the Church and the Papacy as the symbols and instruments of unity accomplished by and in Christ Jesus.

The concept of unity is central in the New Testament. As evidence for this assertion, we submit, for example, Ephesians 4:1-6. Here the Apostle St. Paul speaks succinctly and with clarity of the unity required of those who are to live in a manner worthy of the call they have received, namely to be the followers of Christ. He urges them to strive to preserve this unity, since there is one true Lord, one true faith, and one true baptism, for there is one God and Father of all. This passage exhorting us all to unity in one faith flows from a previous statement in the same epistle that establishes wherefrom this faith can be obtained:

To me, though I am the very least of all the saints, this grace was given, to preach to the Gentiles the unsearchable riches of Christ, and to make all men see what is the plan of the mystery hidden for ages in God who created all things; that through the church the manifold wisdom of God might now be made known to the principalities and powers in the heavenly places. This was according to the eternal purpose which he has realized in Christ Jesus our Lord. (Ephesians 3:8-11)

It is through the Church that "the manifold wisdom of God might now be made known" even "to the principalities and powers in the heavenly places." It is through the Church that the hidden mysteries and unsearchable riches of Christ are manifested.

The Church as a Sign and Instrument of Unity

The Church is so pivotal in the understanding of the faith that the same apostle reminds Timothy, the Bishop of Ephesus, that the Church is the pillar and foundation of truth: "If I am delayed, you may know how one ought to behave in the household of God, which is the church of the living God, the pillar and bulwark of the truth" (1 Timothy 3:15). The Church is the family of God; in this household, we learn how to behave in our relationship with God in the same way as we learn to behave socially in our own human families. The physical is indeed a sign of the spiritual. Intrinsic to the salvific plan of God was the establishment of the Church, accomplished by Christ Jesus, to teach us the faith so that we could know the manifold wisdom of God.

But how and when did Christ accomplish this? The Gospel of Saint Matthew provides the answer:

Now when Jesus came into the district of Caesarea Philippi, he asked his disciples, "Who do men say that the Son of man is?" And they said, "Some say John the Baptist, others say Elijah, and others Jeremiah or one of the prophets." He said to them, "But who do you say that I am?" Simon Peter replied, "You are the Christ, the Son of the living God." And Jesus answered him, "Blessed are you, Simon Bar-Jona! For flesh and blood has not revealed this to you, but my Father who is in heaven. And I tell you, you are Peter, and on this rock I will build my church, and the powers of death shall not prevail against it. I will give you the keys of the kingdom of heaven, and whatever you bind on earth shall be bound in heaven, and whatever you loose on earth shall be loosed in heaven." (Matthew 16:13-19)

In this passage, we see the deliberate intent of Jesus, who took his apostles thirty miles north of their general area of operations (Galilee) to a region bearing a Roman regal name, Caesarea Philippi. That men such as the Romans would treat this area with such deference should give us pause, but it should not surprise us after we apprehend the geological significance of the area. Caesarea Philippi features a mountain of solid rock in the middle of the desert rising to approximately 200 feet. Water gushing out from its base forms one of the tributaries to the Jordan River, the river that gives life to this region. The Romans had built a temple to one of their gods upon it. It is here that Jesus asked them about His identity. We can visualize the apostles, sweaty and tired from the walk, marveling at their new surroundings. It is here where Jesus asked them the question: "Who do men say that the Son of man is?" The answers flowed easily; however, Jesus was not satisfied. He asked again, but this time at the personal level: "But who do you say that I am?" Now, prudence is always a good option, and their apparent silence would indicate as much. Yet, there was one who dared to speak – Simon, the son of Jona. (This fisherman always did most of the talking at any crucial moment.) He answered correctly and Jesus blessed him, asserting that it was the Father who provided the answer. Seeing that His Father chose Simon as the channel of the answer, Jesus, in turn, responded by giving Simon a new name: Peter.

Name-changing by God is rare, and it implies newly acquired responsibilities and authority by the individual. One such case occurred when God changed the name of Abram to Abraham (see Genesis 17:5). It is at this juncture that God established the Old Testament circumcision-covenant with Abraham and through him with his descendants (see Genesis 17:8-11). The change in name of Abraham was a condition immediately preceding the circumcision-covenant established by God with Abraham and his descendants – a momentous time in the history of the people of God.

Nothing less than that is what occurs in the Aramaic (the language spoken in that region at the time) when Simon was renamed "Cephas", and was made the ROCK upon which the Church of Christ would rest. This is the Church with which Christ, at the Last Supper, would establish His new covenant or "testament" (see Matthew 26:27-28). The translation of the Aramaic "Cephas" as "Peter" (or "Rock") can be deduced from John 1:42: "He brought him to Jesus. Jesus looked at him, and said, 'So you are Simon the son of John? You shall be called Cephas' (which means Peter)".

Hence, it is in this region that Jesus named Simon the ROCK upon which He (Jesus) would build His Church, in a fashion similar to the Romans who had built their temple upon the Rock in Caesarea Philippi. Simon Peter was made the ROCK foundation of the Church (in the singular) to be built by Christ. By Christ's own design, this Church, built upon Peter, would have the gift of indefectibility, meaning that no power could destroy it or lead it into error – as stated by Jesus: "the gates of hell shall not prevail against it." Making Peter the rock foundation of His new Household was only the beginning, for Jesus required an administrator with supreme authority to run His new Household. So He proceeded to give Peter the KEYS to the true Kingdom (Heaven), and whatsoever (a very ample word) Peter binds on earth would be so bound in Heaven and whatsoever Peter loosens on earth would be loosened in Heaven. This is authority!

We also note the significant word play between "Caiaphas" (the name of the high priest during the time of Christ's Passion, as recorded in John 11:49-51; 18:13-14, 24) and "Cephas" (which comes from the Greek for "head"). In other words, through this richly symbolic name-change Christ was anticipating the abrogation of the old covenant priesthood. He was implicitly removing the authority of this office from its previous rulers by bestowing the New Testament high priesthood on Peter in making him the visible head of His Church.

The Keys are Key to Understanding the Papacy

The fact that Jesus gave a key to Peter veils a deeper meaning, which is revealed in two other passages of Scripture – in the books of Isaiah and Revelation. These passages highlight the concept of authority, a concept crucial to the understanding of the Christian faith. The richness of detail in the Isaiah passage allows the reader to visualize the steward of the palace, the one "who is over the household" as an awesome representative of the king's authority. One would recognize him instantly, due to his unique robe and sash; also, he would be found carrying the key of the city of Jerusalem on his shoulder as a sign of his unmistakable position. This was evident to all the inhabitants of Jerusalem, high and low. The palace steward had the utmost confidence of the king and would act implicitly with the king's authority. His control of the key to the gates of the city (the most vulnerable section on the city's defense in the case of a siege) was crucial to the city's survival; if the key were to be taken by the enemy or the steward were to betray his countrymen, all would be lost. The pertinent passage in Isaiah follows:

> In that day I will call my servant Eliakim the son of Hilkiah, and I will clothe him with your robe, and will bind your girdle on him, and will commit your authority to his hand; and he shall be a **father** to the inhabitants of Jerusalem and to the house of Judah. And I will place on his shoulder **the key of the house of David; he shall open, and none shall shut; and he shall shut, and none shall open**. And I will fasten him like a peg in a sure place, and he will become a throne of honor to his father's house. (Isaiah 22:20-23, boldface emphasis added)

We recall that Shebna (the displaced steward) was unfaithful to God by relying on the military power of the king of Egypt to save Judah from the attack of the Assyrians, instead of trusting in God for their deliverance as advised by the prophet. So, God replaced the unfaithful servant with Eliakim, son of Hilkiah, and set him as a FATHER to the inhabitants of Jerusalem. This is the significance of the position; the steward was to serve a fatherly role to the chosen people, which is akin to the function of the Pope to all Catholics. The word "Pope", after all, comes from the Italian word "Papa", which means "Father". Eliakim received the key to the House of David in a manner similar to Peter's receipt of the key to the Kingdom of Heaven, so that when one opens, no one else could shut (the play on words between open and shut and bind and loose indicates authority). This authority is akin to and derived from the authority of the ultimate owner of the key – Jesus Christ. We see this in the book of Revelation: "And to the angel of the church in Philadelphia write:

'The words of the holy one, the true one, who has **the key of David, who opens and no one shall shut, who shuts and no one opens.**" (Revelation 3:7, boldface emphasis added)

Jesus Christ, a wiser man than Solomon (Matthew 12:42), must be expected to follow His own advice when building His own House (Church), as indeed He does:

> "Every one then who hears these words of mine and does them will be like a wise man who built his house upon the **rock**; and the rain fell, and the floods came, and the winds blew and beat upon that house, but it did not fall, because it **had been founded on the rock.**" (Matthew 7:24-25, boldface emphasis added)

The Authority of the Pope

Having solidly established the need for the Church in the salvific plan of God with Peter as its foundation, we need now to show the convergence of Scripture regarding Peter and his authority, lest we be accused of verse-slinging. Christians generally understand that the author of Scripture is the Holy Spirit, and, as such, we must see His wisdom and purpose even in the most simple of occurrences, such as the listing of the apostles, which appears three times in the Gospels (Matthew, Mark, and Luke). In all three lists, Peter is always first and Judas Iscariot (the one who betrayed Jesus) is always last, with the names of the others changing in position depending on the particular Gospel (Matthew 10:2-4, Mark 3:16-19, Luke 6:14-16). Is there an explicit intent by God in using this particular order? We think so, for we observe that even after Judas is no longer one of the twelve, Peter is still first (see Acts 1:13).

At crucial events (for example, the Transfiguration, the Agony in the Garden, and elsewhere), when Christ permitted only three Apostles to accompany Him, Peter is listed before James and John (see Matthew 17:1; 26:37, Mark 5:37; 9:2; 14:33, Luke 8:51; 9:28; 22:8). Even when not a single one of the other disciples is explicitly mentioned by name, Peter's importance ensures that, if anyone at all is going to be named, it will be he. For instance, when an angel ordered the women who arrived at the empty tomb on Easter morning to relay this glad news to the

Apostles, the angel explicitly named only Peter, who therefore stands out from the rest (see Mark 16:7). Moreover, St. Paul mentions that after His Resurrection Christ appeared to Cephas before appearing to all of the Apostles collectively (see 1 Corinthians 15:5). Indeed, Peter's name is the name mentioned the second most often in the New Testament; only Jesus Himself is named more frequently than Peter.

In addition to his new name and the possession of the key to heaven, Peter (and only he) was given a unique role regarding the faith:

> "Simon, Simon, behold, Satan demanded to have you, that he might sift you like wheat, but I have prayed for you that your faith may not fail; and when you have turned again, strengthen your brethren." And he said to him, "Lord, I am ready to go with you to prison and to death." He said, "I tell you, Peter, the cock will not crow this day, until you three times deny that you know me." (Luke 22:31-34)

Jesus, knowing that Peter would deny him, told Simon Peter that He had prayed that Peter's faith would not fail, so that once he "turned again" (repented) Peter would have the responsibility to strengthen the faith of the brethren. This responsibility was exercised through his strengthened faith, the result of the efficacious prayer of Jesus.

The gift of infallibility in the Faith thus conferred by our Lord on Peter (and his successors) should not be confused with impeccability. Peter, as well as each of his successors (see below), is protected by the Holy Spirit from teaching error in matters of faith and morals; however, they are susceptible to sin as much as any of the faithful. This explains how throughout the years we have seen sinful popes, yet there has been not a single documented case where a pope has taught error or where one pope has contradicted another. This alone is a testimony to the promise of our Lord and the action of the Holy Spirit in His Church.

An objection could be raised that, due to Peter's denial, he lost the right to the keys of the kingdom in a fashion similar to the unfaithful Shebna in the Isaiah passage; however, the contrary is seen in John 21:15-17. Note in this passage the subtlety in the first question that Jesus asks Simon Peter: "Do you love me more than these?" The primacy of Peter is conditioned on love, a God-like love that takes precedence over the love of humanity and also demands a greater love from Peter than from the other disciples. That Christ asked Peter the question three times was directly related to Peter's triple denial of Jesus, and Saint John alerts us to this relationship when he utilizes the "fire of coals" motif. Indeed, in John 18:16, we behold Peter warming himself at a charcoal fire during Christ's arraignment. But here, in John 21:9, just prior to the thrice asked question resulting in Peter's consistently repeated affirmations of love, St. John reports: "When they got out on land, they saw a charcoal fire there, with fish lying on it, and bread". The charcoal fire motif is not necessary elsewhere; it appears only twice in the entire Gospel of John. Interestingly, though, it brings to mind the purification by burning coal of the prophet's mouth in Isaiah 6:5-8 prior to his mission. Thus, instead of taking Peter down from his position, Jesus secured Peter in his position in front of all the others, so that Peter could, with his strengthened faith, feed the faithful. Peter was made the good shepherd who with a God-given love would feed the family of God in His Household, the Church.

Peter, Named the Undisputed Leader of the Christians by Christ

The Holy Spirit descended upon the Apostles during the feast of Pentecost and emboldened the previously timorous group to preach the Gospel with great fervor and courage. Again, during this event, we see Peter rising as the holder of the key to increase the family of the Household of God by making new converts from the Jews who were witnesses to the death and resurrection of Jesus Christ. He gave the first sermon after the Ascension of Christ into heaven (Acts 2:22-41), which included a receptive reaction on the part of those present (see Acts 2:37-41). Peter was not only first in bringing Jews into the Church, but he was also first in bringing Gentiles into the Church, as seen in Acts 10:25-48, which narrates the story of the conversion of Cornelius and his household.

The early Church was not free from controversy, yet it knew how to resolve disputes by going to Peter. We see how even an Apostle as Saint Paul did not appeal to his own authority regarding a crucial dispute, that of circumcising the new Gentile members of the family of God. Circumcision had been up to that moment the definitive act by which a male was to be received as a member of the chosen people of God. This was the sign of the covenant established by God and not revoked by Christ. So, this was not a small matter and it required the Pope to solve it; and solve it he did, as seen in Acts 15:1-12. After "much debate" had taken place (verse 7), Peter stood up and made his case. Scripture witnesses to us that, once Peter spoke, "the assembly kept silence" (verse 12) and the contentious issue was resolved. The assembly then moved along to the business at hand of making converts, and decrees were issued according to Peter's direction. Peter spoke and the matter was closed.

We can further elaborate on the theme of leadership by considering Matthew 17:24-27. In this passage Jesus wound up paying the temple tax after explaining to Peter why He was not really bound to do so: essentially because He, the Son of God, was the very foundation of the temple. But the critical point to observe is that He paid the tribute money through the mouth of a fish caught by Peter the fisherman. This incident exemplifies Christ's authority over the Church exercised via Peter, whose mouth would enrich the world with his teaching. Even more, Jesus virtually identified Himself with Peter by telling him that the single coin drawn from the fish would suffice to pay the tax for *both* of them together: He saw Himself as one with Peter. This event demonstrates that even outsiders appreciated the tacit leadership of Peter. An interesting sidelight is that Jesus preached from Peter's boat (see Luke 5:1-3), signifying that the Church, which voices the teaching of Christ for us, is truly the bark of Peter.

Finally, Peter shared in Christ's power, working the first miracle after the Ascension (see Acts 3:6-7). Peter imitated Jesus even in the details of the performance of miracles. We can see this by comparing Mark 5:22-24, 35-42 with Acts 9:36-41. In the passage from Mark, Christ raised a girl from the dead by uttering (in verse 41) the words "Talitha cumi" ("Little girl, arise"). There is literally a *sound* connection here through the Aramaic, because, in the passage from Acts, Peter restored to life a woman named "Dorcas" in Greek – pronouncing (in verse 40) the words "Tabitha, rise", which reflect her original Aramaic name.

Apostolic Succession

As the new shepherd, Peter well understood Isaiah 22. Seeing the need to fill the vacant position left by Judas Iscariot, he proceeded to act accordingly. A natural reaction would be to retire that position, due to the ignominy associated with the evil act of betrayal by Judas. So, when Peter made this announcement, it would be natural to expect a reservation (perhaps protest) by some of the disciples. But this was not the case. In Acts 1:17, Peter alludes to the "ministry" in which Judas shared. He then continues:

> For it is written in the book of Psalms, 'Let his habitation become desolate, and let there be no one to live in it'; and 'His **office** let another take. So one of the men who have accompanied us during all the time that the Lord Jesus went in and out among us, beginning from the baptism of John until the day when he was taken up from us – one of these men must become with us a witness to his resurrection." And they put forward two, Joseph called Barsabbas, who was surnamed Justus, and Matthias. And they prayed and said, "Lord, who knowest the hearts of all men, show which one of these two thou hast chosen to take the place in this ministry and apostleship from which Judas turned aside, to go to his own place." And they cast lots for them, and the lot fell on Matthias; and he was enrolled with the eleven apostles. (Acts 1:20-26, boldface emphasis added)

The ease by which this succession occurred points to the clear understanding the disciples had of the authority of Peter. This also underscores the logical appeal of the succession concept itself. The leadership exhibited by Peter above took place prior to the descent of the Holy Spirit upon the Church. The English translation of Acts 1:20 above renders the Greek word *"episkopei"* (from which the word "episcopal", or "related to the bishop", derives) as "office", implying the office of a Bishop. This office of the bishop or his ministry is what constitutes the hierarchy of the Church to this day.

From the necessity of the succession to the position of Judas, we can grasp that the more important position of Peter also needed succession. Nevertheless, an objection could be raised that, although we can clearly see the necessity of the succession to Judas, it does not follow that the succession of Peter was assured. In other words, whereas the primacy and authority of Peter was indisputable, someone may protest that this fact in no way guarantees that the primacy of his office was to remain until the end of time. To counter this objection, let us recall that the prayer of unity by Christ was by design applicable throughout time and that the Church built by Christ was never to cease ("the gates of hell shall not prevail against it"). Therefore, it follows that if the Church were to survive in time, it was even more critical to name a successor to Peter than it was to have a successor to Judas.

That there should be a continuous handing down of authority in Christ's Church of the New Covenant is not surprising. The New Dispensation of grace possesses an integral perfection incomparably beyond the Old. Yet, even in the Old Covenant, God made provision for the passing on of spiritual leadership – with special charisms attached. In fact, the apostolic succession is foreshadowed in the Old Testament by two key incidents.

First, God commissioned Joshua to take the place of Moses in leading the chosen people into the Promised Land (see Deuteronomy 31:23). In particular, we read in Deuteronomy 34:9: "Joshua the son of Nun was full of the spirit of wisdom, for Moses had laid his hands upon him; so the people of Israel obeyed him, and did as the Lord had commanded Moses." The laying on of hands is a sign of consecration, being set apart for a special role. Here, the rank of full authority is conferred, with the power and right to command everyone's obedience. Note that this office, which was handed on to Joshua upon the impending death of Moses, also included a charism of wisdom and prophecy, associated with the Holy Spirit.

Second, there is the famous transition in the office of principal prophet, when Elisha succeeded Elijah. We recall that Elisha, upon the imminent departure of Elijah, had asked Elijah: "I pray you, let me inherit a double share of your spirit" (2 Kings 2:9). The sign that this request would be granted consisted in Elisha's witnessing of Elijah's exit from this world. Not only did Elisha observe Elijah's passage, but he also beheld much more: the assumption of Elijah into heaven amidst a fiery whirlwind (see 2 Kings 2:10-12). The fire and the wind are symbols that serve, at least in part, to indicate the action of the Holy Spirit in choosing His new chief spokesman. Indeed, the other prophets confirmed Elisha's rightful succession in the role previously occupied by Elijah: "The spirit of Elijah rests on Elisha" (2 Kings 2:15). Moreover, just as Elisha watched Elijah leave earth in this astonishingly supernatural manner, so also did the Apostles gaze into heaven at Christ's Ascension (see Acts 1:9-11), which was followed later by the descent of the Holy Spirit in the form of fire accompanied by "the rush of a mighty wind" (see Acts 2:1-4).

Our Lord Himself ratified the legitimacy of a continuous succession of religious authority stemming from the time of Moses: "Then said Jesus to the crowds and to his disciples, 'The scribes and the Pharisees sit on Moses' seat; so practice and observe whatever they tell you" (Matthew 23:1-3). This is an important text, because the Greek word for "seat" is *kathedra*. This is exactly the term, Latinized as *"ex cathedra"*, that is employed by Catholic theology to denote solemn definitions of Church dogma promulgated by the Popes who sit on the throne of St. Peter. They are the successors of Christ, the New Moses, and hence of the chief Apostle whom Jesus made the first visible head of His Church on earth. Like Moses and Joshua, like Jesus and Peter, the Popes have the authority to command the obedience of the whole Church when they pronounce decisions on matters of faith, morals, or mandatory ecclesiastical disciplines. Like Elijah and Elisha, they also possess a certain charism of wisdom and even prophecy, in order to know the prudent way in which the deposit of Faith should be handed on and applied to new circumstances: "Every scribe who has been trained for the kingdom of heaven is like a householder who brings out of his treasure what is new and what is old" (Matthew 13:52; see also 24:45). The Popes are the heads of "the household of God, which is the church of the living God, the pillar and bulwark of the truth" (1 Timothy 3:15). Guided by the Holy Spirit, they are the official guardians of the treasure of the Christian Faith; they are the ones who, while preserving this treasure intact, can bring out facets of it that shine with the brightness of truth appropriate for answering each age's challenges. Protected by the Holy Spirit, "the Spirit of truth" (John 15:26), their official pronouncements in matters of faith and morals, when addressed to the universal Church, must be infallible.

Christ urged all disputes to be brought before the Church for adjudication, at least as a last resort:

> "If your brother sins against you, go and tell him his fault, between you and him alone. If he listens to you, you have gained your brother. But if he does not listen, take one or two others along with you, that every word may be confirmed by the evidence of two or three witnesses. If he refuses to listen to them, tell it to the church; and if he refuses to listen even to the church, let him be to you as a Gentile and a tax collector.

> Truly, I say to you, whatever you bind on earth shall be bound
> in heaven, and whatever you loose on earth shall be loosed in
> heaven." (Matthew 18:15-18)

We see in this passage that Christ grants the Church (as God gave Moses and Joshua) plenary power to serve as the court of last recourse. The Church's decisions oblige us in conscience, whenever the Pope (sometimes acting through his hierarchical delegates) clearly intends to bind the Church's members in matters of faith, morals, or discipline.

At this juncture, we should integrate two pertinent verses: Christ's admonition about listening to the Church in Matthew 18:15-18 (quoted above) and St. Paul's admonition to Timothy (quoted previously): "If I am delayed, you may know how one ought to behave in the household of God, which is the church of the living God, the pillar and bulwark of the truth" (1 Timothy 3:15). The natural, as well as supernatural, response to those admonitions ought to be: very well, I will adhere to what the Church has dictated. However, the obvious follow-up question is: how do I recognize this "church"? If one is to abide by the Church's decisions, it is essential that he know which "church" to follow. Therefore, this true Church must be *visible and recognizable*. One church and only one church can overcome this impasse: the Most Holy Roman Catholic Church. No other church can measure up to these critical standards. In fact, the Catholic Church, alone among the "denominations" of Christianity, has been present since the beginning, the time of the Apostles; that is, only the Catholic Church is "apostolic" in the strictest sense. And being apostolic is inextricably connected with historical succession in the Petrine office.

Scripture bears witness to the succession of "office" in the various mandates that St. Paul issues to St. Timothy regarding priests and bishops (see 1 Timothy 3:1-3).

These stringent requirements are reinforced in the letter of St. Paul to St. Titus (see Titus 1:7-9). The episcopal position should not be conferred lightly, for upon it will rest the continuity of Truth and Faith (see 1 Timothy 5:21-22). We can infer that these are Paul's instructions to bishops (Timothy and Titus) to designate future bishops in order to assure an orderly progression of authority in the Church. And who is the chief bishop? The Pope is the Bishop of Rome, as the Bishop of Rome is the Pope.

In his letters to St. Timothy and St. Titus, St. Paul attests to the Tradition that has been kept alive in the Catholic Church, as the Apostle himself states in his letter to the Thessalonians: "So then, brethren, stand firm and hold to the **traditions** which you were taught by us, either by word of mouth or by letter" (2 Thessalonians 2:15, boldface emphasis added). The Catholic Church, founded by Christ on Peter, the first Pope, follows in this Tradition; her faithful members practice obedience to all the Bishops of Rome (265 to this date).

CHAPTER THREE
The Holy Trinity

We Have Received a Great Revelation

The reader of these pages, if Christian, should accept with thanks the words of our Lord: "Blessed are the eyes which see what you see! For I tell you that many prophets and kings desired to see what you see, and did not see it, and to hear what you hear, and did not hear it" (Luke 10:23b-24). The Lord's very presence was a verification of these words, for who amongst the Jews expected God to take flesh? Yet Peter, speaking at Caesarea Philippi to Jesus on behalf of the entire apostolic band when asked by the Lord "Who do you say that I Am?', recognized that the Lord was not only the Messiah awaited by Israel, but indeed the "Son of the Living God" (Matthew 16:16). These words of Peter were inspired by the Holy Spirit, as is clear in the reply of Jesus, "Blessed are you, Simon Bar-Jona! For flesh and blood has not revealed this to you, but my Father who is in heaven" (Matthew 16:17). We are truly blessed, because we do not have to wait for the unveiling of so much of what was promised through the prophets (although we still await the completion of that unveiling!), but rather we can marvel at what God has wrought. God has more generously fulfilled His promises than anyone, before the said fulfillment, could have imagined.

Certainly one of the most astounding truths of the Christian Faith is that God has allowed us to peek into the mystery of His Trinitarian existence. The event at Caesarea Philippi, referred to above, is rich in significance, for Jesus' acceptance of Peter's response in itself reveals that God is more than one simple divine person. Indeed, this truth of Jesus' divine nature was so powerful that the Apostles had to be temporarily cautioned not to mention it to anyone (see Matthew 16:20). Later on, they would be instructed to spread this and all of the doctrine taught by the Lord to the ends of the earth (see Matthew 28:18-20; Mark 16:15-16; Acts 1:8). It is not possible to know the Holy Trinity unless we first acknowledge the divine Sonship of Jesus. For He is the Word, the truth of God; what He says we must completely accept and live by. We will return to the divine Sonship of Jesus further on, but now we must first ask the question: "Is the *doctrine* of the Holy Trinity found in Scripture?" The short answer is "yes".

Of course, the reader is not encouraged to look for the *word* "trinity" in the Holy Bible; it is not to be found even once. We must understand that the word belongs to the discipline of biblical theology. In the human attempt to understand anything, we invariably restate and organize what we learn in order to grasp the topic better with our intellect. For example, we use the term "biological father" in today's parlance. This term is not found in Scripture, but there are surely many "biological fathers" to be found there! In the case of the term "Holy Trinity", this is a term that has been used for many centuries by Christians to point to the mystery of the Father, Son, and Holy Spirit that is presented to us in the Bible. In fact, the word "bible" itself is not found in the Bible. So we need to realize that, in order to understand God better, we must abandon rigid models of literalism that would limit our discovery of the Truth.

The Holy Trinity in the Old Testament

No one could conclude from the Hebrew Scriptures alone that the Holy Trinity exists. There are only a few hints that one can see if the reader possesses Christian faith. At the culmination of creation when God creates man, He says: "Let **us** make man in **our** image, after **our** likeness" (Genesis 1:26, boldface emphasis added). This seems to be a singular example, since all the surrounding pericopes refer to God in the singular. Also of interest are scriptural texts that point to the Son of God in the prophet Isaiah (see Isaiah 9:6) and in the Psalms. For instance, Psalm 2:7 reads: "He said to me, 'You are my son, today I have begotten you'" (see also Psalm 110:1-3). The unique relationship to this "Son" described in those places implies that the God we know is not a singular divine person. Regarding the Holy Spirit, see Isaiah 63:10.

One of the most intriguing foreshadowings of the Trinity can be seen in the apparition of God to Abraham at Mamre in Genesis 18:1-14. We are told specifically in the sacred text that God appeared and that the lifting of Abraham's eyes brought him the sight of three "men". Christian tradition has consistently viewed this as a sign of the Trinity; Jewish opinion is that two of the "men" stand for angels. It is during this apparition that Abraham is promised a child, through whom all the promises made to Abraham were to be fulfilled (Genesis 18:10; see also Romans 9:6-9). There is a certain but imperfect symmetry between this experience of Abraham and Sarah — who, of course, was barren — and that of Mary (more on this further below).

Another rather startling intimation of the Blessed Trinity can be gleaned from Isaiah 48:12, 16:

> "Hearken to me, O Jacob, and Israel, whom I called! I am He, I am the first, and I am the last.... Draw near to me, hear this: from the beginning I have not spoken in secret, from the time it came to be I have been there." And now the Lord God has sent me and his Spirit.

Since Jesus says of Himself: "I am the Alpha and the Omega, the first and the last, the beginning and the end" (Revelation 22:13), the speaker in the above passage can be identified with Christ. Therefore, the "Lord God" who "sent" Him is the Father, who also "sent" the Holy Spirit.[1]

Yet hints, by their very nature, are not verifiable proofs. The Holy Trinity is an example of a doctrine that the faithful Christian can say is implicit in the Old Testament, but is only brought to light in the New. Because we have the faith of the New Covenant, we know that all the actions of God in the Old Testament were *Trinitarian* by necessity — man was created, chastised, covenanted, and promised salvation by the Father, Son, and Holy Spirit. The call to righteousness of life and final unity with God has always been an invitation to sharing in the life of the Holy Trinity, which is why Christians are baptized in the name of the Father, the Son, and the Holy Spirit. Yet, those under the old dispensation had no way of knowing this until the time of Christ.

One logically asks: "Why did not God explicitly reveal His Trinitarian nature in the Old Testament?" The answer to this must partly be seen in the need to battle *polytheism*.[2] We might say that the Christian doctrine of the Holy Trinity is a delicate truth, which can easily be confused with error by some Christians and become the reason for the outright rejection of Christianity by others. Of course, those of the Jewish Faith find the Trinity to be an obstacle in their acceptance of Christianity. Moreover, we note in history the early Church councils that had to deal with the various aspects of the truth of the Trinity in order to ward off various errors in doctrine.[3] One of the most pernicious heresies of the early Church was *Arianism*, which denied the divinity of Our Lord – which, of course, meant that it denied the Trinity also.[4] Nor can Muslims make sense of the doctrine.[5] So, if after the grace-filled advent of the Savior it is so easy to be confused about the Holy Trinity, then *a fortiori* it would have been no easier to understand this mystery in the Old Testament era. There was enough to do to eradicate the tendency of the chosen people to go after strange gods (note the "golden calf" episode in Exodus 32). The divinely appointed time within which God revealed His Trinitarian nature came when the Savior became incarnate.[6]

The Holy Trinity in the Gospels

The Apostle John tells us that "No one has ever seen God", but that it is "the only Son, who is in the bosom of the Father" who "has made him known" (John 1:18). We may then conclude that by "God" John is referring to the Father, since of course he *saw* Jesus, the son of Mary, and certainly believed Him to be the Son of God. (Lest the reader in any way doubt St. John's belief in the divinity of Jesus, see John 1:1-16.)

It is in the announcement of the Incarnation of the Son of God that the presence of the Trinity is first seen in the New Testament. In St. Luke's account (see Luke 1:26-38), we learn that the angel Gabriel, sent by the Father, reveals that the one born will be called "Son of the Most High", and also "the Son of God", because the Holy Spirit will come upon the virgin, Mary. It is not the Father or the Spirit that is to be born, but the Son. It is not the Father that comes upon Mary, but it is the Spirit. So, presented in this Scripture passage are the three divine Persons with three different works being accomplished: (1) the Father sends the angel; (2) the Spirit achieves the conception by "coming upon" Mary; and (3) the Son becomes incarnate in fulfillment of the will of the Father.[7] Of course, orthodox Christians would understand that all three divine Persons are united in these actions.

In this unity and distinction of the three divine Persons, we encounter the mystery of the Holy Trinity. God is a perfect spiritual being with no parts. The Persons of the Trinity are not parts of God; rather, they are *divine Persons*. We should not confuse divine Persons with human persons. Human persons are created and limited individual beings, with the identity and being existing as the same thing. One human person equals one human being. In general, "person" answers the question "who?" regarding individual identity, whereas "nature" answers the question "what?" with reference to the *kind* of being something is.

For example, take Bill. He is a human being of the type that we observe every day. That is, Bill is a unique member of the human race, and no other human individual acts through his instance of human nature, although each has an equal "share" in human nature – equal in what it means to be human. If Bill were to think that he is two persons, we would know that he has a problem. A psychiatrist might diagnose him with a "split personality". This is because we know that one human being has only one true identity.

But it is simply a mistake to assume that what applies to individual human beings like Bill applies to God. We should not try to see divine Persons within the parameters of human persons; if we do, we surely end up in error. So, if we were to think, drawing from our experience of human persons, that it is not possible for one God to be three Persons, that it is not possible for three distinct individuals to act in a unified manner through the same singular nature, then we would have refused to accept the mysterious character of the Master of Creation. God made Bill; Bill did not make God. We would also be ignoring the clear testimony of Sacred Scripture that God is three Persons, as is being shown in this chapter.

A divine Person is unlimited and uncreated. Now, we only know what a divine Person is from what we have received from the Old Testament, from the preaching of the early Church handed down in Tradition, and from the New Testament that was given to God's people through her. These sources tell us some things about the divine Persons from their operations, as we see in the Annunciation. Yet we can never know them completely – they remain a mystery. We do know from Sacred Scripture that the Father, Son, and Holy Spirit are all *united* internally in their actions as one God and at the same time are *distinct* Persons. Yet, it cannot be said in any way that the Father or the Spirit became incarnate; this salvific action is particular to the Son, for only He took on a human nature. Nor can it be said that the Son is[8] "less" divine because of the union of His divine personhood and nature with a human nature. We will consider this further on when we look at the evidence for the divinity of Jesus.

When we compare the announcement of the birth of the Messiah to the announcement that Abraham will have a child through Sarah, we observe some interesting similarities. In both cases there is an "impossibility" of having a child: on the part of Sarah, because she is barren, and on the part of Mary, no child is possible in the natural way due to a vow of virginity that she had made prior to her betrothal to Joseph.[9] In both instances, there are divine promises made by God that will benefit the chosen people and all of mankind. And in both miraculous pregnancies, there is a "three-ness" to the mode of the divine announcement.

Just as there is a Trinitarian presence expressed at the beginning of Our Lord's earthly life, so is there the same at the start of His public ministry. At the Jordan River when Jesus is baptized, a true *theophany* (manifestation of God) takes place. Matthew 3:13-17 attests to three signs discernible to the senses of vision and hearing. Those present saw (1) the Son and (2) "the Spirit of God descending like a dove" and coming down on Him; then they heard (3) the voice from the Father, "This is my beloved Son, in whom I am well pleased". St. John the Evangelist records, as well, what St. John the Baptist witnessed at the Jordan (see John 1:32-34). Later on in the synagogue at Nazareth, Jesus would refer back to this pivotal point in His receiving the mission through the Spirit: "The Spirit of the Lord is upon me, because he has anointed me.... He has sent me" (Luke 4:18; see also Isaiah 61:1). Indeed, all four evangelists attest to the Trinitarian apparition at the Baptism of Jesus (see also Mark 1:9-11 and Luke 3:21-22).

This does not mean that those present at the Lord's Baptism came to the conclusion that God had a triune nature; for this doctrine to be accepted, one needs the gift of Christian faith. Indeed, it took quite a while for the disciples of Jesus to come to belief in the fact that Jesus was divine.[10] But what we can say is that God was presenting signs, the full weight and significance of which Christians would later more completely understand.

That such a Trinitarian theophany took place at the Baptism of Jesus is a sign to all Christians of the importance of that Sacrament that begins the life of the Christian. Jesus commanded that the Apostles baptize at the Great Commission (see below), because, as Jesus told Nicodemus:

"Truly, truly, I say to you, unless one is born of water and the Spirit, he cannot enter the kingdom of God. That which is born of the flesh is flesh, and that which is born of the Spirit is spirit. Do not marvel that I said to you, 'You must be born anew.' The wind blows where it wills, and you hear the sound of it, but you do not know whence it comes or whither it goes; so it is with every one who is born of the Spirit." (John 3:5-8)

When we as Christians fulfill this command of the Lord to be born anew, we begin our life in the Trinitarian embrace, receiving the Word of God, being guided by the Spirit, so as to reach the house of Our Father in Heaven. The "wind" that "blows where it wills" brings the breath of God's spiritual life into our souls; we are recreated by His grace to be sons and daughters of God.

The Transfiguration of the Lord, as we read of it in Matthew 17:1-9, Mark 9:2-9, Luke 9:28-36, 2 Peter 1:16-18, is a Trinitarian theophany that shows the divine nature of Jesus. (The testimony of St. Mark retells the experience of St. Peter.) In their accounts all three evangelists attest to the fact that this event witnessed by three Apostles occurred upon a mountain, that Jesus shone brightly in the presence of Moses and Elijah, that a voice spoke saying that "this is my Son" and that they should "listen to Him", and that a cloud overshadowed the Apostles. St. Peter, in his Second Letter, recounts seeing the glory of Jesus on the mountain and hearing the heavenly voice:

We were eyewitnesses of his majesty. For when he received honor and glory from God the Father and the voice was borne to him by the Majestic Glory, "This is my beloved Son, with whom I am well pleased," we heard this voice borne from heaven, for we were with him on the holy mountain." (2 Peter 1:16-18)

The presence of the Son and the voice of the Father are easy to distinguish, but where is the Holy Spirit? It is signified by the cloud that overshadows them (recall how the Holy Spirit "overshadowed" or came upon Mary in Luke 1:35).

In order to understand better the importance of the cloud, we must go from Mount Tabor, the traditional site of the Transfiguration, to Mount Sinai (also known as "Mount Horeb"). When Moses ratified the covenant that Yahweh gave to the chosen people, he was called up to Mount Sinai to receive the stone tablets of the Decalogue. We are told that, upon his ascent, a cloud covered the mountain for six days (see Exodus 24:15-16; 33:9-11; see also Sirach 45:5). Nor should we forget the pillar of cloud that led and protected the Hebrews as they traveled through the Sinai desert (see Exodus 13:21-22; also Exodus 14:19-20; 40:38; Numbers 9:15-23; Psalm 78:14; Wisdom 10:17). Particularly interesting in the identification of the cloud with the Holy Spirit is the way in which it guided the people through the Sinai Desert. Of course, Christians trust in the Holy Spirit to guide them to the truth, per the words of Jesus in John 16:13-14. The trust of the faithful Christian in the Holy Spirit is analogous to the obedience of the faithful Hebrews who did the bidding of God in the desert. As His will was exemplified by the movements of the pillar of cloud, so also for the faithful Christian the Spirit "blows where it wills" (John 3:8). Notice also that according to the Exodus excerpt above, the pillar of cloud never left the Hebrews – just as the Holy Spirit will never leave the faithful disciples of Christ in His Church.

Indeed, Jesus prayed and promised that the Holy Spirit to be sent from the Father would always dwell with the Church:

> "I will pray the Father, and he will give you another Counselor, to be with you for ever, ... the Spirit of truth, whom the world cannot receive, because it neither sees him nor knows him; you know him, for he dwells with you, and will be in you." (John 14:16-17)

This passage clearly implies that this "other Counselor" or "other Paraclete" (in Greek, "*allon parakleton*") is a distinct personage from both the Father and the Son. Jesus goes on to explicitly identify this "Counselor" with the Holy Spirit, who would ever refresh the Church's living memory on all aspects of Christ's doctrine: "But the Counselor, the Holy Spirit, whom the Father will send in my name, he will teach you all things, and bring to your remembrance all that I have said to you" (John

14:26). The Holy Spirit is therefore a Person distinct from both the First and Second Persons of the Trinity.

We have seen a pattern in which a Trinitarian theophany was involved in the pivotal points of Our Lord's earthly life: the Annunciation, the Baptism at the Jordan River, and the Transfiguration on Mount Tabor. This theme is continued and brought to fulfillment in the giving of the authority to forgive sins and the Great Commission, both being post-Resurrection events.

No orthodox Christian could deny that the Resurrection was a Trinitarian event. This is because in all of Christ's activities, indeed during His entire earthly life, He was (and of course remains so eternally) united with the Father and the Holy Spirit in His divine nature. On the evening of Easter Sunday, this Trinitarian aspect was made explicit in the giving of the power to forgive sins to the Apostles. John remembers the words for us:

> "Peace be with you. As the Father has sent me, even so I send you." And when he had said this, he breathed on them and said to them, "Receive the Holy Spirit. If you forgive the sins of any, they are forgiven; if you retain the sins of any, they are retained." (John 20:21-23)

The gift of forgiving sins is astounding, because only God can forgive sins (see Luke 5:21; Psalm 103:2-3; Isaiah 43:25), unless of course He shares the power with someone whom He wants to use as an instrument of His forgiveness: the Apostles and their successors (see Matthew 16:18-19; 18:18).

As can be seen in the passage above, this power to forgive sins is surely given, and in a Trinitarian way. First, the Father sends the Son, who then breathes on the Apostles so that they will be so disposed by the grace of the Spirit that they can receive the awesome power to forgive sins from Jesus. The prerogative of pardoning sins is a power of the Trinitarian God; hence, it must be given in a Trinitarian way. We may surmise that the power to forgive sins is given on the day of Resurrection before the Great Commission, because it is uniquely a result of Christ's Easter triumph.

At the Great Commission, again the Holy Trinity is central. Matthew records for us the Lord's instruction:

"All authority in heaven and earth has been given to me. Go therefore and make disciples of all nations, baptizing them in the name of the Father and of the Son and of the Holy Spirit, teaching them to observe all that I have commanded you; and lo, I am with you always, to the close of the age." (Matthew 28:18-20)

To enter into a Christian relationship with God we must be baptized into His name. The name of the Son and the Spirit could not have been included unless they shared divinity equally with the Father. Think how ridiculous it would be to be baptized in the name of John the Baptist, or Moses, or Abraham! The fact that "in the *name*" rather than "in the *names*" is used is also highly significant. This very wording of our Lord is an assertion by Him that this three-ness of God in no way takes away from God's oneness. In this way, Israel's monotheistic faith is ratified.

In the Acts of the Apostles, Luke does not include the aforementioned baptismal formula, but in his account of the Ascension the Lord tells His disciples about the authority of the Father fixing the end time and the gift of the Holy Spirit that they will receive: "You shall receive power when the Holy Spirit has come upon you; and you shall be my witnesses in Jerusalem and in all Judea and Samaria and to the end of the earth." (Acts 1:7-8) Luke thus confirms the testimony of Matthew regarding the Trinitarian nature of the Great Commission.

The Holy Trinity in the Rest of the New Testament

The Acts of the Apostles and the various letters of the New Testament show that the Trinity was integral to the early Christians' understanding of their faith received from Jesus. This is evident in the very first Christian sermon, given on the feast of Pentecost by St. Peter. In this explanation of faith given to those who had just witnessed the onrush of the Holy Spirit, Peter said (in Acts 2:32-33): "This Jesus God raised up, and of that we all are witnesses. Being therefore exalted at the right hand of God, and having received from the Father the promise of the Holy Spirit, he has poured out this which you see and hear." By this proclamation, he made clear that the workings of the Trinity are central to the Christian understanding of God's plan of salvation. Later on in his ministry, St. Peter would express in Trinitarian terms the apostolic mission he was given (see 1 Peter 1:1-2).

The first Christian sermon was Trinitarian, and so was the first martyrdom marked by a Trinitarian vision. St. Luke tells us that St. Stephen, who had been chosen as one of the first deacons (see Acts 6:1-6), was arrested and gave a vibrant speech of witness before the Jewish high court. He spoke of the opposition of many of the chosen people to the word of God – which angered the council so much that they brought him out to be stoned. (The whole story about St. Stephen is reported in Acts 6-7). In the description of the events leading up to his death, we are told: "But he [Stephen], full of the Holy Spirit, gazed into heaven and saw the glory of God, and Jesus standing at the right hand of God" (Acts 7:55). Thus, Scripture tells us that the Trinity consoled him in his last moments.

St. Paul roots his teachings in a Trinitarian understanding of God, as is evident in his First Letter to the Corinthians: "Now there are varieties of gifts, but the same Spirit; and there are varieties of service but the same Lord; and there are varieties of working, but it is the same God who inspires them all in every one" (1 Corinthians 12:4-6). Here "Spirit", "Lord", and "God" refer to the three divine Persons. The Trinity is also part of his description of Christ's mystical body: "There is one body and one Spirit, just as you were called to the one hope that belongs to your call, one Lord, one faith, one baptism, one God and Father of us all, who is above all and through all and in all" (Ephesians 4:4-6; see also Romans 1:1,3,4). Also, he naturally invokes the Holy Trinity when he prays for his fellow Christians: "The grace of the Lord Jesus Christ and the love of God and the fellowship of the Holy Spirit be with all of you" (2 Corinthians 13:13). In Romans 8:15-17, he declares that the Holy Spirit bears witness to the adopted sonship of Christians, who become children of God and therefore "fellow heirs with Christ". In Ephesians 2:18, he links the three Persons: "Through him [Christ] we ... have access in one Spirit to the Father."

The Apostle John writes of the three divine Persons together in two places. In Revelation 1:4-5, He "who is and who was" refers to the Father, the "seven spirits" refers to the Holy Spirit (because of the seven gifts of the Holy Spirit – see Isaiah 11:2-3), and the Lord Jesus is directly mentioned. Since those in the seven churches had been baptized into the new life of the Blessed Trinity, they are being called to account for their actions by the same Trinity.

The other place where St. John makes explicit the Trinitarian operation in Christian faith is in his first letter:

> This is he who came by water and blood, Jesus Christ, not with the water only but with the water and the blood. And the Spirit is the witness, because the Spirit is the truth. There are three witnesses, the Spirit, the water, and the blood: and these three agree. If we receive the testimony of men, the testimony of God is greater; for this is the testimony of God that he has borne witness to his Son. (1 John 5:6-9)

In this passage, the Spirit witnesses to the supernatural actions of Christ in His passion, and as such becomes the testimony of God (the Father).

There are, of course, multiple references to the divine Persons of the Holy Trinity throughout the Scriptures. We will see some of them as we consider the Fatherhood of God, the divine Sonship of Christ, and the divine nature of the Holy Spirit. This examination will in no way be exhaustive.

The Fatherhood of God

The Fatherhood of God is a reality that comforted the chosen people, knowing that they had a filial relationship with their God. From the burning bush, God told Moses (in Exodus 4:22-23; see also Jeremiah 31:9) to state this truth to Pharaoh. The Israelites learned to pray with confidence to their Father-God (see Sirach 23:1,4,6). The experience of the Fatherhood of God in the old dispensation would be brought to fulfillment in Jesus Christ's announcement of the Kingdom.

Our Lord presented the Father in many ways. There are many instances of Jesus praying to the Father; for example, all of John 17 is a prayer addressed to the Father. He gave His disciples the "Lord's Prayer", thus teaching them to address God as Father in *the* Christian prayer (see Matthew 6:9-13 and Luke 11:2-4). He taught them in His various sermons about how the Father would care for all their needs (Matthew 6:25-31), that He was merciful (Luke 6:35-36), and that He wishes to lose no one (John 6:39-40).

Jesus also taught about the Father by way of parables. In that of the Prodigal Son (see Luke 15:11-32), He assures us that the Father is always waiting to embrace us with His mercy, whereas in the parable of the Unforgiving Servant we learn that we must emulate that same mercy of the Father in order to be saved (Matthew 18:23-35). Yet, it is in the relationship of Jesus to the Father that we learn how to live out what is meant to be a guide for us.

As a child, Jesus knew that He had a special and unique relationship to the Father. The youthful Jesus gives us example by His conviction that He belongs in His Father's house, saying to Mary and Joseph, "Did you not know that I must be in my Father's house?" (Luke 2:49b). Throughout His entire public life He shows that He came to do the work of His Father: "I do nothing on my own authority but speak thus as the Father taught me. And he who sent me is with me; he has not left me alone, for I always do what is pleasing to him." (John 8:28b-29; see also John 5:19-24) This trust and filial obedience lasts through the Passion, and is evidenced by His prayer in the Garden of Gethsemane (see Mark 14:36) and even on the cross (see Luke 23:46). Because He is the true Son of God, He can teach us how to be adopted children of God, as St. Paul taught (in Galatians 4:4b-5) that we are (see also Romans 8:15, 21).

All of St. Paul's epistles open with a characteristic greeting referring to God as "our Father" or "the Father", distinguished from the (or our) "Lord Jesus Christ" (see Romans 1:1,3,4,7; 1 Corinthians 1:3; 2 Corinthians 1:3; Galatians 1:1,3; Ephesians 1:2,3; Philippians 1:2; Colossians 1:2,3; 1 Thessalonians 1:1,3; also 3:11,13; 2 Thessalonians 1:1,2; 1 Timothy 1:2; 2 Timothy 1:2; Titus 1:4; Philemon 3). According to Ephesians 3:15, "every family in heaven and on earth is named" from "the Father" (see also Ephesians 4:6), and, according to James 1:17, "Every good endowment and every perfect gift is from above, coming down from the Father of lights with whom there is no variation or shadow due to change." St. James tells us that God the Father is the source of all good things, and implies that we can rely on His goodness because He is unchanging.

The Divinity of Jesus

Jesus spoke of Himself as having a special relationship with the Father – a relationship beyond that which the prophets had with God – saying such things as, "I and the Father are one" (John 10:30) and "I am in the Father and the Father is in me" (John 14:11a; see also verse 10, as well as John 16:15a). Indeed, the entirety of John 17 is a claim to unity with the Father and, hence, divinity. No such words had ever been voiced by the prophets who preceded Jesus, nor could they be spoken by anyone, unless he believed himself to be God. For such claims made by a creature of Yahweh would be blasphemy. Jesus did say such things because He wanted to make clear, in terms understandable to the chosen people, that He indeed was and is divine.

This claim to divinity is clearly made in the *"I Am"* passages of the Gospels. In order to understand the significance of these, we must return to the Book of Exodus and the call of Moses by Yahweh on Mount Horeb. While tending sheep, Moses saw the burning bush on the top of the mountain, and then ascended in order to investigate. He saw that the bush was burning but not being consumed. As he marveled at this sight, God spoke to him from the bush and told him that he would be His instrument through whom the chosen people would be freed from slavery in Egypt. When Moses asked who should he say had sent him, God responded, "I Am" (see Exodus 3:1-14, especially verse 14).

We do not have the space to discuss the deep philosophical and theological implications of this name, God's own self-given name. It is sufficient for our purposes to remark that this name uniquely points to the divine: the source, center, and goal of all that is. And this is exactly the name that Jesus invokes in His discussion with His opponents: "Truly, truly, I say to you, before Abraham was, I am" (John 8:58; in order to get the true import of this response, one should read the entire exchange in John 8:39-59). The reaction of those hearing this reply was indignation, and they took up stones in order to punish Him for what they thought was blasphemy, since He was claiming to be God. (The punishment for blasphemy, of course, is stoning to death – see Leviticus 24:16.) Of course, if one is God, then He cannot be guilty of blasphemy; Jesus is God and therefore rightly claims the biblical name uttered from the burning bush on Mount Horeb. He would use the power of this name at the time of His arrest (see John 18:3-6). And so, for a moment, the glory of the name of God (the "I Am" of "I am he") would throw back His attackers, causing them to fall to the ground, before He willingly submitted to their plans (which would ultimately be in fulfillment of the divine purpose).

Jesus claimed divinity by using the prerogatives of divinity. For example, He forgave sins (Matthew 9:1-8; Mark 2:1-12; Luke 5:17-26); He walked on water (Matthew 14:24-27; Mark 6:47-52; John 6:16-21);

He claimed lordship over the Sabbath (Luke 6:1-5; Matthew 12:1-8; Mark 2:23-28) that God had given to His chosen people (see Exodus 20:8-11); and, of course, He rose from the dead.

The Resurrection, the culmination of each of the four Gospels, proves everything to be true about the claims of Jesus. This is the central fact around which all of the Gospels revolve. It is most unsettling to the skeptics that this truth was propagated from the only place in which it could not be denied, Jerusalem. But the truth of the Resurrection could not be denied for a simple reason: too many people saw the risen Lord and hence knew by personal experience that the reason why the tomb was empty (which was not denied by the Romans or the Sanhedrin) was that it could not contain its Lord. According to Acts 1:3, "He presented himself alive after his passion by many proofs". We are told that Jesus appeared to Mary Magdalene (Mark 16:9; John. 20:11-18), to other women (Matthew 28:5-10), to Peter (Luke 24:34), to ten disciples (Luke 24:36-43; John 20:19-25), to the Eleven, including Thomas (Mark 16:14; John 20:26-29), to the disciples on the road to Emmaus (Mark 16:12-13; Luke 24:13-35), to a group of the disciples in Galilee (John 21:1-24), to James and the other Apostles (1 Corinthians 15:7), to five hundred people in one incident famous to the early Church (1 Corinthians 15:6), to the disciples at His Ascension (Matthew 28:16-18; Luke 24:50-53; Acts 1:4-11), and of course to St. Paul on the road to Damascus (Acts 9:1-6; 22:1-10; 26:12-18; 1 Corinthians 15:8).

It is no surprise, then, that the claim of the Jewish authorities that the body of Jesus was stolen could be taken seriously only outside the Holy Land, or in a later time as our own when books such as the *Passover Plot* can be published.[11]

Additional proof of the divinity of Jesus is found in the Trinitarian theophanies of the Baptism of the Lord and the Transfiguration, referred to above. Probably the most concise profession of the Christian belief that Jesus Christ is God can be found in the prologue of St. John's Gospel:

> In the beginning was the Word, and the Word was with God, and the Word was God. He was in the beginning with God; all things were made through him, and without him was not anything made that was made. (John 1:1-4)

The term "in the beginning" is meant by St. John – and God, the inspirer of all scripture – to bring the mind of the reader back to the first words of the account of creation in Genesis 1:1: "In the beginning God created the heavens and the earth." For only God could have been there then, since there was no thing yet created. The phrase "the Word was God" identifies the Son with the Father without confusing the persons. St. John makes clear the identification of the "Word" with Jesus in his first Letter:

> That which was from the beginning, which we have heard, which we have seen with our eyes, which we have looked upon and touched with our hands, concerning the **word** of life – the life was made manifest, and we saw it, and testify to it; and proclaim to you the eternal life which was with the Father and was made manifest to us – that which we have seen and heard we proclaim also to you, so that you may have fellowship with us; and our fellowship is with the Father and with his Son Jesus Christ. (1 John 1:1-3, boldface emphasis added)

That "all things were made through him, and without him was not anything made that was made" is clearly a divine claim. So also is the assertion "In him was life", which refers to the meaning of the name "I Am" that Jesus claimed: "I am the way, and the truth, and the life" (John 14:6). This congruence of "the Word" with Jesus is seen as well in the Book of Revelation: "He is clad in a robe dipped in blood, and the name by which he is called is The Word of God" (Revelation 19:13). Furthermore, He shares the Father's glory: "And the Word became flesh and dwelt among us, full of grace and truth; we have beheld his glory, glory as of the only Son from the Father" (John 1:14).

St. Paul writes of Jesus in a similar manner:

> He is the image of the invisible God, the first-born of all creation; for in him all things were created ... – all things were created through him and for him. He is before all things, and in him all things hold together.... For **in him all the fullness of God** was pleased to dwell (Colossians 1:15,16,17,19, boldface emphasis added).

Again, St. Paul writes: "In him [Christ] the whole fullness of deity dwells bodily" (Colossians 2:9). It would be a strained interpretation to read these passages as though Christ were anything less than divine, and, in fact, equal to God the Father in His deity – despite the term "first-born", which some may be tempted to understand in an Arian (or semi-Arian) way. Further confirmation is found in the Letter to the Hebrews:

> For to what angel did God ever say, "Thou art my Son, today I have begotten thee"? Or again, "I will be to him a father, and he shall be to me a son"? And again, when he brings the first-born into the world, he says, "Let all God's angels worship him." (Hebrews 1:5-6)

Despite the fact that the angels are also called "sons of god" (see Daniel 3:25), the eternally begotten "first-born" cannot be a mere creature, since it would be idolatrous for the angels to worship anyone inferior in divinity to God the Father.

Even the demons confessed Jesus' divinity (see Luke 8:28). This was only one episode fulfilling St. Paul's declaration in Philippians 2:9-11:

> Therefore God has highly exalted him and bestowed on him the name which is above every name, that at the name of Jesus every knee should bow, in heaven and on earth and under the earth, and every tongue confess that Jesus Christ is Lord, to the glory of God the Father.

Some Christians have difficulties "squaring" the divinity and the humanity of Christ. For example, St Luke tells us that the child Jesus "increased in wisdom and in stature, and in favor with God and man" (Luke 2:52). How is it possible, some ask, for *God* to increase in anything? Then there are the examples of Jesus' "ignorance" of things, such as when He did not know who touched Him as He traveled to heal the daughter of Jairus (see Luke 8:45) or when He did not know when the world would end (see Matthew 24:36). If Jesus is God, then how can He not know a single thing? The knowledge of Jesus involves deep theological questions and is ultimately a mystery. Christian orthodoxy has consistently held from the time of the early Church that Jesus has two natures. In order for us to understand the significance of this teaching, let us go to the saving act of the Lord that redeemed humanity – His death. Who was on the cross? One person, Jesus Christ. But what was He? God? Yes. Man? Yes again. He was both; indeed, He *had* to be both for God's plan to be fulfilled. The cross of Christ is an example of both the mercy of God and the justice of God, both of which are perfect, because everything about God is perfect. The perfect justice of God requires that our sins be, as it were, "paid" for. By our sins we, who are finite creatures, take on an infinite debt, since our sins offend One who is infinite. But we cannot pay an infinite debt in our mere humanity. Hence, it seems that justice must be done and we must be condemned.

But on the cross One who is infinite – the Second Person of the Blessed Trinity, who has taken on a human nature – can and does represent us (see 2 Corinthians 5:21; Ephesians 2:16; Colossians 1:20; 2:14). His death in His human nature therefore has an infinite value before the Father, because that human nature is held by His own infinite Son. Thus, in Christ God takes upon Himself our own punishment, and so the infinite mercy of God is displayed, as well as His justice.

Now let us get back to our original question: How could Jesus grow or be ignorant? We have seen the unity of Jesus' two natures (divine and human) in His divine personhood. But to be human, one must have a human will, intellect, etc. Jesus had all these. This is why in a way that is truly mysterious, Jesus, who in His divinity knew all things, could be ignorant in His human intellect. Indeed, He had to be ignorant of things in His human intellect, because a human intellect by definition is limited, but the knowledge of God is not limited. So, when there is any question about the knowledge of Jesus, it is always about His human intellect.

For reasons that are obvious from the foregoing, we also must say that Jesus had to be able to grow in any way that would be appropriate and normal for someone having a human nature. But does this possession of a human nature make Jesus "less" than the Father? You can draw such a conclusion only if you somehow isolate that human nature from the rest of Jesus. But such thinking is not real, for Jesus is one divine Person with two natures that will always be united – the God-man exists forever! He reigns forever with the Father and the Spirit, and is equal in majesty, power, and splendor.

Now, once some of the evidence of Jesus' claims to divinity has been considered, each individual must make a personal response. For, in fact,

Jesus asks each of us as we read the Gospels, "Who do **you** say that I am?", just as He asked Peter (Matthew 16:15). One cannot hide behind the idea that He was simply a great prophet, because a great prophet, who was only a human prophet, would not claim to be God. Indeed, such a person would be a false prophet! Nor can we say that He was out of His mind. The profoundly wise and unearthly words that are spoken by Jesus in Sacred Scripture are evidence of the sanest person who has ever lived, a man subject to no delusions. No, Jesus is either a bad man – a blasphemous man who should have been stoned to death – or He is God. Who do *you* say that He is?

The Divinity of the Holy Spirit

There are many mentions of the "Spirit of God" in the Hebrew Scriptures, but it seemed never to occur to the chosen people that the "Spirit" was a Person of God. Indeed, how could it? What was clear in the early revelation is that the "Spirit" is essential when God is creating something new. In Genesis 1:1-2, we read that the "Spirit", rendered from the Hebrew word *"ruah"*, which means "breath", moved over the waters as creation began: "In the beginning God created the heavens and the earth. The earth was without form and void, and darkness was upon the face of the deep; and the Spirit of God was moving over the face of the waters."

The Spirit's movement over the waters, sometimes translated as a "mighty wind", signifies the divine creating power that brings about the stages of creation described in Genesis. This Spirit (*"breath* of God") would effect the culmination of creation, when "the Lord God formed man of dust from the ground, and breathed into his nostrils the breath of life; and man became a living being"(Genesis 2:7). Recall how Jesus breathed on the Apostles when He gave them the power to forgive sins. This was also a "creative" action, for when we sin seriously we lose God's life in us; hence, to forgive sin is to breathe life anew into our souls. The Psalmist in Psalm 104:30 also attests to the part that the Spirit has in creation: "When Thou sendest forth thy Spirit, they are created; and thou renewest the face of the ground."

Just as the Spirit is present at the creation of the old Adam and at the creation (conception/incarnation) of the New Adam,[12] our Lord Jesus Christ. The Spirit is also present at the creation of the Church, the Body of Christ, which essentially happened at the Annunciation, but was brought to full form at Pentecost. We read in Acts 2:1-4 how the Holy Spirit came like a powerful wind into the room where the disciples were gathered. This was the *"ruah"*, the breath of God, creatively bringing the muscles, bones, sinews, and flesh of the Church together so that it would be in full form, analogous to the prophecy of Ezekiel 37:3-10.

During His Last Supper parting discourse, Jesus had promised that the Church would receive the Holy Spirit:

> "And I will pray the Father, and he will give you another Counselor, to be with you for ever, even the Spirit of truth, whom the world cannot receive, because it neither sees him or knows him; you know him, for he dwells with you, and will be in you.... But the Counselor, the Holy Spirit, whom the Father will send in my name, he will teach you all things, and bring to your remembrance all that I have said to you." (John 14:16-17, 26; see also John 16:13-15)

It may seem from these passages that the Holy Spirit is inferior to the Father and the Son. Yet, since Christ calls Him "the Spirit of truth" who "will guide into all truth" (John 16:13), and since Truth is a divine attribute essentially identical to the infinite God Himself (see John 14:6; 17:17), the divinity of the Holy Spirit is a necessary corollary.

Jesus had also insisted (in Luke 24:49) that the Apostles wait for the Spirit before they begin their mission of evangelization. The "power from on high" in this verse was precisely the breath of God giving new life to a new thing, the Church, which must be alive with the Spirit in order to preach the Gospel, as she was commissioned to do by the Lord. This new creation is still guided by the Holy Spirit, the Counselor, who supernaturally animates or vivifies the Church – and thus is divine.

Once we accept the existence of God and the Lordship of Jesus Christ, we must accept the divinity and guidance of the Holy Spirit. The reader is referred to the earlier parts of this chapter as they pertain to the Spirit. This cannot be an exhaustive study, but the main points are clear. The Father has sent the Son; the Son in turn has attested to His relationship with the Father and has made clear the essential role that the divine Person of the Holy Spirit has in leading us along the Christian path. The Spirit in turn confirmed with many signs and wonders the teaching of Christ by way of the evangelical work of the Church throughout the centuries. At the same time, the Spirit inspired the writing of the New Testament and the recognition of the canon of Scripture by the Church, so that all Christians could both see with their eyes and hear with their ears the Word of God that His Church presents for the salvation of all. Central to that Word of God is the truth of the Holy Trinity, which wishes to embrace us with love for all eternity. We have indeed received a great mystery!

CHAPTER FOUR
Justification and Salvation

Meanings of "Justification" and "Salvation"

The average religious person in the Western world has heard much about salvation, and often has grasped something of its meaning and importance. The most common questions about religion are questions about salvation. It is a vital word, a word that belongs to popular religion and culture. It is otherwise with the word "justification". The average person has no clue as to its meaning, and has little or no desire to find this out. As a technical term, it belongs mainly to the shoptalk of Christian theologians. Perhaps justification can be made interesting if we first gain a better grasp of salvation itself.

What teachers mean by salvation varies greatly from religion to religion, and even from one form of Christianity to another. There are two well-accepted Catholic meanings. One is narrower than the other. In the narrower sense, one has salvation only when one who needed to be rescued from sin and destruction finally sees God forever in glory, after the journey of this life is past. In this respectable usage, justification is clearly distinct from salvation, because justification is part of God's preparing us in this life for saving us in the next. But in the wider sense, salvation means whatever God has done, is doing, and will do to rescue us from sin and its destruction and to transform us gloriously into the likeness of His glory – that is, God's entire rescue-and-renovation operation, including justification and glorification (see Romans 5).[1] The Scriptures themselves teach of salvation in all three tenses, not only the future (see Romans 8:24, 1 Corinthians 1:18, 3:15, 15:2). Since this book focuses on the Bible, my chapter will be using "salvation" and "saved" in the wider Catholic meaning of these terms, for the sake of promoting easier communication with the average Protestant reader.

Baptism

Let's begin at the beginning of the Gospel of our Lord Jesus Christ. All four Gospels mention John the Baptizer as the herald of our salvation in Jesus Christ, calling Him "the Lamb of God, who takes away the sin of the world" (John 1:29). Simple mention of the Catholic religion often conjures up in the minds of our Protestant brothers and sisters some rather distorted images of a Catholic kneeling and confessing, in rather mechanical fashion, his most embarrassing sins, to a priest. Sadly, Protestants are rarely conscious of our other type of confession. Like John the Baptizer, we Catholics are bearing witness in the Holy Spirit to the saving power of Jesus Christ.

"Lamb of God, You take away the sins of the world. Have mercy on us." Every day, at every Catholic Mass throughout the world, Catholics pray these words. We pray them to our Risen Lord while He is Really Present on our altars. Ever since John the Baptizer stood on Jordan's banks almost two thousand years ago, God's people have known the Good News that is proclaimed in these powerful words (John 1:29). Jesus of Nazareth is God's spotless Lamb of sacrifice for the salvation of the whole world.[2] He alone is God's merciful provision to rescue us all from all of our sins. Christians, and thus Catholics, have never forgotten this precious truth. It is central to our Christian religion. One can hardly read the Bible and miss the theme of salvation when it is painted with very broad strokes, the theme of "macro-salvation". The God who created us for Himself came into the world to "save his people from their sins" (Matthew 1:21). It is very merciful for the Risen Son to take our sins from us, because they threaten to ruin us eternally. In the Son, in this true God, spiritual life abounds for all who sincerely cry out for His mercy (1 John 5:20). The Spirit came down on Him when John baptized Him with water, immediately before the Father declared His delight in the righteousness of His beloved Son. Notice the revealing actions of the Trinity, the three distinct divine Persons mentioned in Christian baptism (Matthew 28:19-20). Notice also the divine declaration, a harbinger of the justification that first occurs when a person is baptized in the name of the Trinity.

It is no secret that Roman Catholics believe that baptism plays an essential part in our salvation. After all, the Apostle Peter states, "Baptism, which corresponds to this [the salvation of Noah's family from a sinful world through water], now saves you, not as a removal of dirt from the body but as an appeal to God for a clear conscience, through the resurrection of Jesus Christ" (1 Peter 3:21). We know that Jesus saves us through His risen power present in Baptism. This is true for our children as well as for us. St. Peter proclaimed to the inquiring crowd on the first Christian Pentecost: "Repent [men of Israel], and be baptized every one of you in the name of Jesus Christ for the forgiveness of your sins; and you shall receive the gift of the Holy Spirit. For the promise [of the Spirit through baptism] is to you and to your children and to all that are far off, every one whom the Lord our God calls to him" (Acts 2:38-39). It is no secret that Catholics wholeheartedly believe the Spirit comes upon us through the waters of Baptism. It is much more of a secret to others that this is what the Bible really teaches, but here it is. Of course, Baptism played no role in salvation under the Old Covenant. It is clear that Jesus Christ first instituted this Sacrament for the salvation of all nations under the New Covenant.

"Water" and "Spirit" relate the passage John 1:29-36 to another passage, only two chapters later. This is the very next mention of "Spirit" in the fourth Gospel. Much of John 3 appears to be dealing with the baptism practiced by the followers of Jesus:

> Jesus answered him [Nicodemus], "Truly, truly, I say to you, unless one [literally, anyone] is born anew, he cannot see the kingdom of God." Nicodemus said to him, "How can a man be born when he is old? Can he enter a second time into his mother's womb and be born?" Jesus answered, "Truly, truly, I say to you, unless one [literally, anyone] is born of water and the Spirit, he cannot enter the kingdom of God." (John 3:3-5)

It is difficult to deny that this passage is referring to Christian Baptism. Because "water and Spirit" are both governed by only one Greek preposition, this passage is teaching a universal need for spiritual purification through one and the same baptismal birth. Later in this same chapter of the fourth Gospel, purification is associated with baptism (3:25-26). The very next mention of "water" refers to baptism (3:23), and the very next mention of "Spirit" refers back to the baptism of Jesus (3:34). It seems clear from the Bible that God has ordained baptism for the sake of the salvation of us all.[3] As St. Augustine once noted, Jesus here permits no exceptions, not even for babies.[4] This is why we Catholics can claim to be Christians. We belong to Christ in a very special way by virtue of our spiritual birth. Not only do we bear witness to the fact that Christ is our Risen Lord and Savior, we also have been through the purifying waters. Like our non-Catholic brothers and sisters, we all had a sin problem from conception and birth, until we all became God's adopted children through the Son's saving power. This happened to us when, similarly to the case of Jesus, the Holy Spirit descended upon us at our baptism, and the Father took great delight in us as His dear children (our justification).

The letter to Titus repeats this sacramental teaching, which is strangely ignored in many Bible-reading circles:

> He [God our Savior] saved us, not because of deeds done by us in righteousness, but in virtue of his own mercy, by the washing of regeneration and renewal in the Holy Spirit, which he poured out upon us richly through Jesus Christ our Savior, so that we might be justified by his grace and become heirs in hope of eternal life. (Titus 3:5-7)

In the Scriptures, when salvation is mentioned, justification, under various terms and images, is never far behind. In this passage, we notice that the Holy Spirit brings about our regeneration (our new, spiritual life) and justification (our new, holy relationship with God) through the purifying, initiating ritual-bath we call baptism.

St. Paul undoubtedly bears witness to this central belief. He warns about serious sins, which exclude one, even a Christian, from God's Kingdom, and then he contrasts some of his Corinthian converts with their past, seamy, sinful lifestyles (see 1 Corinthians 6:9-11). In particular, let us examine the last verse (verse 11) of this passage: "You were washed, you were sanctified, you were justified in the name of the Lord Jesus Christ and in the Spirit of our God." These three forceful expressions ("you were washed, you were sanctified, you were justified") are parallel in structure. The three Greek verbs refer to something that has taken place "in the name of the Lord Jesus Christ and in the Spirit of our God." The Greek prepositional phrases, both beginning with "in" in the English translation, weigh down each one of these verbs and tie them to the same sacred action. This is because these modifying phrases work together to convey to the verbs a tone of authority, sobriety, and dignity – likely liturgical in nature. Since by "washed" it seems clear that "baptized" is meant (see Ephesians 5:26), all three verbs are almost certainly a description of what happened to the unjust Corinthians when they were baptized. During this sacred action, each sinner was washed, sanctified, and justified all at once. Since these three expressions converge on the same liturgical moment, they most naturally converge in their meanings, even if they are not completely synonymous. In this context, the three verbs nuance one another, and give perspective to the same reality that they signify: what baptism accomplishes. It is baptism that makes the difference between what the Corinthian believers once were and what they have now become. Here we once again notice a washing of the sinner from his sins and a renewal in righteousness through the Holy Spirit with the result of justification. To be justified is, in concrete reality, to be washed and to be sanctified.

When St. Paul became a Christian, all his sins were washed away in baptism. This is what the disciple Ananias said to him on that day: "And now why do you wait? Rise and be baptized, and wash away your sins, calling on his name" (Acts 22:16). Baptism is the proper context for calling on the Lord's name for salvation; indeed, this context provides the correct interpretation of Romans 10:9-13, where St. Paul relates salvation to believing in and outwardly professing the Lordship of Jesus. Now St. Paul reminds the Corinthians that this happened to them as well, when they were baptized "in the name of the Lord Jesus Christ and in the Spirit of our God" (see also 1 Corinthians 1:2, 13). Like Jesus Himself (see 1 Timothy 3:16), these Christians were "justified in the Spirit." We note that God's act of justification is dynamic. He did not merely change His mind about the Corinthians because of Christ. He changed *them*. As they were submerged in the water,[5] their sins were washed away, in union with the death and burial of Christ, and as they emerged from the water, they were reborn, in union with the Risen Christ, to become God's holy children in and through the adoption provided by the Holy Spirit (see Romans 6; Galatians 3:26-27; 4:4-7).

Justification as Transforming

God's activity of justification includes two aspects: the negative one (removal of sin) and the positive one (sanctification through the Spirit). Justification is a transformative process, a holy relationship with God, one totally dependent upon God's grace and free human cooperation with this grace. St. Paul uses some vivid images to describe in his converts the "before and after" of justification, the absence and presence of God's gift of a righteous relationship with Him. Once they were sinners stumbling in the dark, but now they are saints walking in the light (Ephesians 2:1-2; Colossians 1:11-14). Once they were servants of sin, but now they are God's holy, adopted sons (Romans 6:17; Galatians 4:4-7). Once they were God's foes, but now they are His friends (2 Corinthians 5:17-19; see also James 2:23). Once they were criminals who broke the letter of the Law of Moses, but now they are heavenly citizens who obey the spirit of the Law of Christ (Romans 8:1-4; 1 Corinthians 9:20-21; Philippians 3:18-20). Through His appointed ministers, Jesus Christ offers to bring every human being into this newness of life and light and love and law. By offering us growth in His grace (2 Peter 3:18), our Savior offers us ever greater light, an ever greater inheritance, ever greater intimacy, and an ever greater glory.

Justification is a technical matter. When it comes to technical matters about salvation, what I call "micro-salvation", a human being naturally tends to be skeptical of whatever the Bible appears to teach, if it seems to go against the teachings of the theologians of his own faith community. In such cases, average adults tend to disqualify themselves to make reliable judgments.[6] We beg off by insisting that we do not understand all the technicalities, or, at least, that we do not trust ourselves to conclude safely that we do. In order to keep the Bible's voice from being silenced or muffled from now on, it may be helpful at this point to inform the Protestant reader of his own faith-tradition about justification. I will strive to be brief and fair. We can then return to the Bible to listen more carefully to it, with a greater confidence in our own abilities to make sound judgments.

The Protestant reformation (Protestants would call it "the Reformation") began with Martin Luther. It quickly became a dispute that revolved around the biblical teaching of justification. Luther insisted that "faith alone" puts someone and keeps him in a right relationship with God. To be fair, careful study of his voluminous writings has shown that he meant more by faith than merely assenting to the truth of what God has revealed. His faith-trust was an optimistic combination of assent and hope. With St. Paul as his alleged main support, Herr Doktor Luther rather boldly asserted that the Church belonging to Jesus Christ must either embrace his own teaching of "justification by faith alone", and therefore stand, or reject it and fall, thereby ceasing to belong to Christ.[7]

What is the gist of what Luther taught about the sinner's justification? Once the sinner truly believes, God imputes to him the righteousness that belongs to Christ alone. The sinner is then pardoned, that is, God covers over his guilt for the sake of Christ, even though real sin continues to remain within him. Although this pioneer reformer would hardly ever discover this saving, justifying faith in other than the hearts of *baptized believers* (even in baptized babies!), most promoters today of the teaching of "justification by faith alone" exclude baptism and babies completely from God's activity of justification. Most of them are fervent fundamentalists and evangelicals – sincere Christians who deny that God has in any way ordained the Sacraments for salvation. Luther himself did not make this major mistake. Because Luther believed in the efficacy of infant baptism, he acknowledged the Christian status of virtually everyone in Europe at the time. Since, in classical Lutheran theology, both Word and Sacrament confer saving grace, whichever one of these means of grace makes effective contact with the unjustified person first is the one that causes an immediate justification of the sinner through faith. In unbaptized babies, baptism takes precedence, but in unbaptized adults who have the ability to make sense of preaching, the Word takes precedence, and initial faith is the instrument of immediate justification, even before the adult is baptized. For Luther, faith is the only means to receive justification. Since baptized babies are justified, these babies must in some sense be true believers. God has covered over the inherited guilt of all the baptized, even though the "matter of Original Sin" always remains after baptism.

All of us know that the interior temptation to sin does not disappear from our hearts once we are baptized. It is there throughout our Christian lives, even though we do not need to cooperate with it. Since Luther knew well, from his own honest struggles with sin, that this natural disorder caused by Adam's first sin is sadly a part of our life-long experience (Catholics call this "concupiscence"), the reformer mistakenly assumed that Original Sin[8] remains in the soul during and after baptism, although not in the exact same way that it existed in the soul before the baptism took place. This denied the Catholic dogma that baptism totally washes away each and every sin in the person baptized, including Original Sin, even though the disorder caused by Original Sin remains. As a clear logical necessity, Luther denied that perfect righteousness could exist within the soul of the baptized person from the first moment of justification. This meant that each living Christian in himself continues to deserve the sentence of death before the judgment seat of God, but is saved from this judgment only because of the imputed alien merits of Jesus Christ alone.

Luther was influenced to a great degree by his own interpretations of St. Paul's writings, especially Galatians and Romans. His view appears reasonable. Since God is all holy, He can never acquit a sinner on any other basis than perfect righteousness, yet it is a fact that God does acquit (justify) sinners, even the ungodly. Since God acquits sinners only on the basis of a perfect righteousness, where can this perfect righteousness be found? The perfect righteousness needed for God's action of justification must either be within the person who is justified or outside of him. Whatever righteousness is within the justified person is never perfect. Because concupiscence is always sinful, no one ever ceases to be a sinner before death, even during and immediately after his baptism. Since justification takes place before death, the one who is justified never has a perfect righteousness within himself. Therefore, God must count such a person as just solely on the basis of an alien righteousness that is perfect. All Christians agree that the righteousness of Christ outside of the believer is perfect. Martin Luther concluded that, among all who have lived or are living in this sinful world, Jesus is the only one who was perfectly holy and righteous, for He is "the Holy and Righteous One" (Acts 3:14). By a process of elimination, based upon a resolute type of scriptural and theological thinking, the righteousness of Christ outside of us seemed to this zealous reformer to be the only possible source for God's acceptance of us sinners at the time of justification.

According to Luther, God imputes the entire alien righteousness of Christ on the sinner's behalf because of his faith-trust in God to do so. God treats the justified sinner as if he were Christ Himself, who is indisputably perfect. Repeating a rather clever memory device, a modern-day evangelical may sometimes be heard to remark, "Because Christ never sinned and I am trusting in Him, God is treating me *Just as if I'd* never sinned. This is what it means for me to be *justified*." Because the alien righteousness of Christ is perfect, there are no degrees of justification in this classical Protestant manner of thought. No one can improve on the degree of Christ's righteousness, and so, for Martin Luther and his followers, the justified person has all of this righteousness in God's sight at once and forever, as long as he truly believes. Justification is identical in all the justified. The German reformer admitted that even the best of all the Church Fathers, his beloved St. Augustine, somehow overlooked these important aspects of the truth about this most important doctrine. No one before Luther seemed to notice that St. Paul taught that faith all by itself appropriates the alien righteousness of Christ on the sinner's behalf in God's sight. How could Jesus Christ's Church have been so wrong for so long about so important a doctrine? Many of Luther's contemporaries could not believe this to be possible. They construed all that seemed to originate with Luther to be false. Without any exception, the bishops at the Council of Trent followed St. Augustine's theology of justification wherever and whenever Martin Luther departed from that saint's teaching.

Because of his pivotal understanding of concupiscence as sinful in itself, even in all the justified, Luther developed other ideas as well. He thought, because a corrupt sinful nature remains in everyone despite baptism, every Christian action on this side of the grave, even the very best, is in some way displeasing to God when considered in itself. According to him and other reformers, all our choices and actions, unlike the deeds of Jesus, are sin-tainted and, therefore, can never merit anything in God's sight. Since we can never merit heaven, the choices of our will cannot really alter our eternal destinies; indeed, we do not even have free will at all, and whether we will be saved or lost is God's choice alone. Martin Luther believed that his view of justification and salvation gave far more glory to God than traditional theology did. But his Catholic foes vigorously argued that his teaching actually detracted from God's glory, since it did not honor God for His present activity in gloriously transforming His creatures through His grace. Because of his own interpretations of the Scriptures, Luther exalted God the Creator by devaluating justified humanity. Because of Scripture and Tradition, the Catholic Church exalts both God and the humanity that is being restored to His image and likeness through Christ.

While Luther had a highly nuanced theological understanding of faith, many of his immediate followers, many untrained in the subtleties of theology, understood him simply to be teaching that a solitary, continuing, unwavering trust in God's offer of mercy in Christ to each of them personally, and nothing more, is what directly brings about their salvation, and that this is known with infallible certainty. Many of these early Protestants ignored the teaching of Luther and Calvin that a change in heart and life is the only sure test that one has really been justified by faith alone. While Luther and Calvin did not teach "easy believism", many of their average Protestant followers took this shortcut. Luther himself said, "After throwing off the yoke of the Pope, everyone wishes to live as he pleases."

Today ecumenism is very popular, with its charitable dialogues and peace-making. In 1999, after almost thirty years of dialogue with the Catholic Church concerning doctrinal issues, theologians belonging to liberal forms of Lutheranism and some leading Catholic theologians issued a "joint declaration" that their current understandings of justification so greatly overlap that the remaining differences "are no longer the occasion for doctrinal condemnations." Although none of these participants disavowed the previous doctrinal positions of his own faith community, it is lamentable that the joint declaration does not address the question of whether or not Martin Luther's own teachings about justification escape the condemnations of the Council of Trent. Ecumenism, however, is practical; it articulates the past only to the extent that it is helpful to a future reunion. Although the Catholic bishops at this sixteenth-century council did not single out any Protestants by name for condemnation, it seems rather clear that they intended to define against official Lutheran beliefs about justification and salvation. Their doctrinal decrees seem to follow the order of treatment in the earlier Augsburg Confession,[9] a key Lutheran confessional document.

Recently, conservative Lutheran bodies, such as the Missouri Synod and the Wisconsin Synod, have issued a few strongly worded rejections of the "Joint Declaration on the Doctrine of Justification." They consider it to be a betrayal of some of the vital scriptural and Lutheran concerns of the reformation era. Although many Lutheran bodies take a conciliatory approach to the issue of justification, some do not – and virtually none of the thousands of evangelical Protestant sects do so, either. Wisdom coming from God is "first pure, then peaceable" (James 3:17). This is the divine way of proceeding. All Christians must be as conciliatory as possible, without compromising the purity of truth.

By Faith Alone?

Now let's return to the Bible, in particular to Matthew 19:16-22, which recounts the dialogue between Jesus and the rich young man. It is vitally important for all of us as Christians to allow the words of Jesus as well as His works to have their full saving effect in our lives. Our Lord's words seem like a Roman Catholic response to the young man's question about attaining eternal life rather than a Protestant one. "Only believe in me" is not what Jesus told the rich young man to do! He required of him only what God required of him, keeping the commandments. But the one thing that the young man lacked in order to be perfect was total detachment from his wealth in order to join Jesus' company. It was not a sin for him to hold on to his wealth, as long as no injustice was done to others or his own soul. Jesus, however, strongly encouraged him to give this up voluntarily. He commanded him only to keep the commandments of God. In the section that immediately follows, He proceeded to warn his disciples of how great a stumbling block to keeping God's commandments a rich man's wealth can become.[10] It almost always does a grave injustice to the man by costing him the salvation of his own soul. This is too dear a price. If we want to have everlasting life, there can be no true substitute for obeying God. Without obedience and forgiveness for disobedience, no one who claims to be living the Christian life will be saved (see Matthew 7:21). God does not do the obeying for us, but Jesus' merits and His grace make true obedience and consequent salvation possible (see Hebrews 5:7-9).

Obeying Jesus Christ is not an option for anyone who wants to receive eternal salvation. St. Paul frames the Book of Romans, with its grand theme of salvation, in two references to "the obedience of faith" (Romans 1:5; 16:26). With this truth all the New Testament writers agree: the Good News makes it possible for God to rule over our lives. St. John announces the bad news in the midst of this Good News: "He who does not obey the Son shall not see life, but the wrath of God rests on him" (John 3:36).

In the days of His public ministry, Jesus began at the very beginning. He gave two basic commands to His hearers: "Repent, and believe in the gospel [Good News]" (Mark 1:15). It was a call to conversion. God calls each of us to turn from sin (repent) to Him as the Ruler of our lives (believe). This is the kind of message one would expect from the God who is all-holy and all-loving. To allow Him to rule over our lives, we need to believe His Messenger, Jesus Christ. Faith in Christ is foundational for justification (Philippians 3:9) and salvation (Luke 8:12; Mark 16:16; 1 Corinthians 1:21; 1 Timothy 1:16; 1 Peter 1:5,9) – that is, for forgiveness of sins (Acts 2:37-38; 10:43; 13:38-39; 15:9), reception of the Holy Spirit (Acts 11:17), and sanctification (Acts 26:18; Ephesians 3:17). It is written in Hebrews 11:6: "Without faith it is impossible to please him [God]. For whoever would draw near to God must believe that he exists and that he rewards those who seek him." God does not do the believing for us, but His grace makes true faith possible within us (Acts 18:27). By believing, we cooperate with this grace. As St. Augustine said, "He who created you without your help does not justify you without your help" (Sermon 169, 11, 13). There can be no doubt that we are justified by faith. This is St. Paul's teaching in two of his letters, Romans and Galatians (see Romans 3:28 – 4:5 and Galatians 3:5-9).

In St. Paul's inspired perceptions of salvation, both Jews and Gentiles are justified by faith. Abraham is the great example of such justification. Works of the law cannot accomplish it. Nothing that a person believes or does before he is justified merits the grace of his initial justification. Grace alone and works alone necessarily exclude one another as principles of salvation (see Romans 11:6). God gives justification, simply as a gift, out of the abundance of His love and mercy. On the other hand, God's grace allowed Phinehas to do a holy, zealous deed, one that God credited to him as personal righteousness (see Psalm 106:30-31). This is God's infallible evaluation of the quality of the man's deed as it has been sung down through the generations of Israel. God was truly pleased. Similarly, it was the quality of Abraham's faith that moved God to credit it to him as his personal righteousness (see Genesis 15:6). The faith mentioned belonged to Abraham and so did the righteousness that God acknowledged, although both were a gift from God through the abundance of His grace. If we carefully study St. Paul's key source, the Book of Genesis, we can discover that, with very few exceptions, Abraham's faith was heroic, persistent, strong despite adverse circumstances, and obedient. The measure of his faith was also a measure of his holiness in God's sight. St. Paul picks this up and makes Abraham, an Old Testament saint, the focal point of his teaching about justification.

This doctrine of the Apostle did not *make* any of his first readers Christians. The fact that he taught those who were already justified (i.e., Christians living in Galatia and in Rome) about justification shows that someone does not need to know and understand all of this teaching before he can become a true Christian – although everything any biblical writer teaches is most certainly true. What a relief! One who cannot articulate the truths about salvation with a biblical precision may still be saved. In Galatians, St. Paul teaches justification by faith in Christ, against the Jews who rejected the Messianic claims of Jesus because they were, instead, trusting in their own circumcision and legal observance. St. Paul did not emphasize faith to the exclusion of baptism. Only a few verses later, he writes: "For in Christ you are all sons of God, through faith. For as many of you as were baptized into Christ have put on Christ" (Galatians 3:26-27). Clearly, we are justified by faith, but not by faith alone. Though the Bible in many places and in many ways says that adult converts in the context of apostolic missionary activities were saved by faith, never once does it say they were saved by faith alone. The writings of St. Paul mention faith many times in the context of a usage of a Greek word or phrase for "only" or "alone", but not once does he bring both together. The only New Testament writer to do so is St. James. He brings both together only to *deny* that justification is by faith only.

Behold, St. Paul is not the only New Testament author to teach us about justification! Luther had a view of justification and salvation that made more sense of St. Paul's letters than of the rest of the Bible. The inspired writers in the Old Testament seemed far from Lutherans in their viewpoints of righteousness and other sacred realities. According to 2 Timothy 3:16-17, the Christian has a God-given duty to heed all of God's Word, not just a portion of it. A portion can be a distortion of the whole. Because the Catholic Church is truly catholic, that is, truly universal in her commitments and goals, her teachings about justification and salvation fit all the books of the Old Testament as well as the New, the letter of St. James as well as all the letters of St. Paul. Luther, in effect, shrunk the canon of the Holy Scriptures, even though it was he who accused the papists of embracing the letter of St. James and leaving out all the rest of the biblical books.

Perhaps an Apostle (see Galatians 1:19), though perhaps not one of the Twelve, St. James writes:

> What does it profit, my brethren, if a man says he has faith but has not works? Can his faith save him? If a brother or sister is ill-clad and in lack of daily food, and one of you says to them, "Go in peace, be warmed and filled," without giving them the things needed for the body, what does it profit? So faith by itself, if it has no works, is dead. But some one will say, "You have faith and I have works." Show me your faith apart from your works, and I by my works will show you my faith. You believe that God is one; you do well. Even the demons believe — and shudder. Do you want to be shown, you shallow man, that faith apart from works is barren? Was not Abraham our father justified by works, when he offered his son Isaac upon the altar? You see that faith was active along with his works, and faith was completed by works, and the scripture was fulfilled which says, "Abraham believed God, and it was reckoned to him as righteousness"; and he was called the friend of God. You see that a man is justified by works and not by faith alone. And in the same way was not also Rahab the harlot justified by works when she received the messengers and sent them out another way? For as the body apart from the spirit is dead, so faith apart from works is dead. (James 2:14-26)

Can a person be saved at the coming of the Lord of glory if he keeps on believing yet never does a blessed thing to help needy strangers at the door? If you believe but do not practice, then you are poor in faith and lacking in love, and should not hope to inherit the Kingdom (James 2:5). St. James' response to this failure in Christian conduct is clear and forceful. He cries out, in effect, "How can you call yourself a son or a daughter of Abraham and do nothing? Even a harlot can do better!" St. James writes in order to jolt his first readers out of their damning complacency. This passage is very much about justification and salvation, and the righteous indignation of St. James.

For the Christian already in the state of grace, good works cause justification. As we have seen in Luther's case, Protestants do not believe that good works ever cause justification in God's sight. From start to finish, justification takes place by faith alone. Also, Protestants do not believe that biblical justification is an on-going process of personal, interior righteousness that allows for degrees. It is the imputation of Christ's perfect, alien righteousness to the believer's account. They insist that there is indeed a process of growth in holiness for a Christian, but that this is rightly called sanctification, not justification. These views are incompatible with St. James' statement that Christians are "justified by works" (verse 24). James never says: "We are justified by faith alone, apart from works, while, later, we are sanctified by works." Rather, he uses the same Greek word for "justified" that St. Paul always uses in his own descriptions of justification without works.

Naturally enough, Martin Luther believed that he could not harmonize St. James with St. Paul. On the contrary, the Catholic Church insists that there is no contradiction. Both writers were inspired by the same Holy Spirit. Therefore, there must be a stage of justification by works (St. James) as well as a stage of justification without works (St. Paul). Since St. James is very practical, he is not simply sharing his theology about the matter. Unlike St. Paul, he is not explaining the theology behind his missionary message. Rather, St. James exhorts. He thinks his Christian readers, people already justified without works, need to proceed to another justification, one because of works of love done through grace. The more good works one does, like Abraham and Rahab, the more a friend of God one is.

Both inspired writers hold up the example of Abraham to make their point. St. Paul uses Abraham to illustrate the merciful first stage of justification, which works cannot earn, and here St. James uses a later event in Abraham's life to illustrate the just second stage, the gift of justification because of good works performed by Christians in a state of grace. Abraham, our forefather in faith, was justified more than once. According to the writer to the Hebrews, traditionally thought to be St. Paul, Abraham possessed an exemplary faith when he obeyed the Lord at the time that he was called to leave the city of Ur (see Hebrews 11:8-10). Since this faith was pleasing to God (Hebrews 11:8), this clearly suggests that Father Abraham was already regenerated by this time, and since there is no spiritual regeneration without justification, Abraham seems to be already justified during the events of Genesis 12. Twenty-five years and some sins later, he was justified again (see Genesis 15:6), according to St. Paul in Romans 4:1-5. Genesis 15:6 seems to be the first explicit biblical reference to the divine action of justification. About thirty years after this, Abraham offered Isaac to God on the altar (see Genesis 22), although it turned out that God did not require his slaying. St. James informs us that this was yet another time of justification for Abraham, one in keeping with his character as manifested earlier, at the time of Genesis 15. The sacrifice of Abraham's beloved son, Isaac, out of love for God, led Him to repeat His high estimate of Abraham's faith and personal righteousness, a faith already commended in Genesis 15:6, which St. James construes to have a future dimension. (Note also 1 Maccabees 2:51-52: "Remember the deeds of the fathers, which they did in their generations; and receive great honor and an everlasting name. Was not Abraham found faithful when tested, and it was reckoned to him as righteousness?")

St. James gives this teaching about justification in the context of his exhortation to works of love for one's poor brothers and sisters. Similarly, St. Paul teaches that faith without such works is nothing. He writes: "For in Christ Jesus neither circumcision nor uncircumcision is of any avail, but faith working through love" (Galatians 5:6). And in another place, he says: "If I have all faith, so as to remove mountains, but have not love, I am nothing" (1 Corinthians 13:2). Because St. Paul is here writing about the faith that normally attends hope and charity (1 Corinthians 13:13), he is commenting on the faith that belongs to every Christian's salvation (see 1 Thessalonians 1:3; 5:8, and other passages in which these three virtues appear together – Romans 5:1-5; Galatians 5:5-6; Ephesians 1:5-18; Colossians 1:3-5; 1 Peter 1:21-22). This faith is able to grow (see 2 Corinthians 10:15) and even become great in some Christians, yet be totally useless except for moving mountains! For St. Paul, it is not so much that true faith includes hope and love, as that true love includes faith and hope (see Luke 7:47-50). Love "believes all things, hopes all things, endures all things" (1 Corinthians 13:7). Love is the master virtue (see Colossians 3:12-14). On this point, St. Peter writes: "For this very reason make every effort to supplement your faith with virtue, and virtue with knowledge, and knowledge with self-control, and self-control with steadfastness, and steadfastness with godliness, and godliness with brotherly affection, and brotherly affection with love" (2 Peter 1:5-7).

True faith is still faith, whether it is alive or dead, great or small. A living faith is always accompanied by hope and charity, and leads to good works; and faith without charity is genuine faith, but it is not at all alive or saving. Luther[11] and Calvin[12] were dogmatic that the divine gift of charity contributes absolutely nothing at all to the saving power of faith, although at least Calvin believed true faith is never disjoined from love for God ("pious affection").[13] Luther as well as Calvin believed that genuine faith would automatically produce love and "good" works. There could never be someone such as a completely inactive, true believer. St. James contradicts Luther's teaching on this score, and Luther was honest enough to admit it. St. James notes that one must try hard to make sure that genuine faith does not remain alone. True faith can exist in the soul without good works, but it cannot stay alive without them. St. James clearly teaches that genuine faith alone cannot save a person on the Last Day. The choice to cooperate fully with God's grace in producing some good works is a choice added to true faith. It is a mandated choice no Christian is ever forced to make, but a fully informed choice not to make this choice will cost us our eternal salvation. St. Paul and St. James are not the only Apostles who make clear that faith devoid of works of love is not sufficient for salvation. St. John reminds us that Jesus taught two complementary truths in the analogy of the Vine and Branches: (1) we can be fruitful only insofar as we remain in Christ, and (2) we can remain in Christ only if we are fruitful (see John 15:1-5). In his first letter, St. John insists that every child of God not only believes in the Son of God but also does loving deeds of righteousness: "Whoever does not do right is not of God, nor he who does not love his brother" (1 John 3:10).

St. James teaches that Abraham was "justified by works" (*plural*), but he mentions only the offering of Isaac. St. James seems to expect his readers to fill in the gaps from their own acquaintance with the holy life of Abraham. Although Genesis 22 does not explicitly mention Abraham's faith, it was present there, along with his works, just as Genesis 15 does not explicitly mention his good works, though they were present there, along with his faith. Abraham's faith and good works perfected one another so that they were both pleasing in God's sight. Abraham put his religion into practice by offering sacrifices and by doing acts of kindness. By the oaks of Mamre, the needy strangers at his tent door were divine visitors, and, before he sent them on their way, he gladly offered them fresh food and refreshing shade under a tree (see Genesis 18:1-16). Another of Abraham's loving deeds, for a brother of his, was his rescue from kidnappers of his nephew Lot (called his "brother" in the Hebrew of Genesis 14:14). More than once the Lord has declared through the inspired biblical writers that Abraham is His friend (see 2 Chronicles 20:7; Isaiah 41:8). Isaac could have declared his own father to be righteous after the ordeal on Mount Moriah, but what clearly matters to St. James is God's own declaration of Abraham's friendship with Him.

Was Abraham always God's friend after his call in Genesis 12? Neither St. James nor St. Paul addresses this question, but there are biblical hints pointing in the other direction. Between the time of Genesis 15 and Genesis 22, Abraham, who was master of his own household (1 Peter 3:6), once wrongly obeyed his wife Sarah, when he took Hagar to be his second wife. By doing this, he was sinning. He was relying on Sarah's plan to gain offspring for him instead of relying on God's promises through faith. In Genesis 16:2, Sarah prefaced her scheme by blaming God for her barrenness. Although God later told Abraham to follow the advice of Sarah when it accorded with His plan (Genesis 21:12), there is no such divine endorsement in Genesis 16. In this place, God reinforces Sarah's authority over Hagar by means of Abraham's words (16:6) and the angel's words (16:9), but not her bold usurpation over Abraham, the cause of the sad situation in the first place. If this sin had been more obvious in the Scriptures, it would have readily come to mind for James' first readers and so would have defeated his immediate purpose.

This sin of Abraham and Sarah was similar to the sin of Adam and Eve. The first man obeyed his wife and so took the forbidden fruit and ate it. In doing so, Adam was relying on Eve's plans for them to become like God, because of a new experiential knowledge of good and evil, instead of fully appreciating that they were already like God, because they were created in holiness (Genesis 3:5-6, 22; Ecclesiastes 7:29; 2 Peter 1:3-8). After this human trespass, God clearly reinforced Adam's authority over Eve (Genesis 3:16-17). There is no explicit mention of God forgiving Abraham, or Adam and Eve, but these are implied. The Lord clothed our first parents in animal skins in place of their fig leaves and gave them the promise of the Savior (Genesis 3:15). This divine action hints that God forgave them and gave them grace again to become holy, although He did not re-admit them to Paradise. By their enduring eviction we know that God did not remit all of their "temporal punishment", including the humiliating labors, sweat, labor pains, and domestic male dominance, in short, their earthly "purgatory". A sorry sinner can be forgiven and restored to God's friendship, yet in His wise ways, He often chastises the forgiven sinner for a time because of what he did. Just because the nail of sin is yanked from the plank of life does not mean the board is as good as new.

St. James moves from Abraham to Rahab. He says that they were justified "in the same way". Earlier, Jesus warned the self-righteous religious establishment about their lack of belief and repentance subsequent to the holy preaching of John the Baptist, in contrast with the belief and repentance displayed by tax collectors and harlots (see Matthew 21:31-32). According to Hebrews 11:31, "By faith Rahab the harlot did not perish with those who were disobedient, because she had given friendly welcome to the spies." The pagan inhabitants of Jericho who perished, unlike Rahab, merely feared the Israelites and only heard of their God, but they did not have the type of faith in Him that sought to obey Him. Rahab's fear was mixed with true faith in God. In Joshua 2:8-11, she seems to be confessing to the Israelite spies a faith that previously found a home in her heart. She was a repentant Gentile believer, and they appeared to be strangers at her door. But they were really brothers in the same faith. She feared God and kept her conduct with the spies chaste. St. James mentions her good "works" (*plural*). She was righteous in receiving the spies, and righteous in sending them out by another way. The initial justification of Rahab, like that of the father of the Hebrews, Abraham, was fruitful and exemplary. Since they lived in Old Testament times, baptism did not play any part.

In the Hebrew Scriptures, God declared Abraham to be His friend. St. James informs us that Rahab was like Abraham in this respect. Friendships allow for varying degrees and can even be broken. At the end of his letter, St. James writes: "My brethren, if any one among you wanders from the truth and someone brings him back, let him know that whoever brings back a sinner from the error of his way will save his soul from death and will cover a multitude of sins" (James 5:19-20). The soul of a Christian brother can die. When one turns away from God through serious sins, one becomes His enemy and is punished with the death of one's soul. By mentioning Rahab, St. James moves his readers back to the early days of the history of Israel, when the nation was making its journey through the desert to the Promised Land. Rahab, a Gentile, was more faithful to God than the wilderness generation of Israelites. Elsewhere, the writer of the Letter to the Hebrews blames the wilderness generation for only temporarily having a faith that is pleasing to God (see Hebrews 11:29). Their unbelief in the good news brought by the two just spies, Joshua and Caleb, is but one example of a mortal sin. They shrunk back and so were destroyed in the course of their forty-year march in the desert (see Hebrews 10:39; Jude 5; 1 Corinthians 10:1-11). They had grieved the Holy Spirit and became God's enemies (see Isaiah 63:10). In this regard, St. Paul draws a lesson for us all (see Ephesians 4:30).

Although St. James does not mention David in his letter, the Shepherd-King has never been far from this Jewish Christian's mind. St. James' immediate purpose is to present powerful paragons of justification, not notorious examples of the loss of it. He wants to exalt in his readers' eyes Old Testament saints known for helping needy strangers at the door through their acts of love and mercy. He carefully selects Abraham and Rahab, and seems deliberately to exclude David. The story of King David's adultery is simply too well known to St. James' readers. God, through Nathan the Prophet, cites David as an egregious example of the lack of hospitality for a stranger, a grave injustice done in the name of providing hospitality to another. By taking Uriah the Hittite's wife to his own bed, King David, who is like a greedy, rich man, with "very many flocks and herds" and a guest to feed, has shamelessly stolen from "a poor man", Uriah, who "had nothing but one little ewe lamb, which he had bought", his only legal wife, Bathsheba (2 Samuel 12:3). Perhaps also contributing to St. James' silence about King David is the author's emphatic teaching in 1:13 that God does not tempt anyone to sin. The book of 2 Samuel seems to teach that God, in His anger, stirred up David to commit the very serious sin of counting God's people in a prideful way (see 2 Samuel 24:1; contrast 1 Chronicles 21:1).

After Israel was settled in the Promised Land for centuries, King David mourned the loss of the Holy Spirit because of his adultery with Bathsheba. He prayed for the Spirit's restoration and continuance (Psalm 51:10-12). In another place, Psalm 32, he expresses his appreciation for justification after the loss of his friendship with God through this grievous sin. St. Paul uses David's words to describe the joy of a person who is justified (Romans 4:6-8). Since the young David is uniquely described as "a man after God's own heart" (1 Samuel 13:14; Acts 13:22) and could honestly sing in the Spirit of his personal righteousness (Psalm 18:20-24), he was justified years before his mortal sin with Bathsheba. Later, he was justified again. According to Nathan the Prophet, the Lord mercifully forgave King David for committing this great sin. David regained the relationship with God that he had lost. Nevertheless, God also commanded Nathan to inform him that he would be punished in this life for committing this sin (see 2 Samuel 12:9-13). Afterwards, he underwent "temporal punishment" in his family affairs and his political endeavors (many domestic and national troubles) because of this forgiven sin. Merely because David once lost God's friendship does not mean that everyone will do so.

Finally, St. James is concerned about anyone boasting that faith is sufficient to be a good Christian. Many evangelicals boast that they are saved by faith alone and that they are saved for sure. They boldly proclaim that one cannot be saved without "a full assurance of salvation", although most of them are willing to grant that a saved person might have frequent attacks of doubt. St. Paul saw matters quite differently, refusing to put much trust in merely human judgment (even his own personal sense of justification), preferring to let God do the judging (1 Corinthians 4:3-5). Paul sternly commands us: "Work out your own salvation with fear and trembling" (Philippians 2:12). He further warns us: "Therefore let any one who thinks that he stands take heed lest he fall" (1 Corinthians 10:12). These admonitions should reinforce our humility and our good actions. According to Jesus Himself, the humble and contrite tax collector, the hero in one of His parables, went home justified (Luke 18:14). According to St. James, God keeps on giving even "more grace" to those who remain in this humble state of grace (James 4:6). St. John also speaks of the growth of grace (see John 1:16). We can and should grow in grace, as well as in Christ-like humility. Grace can and should increase in our humble souls.

Nowhere in the Gospels does Jesus make forgiveness depend upon the sinner being sure that Jesus will forgive him. During Jesus' public ministry, He assured a paralytic of forgiveness only after the sick man had already been forgiven (Matthew 9:2). He revealed this to the man in order to lift his spirits and rebuke His own opponents. Salvation came to the home of Zacchaeus even before he was made aware of it. Jesus revealed it to him in order to encourage him and to instruct the crowd. The point is that this publican was saved before he knew it. Christians are able to have a *moral* certitude of being in a state of justification, but we can have an *infallible* certitude of this only if God reveals this in a special way to us. St. John wrote the following words about Christian moral certitude: "I write this to you who believe in the name of the Son of God, that you may know that you have eternal life" (1 John 5:13). Ironically, St. John wrote these words after devoting most of his letter to clarifying what should cause some Christians to tremble with fear. This is St. James' point as well as St. John's point: there may be some very good reasons for us to doubt, not God's Word or His mercy in Christ, but our own personal qualifications for life in the world to come. This should cause us to shape up.

"Strive for peace with all men, and for the holiness without which no one will see the Lord" (Hebrews 12:14). This biblical writer is addressing Hebrew Christians, whom he, of course, charitably presumes to be justified. He reminds them that they do not yet have everything they need to enter heaven and to live with God forever. Why would the Lord have one standard of salvation for time (namely, faith alone) and a different one for eternity (namely, holiness)? This hardly makes sense.[14] Rather, God's unchanging standard for both time and eternity is holiness, begun and continued in faith, hope, and love. If God justifies the ungodly in the manner that most Protestants believe (by a sort of legal fiction), then we would expect God to cover our sins for all eternity for the sake of our faith-trust in the eternal Christ and not bother with sanctifying our very being. But God has an approach befitting of God Himself, one everlasting standard of salvation: holiness through grace.

Infusion of Grace

Justification involves an internal change of the person, not merely an external change in God's viewpoint of the person. This truth is a key difference between official Roman Catholicism and many forms of Protestantism today. On this issue, St. Paul seems to be on the side of the Catholic Church, which seems to be on the side of the angels. After contrasting righteousness and sin, he writes:

For the judgment following one trespass [Adam's first sin]

brought condemnation, but the free gift following many trespasses brings justification. If, because of one man's trespass, death reigned through that one man, much more will those who receive the abundance of grace and the free gift of righteousness reign in life through the one man Jesus Christ. Then as one man's trespass led to condemnation for all men, so one man's act of righteousness leads to acquittal and life for all men. For as by one man's disobedience many were made sinners, so by one man's obedience many will be made righteous. (Romans 5:16-19)

For St. Paul, this parallel in Romans 5 is crucial. Adam's sin changed us internally by bequeathing to us a human nature devoid of sanctifying grace (Original Sin). *In exactly the same way, that is, internally*, our Savior's obedience has made us just and will make many others just. God does this by infusing grace into our nature so that sin is totally removed at baptism, the topic of the very next chapter of the Book of Romans. Before St. Paul shares his teaching about baptism with Roman Christians, however, he teaches that Jesus Christ did far more for our salvation than repair the damage done by Adam. Salvation is not only a rescue-and-restoration operation; it is a rescue-and-renovation operation. Divine, spiritual reality is far greater than the biblical words or metaphors that refer to it. This can hardly be denied, given the limitations of even inspired words.[15]

Protestants normally teach that justification is a different reality from sanctification, but St. Paul seems to make no such distinction. In St. Paul, as in Catholic theology, they refer to the same reality, or two aspects of the same mystery. The entire period between a Christian's initial calling to salvation and his glorification is one of justification (Romans 8:30, 33). Elsewhere, St. Paul calls this middle period one of "sanctification by the Spirit" (2 Thessalonians 2:13). For St. Paul, the Christ who is our sanctification is also our righteousness (1 Corinthians 1:30), and the baptism that justifies us can just as easily be said to sanctify us (1 Corinthians 6:11; 1 Peter 1:2; see also Romans 1:7; 1 Corinthians 1:2; 1 Thessalonians 4:7). According to one well-known Protestant biblical scholar, St. Paul teaches that Christians are holy (because of sanctification) and righteous (because of justification) "in precisely the same eschatological sense" (see 2 Thessalonians 2:13; 1 Timothy 2:15; Hebrews 12:14).[16] Since no biblical scholar seriously disputes that sanctification involves varying degrees, so does justification – *if* one grants the Catholic premise that justification and sanctification are synonymous terms for the same reality.

King David once confessed: "Against thee, thee only, have I sinned, and done that which is evil in thy sight, so that thou art justified in thy sentence and blameless in thy judgment" (Psalm 51:4). What does it mean for God to be blameless in His judgment? In the Law of Moses, God solemnly demands that human judges represent His own blameless standard of judgment: "You shall not pervert the justice due to your poor in his suit. Keep far from a false charge, and do not slay the innocent and the righteous, for I will not acquit the wicked" (Exodus 23:6-7). Israel's inspired Wisdom literature also upholds the blamelessness of God's standard of judgment: "He who justifies the wicked and he who condemns the righteous are both alike an abomination to the LORD" (Proverbs 17:15). Before the Lord forgives someone such as King David, the sinner is justly under God's condemnation. After God forgives him, God is also justified in His pardon, and also blameless in His judgment. God's character does not change. It is the gift of sanctifying grace that makes the difference.

Both Protestants and Catholics agree that the first moment one is justified is the moment one's sins are taken away. But did you notice? The Lord promises never to acquit the wicked (Exodus 23:7), yet He does justify the ungodly (Romans 4:5). Both inspired statements must be correct, since God cannot contradict Himself. There is only one way that both assertions can be true. Justification cannot happen without the sinful person being changed by God's grace. This must happen before his acquittal. What the word "justify" means is less important than the real work of God to which it refers. Either God as our Judge makes us righteous and then declares us to be such, or His declaration of our righteousness is the powerful decree that makes us immediately such, or He makes us righteous period, without any declaration at all. But He does not simply declare us righteous because Christ outside of us is righteous and we ourselves are not, as Luther strongly insisted. This doctrine has God, the Righteous Judge, for the sake of bringing about a real relationship with Him, pretending, because of Christ, that we are as perfect as He is, for the rest of our lives, before we in fact are. Although it is grossly unfair to characterize the Protestant position as God acquitting the guilty because He is bribed by the righteousness of Christ (see Isaiah

5:23), it is a fact that no honest jury will knowingly clear a guilty person; yet the Protestant teaching does make sincere human jurors seem to have more integrity than God Himself has. God clearly affirms: "I will not acquit the wicked" (Exodus 23:7). The Catholic Church takes these words very seriously. It has often been colorfully remarked that Martin Luther's most distinctive doctrine treats all the deeds of a Christian, even his very best ones, as so much filthy cow dung covered under the pure snowfall of Christ's own righteousness.

Possibly the only real divine declaration of our righteousness is still waiting in the future, at the Last Judgment (Romans 2:6, 13; 3:20; 1 Corinthians 4:4-5; see also Galatians 5:4-5). Jesus teaches that justification takes place at the Last Judgment (Matthew 12:36-37) as well as during the present life (Luke 18:14). All the biblical depictions of an end-time judgment focus on deeds, not on faith (See Matthew 25:31-46; Revelation 20:11-15; 2 Corinthians 5:10; Romans 2:1-11; 14:10-12; John 5:25-29). A final judgment based on works totally disproves the common notion that faith alone causes all the saving that is necessary. On the contrary, the quality of our works as evaluated by God is what ultimately decides our eternal destiny, heaven or hell. Every New Testament document except Philemon associates good works with salvation. In any case, God Himself never changes (He is always justified in His actions and blameless in His judgments), but He can (and does) change an ungodly man into a godly one and acquit him of sin and guilt while changing him through grace.

If we meet a man who became a Christian as an adult, what happened? How, then, has Mr. Ungodly Man been acquitted? This man's heart was first touched by God's grace as he was called to repentance. He eventually repented, not of all his past actions, but only of his sins. Not every deed done before one's initial justification is a sin, despite the classical Protestant claim. Before someone comes to Christ, the Light, at least some of one's deeds may be "wrought in God" (John 3:21). God was pleased with the devout prayers and generous almsgiving of Cornelius, the Roman centurion, even before he was justified and saved (Acts 10:2, 4, 31, 35, 43, 11:14; see also 15:9, 11). These were only natural good works, and so could never justly establish a right to heaven or a just claim to the grace of justification in his conversion. Nevertheless, it was fitting that God did not ignore these good works. Entrance into the justified state can never be truly merited by the one who is being justified, either initially or after repenting of mortal sins. Before Mr. Ungodly Man was justified, God was already working in the cracks and crannies of his life. The whole orb of salvation as a merciful transfer to a justified state is a totally unmerited gift from God (see Ephesians 2:8). On this fundamental point, Protestants and Catholics fully agree.

With the help of God's unmerited grace, Mr. Ungodly Man in the process of conversion freely accepted this totally unmerited call from God. By himself, he could have also freely rejected this grace. But he feared God's justice and also hoped for God's mercy because of Christ. He then began to love God and hate his sins. This was the point of true sorrow for sin. God did not repent for him or believe for him, but he could not have met these requirements without God's grace. Repentance and faith led this man to baptism, through which the Spirit came to dwell within him and gave him spiritual birth through sanctifying grace. Since we have seen above, in St. Paul's case, that baptism truly washes away sin, the man freed from his sins through baptism certainly was not justified before his baptism, even though this adult possessed faith in Christ before he was baptized.

So, the most popular, evangelical understanding of justification by faith alone as "by faith before baptism" must be false. Normally, incorporation into Christ's death through baptism is what frees a repentant believer from his sins (Romans 6:7), not faith apart from baptism. At the moment of his baptism, the supernatural gifts of faith, hope, and love were infused into his heart through grace. From God within him, supernatural life sprang forth, along with love and the other virtues. They were not of him, but they were his. At the pouring of water, while the priest or deacon pronounced the baptismal formula "in the name of the Father, and of the Son, and of the Holy Spirit", Mr. Ungodly Man became Mr. Abel T. Christian (the "T" stands for "Tomerit"). A person in a state of grace is able to merit eternal life and an increase of grace for gaining even greater, finite merits. Behold, the miracle of micro-salvation![17]

God transformed the sinful man by making him holy through baptism. God purified his soul by turning it from self-love to love of God. It seems that the moment He made the sinner just in this way was the very moment He declared this baptized person to be just. Crowning the sanctifying grace within him was the indwelling of the Holy Spirit Himself. Sanctifying grace brought other gifts from God in its train. These are the infused virtues, including the "theological virtues" (faith, hope, charity), the four "moral virtues" (prudence, justice, fortitude, temperance), and the seven "gifts of the Holy Spirit" (wisdom, understanding, counsel, fortitude, knowledge, piety, fear of the Lord). Grace is not the external cause of faith, hope, and charity. Grace is not only God's favorable viewpoint of the sinner. Grace is infused to *make* him holy. While many Protestants today believe that "infusion is confusion", many of the early Protestants were willing to admit that an infusion of faith and sanctifying grace occur. But they were most unwilling to call the result of this action justification instead of sanctification. For them, justification never correctly refers to an interior righteousness that is the baptized person's own as a result of the activity of God's grace within the soul.

Repentance

Unfortunately, Christians sin after baptism. A Christian may lose the state of grace if he commits a mortal sin, as did the wilderness generation and King David. In Old Testament times, justification could be regained by an act of perfect contrition, the kind of sorrow for sin out of love for God that we see in the Psalms of David. Today this also happens. The Sacrament of Penance, however, is the normative way for regaining justification whenever it is lost through one's mortal sin. Protestants do not have this special gift. This is one great advantage to being a Catholic. All sins do not have the same seriousness in God's sight (see John 19:11). There are greater sins and lesser sins. Except for a mortal sin, the worst thing in the world is a venial sin. Such a sin can be forgiven without the Sacrament of Penance, although it is very commonly forgiven through it. A venial sin by itself cannot deprive a person of the state of grace and the justification that accompanies it, but as venial sin is added to venial sin and the guilt grows and grows, the degree of one's justification (friendship with God) decreases. A mortal sin is necessary for it to reach the zero point. Calvinistic Protestants do not believe that justification can be lost. Lutherans believe that one can lose justification only by losing one's faith. They do not believe that Sacraments are necessary to regain justification. One simply needs to believe again. Some more recent Protestant groups believe that serious sins can so separate a justified person from God that he loses justification. For Luther, a justification that can co-exist with sinful concupiscence can also co-exist with any sin that the believer commits, as long as he really believes.

The truth is rather that there are many more mortal sins for a Christian to flee than only deliberate loss of faith. In fact, St. Paul's writings have four partial listings of sins that separate us from God (see 1 Corinthians 6:9-11; Galatians 5:19-21; Ephesians 5:5; Colossians 3:5-6). "Once saved, always saved" is a false sectarian slogan that encourages a very dangerous spiritual presumption. The promise of eternal life is conditional (see 1 John 2:24-25 and Colossians 1:21-23). Let us not be deceived!

St. John explains: "If any one sees his brother committing what is not a mortal sin, he will ask, and God will give him life for those whose sin is not mortal. There is sin which is mortal; I do not say that one is to pray for that…. Little children, keep yourself from idols" (1 John 5:16, 21). Thus, the soul of a Christian brother can die. If you looked up and read the above Pauline citations, did you notice that St. Paul mentions the sin of idolatry in all four of his listings of mortal sins? Now St. John ends his letter with a warning against it.

Other than the sinner making an act of perfect contrition, after he repents, only a man with the apostolic powers of priesthood like St. John can effectively ask God for forgiveness and spiritual life for a believer who has fallen back into the spiritual death of idolatry, or of some other mortal sin: "If you forgive the sins of any, they are forgiven; if you retain the sins of any, they are retained" (John 20:23). Here is the scriptural authority for priestly absolution. Catholics rejoice that no type of sin seems to be excluded from these merciful words of our Lord. Only a persistent failure to be contrite for one's sins excludes a person from forgiveness. The "blasphemy against the Holy Spirit" is the refusal to repent of at least one mortal sin as long as this life lasts. Final impenitence in the case of a mortal sin is an eternal sin. Like the common people of Jesus' day, we Catholics rejoice that God has given "such authority [to forgive sins] to men [plural]" (Matthew 9:7). The Protestant reformers' most basic criticisms of the Catholic view of justification focused on the justification process within the Sacrament of Penance. The Council of Trent first mentioned this Sacrament in its *Decree on Justification*. Far more Protestants seem to object to the Catholic teaching of justification through the Sacrament of Penance than through Baptism. Honestly, Protestants do not know what they are missing.

Clever teachers, with ulterior motives, sometimes use the Bible to razzle-dazzle average people. St. Peter warns his readers living in perilous times about those who distort the meaning of scriptural passages that are difficult to understand (see 2 Peter 3:15-16). The quest for the unerring truth about God's eternal plan to rescue mankind from sin and its soul-destroying qualities calls for the very wisest approach. Indeed, the shortest way to a totally accurate and reliable knowledge of salvation is to discover carefully which church specially belongs to Christ and to heed all of her teachings on this most vital subject. Near the end of the Bible, we find these words of exhortation: "Beloved, being very eager to write to you of our common salvation, I found it necessary to write appealing to you to contend for the faith which was once for all delivered to the saints" (Jude 3). Salvation belongs to the people to whom God has committed the true Faith once for all. Chapter Two of this book has already presented the case that this community is the Roman Catholic Church. Therefore, I will make only a few relevant remarks.

Matthew 16:18-19 is a passage about salvation. To have the "keys" to open and to close the kingdom of Heaven to others is to have great power and authority to affect the salvation of multitudes. We see that Christ promised to "build" only one church, and that He promised to "build" His Church on Peter. You can read every word of the New Testament, and you will never find Jesus promising these "keys" to anyone else – only to Peter. St. Peter does share the binding-and-loosing power with all the other Apostles (Matthew 18:18), but he alone is said to receive the "keys of the kingdom of heaven". What is true of Jesus, "the Way, the Truth, and the Life" (John 14:6), is also true of His Church. In several places in the Acts of the Apostles (9:2; 19:9, 23; 22:4; 24:14, 22), this original church is called "the Way".[18] According to Thomas a Kempis, "Without the Way there is no going. Without the Truth there is no knowing. Without the Life there is no living." So we may safely conclude that, just as it is normatively necessary to be a Christian in order to be saved, so it is normatively necessary to be a Catholic in union with Rome in order to be saved.

The Holy Scriptures guarantee that *some* members of the original

Church, the one that continues to belong specially to Christ, will be saved on the Last Day. Nevertheless, they provide no similar assurance for other, more recently established groups of Christians who are living among us today. At the same time, God is not hard-hearted. He does not refuse grace to anyone who does His will to the degree that he is able to know it and to do it. But obeying God in a serious matter such as this is necessary for salvation.

What is necessary is necessary. Nevertheless, to understand this necessity better, we need to understand the easily perceived distinction between "normative necessity" and "absolute necessity." For example, it is normally necessary to stop at stop signs. It is the law. Period. Even at three o'clock in the morning, when no other vehicle is on the road. But it is not absolutely necessary. One exception is a funeral procession. On the way to the cemetery, car after car goes through stop sign after stop sign, often with a police escort. But if a driver in an approaching car "runs" a stop sign in order to "beat" the funeral procession, he greatly risks paying a very dear price for failing to do what is necessary. All of this might apply to the salvation of those who are invincibly ignorant.

The Catholic Church is a very special church. It is the one church that specially belongs to Jesus Christ. He has given her authority to speak for Him. Because of this fact, God has promised to protect whatever she teaches. God wants everyone to be Catholic, even though it is not always easy to live up to all that the Church teaches. On account of the promises of Christ, His Church can never mislead us about salvation. Some Church leaders can be misleading, but not every teaching *in* the Church is the teaching *of* the Church. God guarantees the truth of all official, definitive teachings of the Church.

The following is macro-salvation, salvation made simple. We needed to be rescued from the eternal destruction that results from sin. God has come to our rescue in Jesus Christ, and Jesus continues to rescue us for His heavenly Kingdom by means of the Catholic Church: "He has delivered us from the dominion of darkness and transferred us to the kingdom of his beloved Son, in whom we have redemption, the forgiveness of sins" (Colossians 1:13-14). Today, Pope Benedict XVI, St. Peter's successor in the long line of Roman pontiffs, alone possesses the keys to this Kingdom. His teachings promote a reliable knowledge of salvation. The Catholic Church reliably teaches the chain of micro-salvation, with all its complexities. Where the Pope is, there is Peter. Where Peter is, there is the Church. Where the Church is, there is Christ. Where Christ is, there is sanctifying grace. Where sanctifying grace is, there is predestination to grace.[19] Where predestination to grace is, there is justification. Where justification is, there is merit.[20] Where merit is *at death*, there is predestination to glory. Where predestination to glory is, there is glorification. We need to pray constantly for the unmerited gift to remain and die in a state of grace, the state of our worthiness in God's sight. Although Catholics are unfairly criticized for repeating the Lord's Prayer and the Hail Mary as often as we do, both of these special prayers ask for this grace of final perseverance.

There is much that Catholics know about salvation. We know that only within the visible bounds of the Catholic Church may anyone find the fully secure road to salvation. There we have the sure guarantee of revealed truth, the Faith once for all delivered to God's people. To the extent that someone is not in full communion with the Catholic Church, he faces disadvantages, greater obstacles and burdens to his own salvation. It is hard for Catholics to attain heaven, but it is easier for them than for others. In the last analysis, only God can judge who will be saved and who will be lost (see 1 Corinthians 4:3-5). Our God-given mission is to be faithful in bringing as many people as we can into full communion with the Church, "the pillar and bulwark of the truth" (1 Timothy 3:15). It is a sin against charity to know that we have this serious duty of love to perform in God's sight, and then freely to refuse to perform it.

There is much that Catholics do *not* know about salvation. The Lord has not revealed who or how many will be saved, and so we do not and cannot know these curious details. We should charitably commend the deceased, non-Catholics as well as Catholics, to the mercy of God in Jesus Christ, even as St. Paul did in the case of his deceased friend Onesiphorus (see 2 Timothy 1:16-18). This, of course, assumes that those who have died might need God's mercy and might benefit from it. Obviously, the departed souls in heaven do not need God's mercy and those in hell cannot benefit from it. So St. Paul's prayer for Onesiphorus makes sense only if there is a third possibility, which Catholics call "purgatory".[21] Protestants pray only for the surviving family members, not for the deceased. In truly Catholic – and Jewish – fashion, St. Paul prays first for the grieving family of Onesiphorus, and then he goes on to pray solemnly for the dearly departed Onesiphorus. The doctrine "Outside the Church, No Salvation" does not make Catholics hard-hearted.

So far, we have discussed both variations on the *merciful, first* stage of justification, which works can never earn or truly merit. They are baptismal justification (first justification discovered) and penitential justification (first justification recovered). This first stage of justification takes place whenever a sinner passes from spiritual death to spiritual life. I have called this stage "first justification" even when it occurs in penitential justification, because the sinner starts his life in grace over again (except that the merits of his previous supernatural life are revived). This stage occurs only once through the Sacrament of Baptism, but it can occur repeatedly through the Sacrament of Penance or an act of perfect contrition. The first stage happens to someone who is not in a state of grace at the time that he is justified, normatively by one receiving the proper Sacrament with a proper disposition.

Merit and Divinization

We now turn to the *just, second* stage of justification. This could well be called "further justification", because it increases one's righteousness. Greater justification happens to someone who is already in a state of grace; an increase in righteousness is justly earned by good works done through grace.[22] Although God gives this righteousness as a matter of justice, the ability to earn it is itself a gift of God's mercy. Behold, the divine irony! The more one is justified, the greater one's spiritual wholeness. Sanctifying grace is like good food, which changes people, not only by removing the sick from a state of sickness to a state of health (compare the first stage of justification), but also by making the healthy even healthier (compare the second stage of justification).[23] This second stage requires human merit.

To deny each and every form of human merit, the mainline Protestant reformers, Martin Luther and John Calvin, taught a very rigorous species of predestination, in order to exclude totally from the realm of salvation any "power of choosing contraries" (free will) within any human creature.[24] If, as every full-fledged Calvinist asserts, everything that occurs has been foreordained by God, then all the sins of every true Christian done last week were predestined to be done. But this clearly contradicts St. Paul's teaching that God makes the way for us to escape from sinning, a way to avoid giving into temptation. He writes: "No temptation has overtaken you that is not common to man. God is faithful, and he will not let you be tempted beyond your strength, but with the temptation will also provide the way of escape, that you may be able to endure it" (1 Corinthians 10:13). Here is the truth. We can be either saved or lost for all eternity. What we, under the influence of God's grace, choose to do with the teachings and deeds of Jesus Christ is really what decides our eternal destiny in the predestinating foreknowledge of God. The quality of our free choices and the actions flowing from them will send us to heaven or hell, even though Luther and Calvin strongly rejected this traditional understanding of salvation.

At the Last Judgment, all the saved ones of all ages in human history will be totally conformed in perfect holiness to the glorious image of the Son (see Romans 8:29-30; 2 Corinthians 3:18; 1 John 3:2-3; 1 Thessalonians 5:23). On that day, "final justification" will be based upon meritorious deeds, for the Jews (see Romans 2:13) as well as for the Gentiles (see Romans 2:14-15), since God is totally just and fair in meting out the reward of eternal life to those who have persevered in doing good and the punishment of everlasting misery for those who have persisted in doing evil (see Romans 2:7-11). Because of their merits, God will praise each one of the righteous (see 1 Corinthians 4:5).

It is the Catholic doctrine of merit that many find most galling. It greatly offends Protestant sensibilities, even though belief in merit is a tradition that goes back to the earliest ages of Christianity. They think belief in merit is inconsistent with any claim that salvation is God's gift of mercy to us. They say, "On the one hand, Catholics believe that salvation is by grace through faith, but on the other hand, Catholics believe that they can earn their salvation by doing good deeds." How can both be true? Well, consider two scenarios.

If I promise a stinking beggar that I will give him five dollars, it would be wrong for me to fail to give him the money, but he cannot justly say to me, "You owe me five dollars, Bud." He did not merit or earn it. But if I promise one of my sons a full wage for a full day of work in the family business, and he freely accepts my offer and then freely does a full day of work for me, he can justly exclaim, when the factory whistle blows, "Dad, I have earned a full wage today!" The Protestant view of salvation is that we all remain beggars throughout life, even Mr. Abel T. Christian.[25] We can merit nothing now or ever. Heaven is a gift to the unworthy. The Catholic view is that we started out as beggars, but God has mercifully cleaned each of us up, even adopting us into His family, and then made us His loyal employees in the family business. Apart from God's grace, we would still stink and beg. We would remain Mr. Ungodly Man. We would not truly merit a thing. Through God's grace, we can merit life in heaven forever. For Protestants, God never gives the justified sinner what he truly deserves, only what Jesus Christ truly merited for the sake of the justified person; justice operates only on the level of Christ.

Our Creator has no need of us and our works. Creation is for the glory of its Creator. We already owe Him our service as His creatures. He not only created us, He also keeps us in existence. All of this is a gift to us from our Creator and should humble us deeply (see 1 Corinthians 4:7-8). A servant does not receive a reward for merely doing his duty. God could have called us to serve Him without any reward at all. This was His right. If He had done so, He would not have been unjust. But God has graciously promised to reward the good works of His children with eternal life. Since God is faithful and just, we know that He will not fail to keep His promises. The least good act done out of love by a child of God merits heaven. The reward of heaven far exceeds anything that we can imagine (see 1 Corinthians 2:9). For a child of God, every external good deed can be a truly meritorious act, but not every truly meritorious act is something done externally. A Catholic who is totally paralyzed can pray and make an act of love within his heart. The hands of the good thief to whom Jesus promised Paradise were literally tied, but his mouth and heart were free (see Luke 23:39-43). He humbly acknowledged his sinfulness and Jesus' righteousness. In addition to repentance, he had faith that someday Jesus would reign over God's Kingdom. He confessed Jesus in public after he was justified. After his soul was in a state of grace, he continued to express on his lips the faith, hope, and love in his heart. He died before Pentecost, when baptism became a requirement for salvation.

Even just being a child of God confers a right to heavenly glory. This is why deceased baptized infants enter heaven, even though they have not done anything with the grace given in baptism. Even though grace is a sharing in divine life that develops and brings forth meritorious deeds over time, they could not do anything. Although they died before they were even conscious of God, they are God's children with the right of inheritance: "and if children, then heirs" (Romans 8:17). We owe our adoption as God's children to the merits of Christ freely bestowed and freely received. Therefore, we owe our ability to merit heaven to the merits of Christ as well. The life of grace, if never lost, continues and becomes eternal life. Our merits help our divine life to continue unto eternal life. We merit in the strength of Christ alone, and our good deeds, if done in a state of grace, confer a second but even greater claim to heavenly glory. Apart from Jesus Christ, we can do nothing (see John 15:5). Whatever truly glorifies God's children also glorifies the Father, Son, and Holy Spirit, who have made us glorious (see John 17:1, 22).

Our merits are God's gifts to us through our cooperation with His grace. They accrue from free actions that are pleasing to God, precisely because they have been caused by the merits and grace of Christ. Some things cannot be merited. Just as no one can merit his own existence, no one can merit one's own passing from spiritual death to spiritual life at any time. One cannot strictly merit this for anyone else, either.[26] Also, none of us can merit that we will be in a state of grace tomorrow or at the moment our souls leave our bodies. Otherwise, we could never lose our justification. We can only pray daily for these unmerited gifts from God, who will surely prove Himself to be the merciful and just God of our salvation, if we continue to pray and do not lose heart (see Luke 18:1).

It is a common misunderstanding to think that eternal life at the end of the world is not itself a reward, but is only a gift acquired by faith alone, a pure gift of life lived in the midst of various rewards. Yes, eternal life is a true gift, but it is also a true reward. Speaking of compensation for the sacrifices of true discipleship, Jesus guarantees His followers great blessings in this world and eternal life in the world to come (see Mark 10:29-30). A child of God will "inherit eternal life" (Mark 10:17), and his inheritance is a just reward for pleasing God (see Colossians 3:23-25), as well as a gift. God actually repays the justified with life, as well as with blessings attending that future life. Jesus promises: "You will be repaid at the resurrection of the just" (Luke 14:14). St. Paul views this resurrection as a prize to be won (Philippians 3:7-14). Luther and Calvin taught that Jesus merited for us. They did not even mention that He could merit anything for His own human nature, so ardent was their conviction that no one could merit anything for oneself.

Clearly, the Protestant rejection of merit cannot make sense of some Bible verses. They say no one, not even a Christian, can live well enough to be worthy of eternal life. But St. Paul clearly disagrees. He writes:

> This is evidence of the righteous judgment of God, **that you may be made worthy of the kingdom of God,** for which you are suffering – since indeed God deems it just to repay with affliction those who afflict you, and to grant rest with us to you who are afflicted, when the Lord is revealed from heaven with his mighty angels in flaming fire. (2 Thessalonians 1:5-7, boldface emphasis added)

St. Paul does not pray make-believe prayers, either. Yet, he prays that the Colossians would "lead a life worthy of the Lord, fully pleasing to him, bearing fruit in every good work and increasing in the knowledge of God" (Colossians 1:10). St. Paul does not waste his breath. Yet, he reminds the Thessalonians that he has previously exhorted them "to lead a life worthy of God, who calls you into his own kingdom and glory" (1 Thessalonians 2:12).

Of course, all our good works have blemishes, as well as much that is pleasing to God. Since these little defects are in no way intentional, God mercifully overlooks them out of love for His children. We are confident that He does so. St. Luke probably understood St. Paul's doctrine of grace better than most of us ever will in this life, yet he summarized the quality of the lives of John the Baptist's parents with the statement: "They were both righteous before God, walking in all the commandments and ordinances of the Lord blameless" (Luke 1:6). Many times in the Old Testament, too, God or the inspired writer commends a living or dead king for having done everything that is good and right in God's sight (see 1 Kings 11:38; 14:8; 15:5; 22:43; 2 Kings 10:30; 12:2; 14:3; 15:3, 34; 18:3; 22:2; 2 Chronicles 14:2; 17:3; 20:32; 24:2; 25:2; 26:4; 27:2; 29:2; 31:20; 34:2). Such divine commendations often occur in the immediate context of the king's chief human failures. The reformation polemics insisting that Christians in a state of grace can never merit anything from

God because none of us has ever yet loved Him with our whole heart, soul, mind, and strength thus proves itself to be sophistic and ultimately unbiblical in spirit. This is not to say that everything a person believes is a good work really *is* such in God's sight. We need to judge all of our deeds by the light we have. Under the Old Covenant, because of their own fault, God's people as a whole often descended into thick darkness, although God always kept a remnant holy through His grace. Often, they offered sacrifices and went through the motions of doing what God required, but their hearts were far from Him. Their "righteous deeds" were not really good; they were filthy rags (see Isaiah 64:6).

On the Day of Judgment, God will judge those who do truly good deeds to be worthy of eternal life and the others to be unworthy (see Romans 2:7-10). It is only those persons persistent in rejecting St. Paul's saving message who judge themselves "unworthy of eternal life" (Acts 13:46), not Christians who live in accord with its precepts:

> Do not be deceived; God is not mocked, for whatever a man sows, that he will also reap. For he who sows to his own flesh will from the flesh reap corruption; but he who sows to the Spirit will from the Spirit reap eternal life. And let us not grow weary in well-doing, for in due season we shall reap, if we do not lose heart. (Galatians 6:7-9)

As he bravely approaches the end of his own life, St. Paul knows that God will judge him justly. He knows by divine revelation that he will be saved, and he knows that he has merited the eternal glory (the crown) that is the reward of righteous, faithful living. Of this he speaks triumphantly in 2 Timothy 4:7-8. He also knows all faithful Christians will justly merit this reward. To fight the good fight of faith is to "take hold of eternal life" (1 Timothy 6:12). Hebrews 6:10 echoes this theme: "For God is not so unjust as to overlook your work and the love which you showed for his sake in serving the saints, as you still do". The reward that God justly promises is "salvation", mentioned in the previous verse (Hebrews 6:9). Though Jesus Christ is far worthier of glory, Moses, too, is "worthy of glory" (Hebrews 3:3), and so shall every holy, persevering Christian be. Sin makes everyone fall short of the glory of God before justification (see Romans 3:23), but it is never true that anyone who is and remains justified falls short of God's glory (see 1 Corinthians 4:5). With grace and its fruits, good works, come a deserved glory. While grace alone and works alone necessarily exclude each other as principles of salvation, grace does not exclude works, and works do not exclude grace in our glorious progress toward eternal salvation.

What is most often overlooked or seriously misunderstood[27] in the reformation polemics against merit is that *DIVINIZATION* is the reality that makes our true merit possible.[28] Mr. Abel T. Christian, a man living in a state of grace, is not living on the natural level. He is living on the supernatural level. He is not a natural man, as Mr. Ungodly Man was; he is a supernatural man through God's grace (see 1 Corinthians 2:14-15). Sanctifying grace divinizes the being and actions of the justified person, who is living supernaturally in a state of grace: "For it is the God who said, 'Let light shine out of darkness,' who has shone in our hearts to give the light of the knowledge of the glory of God in the face of Christ" (2 Corinthians 4:6). A good illustration of this transformation of nature is the incandescent bulb. A child who has never observed that a flick of a switch in the dark will make a glass bulb glow experiences this for the first time with great surprise and delight. The flowing of electricity makes a huge difference. Similarly, sanctifying grace elevates our human nature. The difference between natural and supernatural living is far greater than the difference between a new unlit bulb in its package and one glowing brightly in a lamp (see 2 Corinthians 3:18).

The Sacraments have awesome power to divinize us. Receiving a Sacrament with a proper motivation while in a state of grace, especially Holy Communion, is itself a meritorious act. Apart from the merit of the act itself, the increase of sanctifying grace that the Body and Blood of Christ directly brings into one's soul through worthy reception greatly increases the meritorious value of every good deed that one performs afterwards while this renewal of sanctifying grace is still present: "He who eats my flesh and drinks my blood abides in me, and I in him. As the living Father sent me, and I live because of the Father, so he who eats me will live because of me" (John 6:56-57). Holy Communion gives us a share in the life of the Trinity and helps us to be fruitful by strengthening our union with Christ.

The Blessed Virgin Mary and the saints in heaven are divinized beings, yet they will never cease to be humans who are full of grace and love. In heaven, faith gives way to the Vision of God, hope gives way to possession, but love and sanctifying grace remain forever. This glorious state of affairs can begin in this life. St. Stephen, deacon and first martyr, is reputed to have been "full of grace" (Acts 6:8), something that clearly is not true of every Christian. This shows that there are degrees of grace as well as degrees of glory.[29] While it lasts, such fullness necessarily excludes sin. St. Stephen was not always full of grace, but, according to official Catholic teaching, the Blessed Virgin Mary has always been full of sanctifying grace, throughout her earthly life, even from the very first moment of her existence. The good deeds of someone who is truly full of grace when he is doing them cannot, in the least, be tainted by sin. On the contrary, because of Mary's great degree of divinization through grace, the merit of even her very slightest good deed was so magnificent, and marvelous, and awesome, as to be beyond our abilities to comprehend or imagine. It is entirely the grace and power of Christ mightily possessing her soul that gives all of her freely-chosen actions all of their value in God's sight.[30] The exact same principles apply to the other saints, even though they possess a lesser degree of divinization.[31]

We have not been in any way describing a New Age or pagan belief. The Church Fathers, especially in the East, stressed the importance of the process of divinization (or deification) in the Christian life.[32] Their teaching is as old as St. Peter himself. Just before he exhorts us to greater and greater holiness, he asserts that by God's power we can actually participate in His divine nature (see 2 Peter 1:3-4). This means that our glorious destiny as God's children is to become as much like God as is possible for a creature to become without ceasing to be a creature. We do not become God, but we become God-like children of God (see 1 John 3:2, 9). Mortal sin is totally incompatible with this supernatural life and robs a justified person of his divine adoption and the ability to merit. Mortal sin makes us "worthless servants" in the dark (Matthew 25:30).

If we look back on the years between our baptisms and today, many of us have much reason to be ashamed. Often we Christians have foolishly decided to throw away our most precious gift, God's sanctifying grace. We commit spiritual suicide whenever we commit a mortal sin (that is, whenever we reflect on a contemplated action as one that we judge seriously offensive to God and freely choose to do it anyway). When most of us soberly review our record of service to God, we must quite honestly admit that we have been His "unworthy servants" times without number

(Luke 17:10). But an impartial reading of our record should also show that sometimes we have really been worthy ones. Unworthy servants will be treated naturally (see Luke 17:7), but Jesus promises that worthy servants will be treated supernaturally. He will treat them as His children instead of as His slaves (see Luke 12:37). This is precisely the way loving parents feed their little children at the end of a long and busy day. Because we are children of God, our divinized actions follow from our divinized being – actions truly meriting a supernatural and eternal reward. No wonder Jesus exhorts us to act as beacons to the world through our good deeds (see Matthew 5:16)! This is how it is possible for us to exceed the righteousness of the scribes and Pharisees (see Matthew 5:20). By doing supernatural, meritorious works of love,[33] not merely natural good works or worse in an unjustified state, we truly merit life in God's Kingdom, as Christ declares in Matthew 25:31-46 regarding the Final Judgment at the end of time.

CHAPTER FIVE
The Sacraments of Baptism and Confirmation

Sacramental Symbolism in General

God communicates with us through symbols. A symbol is a perceptible sign that points to something beyond itself – a reality that the sign resembles in some way. The sign is some ordinary material object or physical action with which we are familiar, whereas the reality it signifies is generally more remote from our usual level of awareness. But the similarity between them is close enough so that the sign is capable of directing us to a notion of the higher reality.

God employs symbols to speak to us, because, although we are rational beings possessing spiritual souls, we also have physical bodies endowed with sensory organs. Therefore, all our knowledge during this life on earth is based on sense experience and the objects of the senses: what we can see, hear, smell, taste, and touch. Our minds are not naturally geared toward lofty supernatural truths.

On a cosmic scale, God uses the awesome splendor of the whole physical universe as a gigantic sign to reveal Himself to us. Sacred Scripture tells us this in both Psalm 19:2 and Romans 1:20. The entirety of Psalm 104 is a hymn of joyful praise and gratitude to God for His wondrous creation; in particular, verses 27-28 proclaim the truth of God's providential care for all His living creatures.

In the case of mankind, though, divine providence extends beyond material necessities to include our spiritual needs. In fact, the Catholic Faith teaches that our Lord Jesus Christ, the Second Person of the Blessed Trinity and the Word of God who incarnated Himself to redeem us (see John 1:1-14), instituted *Sacraments* for our sanctification. According to the traditional Catholic definition, a "Sacrament" is an outward sign instituted by Christ to give grace. The Catholic Church holds that there are seven Sacraments: Baptism, Confirmation, the Holy Eucharist, Penance or Reconciliation, Anointing of the Sick or Extreme Unction,

Holy Orders, and Matrimony. All seven Sacraments consist in symbolic exterior actions (visible) and prayerful words (audible) that God uses as instruments to actually bring about within the human soul the inner spiritual effects that these external ceremonies represent. The purpose of each Sacrament is to render worship to God through sanctifying individuals and building up the Body of Christ.

Many of the Sacraments (particularly Baptism, the Holy Eucharist, Confirmation, Anointing of the Sick) involve simple, commonplace material substances (respectively, water, wheat bread, grape wine, olive oil) exhibiting the remarkable power to raise our minds to the realm of divine mystery.[1] Every Sacrament, however, can be analyzed into a "material" aspect and a "formal" aspect. In other words, a Sacrament is a symbolic rite, containing some basic physical substance or condition (its *matter*) along with a structure of words and actions (its *form*), which actually brings about the very gift (or *grace*) that it signifies. We need to experience such perceptible signs because of our natural mental debility for grasping spiritual truths directly, especially after the damage wrought by Original Sin.

It is the burden of several subsequent essays in this book to establish (or at least defend) from scriptural sources the thesis of the existence of the seven Sacraments, as well as to discuss their nature based on the relevant sacred texts. In this chapter, we consider the Sacraments of initiation called "Baptism" and "Confirmation".

(I) Baptism

The Effects of Baptism

One of the main disputes about Baptism revolves around what it accomplishes for the recipient. Is it merely an ordinance of initiation for membership in the Church? Or does something more profound occur when this Sacrament is administered?[2]

In John 3:5 our Lord Jesus Christ affirms: "Truly, truly, I say to you unless one is born of water and the Spirit, he cannot enter the kingdom of God." Although St. John the Baptist had prophesied that the Messiah would "baptize with the Holy Spirit and with fire" (Matthew 3:11; Luke 3:16), the "fire" of Christ's baptismal ministry obviously did not exclude water, for we encounter Him baptizing with water in John 3:22-23 – at least through the ministry of His disciples (see John 4:1-2).[3]

Let us return to John 3:5, where Jesus tells us (via His conversation with the Pharisee Nicodemus): "Unless one is born of water and the Spirit, he cannot enter the kingdom of God." In John 3:7 He amplifies on His meaning: "You must be born anew". Instead of "anew", however, an alternative (perhaps better) translation of the Greek ἄνωθεν might be "from above". Moreover, John 1:12-13 supports the substitution of "born above" for "born again", because "the power to become children of God" is a heavenly rebirth stemming from God Himself. At any rate, in His gentle reprimand of Nicodemus in John 3:7-12, Jesus corrected some mistaken notions of a man whose name derives from the Greek for "crusher of the people" (νικώ = "vanquish", δέμος = "people"); in other words, He refuted some potential doctrinal misinterpretation about the nature of salvation that could have caused widespread confusion from the mouth of an influential religious leader.

At any rate, on account of the significance of water, which washes away contamination from what is soiled, our Lord's declaration implies that the soul of the recipient is somehow besmirched prior to the baptismal rite. It thus requires the supernal action of the Holy Spirit, working instrumentally through the physical substance of water, to purify it and regenerate it, rendering it fit for a supernatural mode of life. For, as Revelation 21:27 insists, "nothing unclean shall enter it [the heavenly city]."

Hence, Baptism, though employing a powerful sign of purification, does not merely symbolize admission into the Christian community. Indeed, in 1 Peter 3:21, St. Peter clarifies that "Baptism ... now saves you, not as a removal of dirt from the body but as an appeal to God for a clear conscience". Now, a clear conscience entails an interior transformation from a condition of sin to a state of righteousness before God – not merely an externally imputed or legal justification leaving one as depraved as before, but rather a real internal elevation from deprivation of divine life to its possession. St. Peter emphasizes that we are called to "become partakers of the divine nature" (2 Peter 1:4) – which is not possible unless we undergo a genuine renovation of our very inner being (i.e., an ontological change).

In the same vein, St. Paul writes in Titus 3:5-7:

> He [God] saved us, not because of deeds done by us in righteousness, but in virtue of his own mercy, by the washing of regeneration and renewal in the Holy Spirit, which he poured out upon us richly through Jesus Christ our Savior, so that we might be justified by his grace and become heirs in hope of eternal life.

These verses echo John 3:5 with their thematic notes of baptismal water and the concomitant action of the Holy Spirit, who justifies the soul – regenerating it unto the new supernatural life of sanctifying grace. These key baptismal terms in their sequential relation also appear in 1 Corinthians 6:11: "You were washed, you were sanctified, you were justified in the name of the Lord Jesus Christ and in the Spirit of our God." (Observe the Pauline theological explication of the Trinitarian baptismal formula that our Lord enunciated in Matthew 28:19.)

We find further corroboration in Romans 6:3-4 (see also Colossians 2:12):

> Do you not know that all of us who have been baptized into Christ Jesus were baptized into his death? We were buried therefore with him by baptism into death, so that as Christ was raised from the dead by the glory of the Father, we too might walk in newness of life.

St. Paul here capitalizes on the aquatic imagery of the baptismal ceremony, which literally immerses the recipient in water. This watery engulfment is the visible sign of the spiritual drowning of sin. St. Paul teaches that Baptism is a Sacrament that puts sin to death through submergence in Christ's meritorious suffering, death, and burial. Saul of Tarsus (the future St. Paul) himself experienced this spiritual rebirth through the medium of water, after hearing Ananias tell him: "Rise and be baptized, and wash away your sins, calling on his name" (Acts 22:16). This Sacrament thus enables us to participate in Christ's resurrection unto a new life from which sin has been washed away: in particular, restoration from the loss of sanctifying grace inherited due to Adam's Original Sin, as St. Paul brilliantly explains in Romans 5:12-21.

Hence, when St. Paul says in Galatians 3:27 that "as many of you as were baptized into Christ have put on Christ", he does not mean a clothing with Jesus as a mere covering over of residual spiritual corruption, but rather a penetration of the soul by the Lord with the vesture of His divine light. Our configuration to Him entails our undergoing "sanctification by the Spirit" (2 Thessalonians 2:13). If we persevere in this state, we shall be rewarded with the Beatific Vision, wherein grace is manifested as glory. But this result is possible only because the cleansed soul is already, in a way, Godlike (see 1 John 3:2).

In sum, Baptism satisfies the traditional definition of a Sacrament. It was instituted by Christ, explicitly in the command recorded in Matthew 28:19-20. Its purpose is to restore the sanctifying grace lost through the inheritance of Original Sin, accomplishing this aim via outward signs (pouring with water, accompanied by the standard Trinitarian formula).

Necessity of Water Baptism

Some controversy has arisen over the question of the necessity of water baptism for salvation. After all, Christ did say in John 3:5 that "unless one is born of water and the Spirit, he cannot enter the kingdom of God." The issue here revolves around the degree to which this command is absolute.

Our Lord could have meant His statement in a conditional or provisional sense. In other words, water baptism is necessary to remove the stain of original sin for those who know about this mandate and are able to fulfill it. But it is reasonable to assume that, for those who are invincibly ignorant of this requirement or who know about it but are involuntarily prevented from achieving their aim, the desire to receive water baptism would suffice to produce the effect of the remission of original sin. This seems to follow from what St. Paul teaches in Romans 2:14-16, which could be applied to all those inhabiting pagan lands. St. Paul indicates in this passage that there may be extenuating circumstances excusing certain people from completely abiding by or thoroughly conforming to regular divine norms.

Thus, the desire for water baptism could be either explicit or implicit. It would be explicit, for example, in catechumens who are studying the Faith in preparation to receive Baptism. If some misfortune overtakes them and they are unable before death to realize their express intention, it seems logical to conclude that God would take this into account and not hold them responsible for any dereliction in duty.

On the other hand, the desire for Baptism (including the material factor of a pouring with water) may be present in someone's mind, not expressly, but by some sort of equivalent intention. If certain people have never heard the Gospel preached and therefore have no natural means of finding out about the necessity of water baptism for salvation, yet seek the one true God as manifested by living in a morally upright manner according to their interior lights, then such persons may come under a mysterious divine dispensation that will secure their deliverance from the bondage of original sin. God, after all, is not bound by the Sacraments He has instituted for mankind's benefit.

Infant Baptism

Another controversy surrounding Baptism centers around the qualifications of the recipient subjects: in particular, whether children who have not reached the age of rational consent ought to be baptized.

Of course, the early Church zealously obeyed Christ's command in Matthew 28:19: "Go therefore and make disciples of all nations, baptizing them in the name of the Father and of the Son and of the Holy Spirit." For example, Acts 2:38 tells us that St. Peter urged a large crowd: "Repent, and be baptized every one of you in the name of Jesus Christ for the forgiveness of your sins; and you shall receive the gift of the Holy Spirit." We are then informed in Acts 2:41 that his preaching was immensely efficacious, since many people were baptized. In Acts 10:47 we once again encounter Peter promulgating Baptism: "'Can any one forbid water for baptizing these people who have received the Holy Spirit just as we have?'"

But someone may protest that these numerous recipients of Baptism were all adults. How about children? Let us examine some pertinent texts in this regard.

It is recorded in Acts 16:33 that one of the jailers of Paul and Silas "was baptized at once, with all his family". Acts 18:8, reporting that "many of the Corinthians hearing Paul believed and were baptized", implies that the synagogue ruler Crispus was also baptized – "together with all his household". In 1 Corinthians 1:16 St. Paul avers: "I did baptize also the household of Stephanas." Other cases that seem to involve the baptism of entire households occur in Acts 11:14-16 and Acts 16:15. It is safe to assume that at least some of these households had children below the age of reason. At any rate, none of these passages make any distinction among the family members under the head of the house. It would be unwarranted to read into them any exclusion from reception of Baptism on account of age or some other condition (such as mental or physical infirmity). Now, if we had only the testimony of silence on the issue, there might be a reasonable basis for contention over it. Instead, on the contrary, we behold the leading disciples of Christ in the early Church practicing the baptism of whole families.

If we think about the effects of Baptism as articulated in the previous subsection, infant baptism makes perfect sense. Baptism is unlike other Sacraments that demand free choice of the will in order to fulfill their purpose (for example, the duties of Matrimony or Holy Orders). For those enslaved under the yoke of Original Sin alone, with no burden of actual sins committed for which they are personally responsible, the immediate result of their baptism would be the cleansing of their souls from this Adamic stain and their simultaneous endowment with God's friendship. They would not be expected to proclaim their own personal faith in Christ as an antecedent condition for baptism, because the baptismal grace operates by virtue of the enacted rite itself. Since this internal transformation does not necessarily require the liberty of informed consent, it would seem unjust to deny a child the automatic benefits of Baptism – at least if it is foreseen that a favorable family environment will later enable the baptismal gift to blossom into personal acts of faith, hope, and charity.

But let us review some Old Testament prefigurements of Baptism in order to settle the matter.

Old Testament Typology

A number of events in the Old Testament foreshadow Baptism.[4] We recall the Spirit of God moving over the waters in Genesis 1, the story of the Great Flood in Genesis 6-9, the passage of the Israelites through the Red Sea in Exodus 14-15, and the crossing of the Jordan River by the chosen people in Joshua 1, 3-4. (See also the prophecies of Ezekiel 36:25-27 and Isaiah 12:3; 45:8, the latter verse pleading for the heavenly descent of the rain of righteousness, which signifies the advent of the Savior who would purify earthly humanity from sin.) In fact, reverting to the Deluge narrative, St. Peter explicitly links the Sacrament of Baptism with the salvation of Noah's family via the ark that bore them through the waters of the Flood, telling us that "Baptism ... corresponds to this" (see 1 Peter 3:20-21). In other words, the earth-cleansing catastrophe, in conjunction with the subsequent Noahic covenant re-establishing peace between heaven and earth, is a clear *type* of Baptism. For our purposes, however, we concentrate our attention on the passages of Exodus and Joshua.

In 1 Corinthians 10:1-2 St. Paul reminds his audience: "I want you to know, brethren, that our fathers were all under the cloud, and all passed through the sea, and all were baptized into Moses in the cloud and in the sea." Notice that **all** the chosen people underwent this "baptism" of safe passage through the waters of the Red Sea; it did not require the express consent of any of them, particularly not the children. The same verdict can be rendered about the crossing of the Jordan River, which Christ would sanctify centuries later through His own baptism and which therefore represents the baptismal waters of the New Covenant: once again, **all** the chosen people alive at that time, without exception, passed unharmed into the Promised Land through the waters of the Jordan.

Another Old Covenant *type* of Baptism is the circumcision ritual prescribed by God for the Israelites through Abraham in Genesis 17 and through Moses in Leviticus 12. (See St. Paul's validation of this sacramental association in Colossians 2:11-12.) This ritual act was to be executed on infants solely in accordance with the permission of the parents.

One of the corollaries of the corporate unity of the human race (see again Romans 5:12-21) is that children are subject to the authority of their parents (see Colossians 3:20; Ephesians 6:1). During the period of their youth, human offspring are borne along on the trail marked for them by their parents. The consequences can be for better or worse; children share non-voluntarily in both the sufferings arising from their parents' faults and the blessings merited by their parents' wise decisions. Hence, the faith and sincere wishes of the parents suffice for a valid and efficacious conferral of Baptism.

(II) Confirmation

Distinct from Baptism

The main apologetical difficulties with Confirmation seem to consist in demonstrating that Christ truly instituted it as a Sacrament and that it is really distinct from Baptism. We have seen that the principal effect of Baptism is to efface Original Sin from the soul. We must adduce scriptural texts implying the existence of a different Sacrament to strengthen the recipient with the power of the Holy Spirit for the purpose of giving Christian witness.

We know from John 3:5 that the Holy Spirit regenerates the recipient of Baptism through the instrumentality of water, and we note from Matthew 28:19 that our Lord commanded this Sacrament to be administered with an accompanying Trinitarian formula. Since Jesus Himself baptized early in His public ministry, at least through His disciples (see John 3:22; 4:1-2), the Holy Spirit must somehow already have been at work in sanctifying souls.

But St. John the Baptist prophesied that the Messiah would baptize "with the Holy Spirit and with fire" (see Matthew 3:11; Luke 3:16). The physical element of "fire" suggests an action of the Holy Spirit different from the removal of Original Sin through the material agency of water. Hence, Christ's promise in John 14:16-17 to send the Holy Spirit in a special manner seems to go beyond Baptism:

> "And I will pray the Father, and he will give you another Counselor, to be with you for ever, even the Spirit of truth, whom the world cannot receive, because it neither sees him nor knows him; you know him, for he dwells with you, and will be in you."

Evidently, according to Christ's words, the Holy Spirit already abided with the Apostles. Yet, our Lord foretold the future coming of the Holy Spirit! Moreover, in John 16:7, He repeated His promise, adding: "If I do not go away, the Counselor will not come to you; but if I go, I will send him to you." Thus, the Holy Spirit had already come, but nevertheless had still not come.

How can this apparent contradiction be resolved? There is no conflict here if the first coming of the Holy Spirit refers to the divine operation transpiring in Baptism (or its Old Covenant precursor), whereas the second coming of the Holy Spirit refers to an additional outpouring of grace for a different end – which would imply a distinct Sacrament.

The words of our Lord reported in Acts 1:4-5 are even more explicit (see also Luke 24:49):

> And while staying with them he charged them not to depart from Jerusalem, but to wait for the promise of the Father, which, he said, "you heard from me, for John baptized with water, but before many days you shall be baptized with the Holy Spirit."

The Apostles and disciples had already received the Holy Spirit, just as other early Christians would later receive the Holy Spirit in the Sacrament of Baptism through water (see, for example, Acts 2:41; 8:36-38). But here Christ was informing His first followers that they were about to be "baptized" in a different manner, which seems to hark back in a specific way to the vivid prophecy of St. John the Baptist in Matthew 3:11 and Luke 3:16.

Indeed, the dramatic account of the descent of the Holy Spirit under the form of tongues of fire in Acts 2:1-3 shows the literal fulfillment of the Baptist's prophecy. The results were immediate and astonishing. Despite the presence of the Holy Spirit in the lives of the Apostles prior to Pentecost Sunday (with a state of righteousness prevailing in their souls), they were nonetheless a timid band of men – too weak to proclaim the Gospel to the world. But after they experienced this new and powerful manifestation of the Spirit, they were emboldened to witness about Jesus Christ, preaching to the multitude and prophesying in the name of the Lord (see Acts 2:4-40). The radically different effect produced in them indicates their reception of a Sacrament distinct from Baptism, though undoubtedly an extension of it by virtue of a more intense participation in the activity of the Holy Spirit.

When St. Peter exhorted the crowd in Acts 2:38, saying: "Repent, and be baptized every one of you in the name of Jesus Christ for the forgiveness of your sins; and you shall receive the gift of the Holy Spirit", the Prince of the Apostles was apparently alluding to the first action of the Holy Spirit in cleansing the soul from sin (whether Original Sin or personal actual sins). Even if the second action of the Holy Spirit in empowering open Christian witness chronologically accompanied the first, the two operations were (and still are) distinguishable.

We can support this assertion by considering Acts 8:14-17:

Now when the apostles at Jerusalem heard that Samaria had received the word of God, they sent to them Peter and John, who came down and prayed for them that they might receive the Holy Spirit; for it had not yet fallen on any of them, but they had only been baptized in the name of the Lord Jesus. Then they laid their hands on them and they received the Holy Spirit.

This passage illustrates the reality of two different Sacraments. The Samarians had already been "baptized in the name of the Lord Jesus". Hence, they had received the Holy Spirit in an incipient way, because Baptism remits Original Sin through the power of the Holy Spirit. Presumably they had been baptized with water, in compliance with John 3:5. (Incidentally, even though the text explicitly mentions only their baptism "in the name of the Lord Jesus", the full Trinitarian formula mandated by Christ in Matthew 28:19 is not necessarily excluded.) But, when Peter and John arrived, the two Apostles conferred the Holy Spirit on them, not through the use of water, but rather by a laying on of hands. We conclude that the Samarians received another Sacrament beyond Baptism — what the Church has for centuries called "Confirmation".

Another "laying on of hands" for the reception of the Holy Spirit, distinct from Baptism, occurs in Acts 9:17-18. In this passage, Saul was baptized apart from the action of the laying on of hands by Ananias, whom the Lord had sent as an instrument to fill Saul with the Holy Spirit. After this Damascus event, Saul underwent a drastic conversion — from being a vicious persecutor of the Church to one of Christ's most militant witnesses: "Saul increased all the more in **strength**, and confounded the Jews who lived in Damascus by proving that Jesus was the Christ"

(Acts 9:22, boldface emphasis added). One lesson to be drawn here is that the Sacrament of Confirmation can furnish the ability to do adequate apologetics through the fortifying enlightenment of the Holy Spirit.

Another passage describing the reception of water Baptism apart from the prophetic gifts of the Holy Spirit (similar to the Pentecost manifestation in Acts 2:4) is Acts 10:44-48. Here the Holy Spirit descended upon a group of Gentiles who were listening to St. Peter preach about Christ (Acts 10:34-43). The Gentiles responded by "speaking in tongues and extolling God" (verse 46). Peter then interrupted (verses 47-48): "'Can any one forbid water for baptizing these people who have received the Holy Spirit just as we have?' And he commanded them to be baptized in the name of Jesus Christ." We may balk at the reversal of order in the reception of the two Sacraments, but God, who is not bound by His Sacraments, apparently made an exception in this case. Anyway, Christ had granted St. Peter, as the first pope, jurisdiction over the Sacraments (see Matthew 16:19).

An even more glaring passage illustrating the distinction between the two Sacraments is Acts 19:1-6. In this narrative St. Paul encountered some Ephesian disciples who had been baptized only with the baptism of repentance administered by St. John the Baptist; they had never even heard of the Holy Spirit. After listening to some instruction by St. Paul, "they were baptized in the name of the Lord Jesus. And when Paul had laid his hands upon them, the Holy Spirit came on them; and they spoke with tongues and prophesied." Notice that, following sufficient catechetical instruction, Paul first had them baptized. Subsequently, he performed another rite for a special advent of the Holy Spirit. Here, therefore, we find convincing evidence that Confirmation, which imparts the possibility for external manifestations of the Holy Spirit, is a different Sacrament from Baptism, which initially configures the soul to Christ.

Because St. John the Baptist was among the greatest of the prophets, we can be sure that he was profoundly accurate in his declaration that Christ would baptize with the fire of the Holy Spirit. Jesus Himself promised the arrival of the Holy Spirit, whom He publicly sent on Pentecost Sunday nine days after His Ascension into heaven. We deduce, then, that the Founder of the Church instituted Confirmation, whose purpose is to intensify the grace of the Holy Spirit, thereby strengthening the ability to give Christian witness. Since it is accompanied by outward signs (tongues of fire, laying on of hands, and anointing with oil, as we shall see below), Confirmation qualifies as a genuine Sacrament according to the traditional Catholic definition.

Anointing with Oil

An interesting aspect about the way in which Confirmation has been conferred for centuries is anointing with oil. The scriptural texts we have examined so far, however, have mentioned the laying on of hands alone. Is there biblical warrant for the use of oil in this Sacrament?

In Ephesians 1:13 St. Paul reminds his audience: "In him [Christ] you also, who have heard the word of truth, the gospel of your salvation, and have believed in him, were **sealed** with the promised Holy Spirit (boldface emphasis added)." The term "seal" suggests an anointing with oil on the forehead (see Revelation 6:6; 7:3; 9:4). Indeed, in 1 John 2:20, St. John writes that "you have been **anointed** by the Holy One" (boldface emphasis added; see also verse 27). The Greek for "anoint" stems from the root *chrisma*; "chrism" is the name of the fragrant oil (olive oil mixed with balsam) used in the Confirmation rite. Perhaps, therefore, the early Church did (at least eventually) employ oil when administering Confirmation.

We can support this verdict by invoking Old Testament typology. Since St. Peter calls Christians a "royal priesthood" (1 Peter 2:9), the appointment ceremonies for priests and kings in the Old Testament provide a foreshadowing of Confirmation.

Let us first consider the ordination rite of priests under the Mosaic Law. In Exodus 22:30, God commanded Moses to anoint Aaron and his sons for divine ministry. In Exodus 30:22-25, we read that the Lord told Moses to make consecrated oil for this purpose by combining fragrant spices with olive oil. The exact prescription for concocting the anointing oil delineated in Exodus 30:23-24 made more precise the implementation of the previous general command of God to Moses in Exodus 29:7-9 concerning the anointing of Aaron and his sons. (Incidentally, in Judges 9:8-9, anointing with olive oil, regarded as very rich, is considered a sign of honor.)

Centuries later, the prophet Samuel anointed Saul with oil as the first king of Israel (see 1 Samuel 10:1-6), foretelling Saul (in verse 6) that "the spirit of the Lord will come mightily upon you, and you shall prophesy ... and be turned into another man." (Samuel's prophecy was fulfilled in verse 10.) Furthermore, regarding Samuel's anointing of David as the second king of Israel in 1 Samuel 16:13, the sacred text relates: "Samuel took the horn of oil, and anointed him in the midst of his brothers; and the Spirit of the Lord came mightily upon David from that day forward." Likewise, in 1 Kings 1:39, Solomon was anointed king with oil by Zadok, a priest. (See also 1 Kings 19:15-16; 2 Kings 9:3, 6; 11:12.)

In the foregoing Old Testament verses, we find a close connection between anointing the forehead with oil and the coming of the Holy Spirit in a special way. In fact, the Holy Spirit can transform "into another man" someone who undergoes this sacramental anointing with oil. Oil therefore substitutes for fire as a symbol of the Holy Spirit.[5] Like the Apostles and disciples after the advent of the Holy Spirit at Pentecost, the recipients of Confirmation can become mature and zealous Christians. Participating in Christ's roles of priest, prophet, and king, they are spiritually fueled by the grace bestowed through this sacramental oil – grace enkindling them to become strong and bright lights in prophetically witnessing before the world to the truth of Jesus Christ as "King of kings and Lord of lords" (1 Timothy 6:15; Revelation 19:16).

CHAPTER SIX
The Sacrifice of the Mass and the Holy Eucharist

Introduction

Within the famous passage recording the encounter between our Lord and the Samaritan woman at Jacob's well (John 4:4-26), Christ tells her: "True worshipers will worship the Father in spirit and truth" (verse 23). What does it mean that one "must worship [the Father] in spirit and truth" (verse 26)? For some people, this kind of worship occurs only when ritual or liturgical expression is absent — as if liturgy can only degenerate into habitual and faithless formalism. There is no question that worshiping the Father in spirit and truth requires hearts and minds oriented toward faith, hope, and love in Him. Nevertheless, does worship "in spirit and truth" ever require us to engage in certain forms of worship that God has handed down to His people: that is, specific rites directed toward bringing us into stronger communion with God Himself? If a Christian answers in the negative, how then can he explain the numerous occasions in the Old and New Testaments in which God expressly lays out a sacred ritual for the community of faith to practice as part of their life of worship? To say that God laid down rituals in the Old Testament, but not in the New, would not concur with the scriptural evidence: for example, Jesus told us to baptize and to celebrate the Last Supper. These commands of Jesus are specific instructions for us to follow, intended to enable us to worship and give thanks to God in the manner He wants. In this passage, the Samaritan woman identified the essence of worship with a place rather than with a person. Christ points to a time when the true worship of the Father will not have its focus on a particular place, but will consist in believing and trusting the one sent from God who will reveal worship in spirit and truth. Hence, on the night before Christ dies, he gives us a ritual whereby we may enter into communion with Him and give thanks to the Father.

While Catholics and Protestants share what is called "the Lord's Supper" in common, they differ dramatically on its proper comprehension. How are we to interpret and properly apprehend Jesus' teachings surrounding the Last Supper? Catholics maintain that the bread and wine are completely changed, so that Christ is present body, blood, soul, and divinity under the appearances of bread and wine. Lutherans hold that Christ is physically present with the bread and wine, but only long enough to be received by the believer – and then that presence evaporates. Those following the tradition of Protestant Reformer John Calvin say that this presence is not physical, but only spiritual; and still others, like Ulrich Zwingli, teach that this whole rite is purely a symbolic gesture in order to help us express our faith in Jesus. In my experience, most Protestants generally regard the celebration of the Last Supper in purely symbolic terms. Emphasis is placed upon the believer's faith and personal appropriation of this sacred rite, rather than upon its objective character.

For many Protestants, what Catholics call "sacraments" are termed "ordinances". These ordinances may help elicit a faith-filled response, but do not themselves impart grace. For Catholics, on the other hand, these are not mere ordinances, but sacraments whose objective character is based in God's action and whose proper performance imparts grace. The sacraments are not magic, however, and for a sacrament to benefit a person it must be received in faith. (Infant baptism is a separate case, which depends on the faith of the parents, for God's saving actions are not contingent merely upon our own ability to do something.) Besides this, why would Christ institute "ordinances" to be obeyed, if those "ordinances" did not objectively do something? Christ did not come to continue giving us rites, whose objective nature is no greater than the Old Testament rites. If he established the "ordinances", then he did so because they actually do something in themselves (through divine power, of course). Hence, these "ordinances" are truly sacred things, that is, sacraments.

The manner of Christ's presence is not the only issue dividing the Christian community with regard to the Last Supper. Is the Last Supper a sacrificial meal? Are we partaking of a real sacrifice? For Catholics the answer is in the affirmative, but this is not the case for many other Christian communities. Some hold that the answer to these questions is not essential to the Faith, but how can one say this when it concerns a practice expressly set forth by Christ Himself? The Catholic Faith maintains that these questions are not unessential, but important ones, because they directly relate to our salvation and growth in holiness.

I remember meeting a Messianic Jew who declared he was a strict literal interpreter of the Scriptures. Unlike many that follow the tradition of the Protestant Reformers, he accepted the real presence of Christ in the Eucharist because the Bible says so. In addition, his Jewish roots enabled him to understand the Jewish meaning of memory and its connection to the Passover. It is this understanding that bequeathed to him a very clear picture of what Christ was doing at the Last Supper. Jesus was not speaking symbolically, and this "born-again" Messianic Jew did not think so either.

The Institution Narratives and Passover

For Catholics, the re-enactment of the Lord's Supper is called the Mass or the celebration of the Eucharist. The word "Eucharist" stems from the Last Supper narratives and means "to give thanks" or "thanksgiving" (literally deriving from the Greek for "good gift"). Catholics believe that in the Eucharist Christ is entirely present. As mentioned earlier, He is present body, blood, soul, and divinity under the appearances of bread and wine. What we see, touch, and taste is perceived to be bread and wine by the senses, but the eyes of faith realize that the essence of both the consecrated Host and the contents of the consecrated chalice is Christ. After the invocation of prayer and the words of consecration, the bread and wine cease to be what they were (ordinary bread and wine), but are changed in their substance to the resurrected Lord Jesus Himself. Hence, Catholics believe Jesus gave the power to change ordinary bread and wine into Himself when He commanded the Apostles to keep a memorial of Himself. The famous Last Supper narratives are recorded in the Gospels of Matthew, Mark, and Luke, and recalled in St. Paul's First Letter to the Corinthians (see Matthew 26:17, 19, 26-29; Mark 14:1, 12-16, 22-25; Luke 22:1, 7-20; 1 Corinthians 11:23-26). While simply making reference to the Last Supper (see John 13:1), John has no such narrative; instead, he includes the Bread-of-Life discourse in which the reality of the Eucharist is articulated (see John 6:32-69).

The three Synoptic Gospels contain what Catholics call the "institutional narratives" in which Christ, during the Passover celebration with His Apostles, leaves for us a memorial to be celebrated in remembrance of Him. It is obvious from reading the texts cited above that the Last Supper is placed in the context of the Passover celebration. This point is extremely important in understanding the sacrificial nature of the Last Supper and the mode of Christ's presence.

First, Christ is likened to the Passover lamb. St. John the Baptist proclaims Jesus to be the "Lamb of God, who takes away the sin of the world" (John 1:29, 36). St. Paul says: "Cleanse out the old leaven that you may be a new lump, as you really are unleavened. For Christ, our paschal lamb, has been sacrificed" (1 Corinthians 5:7). St. Peter declares: "You know that you were ransomed from the futile ways inherited from your fathers, not with perishable things such as silver or gold, but with the precious blood of Christ, like that of a lamb without blemish or spot" (1 Peter 1:18-19). The book of Revelation refers to Christ as "the Lamb who was slain" (Revelation 5:6, 12; 13:8; see also 7:14; 12:11).

There is some scholarly debate about whether the Last Supper should be understood from the standpoint of the Passover or from the standpoint of table fellowship. This debate ought not degenerate into a false either/or dichotomy, because the Last Supper is both of these things. The two emphases are not mutually exclusive, and each focuses on a different aspect of the Eucharistic mystery. The Passover emphasis focuses on the sacrificial nature of the meal itself, whereas table fellowship focuses on the strengthening of bonds between those sharing in the meal.

Second, the words and phrases such as "covenant in my blood", "give", and "poured out" used in the Synoptic Gospels by Jesus are shrouded in sacrificial imagery from the Old Testament (see, for example, Leviticus 4:7). Placing these words in the context of the Passover enables one to understand that what Jesus is doing is a sacrifice itself that is intimately connected to His own death on the cross.

Third, in reading the entirety of the accounts surrounding the Last Supper, we notice the theme of faith versus disbelief. In each of these accounts, Judas personifies faithlessness and lack of love, as he sets out to betray the Lord. Contrarily, in each account Peter personifies faith, though that faith is sometimes weak; for he, while believing, later abandons his Lord. This is an important theme, because to believe in the real presence of Christ necessitates faith. It was the rationalism of the Reformers that led them to reject the long held Catholic teaching on the real presence of Christ.

Fourth, Christ says: "This is my body" – *not* "This represents my body" or "This symbolizes my body". If it were the intention of the inspired author to communicate the merely symbolic nature of this rite, then why did he not choose these more appropriate words? The verb "to be" can sometimes mean "represents" or "symbolize", but only when the obvious context of the passage demands it. For example, Christ said: "I am the door" (John 10:7, 9). Yet, no one interprets Him to mean that He is literally a physical door, but rather that He is *like* a door insofar as it is through Him that we have access to the Father. In addition, the eating of bread and the drinking of wine was already a part of the Passover meal. Jesus was clearly doing something new and different. The signs He had chosen were to indicate the real presence of His own body and blood in a novel manner.

Lastly, and very importantly, in each of these accounts Jesus instructs us to "do this in memory of" Him. This did not simply mean to recollect some past event. It would be helpful to understand what "memory" in the context of the paschal meal really meant, and to do this effectively it is necessary to explore the Old Testament Passover passages of Exodus. After all, it is the Passover context that sheds light upon the meaning and significance of Jesus' words.

For the Jews the celebration of the Passover is an important liturgical event, because it defines them as a people set apart – chosen by God to be a great nation. The Passover celebrates the Israelite flight from the bondage of slavery in Egypt to the Promised Land. The celebration of the Passover supper is a Jewish feast whose origins can be found in the Old Testament. The book of Exodus begins by depicting the enslavement of the people of Israel under Pharaoh. In chapters seven through ten, Yahweh executes nine plagues on the Egyptian Dynasty in order to secure the release of His people. In chapter eleven there is a tenth plague that would result in the death of every first-born male child; this plague would prove to be the definitive action that would move Pharaoh to free the Israelite slaves. In chapter twelve, the Lord speaks to Moses and instructs him to institute a memorial sacrifice commemorating this liberation. Through participating in this sacrificial memorial, the Jewish people would be protected from the deadly tenth plague. The Lord commands the feast to be celebrated by all of Israel, and it would be their most solemn feast (Exodus 12:1-3). The Jews must take a lamb for each household, or share it with another household if the family was too small (Exodus 12:3-4). The lamb must be a year old male "without blemish" whose bones must not be broken (Exodus 12:5, 46). The lamb must be sacrificed and eaten (Exodus 12:6, 8-10). The lamb *must* be eaten and its blood spread on the doorposts of the dwelling, or the sacrifice would be incomplete (Exodus 12:7). When the Jews partake of this sacrifice as God has commanded, the angel of death would pass over them. Those who fail to comply with these stipulations would lose their first-born child (Exodus 12:12-13). This feast would be "a memorial day, and you shall keep it as a feast to the Lord; throughout your generations you shall observe it as an ordinance for ever" (Exodus 12:14). This feast would take a once and for all event and perpetuate it through time so as to enable future Jews to be present to it. This understanding of perpetuation is critical in understanding the Hebrew meaning of "memory", and also for comprehending the celebration of the Holy Eucharist. When the Jews celebrated the Passover, they dressed as if they were on a journey in flight and were somehow mystically present to the original experience their forefathers endured (Exodus 12:11).

Christ is inserted into the Passover context in many passages, even beyond those already cited regarding the Last Supper itself (see, in addition, Luke 2:41-46; John 11:55-56; 12:1-3; 18:28; 19:14, 42). As stated earlier, Catholic doctrine holds that the Mass is the celebration of the Last Supper, the New Testament Passover. Jesus Christ is the Passover Lamb of God, the perfect Lamb "without blemish" (no sin), the sacrificial lamb of Isaiah 53:7-12 whose bones would not be broken (see Psalm 34:20 and John 19:36). When the Jews sacrificed a lamb, they would place it over an altar and secure its arms in an outstretched fashion – much like Jesus on the cross. Then they would sacrifice it by cutting it open and letting the blood flow out until water began to flow from it, thereby verifying its death. Compare with John 19:32-34. To the Jewish audience hearing or reading this passage, the details narrated in it were not superficial, but rather facts calling to mind the sacrifice of the Passover lamb. Jesus is the Lamb whose blood is shed. Hence, the liberation offered by Jesus was foreshadowed in the Old Testament. Of course, we are not being liberated from the bondage of Pharaoh, but are instead being freed from the more oppressive bondage of sin, since Jesus is "the mediator of a new covenant" (Hebrews 9:15; 12:24).

Just as the Jews had to eat the Passover lamb in order for the sacrifice to be effective, so Christians have to eat the body and blood of Jesus Christ who is the Lamb of the New Covenant. This is why Jesus says: "Truly, truly, I say to you, unless you eat the flesh of the Son of man, and drink his blood, you have no life in you" (John 6:53). The follower of Christ keeps His words, for by doing so he will never see death (John 6:51, 54, 58). If a Jewish child in the Old Testament were to take umbrage with the eating of lamb, and his father responded by giving him some symbolic substitute for participating in the sacrifice, that child would not have lived to see the next morning. We do not symbolically partake of Christ's sacrifice, but really and truly partake of the Lamb of God who suffered and died for our sins.

For the Hebrews, to remember the Passover was *to be made present again* to it. If one were to ask practicing Jews what they are doing at the Passover meal, they would tell you that this is the night when God set them free – even though that event occurred thousands of years ago. The Mass is the *re-presentation* of the same sacrifice of Christ on the cross, just like the Passover meal in the Old Testament is a re-presentation of the same once for all liberation of the Jews from Egypt. With respect to Jesus' command "Do this in memory of me", the Catholic Church is utilizing this scriptural understanding of "memory". The sacrifice of Christ on the cross and its memorial supper is to be made present to the entire family of God throughout human history. Christ fulfills the Old Testament Passover when he suffers on the cross and institutes the Eucharist. The Eucharist is now the New Testament Passover.

Hence, the words of Scripture in Exodus 12:17 ("you shall observe this day, throughout your generations, as an ordinance for ever") are still carried out today. The reason why this is so is that the Old Testament Passover is but a foreshadowing of its perfection in the New Testament. Every time we celebrate the Eucharist at the Mass, the reality of Christ's death and the benefits it gives us are made present again, so that the very person of Jesus Christ is tangibly re-presented. One may wonder how this can be. It is important to remember that God is not bound by time, but rather time is a creation of God in which we exist. Any action of God is a "now" event. The sacrifice of Christ (the God-Man) is not merely some event that happened almost two thousand years ago, but one that is always present to God.

The sanctuary lamp, burning day and night beside the tabernacle in Catholic churches in honor of Christ's real presence there, finds its roots in the Jewish temple, where a sanctuary lamp was kept burning in honor of the presence of God in the Ark of the Covenant kept there (see Exodus 27:20-21; 40:4; Leviticus 24:1-4). It should come as no surprise that elements of the Catholic Christian faith have strikingly close counterparts in the Judaic religion. As Jesus said, "Think not that I have come to abolish the law and the prophets; I have come not to abolish them but to fulfill them" (Matthew 5:17).

Following the logic of the Jewish meaning of "memory" and God's duration as the eternal "now", the celebration of the Eucharist is the one and the same sacrifice of Christ on the cross. Every time we celebrate the Mass, we are made present to Christ's own sacrifice. Christ is not being re-sacrificed in the manner of His bloody death. Of course, He does not die again, as Paul says in Romans 6:9. Jesus' self-oblation on the cross is the one eternal sacrifice made present again for us to partake in every time we meet in memory of Him. His sacrificial death is past, present, and future. Jesus, the Lamb, was slain once and for all, but continues to be the slain Lamb in whom Christians can partake until the end of time. This understanding of Christ's sacrifice finds support in Revelation 13:8: "every one whose name has not been written before the foundation of the world in the book of life of the Lamb that was slain" and in Revelation 5:6: "between the throne and the four living creatures and among the elders, I saw a Lamb standing, as though it had been slain". These two quotations from the book of Revelation tell us that Jesus is presented before God as the slain Lamb, yet he is also the risen Lord. Why as a lamb? Because the "lamb" evokes a liturgical and sacrificial understanding in which the community still participates. The Mass is a real sacrifice, because in it the members of Christ's body united to Christ the head offer to God the Father the sacrifice of Jesus Christ, "the Lamb that was slain".

Thus, the Mass is the renewal and perpetuation of the new Passover sacrifice of Christ on the cross. It commemorates the sacrifice of Christ, mystically re-enacts it, and applies the graces of Christ's death to us. When the Jews celebrated Passover, it was a liturgical affair. Every year they did the same thing. They sang the same songs, read the same scriptures, and said many of the same prayers. The only things that changed were small outward externals and the people who were actually present. Just so, the Mass is a liturgical service of worship. Like the Jews of the Old Testament, Catholics maintain the fundamental structure of their religious celebrations. Again, it is another example that Catholicism is the fulfillment, not the abolishment, of Judaism.

While listening to a tape on the Eucharist from a noted Catholic scholar and convert, Scott Hahn, I learned that the unity of the Last Supper with the crucifixion and death of Christ is better understood when one considers the Passover celebration with its four cups of blessing. At the beginning of the Passover celebrations, which started about a week before the Passover meal, and at the beginning of the feast of unleavened bread, the Jews began with a ceremonial blessing of the first of the four cups. They partook of the second cup during the feast of unleavened bread. These first two cups are not mentioned in the New Testament. When the Apostles sat down with Jesus on the night He was betrayed in order to eat the Passover feast, they began with the drinking of the third cup. Those to whom the Gospels were written in the early days of the church were well familiar with the Passover celebration. The Last Supper begins with the third cup, "the cup of blessing" (see Mark 14:22-24). After the cup is passed around, Jesus adds: "Truly, I say to you, I shall not drink again of the fruit of the vine until that day when I drink it new in the kingdom of God" (Mark 14:25). The reason for this is that the fourth cup, not yet drunk from, is the cup of the consummation. The cup of the consummation is the definitive cup marking the completion of the Passover feast. Jesus prays in the garden of Gethsemane: "Abba, Father, all things are possible to thee; remove this cup from me; yet not what I will, but what thou wilt" (Mark 14:36). We read latter on that Jesus does indeed drink, but this time it is on the cross. The Gospel of John records Jesus as exclaiming "It is finished" just after drinking from the fruit of the vine given to Him by way of a spongy plant (John 19:30). Hence, the New Testament Passover feast includes the action of Christ on the cross.

Christ and the Last Supper Foreshadowed by Melchizedek

The foreshadowing of the sacrificial celebration in the Mass of the death of our Lord is found even before the calling of Moses and the giving of the Law on Mount Sinai. In fact, it takes place after Abram defeats Chedorlaomer and his allies (Genesis 14:17). As a token of his thankfulness to God for his victory, Abraham gave tithes to Melchizedek who was a priest of God. Melchizedek, prefiguring Christ, offered up to God gifts of bread and wine on behalf of Abram:

> And Melchizedek king of Salem brought out bread and wine; he was priest of God Most High. And he blessed him and said, "Blessed be Abram by God Most High, maker of heaven and earth; and blessed be God Most High, who has delivered your enemies into your hand!" And Abram gave him a tenth of everything. (Genesis 14:18-20)

Here we see a priest of God appearing, seemingly out of nowhere, to Abram with bread and wine. The context makes it obvious that it is a sacrificial offering, for this is what priests do. The Israelite religion had an abundance of sacrifices – some of them bloodless, whereas others (such as the Passover lamb) were bloody. In the New Testament, Christ shed His blood for the salvation of the world, while leaving behind a sacrificial memorial of Himself that is bloodless in terms of its perpetual re-enactment, in which His sacrifice is re-presented every time we "do this in memory" of Him. The scene above foreshadows both the one who is making the offering and the elements of the sacrifice itself.

The book of Hebrews refers to Christ as a priest after the *type* or prefiguring of Melchizedek:

> So also Christ did not exalt himself to be made a high priest, but was appointed by him who said to him, "Thou art my Son, today I have begotten thee"; as he says also in another place, "Thou art a priest forever after the order of Melchizedek." (Hebrews 5:5-6)

As Melchizedek is a *type* who foreshadows Christ, so must also the sacrifice he offers to God for Abram. When Scripture says Christ is a priest "after the order" of Melchizedek, the sacred text means "after the manner" of Melchizedek. The manner is the *kind* of sacrifice he offers. Melchizedek's appearance occurs only once in the Old Testament, and this appearance occasions the offering (sacrifice) to God of bread and wine. Since this is the case, the offering made by Melchizedek and its uncanny resemblance to the Last Supper should give us pause for reflection. That which foreshadows in the Old Testament is infinitely less perfect than its foreshadowed fulfillment in the New Testament. The fulfillment always supersedes that which preceded it by way of *type*. Hence, bread and wine here in the Old Testament must be more than just mere bread and wine in the New Testament – and they are. Christ took the bread and wine and said they were His body and blood – a perfect sacrifice.

The above passage from Hebrews explicitly states that Christ is the High Priest who makes the offering to God, and that offering would also be Himself. Christ is both priest and victim. The book of Hebrews goes on to describe Melchizedek in a way that shows Christ is the fulfillment of him:

> For this Melchizedek, king of Salem, priest of the Most High God, met Abraham returning from the slaughter of the kings and blessed him; and to him Abraham apportioned a tenth part of everything. He is first, by translation of his name, king of righteousness, and then he is also king of Salem, that is, king of peace. He is without father or mother or genealogy, and has neither beginning of days, nor end of life, but resembling the Son of God he continues a priest forever. (Hebrews 7:1-3)

Only God is without beginning of days or end of life. Therefore, this Melchizedek must be an appearance of Christ Himself, who is "the Alpha and the Omega, the first and the last, the beginning and the end" (Revelation 22:13). Christ is "a priest for ever after the order of Melchizedek" (Psalm 110:4).

Jesus fulfilled the typology of Melchizedek when He took bread and wine and changed them into His body and blood, while commanding the Apostles to "Do this in memory of me". The Protestant Reformers and their spiritual progeny think that Christ did away with the priesthood when He died, because the curtain in the temple of the holy of holies was torn asunder. However, the tearing of the curtain symbolizes the fulfillment of the Levitical priesthood, and the abolishment of it as an institution. The Old Testament priesthood is now changed (see Hebrews 7:12). The Levitical priesthood existed on account of the infidelity of the Jews in the desert, replacing the priesthood of sonship that God had intended. Christ, as Son of God, makes us sharers in His own sonship. We are now brought to God through Him as a family with a true and organic relationship to God and to each other as the Body of Christ (see 1 Corinthians 12:1-27). The body of Christ is structured in such a way as to keep the unity of faith, fellowship, and growth in holiness. The priesthood is a ministerial office of Christ serving this purpose. When Christ commanded the Apostles to "Do this in memory of me", He invited them to participate in His priesthood by offering up the Eucharist for the people of God. The Apostles were to make present again the one eternal sacrifice of Christ by following the command of Jesus to do this in memory of Him. This is the manner in which the Apostles themselves become the first priests (presbyters) of the New Testament with Christ as the High Priest. Through their (and their successors') faithful obedience to our Lord's command, Christians throughout the ages can partake of the holy sacrifice of Christ's body and blood

The Mass Prophesied by Malachi

Typological fulfillment is not the only way in which Christ's sacrifice and its memorial perpetuation is prefigured. The book of Malachi addresses the problem of priestly infidelity, because they offered up sacrifices not in accord with the Law of Moses. The prophet Malachi announces that the sacrifices being offered will never again be acceptable to God (see Malachi 1:10). Foretelling a time when the sacrifice offered to God would be perfect and without fault, the prophet then goes on to say (in Malachi 1:11) that one day there would be a sacrifice among the nations acceptable to Him:

> For from the rising of the sun to its setting my name is great among the nations, and in every place incense is offered to my name, and a pure offering; for my name is great among the nations, says the Lord of hosts.

Notice the plural nature of this sacrifice. It is offered in "every place". It would not only refer to the worldwide and eternal significance of Christ's death on the cross, but also the memorial of His death – the continual celebration of the Last Supper, in which we consume the Lamb of God. This prophecy could not refer to Protestant communion services, because Protestants do not recognize the memorial of Christ's death as a sacrifice. For many Protestants, the death of Christ and His resurrection remain trapped in history as past events upon which we look back and remember. Faith in Christ as the risen Lord is all we need during this recollection. For the Catholic, as already explained, the death and resurrection of Christ indeed happened in history, yet this event is also a transcendent reality accessed by faith-filled liturgical worship of Christ – an event in which we actively participate with our mind, body, and spirit. Across the world today the Mass is being offered, and the reality of Christ's sacrifice is being made present again to the faithful. This is the offering among the nations of which Malachi speaks. It is not a different offering, for we partake of the one Lamb of God.

Some think that Catholics believe Christ is crucified again at each Mass, as if the first time were not enough. This understanding, however, is erroneous. Catholics are emphatic that there is no longer a need for a new offering for sin because Christ, being the perfect victim, has obtained forgiveness for all sins (see Hebrews 10:11-18). The Mass is a participation in the once-and-for-all sacrifice of Christ on the cross. There need never again be a bloody sacrifice, because Christ has accomplished that for us, and "without the shedding of blood there is no forgiveness of sins" (Hebrews 9:22).

So, why then must we celebrate the Mass? Firstly, the Mass is the celebration of the Lord's Supper in which we "do this in remembrance" of Him. By going to Mass, we obey Christ's command, remembering what He has done for us. Secondly, going to Mass on Sundays in particular is the main way in which we keep holy the Lord's Day. Thirdly, the Catholic Church continues to offer the sacrifice of the Mass because our salvation is conditional, contingent upon our continued acceptance of Christ and willingness to live out what that means.

In the Old Testament, a repeated sacrifice was needed. Although Christ the eternal Lamb was sacrificed only once, He is continually offered to the Father. Some may wonder how this can be. In seeking to understand this, we must keep in mind that "Jesus Christ is the same yesterday and today and forever" (Hebrews 13:8). Again, the action of Christ on the cross is present to God now, and God makes the sacrifice on Calvary present to us at the Mass, just as the Passover supper for the Jews makes their liberation from Egypt thousands of years ago present to them. As St. Paul asserts in 1 Corinthians 11:26, "As often as you eat this bread and drink the cup, you proclaim the Lord's death until he comes."

The Bread-of-Life Discourse

In the sixth chapter of John's Gospel, we find Christ speaking words that occasion the first large defection from Him and His teachings. For the first time we see people turning away from Jesus because they found His words to be "hard sayings". Chapter six of John's Gospel begins with the report of the multiplication of the loaves and the fishes. The story was so famous in early Christianity that the Christians used the symbol of the fish to identify themselves. The entire sixth chapter of John's Gospel is linked together like a fine tapestry, and the interpretation of the later parts of the chapter is greatly influenced by its early verses (namely, John 6:4-13).

Just as was the case for the institutional narratives in the Synoptic Gospels, the context of this great and memorable event is the Passover. The Eucharistic significance of this passage can be determined not only by its Passover context, but also by the words "he had given thanks" in verse 11. After seeing the multiplication of the loaves and fishes, the people exclaim over what they perceive is the arrival of the long-anticipated great prophet (see John 6:14). Based on a Mosaic prophecy (see Deuteronomy 18:15, 17, 18-19), the Jewish people had been expecting a messianic prophet who would speak God's words truly. Verse 14 indicates that Jesus is this prophet who would come into the world. After having been miraculously fed, the people would begin to see this truth, but for many of them it would not be for very long. Our carnal nature is ready to believe and follow when the pleasures and needs of the flesh are satisfied. To live by faith, however, is to live by the Spirit and not by the flesh.

Christ is then presented as a new and greater Moses who will eventually give them bread from heaven. Let us consider John 6:16-35 in some detail. In verses 16 through 21 of this passage, John shows Christ to be greater than Moses who parted the Red Sea by God's power, for Christ does not merely part the sea but walks upon the water and miraculously brings His disciples' boat to the other side. Jesus is the new Moses who, like Moses, is able to provide for the Israelites starving in the desert and also able to bring His followers to safety through a miracle involving the sea.

Again, in verse twenty-three the sacred author situates the interaction between Jesus and the people in the place where He "had given thanks". The phrase "given thanks" has now made its appearance twice in the chapter; its purpose is to recall the memorial of the Last Supper that the community continuously performed on the Lord's Day. These two short stories are preparing the reader for the discourse on the Bread of Life and its proper theological understanding. Some try to say that the real miracle was not the suspension of the laws of nature, but rather that Jesus got people to dig into their pockets and share what they had with others. This is an attempt to de-emphasize the miraculous that is integral to understanding the whole of John 6. That interpretation is even more problematic when one reads the text more thoroughly and finds that the people do not really grasp the significance of His miracle. If the true miracle were their sharing what they had, then a lesson would clearly have been learned, but Jesus' reprimand in John 6:26-28 states otherwise. The miracle was to enable people to see that the Kingdom of God was at hand and that faith in Christ would be the criterion for this Kingdom. Do we have enough faith in Jesus to accept *all* His teachings including, and especially, those teachings that are hard to hear?

It is in verse 22 that the Bread-of-Life discourse actually begins. The crowds follow Jesus, while He scolds them for their lack of faith and their failure to understand the meaning of the sign that He has just given them. He tells them in verse 27, "Do not labor for the food which perishes, but for the food which endures to eternal life, which the Son of man will give to you; for on him has God the Father set his seal." In verse 28, the crowds want to know what work of God they must do. Christ responds in verse 29 by saying that their godly work should consist in believing in the One whom God sent them. Christ constantly emphasizes the necessity of faith in Him. But, as if the sign of the loaves and fishes were not enough, the people demand again in verse 30 that He perform some work or another sign that would convince them to believe in Him. Jesus then reminds them in verse 32 that it was not Moses who worked such miracles in the desert, but God Himself. The bread provided by God through the instrumentality of Moses was but a foreshadowing of the Bread of Life: the Eucharist. Christ would provide the Eucharist to the new people of God through the instrumentality of His Apostles. Jesus goes on to tell them in verses 33-35 that the bread of God is that which comes down from heaven and gives life, and that it is He who is this bread.

Let us next consider John 6:36-51. First, before getting to the pinnacle of the discussion, Jesus warns the Jews about their lack of faith in Him. He is from God, here to do His will; those who believe in and act on what He teaches will have life eternal. Lacking understanding, the Jews murmur because He says He is the Bread of Life come down from heaven (verses 41-42). Jesus then explains that all those who listen to the Father will listen to Him and have everlasting life (verses 45-47). Jesus reiterates more forcefully each time that He is the bread of life and that the nature of this bread is His flesh (verses 48-51). At this point, the Jews incredulously ask how it is possible for a man to give his flesh as food to eat (verse 52). Up to this point, we notice Jesus repeating the need for faith in Him and believing the things He will teach. These things are from God. It is clear Jesus is about to give a teaching to follow that will require one to put absolute faith in Him. Only those open to the will of the Father can be drawn by Him and will accept the teaching that Christ is about to give.

The following verses are the most hotly contested between Catholics and some Protestants. How are we to interpret Jesus' words? Are they symbolic or literal? It is often said that Protestants generally take the plain meaning of the words of Jesus to a greater extent than Catholics do, that their interpretations are more literal; however, Chapter six of John's Gospel is a case where this assertion is certainly not true:

> So Jesus said to them, "Truly, truly, I say to you, unless you eat the flesh of the Son of man and drink his blood, you have no life in you; he who eats my flesh and drinks my blood has eternal life, and I will raise him up at the last day. For my flesh is food indeed, and my blood is drink indeed. He who eats my flesh and drinks my blood abides in me, and I in him. As the living Father sent me, and I live because of the Father, so he who eats me will live because of me. This is the bread which came down from heaven, not such as the fathers ate and died; he who eats this bread will live for ever." (John 6:53-58)

It is manifestly clear to Catholics that Jesus is teaching that the nature of this bread from heaven really *is* His own flesh. Following the rabbinic form of argumentation in which a rabbi would repeat himself three times in order to drive home the literal point he is making, Jesus states three times the necessity of eating His flesh and drinking His blood. If His words were merely symbolic, why would He have used this method of argumentation? Besides this, to hold to a symbolic interpretation would necessitate believing that Jesus deliberately misled his hearers so they could not properly understand his words.

Furthermore, the concept of symbolically eating the flesh and drinking the blood of someone, in the Hebrew mind, would mean to assault or even destroy an individual (see Psalm 14:1-4; 53:1-4; Isaiah 9:18-20; 49:26; Micah 3:1-3; 2 Samuel 23:15-17; and Revelation 17:6, 15-16). Therefore, if Jesus were speaking merely symbolically about eating His flesh and drinking His blood, then what He would mean is this: "Whoever persecutes and assaults me will have eternal life". Of course, this absurdity would make nonsense of the passage.

Levitical prohibitions against eating and drinking blood are frequently mentioned to support a symbolic interpretation of this passage. However, the flesh and blood Jesus is talking about here is not that of animals, but of His entire incarnate self. It is the body and blood of the resurrected Lord, not that of some profane beast.

Moreover, if Jesus meant to speak only symbolically, it would seem that He would correct the misunderstanding, as He did in other places in the New Testament. Take, as an example, John 4:31-34 – verses that follow His dialogue with the Samaritan woman at Jacob's well. In this passage, the disciples fail to understand Jesus' usage of the word "food". Jesus clears up the misconception by explaining that the food about which He speaks is doing the will of the Father. Thus, when the disciples apparently lack a proper appreciation of the meaning of Jesus' words, He explains His words so that they may understand Him correctly.

Another passage in which Jesus corrects His followers when they misunderstand Him is Mark 8:14-21. Here the followers of Jesus fail to grasp His usage of a word. This time it is the word "leaven". They somehow think Jesus is referring literally to the agent responsible for fermenting dough and making bread rise, but Jesus corrects this wrong interpretation. He is, of course, referring to the deceptive and corrupting nature of the Pharisees' influence.

If one were to browse the New Testament, one would see a number of instances where Jesus corrects a false understanding of His teaching, but no such clarification is offered in the Bread of Life discourse. No rebuke, no explanation to clear the air; instead, there is only a reiteration of His words. The Jews interpret Him correctly, and Jesus makes no effort to water His saying down. So that no one may misunderstand, He explicitly says in verse 55: "My flesh is food indeed, and my blood is drink indeed." Jesus also attaches eternal life to the eating of His flesh and drinking of His blood. This certainly is not within the sphere of symbolism.

The discourse will take a sudden shift in verse 59, returning to the issue of faith that had preceded the discourse. Let us finish by examining John 6:59-71. Verse 59 is a transitional sentence preparing us for the discussion of faith, for in verse 60 the disciples balk with the retort that "this is a hard saying, who can listen to it?". It would seem that if they have misunderstood Jesus, He would correct them at this juncture; yet He does not, as noted above. He forthrightly asks in verse 61, "Do you take offense at this?". He then reminds them in verse 65 of what He said before in verse 44: that only those who are guided aright by the Father will come to Him.

Jesus then poses an interesting question in verse 62: "Then what if you were to see the Son of man ascending where he was before?". The question is asked as if to mean: "If you find this hard to believe, how will you be able to believe when you see me in my essence?" – or perhaps: "If you find it hard to believe that I can perform this miracle, would you believe in my power if you were to see me in my divine glory?" Earlier in John's Gospel (see John 1:49-51), the mention of the ascension is brought in within the context of Nathanael's faith. Nathanael came to believe in Christ merely because our Lord had told him that He knew who he was without having first met him. The revelation of this simple miraculous knowledge possessed by Christ brought about Nathanael's response of faith. Here in John 6, Christ gives a difficult teaching, but that teaching will not be as hard a saying as His true identity, since God taking on human flesh would be a scandal to any monotheistic Jew.

Jesus is the bread from heaven. The Eucharist looks like bread and wine, tastes like bread and wine, but truly is His body and blood. Assent to this teaching requires faith, whereas a figurative memorial supper makes no such demand on the Christian. By mentioning the ascension,

Jesus confirms the truth of what He has just said, while correcting the misunderstanding of eating His flesh and drinking His blood in a cannibalistic manner. He would ascend into heaven taking His entire body with Him – not leaving it to be chopped-up, mangled, and then consumed. Some have charged that the Catholic doctrine on the Eucharist amounts to cannibalism. But it does not. In order for cannibalism to be an accurate accusation, it would be necessary for the appearances of bread and wine to cease, and the appearances of flesh and blood to emerge. The charge of cannibalism is interesting, because it bears some historical evidence supporting the Catholic belief. One of the popular rumors about Christians was that they were cannibals. The Roman populace, ignorant of Christian beliefs and practices, believed Christians ate their children. This accusation makes sense solely in light of a Roman misunderstanding. We do not eat our children, but we *do* eat the Son of God in the Eucharist – under the appearances of bread and wine.

As in the institution narratives discussed previously, the belief versus disbelief motif is again personified in the characters of Peter and Judas. It is Peter (in verse 69) who expresses trust in the Lord as the divine bearer of the message of eternal life. He is presented as the disciple of faith, while Judas Iscariot is the "devil" and "betrayer". The role of the two apostles in both John 6 and the synoptic Last Supper accounts could not be merely coincidental. The same thematic element of contrasting Peter to Judas is operating here, giving away the obvious juxtaposition of John 6 to those accounts in the Synoptic Gospels.

In verses 63-64 Jesus says: "It is the spirit that gives life, the flesh is of no avail; the words that I have spoken to you are spirit and life. But there are some of you that do not believe." These words are often interpreted by some to mean that all the aforesaid is couched in symbolic terms. In this case, the term "spirit" would mean "symbolic"; that is, Jesus' words are symbolic and not literal. There are problems, however, with this interpretation. The word "spirit" is never used in any way to mean or imply the connotation of the word "symbolic". Being part of the passage on faith, "the flesh" refers to the carnal man and "the spirit" refers to the man guided aright by faith. Jesus never says, "*my* flesh is of no avail", but rather "*the* flesh (ἡ σαρξ) is of no avail". The "flesh" referred to here is not His own as He discussed earlier; instead, "the flesh" refers to those not guided by the Spirit (το πνεῦμά). The "flesh" (that is, man's natural and carnal thinking that refuses to be subject to the Holy Spirit) profits nothing. Immediately afterwards, His words on "the flesh" and "the spirit" are followed by His statement in verse 65: "This is why I told you that no one can come to me unless it is granted him by the Father." The context makes it obvious that Christ is talking about faith, and it is this context that governs the interpretation of the very words "the flesh" and "the spirit".

This interpretation is consistent with John's usage of these terms in other places. For example, consider John 3:2-8, which features a nocturnal meeting between Jesus and Nicodemus, an important man of the Sanhedrin who has a difficult time understanding the truth about spiritual rebirth by water and the Spirit. Christ speaks to him about the new birth that takes place within those who put their faith in Him. In this passage, the usage of the words "the flesh" (*sarx*) and "the spirit" (*pneuma*) is quite obvious. There are those whose comprehension is that of the carnal man without faith; on the other hand, there are those whose understanding proceeds from faith in Christ. Those born of the Holy Spirit are born anew in a mysterious manner.

This contrast is also found in St. Paul's writings, which contain a few passages where "the spirit" is contrasted with "the flesh", in which "the spirit" is represented as pertaining to the man who lives by faith (or according to the truth) and "the flesh" refers to what is still mired in earthly imperfections. By saying that the words He has spoken are "spirit and life", Christ is stating that they are true, come from God, and bring about supernatural life. Note, in addition, the contrast in 1 Corinthians 2:14 – 3:3 between the spiritual and the unspiritual (or fleshly) man regarding their respective abilities to judge wisely according to the mind of Christ. Again, in Romans 8:2-14, Paul contrasts worldly people enslaved by fleshly desires with the righteous who live in the Spirit. For similar passages, see 1 Corinthians 3:1, Galatians 3:3, Galatians 4:29, and Galatians 5:16-17, as well as 1 John 5:7.

Some will object that Christ meant He was only spiritually present in the bread and wine. This reduces Christ's words to metaphor. If He meant that He would be only spiritually present, then why all the discussion about His flesh? Besides, to separate the human nature of Christ, that is, His fleshly existence, from His divine nature would be to contradict the logic of the Incarnation. The Word became flesh (John 1:14), and to follow His teaching through faith in Him requires partaking of Him completely – body, blood, soul, and divinity – in the Eucharist, as He insists in John 6. To separate human spiritual nature from human bodily nature amounts to dualism. In Jesus, the physical is forever united with the spiritual. When we worship Jesus, we worship Him both as God and man. Through misunderstanding the Eucharist in this way, one misunderstands the radical nature of the Incarnation.

Someone may respond with the objection: "Since Jesus lives in *me* spiritually, why does He not also abide in the Eucharist in a purely spiritual manner?" The reason is that Jesus lives in us through our being born anew by the supernatural action of the Holy Spirit. The Eucharist is identified substantially with Christ the Lord Himself – *we* are not!

Catholics are accused of committing idolatry, allegedly because we "worship bread and wine". This is utterly untrue. Although the Holy Spirit did not become flesh, the Son did. Since the fullness of the divinity is present in all three Persons of the Blessed Trinity, Catholics worship Jesus, who is God and whom we discern by grace through faith to be entirely present in the Eucharist, as Christ promised in John 6. Yes, the words of our Lord are shocking, but they are intended to be so because what Jesus seeks is faith. It is fortunate for us that our Savior's flesh does indeed profit for our salvation; and, when we attend the Holy Sacrifice of the Mass, through Christ we *do* "worship the Father in spirit and truth" (John 4:23).

St. Paul on the Eucharist

In 1 Corinthians 11:23-30, St. Paul writes the Corinthian church regarding his own historical revelation about the Eucharist and its proper celebration. Evidently, just prior to the celebration of the Eucharist there was a meal during which those with wealth were able to eat while the poor went hungry. In this passage, Paul condemns the conduct as damnable precisely because this lack of love for others less fortunate was taking place just as the Christian community was about to receive the sacred body and blood of Christ. This was quite an ironic sin, given the fact that the Eucharist is Christ's sacrificial giving of Himself. Those who eat the bread or drink the cup of the Lord in an unworthy manner will be guilty of profaning the body and blood of the Lord. Why? Because what they are eating and drinking is not ordinary bread and wine, but truly Christ's body and blood. How else would such a terrible sin be committed if the bread and wine were not His body and blood? If the bread and wine are only symbolic representations of Christ's body and blood, then why is it such an offense? Not only this, but Paul also asserts that some have become weak and ill and even died because of their sin. If the bread and wine were not Christ's body and blood, why would such a punishment come upon them? What Paul says makes sense only if he believed that what seem to be bread and wine are really the body and blood of Christ.

Moreover, to hold to a symbolic interpretation does not square with Paul's teaching on food in 1 Corinthians 8:1-8. In Paul's day, the food bought and sold in the marketplace had been offered to some god prior to its sale. The eating of this meat presented a scandal to some of the Gentile Christian converts who left behind a life of idolatry in which they would go to the marketplace and buy such foods as a part of their religious practices. Paul warns the Christian community of the need to respect the consciences of such persons, so as to avoid scandal and consequent adverse effects on the faith of those who are weak. Though there is no sin in eating the meat *per se*, it can become sinful if it scandalizes a brother Christian. Hence, one ought to observe the law of charity dictating not to eat the meat for the sake of those whose consciences are weak. Meat sacrificed to idols means nothing, since the idols, which represent false gods, do not exist; but wounding the conscience of another believer is an objectively serious matter. Paul then adds that "food will not commend us to God" (verse 8), yet he says in 1 Corinthians 11:27-30 that those who eat bread and wine unworthily at the Eucharistic celebration will be guilty of the body and blood of the Lord, eating and drinking judgment upon themselves. What kind of God would make it a damnable sin to fail to discern a symbol? Again, this only makes sense if the Eucharist is not ordinary food and drink, but is indeed the body and blood of Christ.

The issue of foods sacrificed to idols and whether or not one should eat them continued as a problem in the Corinthian church for some time. In 1 Corinthians 10:14-21, however, Paul makes a distinction between eating foods bought in the marketplace that may have been sacrificed to idols and actively and knowingly participating in sacrificial feasts of the pagan religions. This passage is interesting for a number of reasons.

First, Paul specifically says that the bread and the cup constitute an actual sharing in Christ's body and blood. The fact that he continues to refer to the Eucharist as "bread" does not mean it is *only* bread. Rather, the usage here fits with the same terminology that Christ employed in John 6:35, 48 and that Catholics sometimes employ – namely, the Eucharist is the "Bread of Life". The "breaking of the bread" evokes the memory of the Last Supper and brings about the reality of Christ's real presence under those simple appearances of bread and wine (see Luke 24:35; Acts 2:42, 46).

Secondly, the passage has a sacrificial character to it. When Paul says that Christians may not partake of the "table of the Lord and the table of demons", he is saying Christians may not partake of two contradictory sacrifices. Your allegiance is either to God in Christ or to the evil one, so you may partake of one or the other only. The word "table" functions in the same way as the word "altar". For the Hebrew, "altar" is a word that designates a place of sacrifice, and for the Gentile, it also designates a place for animal sacrifices. For both Jew and Gentile, it is a site upon which something is offered up to God. For the Christian community, Jesus is the sacrifice procuring our salvation. A Christian need not offer up animal sacrifices in order to gain God's favor, because this has already been accomplished by Christ on the cross. Yet, in this passage we read Paul referring to our participation in a "table of the Lord" or "altar of the Lord". Hence, the celebration of the Last Supper (the Mass) is a participation in Christ's own sacrifice. The explicit use of the word "altar" in verse 18, as opposed to the use of the word "table" in verse 21, can be explained by the fact that the author is making a distinction between the sacrifices of Israel and that of the Christian church. If some people were to quarrel with interpreting the word "table" to mean "altar" because both words occur in the text, yet are employed at different times, they need to recognize that Christians believed they were partaking of an altar sacrifice themselves. In fact, Hebrews 13:10 reads: "We have an altar from which those who serve the tent have no right to eat." Furthermore, extra-biblical evidence for Christians having altars can be found in the catacombs in which pictures and inscriptions have been preserved.

The book of Hebrews was written to Jewish Christians who were in danger of falling back into Judaism. It reminds them of Christ's unique sacrifice and its implications for those who think they may continue to participate in the Old Testament sacrifices (see, for example, Hebrews 8:6-7, 13; 12:24). The unconverted Jews may not partake of the Christian altar. If Christians eat from an altar, then they must be eating a sacrifice. Indeed, Christians *are* eating of a sacrifice – the sacrifice of Christ. The context of this passage is how Christians need to be willing to suffer with and for Christ and, in so doing, "continually offer up a sacrifice of praise to God" (Hebrews 13:15). What better sacrifice of praise can be offered to God than the one Jesus left us in order to give thanks to God: namely, the Holy Eucharist in the Sacrifice of the Mass?

CHAPTER SEVEN
The Ordained Priesthood

This chapter is devoted to resolving three controversies about the priesthood. First, since many people question whether Christ really did establish a hierarchical priesthood (or even deny that He did), this contentious issue is addressed. Second, since many think that the restriction of Holy Orders to men is a mere human precept subject to change by the Church, the second section of the chapter attempts to prove that Christ intended an exclusively male priesthood. Third, since there has been some agitation for permitting a married clergy in the Latin rite of the Church, the third section defends the discipline of priestly celibacy.

(1) The Ordained Priesthood Was Instituted by Christ

Introduction

St. Luke relates the following celebrated scene at the Last Supper of our Lord Jesus Christ on Holy Thursday (Luke 22:19, boldface emphasis added):

> And he took bread, and when he had given thanks he broke it and gave it to them [the Apostles], saying, "This is my body which is given for you. **Do this in remembrance of me.**"

St. Paul (in 1 Corinthians 11:23-26) recounts the same event based on his *own* revelation (see Galatians 1:12), reporting the Lord's command "Do this in remembrance of me" *twice* – the first time in connection with the change of the bread into Christ's body and the second time in connection with the change of the wine in the chalice into Christ's blood, thereby inaugurating the New Covenant.

The Catholic Church holds that, by force of the Lord's command reported in these two narratives, Jesus conferred the "new covenant" ministerial priesthood on His twelve Apostles, ordaining them to offer the Holy Sacrifice of the Mass in the power of His Name.

Yet, some have denied that Christ instituted a hierarchical priesthood ordered to perpetuating the one sacrifice of Himself on the cross on Good Friday in redemptive atonement for our sins. They interpret the memorial celebration of the Last Supper service in a minimalist sense – as though it were merely an external observance symbolically re-enacting a past event. To vindicate their position, they quote, for example, Hebrews 7:26-27. For those who disagree with Catholic teaching in this area, the words "once for all" in this passage are decisive (see also Hebrews 9:11-12, 24-26; 10:10; 1 Peter 3:18). Nevertheless, their interpretation that these words conclusively rule out a special Sacrament of Holy Orders is fraught with problems. We intend to demonstrate that the Bible supports the Catholic doctrine asserting the divine origin of the New Testament priestly office exercised in the Catholic Church (along with the Orthodox branch of Christianity). In other words, the Catholic priesthood was not invented as some sort of corrupt innovation in the early Middle Ages, but rather stems from the Founder of the Church Himself.

Old Testament Prophecies

It is proverbial that the New Testament is the Old Testament revealed, and the Old Testament is the New Testament concealed. Hence, Old Testament prophecy is a relevant point of departure for our defense of the Catholic position on the priesthood. In particular, the Last Supper on Holy Thursday was a Jewish Passover meal. So, like the Passover meal, it needed an unblemished male lamb (see Exodus 12:5) to deliver the people of God from certain death – signifying the everlasting death of humanity in punishment for sin, had Jesus not come to save us (see also Leviticus 4:22-26). He is the promised Isaac, about whom Abraham spoke prophetically that God would "provide himself the lamb for a burnt offering" (Genesis 22:8). The Lord Jesus was the officiating priest holding up His own body at the Last Supper, telling us that it is offered up for us (Matthew 26:28). On Good Friday, He was the altar lifting Himself up (see John 10:17-18; 12:32), sacrificing Himself on a pile of wood (see Genesis 22:6, 7, 9); indeed, He *is* Salvation itself immolated for us (see Matthew 1:21). Thus, the Passover Supper had intrinsic sacrificial undertones, and was not simply a commemorative meal. But how do these facts relate to a New Covenant priesthood consisting of mere men?

A key text is Isaiah 66:18-24, where the prophet foretells the gathering of the nations into God's everlasting reign. Verse 19 promises that He "will send survivors to the nations", who "shall declare my [the Lord's] glory among the nations". Since God "will set a sign among them", these messengers who proclaim God's "fame and glory" are clearly Christian missionaries who carry the sign of Christ's cross. In verse 20 those who enter the kingdom are depicted as arriving via multifarious means at the destination of God's "holy mountain Jerusalem" – i.e., the New Israel inaugurated by Christ's Passion, Resurrection, and Ascension. A Eucharistic dimension is implied, because they are compared to the old Israelites who "bring their cereal offering in a clean vessel to the house of the Lord". Indeed, as was explained in Chapter 2, the "house of the Lord" is the Catholic Church founded by Christ on the Rock of St. Peter, and the "cereal offering in a clean vessel" suggests the Eucharistic body of Christ confected from wheat bread, since He is the "Bread of Life" (see John 6:35, 48, 51, 58; 12:24) and the "lamb without blemish or spot" (1 Peter 1:19; see also Malachi 1:11 below).

But, standing out against this background, the most crucial verse is Isaiah 66:21: "And some of them also I will take for priests and for Levites, says the Lord." Now this prophecy cannot refer to the common "royal priesthood" of Christians, mentioned in 1 Peter 2:5, 9 and Revelation 1:6; 5:10. For in these verses St. Peter and St. John include *all* Christ's faithful members, yet Isaiah 66:21 predicts that God will appoint as "priests" only *some* of those who enter His Church. Thus, a distinct ministry is demarcated here – one that shares in the eternal high priesthood of Christ elaborated in Hebrews.

What would be the role of these specially distinguished priests? To answer this question, we must turn to Malachi 1:11: "For from the rising of the sun to its setting my name is great among the nations, and in every place incense is offered to my name, and a pure offering; for my name is great among the nations, says the Lord of hosts." Now the majority of Christians never engage (especially not on a daily basis) in conducting a ritual sacrifice to the praise and glory of God's name. Hence, in order for this prophecy about "the times of the Gentiles" (Luke 21:24) to be fulfilled, God deemed it suitable for His plans to constitute a class within His Church whose primary duty would be to continually ("from the rising of the sun to its setting") and universally ("in every place") offer this sweet oblation to Him – a fragrant sacrifice that can mean only His Divine Son. Consequently, throughout the era of the New Covenant there would exist a rank of ordained priests who would, acting subordinately in the person of Christ ("the one mediator between God and men", according to 1 Timothy 2:5), offer around the world's time zones the pleasing daily sacrifice of Jesus to the Father, thereby prolonging through time the one sacrifice of Mount Calvary.

For further corroboration let us investigate Psalm 132, which contains some crucial prophecies about the New Covenant. The psalmist (in verses 11-13, 18) mystically refers to Jesus, the son of David (Matthew 1:1; 15:22; 20:30-31; 21:9, 15; 22:42; Mark 10:47-48), as the one whom the Lord swore He would crown and set on the Davidic throne forever (see Luke 1:31-33; Revelation 14:14). This Davidic king would be "anointed" as a "lamp" (verse 17; see also Isaiah 42:6-7; 49:5-6), and hence *must* be Christ (see John 1:4-5, 9; 3:19; 8:12; 9:5; 12:46; Revelation 21:23). Thus, speaking through the psalmist in verses 15-16, God is promising what He will do for His foreshadowed Church under Christ: "I will abundantly bless her provisions; I will satisfy her poor with bread. Her priests I will clothe with salvation, and her saints will shout for joy." (See also Psalm 132:9 with 2 Chronicles 6:41.) These are profound christological and sacramental verses. Let us examine them from both angles.

First, the fact that the "priests" are "clothed with salvation" implies that they are assimilated to Jesus, because His name transliterated from the Hebrew is *"Yeshua"*, which means "savior" (Matthew 1:21). Indeed, in Luke 4:17-21, Jesus proclaims in the synagogue that *He* is the fulfillment of Isaiah 61:1-3. But the Incarnate Word of God, speaking through the prophet in Isaiah 61:10, says: "I will greatly rejoice in the Lord, my soul shall exult in my God; for he has clothed me with the garments of salvation." Therefore, the New Covenant "priests", who are likewise "clothed with salvation" in Psalm 132:16, are acting in the person of Christ. Furthermore, Isaiah 61:6 continues: "You shall be called the priests of the Lord, men shall speak of you as the ministers of our God" – as though the Second Person of the Blessed Trinity were already (through this prophetic mode) mystically ordaining His Apostles and their successors as priests.

Incidentally, the "garments of salvation" are literally mandated in the divine worship rites of the Old Covenant, where ceremonial details abound. God is very demanding about the precise ways in which He is to be worshipped, not leaving such momentous matters to the subjective whims of human beings, lest we veer off into a casual irreverence or even idolatry. For instance, in Exodus 31:10 the Lord reminds Moses of His command about "the holy garments for Aaron the priest and the garments of his sons, for their service as priests" (see the earlier passage Exodus 29:5-9 and the later passage Exodus 40:13-14). Moses faithfully transmits this divine precept in Exodus 35:19, which is implemented in Exodus 39:41. We can infer that this special vesture foreshadows the vestments to be worn by New Testament priests – as is indeed verified during the Mass offered by Catholic (and Orthodox) priests. The ritual washing with water enjoined in Exodus 30:17-21, when "Aaron and his sons ... come near the altar to minister, to burn an offering by fire to the Lord" (verse 20), likewise prefigures the purification of the priest's hands during the Offertory prior to the Consecration of the Mass.

Secondly, the "bread" in Psalm 132:15 signifies the Eucharistic body of Christ, which is completely satisfying (see Isaiah 55:2; Matthew 5:6; John 6:32-35, 48-51, 58). But the proximate source of joy for the Church's members (the "saints") is the fact that they have "priests" in their midst who are privileged to carry in their very persons the means of "salvation": i.e., these ministers have the power to confect the sacraments, especially Baptism (using the "abundant provision" of water) and the Holy Eucharist (using bread composed of widely available wheat). In short, as "other Christs" the priests bring the entire Jesus, who covers them with Himself, to the Lord's favored flock.

Therefore, the re-enactment of the Holy Thursday meal at the Mass is not simply a commemoration in a minimal sense; in addition to being a memorial celebration, the Mass perpetuates the grace of Christ's unique sacrifice on the cross for the members of the Church down through the centuries. Hence, those who re-present this event are not common laity, nor are they presiding "ministers" whose sole function is to preach the gospel and lead the congregation in prayer. As the verses in Joel 1:19, 13; 2:17 indicate, the "ministers of the Lord" are "priests" – "ministers of the altar".

In fact, there is a scriptural connection between "remembrance" (*anamnesis* in Greek) and sacrificial offerings by specially ordained priests. For example, Hebrews 10:3 associates "sacrifices" with "reminder of sin" (see also Romans 15:15-16). Our Lord may have intended His profoundly suggestive "remembrance" terminology to hark back to Numbers 10:10, where God commanded Moses that "at your appointed feasts ... you shall blow the trumpets over your burnt offerings and over the sacrifices of your peace offerings; they shall serve you for remembrance before your God." Now this officiating was to be carried out by the priests, as indicated in Numbers 10:8, where God told Moses that "the sons of Aaron, the priests, shall blow the trumpets." These verses from Numbers 10 foreshadow the Last Supper and subsequent re-enactments of "the breaking of bread and the prayers" (Acts 2:42, 46). Indeed, the trumpet sound symbolizes the voice of Christ, as affirmed by St. John in Revelation 1:10-18, which is a passage reminiscent of the "son of man" scenes in Daniel 7:13-14; 10:5-6 and Ezekiel 1:24-27. (Along with Revelation 1:10, see Revelation 4:1 and 1 Corinthians 15:52.) Furthermore, the "burnt offerings" and the "sacrifices of peace offerings" symbolize Jesus, who is the atoning victim slain for our redemption (see 1 Corinthians 5:7; 1 Peter 1:18-19; Revelation 5:6, 12; 7:10, 13-14) and who is "our peace" (Ephesians 2:14). It follows that the priests who sounded the trumpet over the sacrificial oblations in the Old Testament are *types* of the New Testament priests who speak the words of the Eucharistic institution narrative ("this is my body, this is my blood") vicariously in the voice of Jesus, the high priest who offered Himself as a victim in expiation for our sins (see Hebrews 2:17; 1 John 2:2; 4:10).

Consequently, according to these Old Testament typological prefigurements, the correct way to interpret the phrase "once for all" (in Hebrews 7:27; 9:26) is not to deny the efficacy of the Mass, condemning it as an early medieval accretion that borders on magical superstition (or "hocus pocus"). On the contrary. The subordinate priests who pronounce the supernaturally powerful words of the eternal high priest apply (in a non-bloody manner) His "once for all" bloody redemptive sacrifice for the sanctifying (and ultimately salvific) benefit of the Church's members – all of whom must personally appropriate Christ's unique oblation in their concrete circumstances (see Colossians 1:24). To think otherwise is to downplay (or undermine) the historical prolongation of the Incarnation, suspending it in an abstract vacuum. It will not do merely to accept Christ internally as one's personal Lord and Savior without worshipping Him in the external communal manner He has ordained through the sacramental mediation of His hierarchical ministers, who serve as channels for the dispensation of grace. Of course, God *could* have chosen to dispense with priests and opted to dispense His grace directly, but evidently the Creator of human nature deemed it more fitting for us bodily creatures to receive His grace through physical conduits. Moreover, this divine economy is more conducive to humility for us who tend to be prone to prideful self-sufficiency.

New Testament Fulfillments

Let us begin with Matthew 16:13-19. In making Simon Bar-Jona the head of His Church, the Lord Jesus bestowed on him the new name "Cephas" (see John 1:42), which (not coincidentally) was essentially the name of the high-priest (i.e., Caiaphas) for that year (see John 18:13). Therefore, Peter's status as visible head of the Church entailed both the termination of the Old Covenant priesthood and his concurrent possession of the priesthood of the New Covenant inaugurated in Christ's blood on Holy Thursday and Good Friday.

But what specifically did Peter's priesthood involve? And how about the other Apostles? Even more pointedly, how about the welter of bishops, priests, deacons, elders, and ministers mentioned in the New Testament? There seems to be an interweaving set of terms employed to translate the Greek *episkopos, iereus* (or *hieros*), *diakonos, presbyteros, leitourgos.* It may be difficult to sort these out and discern their exact significance, but we shall try — first by making a glossary of these terms according to their contextual translations. This catalogue, though not necessarily exhaustive, will be representative within its range of ideas.

#1. *episkopos* is rendered as "bishop" (Philippians 1:1; 1 Timothy 3:1, 2; Titus 1:7), as "overseer" (Acts 20:28), and as "guardian" (1 Peter 2:25); hence, the *Revised Standard Version* translation of *episkopei* (in Acts 1:20) as "office" is too generic, weak, and hence inadequate: it should be rendered as "bishopric" (*King James Version, 1611*) or "position of overseer" (*New Revised Standard Version*).

#2. *iereus* is always translated as "priest" in the New Testament — whether referring to the Jewish priests (in the four Gospels and Acts of the Apostles), pagan priests (Acts 14:13), the "priestly service" of St. Paul (Romans 15:16), the priesthood of Jesus (Hebrews 2:17; 3:1; 4:14-15; 5:5; 7:3, 21, 24, 26; 8:1, 3; 10:21), or the priestly character of Christians in general (1 Peter 2:5, 9; Revelation 1:6; 5:10; 20:6). The references in Hebrews 5:6, 10; 6:20; 7:11, 15, 17 to Christ's priesthood according to "the order of Melchizedek" are, of course, based on Psalm 110:4, which employs precisely this terminology to prophesy about Christ. But the Hebrew word for "priest" used in Psalm 110:4 is exactly the same as the word that occurs numerous times in the Old Testament (namely, וְכֹהֵן) – virtually all of these instances in contexts alluding to priests who offer sacrifices at altars (note particularly Genesis 14:18 containing the original reference to "Melchizedek king of Salem" who was "priest of God Most High").

#3. *diakonos* is rendered as "deacon" (Philippians 1:1; 1 Timothy 3:8, 12), as "servant", sometimes in explicit or implicit reference to the Apostles and to Christ Himself (Matthew 23:11; Mark 9:35; 10:43; John 2:5, 9; 12:26; Romans 13:4; 15:8; 1 Corinthians 3:5; 2 Corinthians 6:4; 11:23), and as "minister", chiefly with reference to the Apostles (especially St. Paul) and those whom they appointed (Acts 1:17, 25; 6:4; 20:24; 21:19; Romans 11:13; 2 Corinthians 3:6; 4:1; 5:18; 6:3; Ephesians 3:7; 4:12; 6:21; Colossians 1:7, 23, 25; 4:7, 17; 1 Timothy 4:6; 2 Timothy 4:5). This Greek term can evidently have both generic and specific connotations – generic when translated as "minister" or "servant", but specific when translated as what we know today as a "deacon".

#4. *presbyteros* is translated by the *RSV* as "elder" throughout the New Testament – whether referring to the Jewish "elders" (in the Synoptic Gospels and Acts of the Apostles), to the "elders" appointed by the Apostles among the early Christians (Acts 11:30; 14:23; 15:2, 4, 6, 22, 23; 16:4; 20:17; 21:18; 1 Timothy 5:17, 19; Titus 1:5; James 5:14), to the "elder" Apostles themselves (1 Peter 5:1; 2 John 1:1; 3 John 1:1), or to certain mysterious "elders" in heaven enthroned around the central throne of the Lamb (Revelation 4:4, 10; 5:5, 6, 8, 11, 14; 7:11, 13; 11:16; 14:3; 19:4). It seems to connote the authority associated with maturity (perhaps more spiritual than chronological).

#5. *leitourgos* is differently rendered as "servant" or "minister" regarding the angels (Hebrews 1:7, 14), as "minister" in the sense of civil authority (Romans 13:6), as "minister" in the sense of a religious leader or his auxiliary colleague (Romans 15:16; Philippians 2:25), or as "minister" in reference to the high priesthood of Christ Himself (Hebrews 8:2, 6). This generic term, therefore, is so variously translated in diverse contexts as to appear almost exegetically useless. It can seemingly apply to anyone (Divine, angelic, or human) who performs some official task, whether secular or religious. But perhaps it has a paradigmatic usage.

At any rate, amidst all this complex nomenclature we are most interested in establishing connections with the term "priest" (*iereus*). Let us work our way through the above list, beginning from the bottom with Romans 15:15-16, where St. Paul asserts:

> But on some points I have written to you very boldly by way of reminder, because of the grace given me by God to be a **minister** of Christ Jesus to the Gentiles in the **priestly service** (*ierourgounta*) of the gospel of God, so that the **offering** of the Gentiles may be acceptable, sanctified by the Holy Spirit (boldface emphasis added).

This passage provides a direct association among the terms "minister" (*leitourgos*), priest (*iereus*), and a "sanctified" (or sacrificial) "offering" – the latter term (*prosphora*) identical to the one used in Ephesians 5:2 about Christ, who "gave himself up for us, a fragrant **offering** and sacrifice to God" (emphasis added). Furthermore, this Greek word for "offering" occurs in Hebrews 10:10, one of the passages often invoked to deny the efficacy of the Mass offered by a sacrificing priestly class in the New Covenant: "We have been sanctified through the **offering** of the body of Jesus Christ once for all" (emphasis added). Despite the fact that Christ offered up His body in atonement for our sins "once for all", St. Paul (in Romans 15:15-16) still views his liturgical ministry as a priestly service enabling the Gentiles to participate in the sacrificial oblation of Christ, for the sake of their own sanctification. Christ did *His* part (so to speak) in His objective redemption of mankind; it is up to the members of the Church to incorporate themselves subjectively into His "once for all" offering (see Colossians 1:24-25; 2 Timothy 4:6) – and for this purpose we need priestly intermediaries. In Romans 15:15-16 St. Paul is definitely distinguishing himself (and, by extension, similar "priests") from Christians in general who share in a "royal priesthood" (1 Peter 2:5, 9). Thus, it seems that the class of "priest" to which the Apostles and their successors belong is the quintessential species within what might be considered a broader genus of "liturgical minister". But perhaps, given the offertory or sacrificing role of the Apostles (as exemplified in Romans 15:15-16), such a priest is really identical with the only genuine kind of "liturgical minister", on account of an affiliation with the high priesthood of Christ, who is the archetypal *leitourgos* (see Hebrews 8:2-3).

But what public functions do these priests perform for our sanctification by the Holy Spirit? The verses in Acts 2:42, 46 furnish a clue: "They devoted themselves to the apostles' teaching and fellowship, to the breaking of bread and the prayers.... And day by day, attending the temple together and breaking bread in their homes, they partook of food with glad and generous hearts."

The allusions to "the breaking of bread and the prayers" are unmistakably non-coincidental, harking back to the Last Supper narratives of Luke 22:19 and 1 Corinthians 11:23-26, as well as 1 Corinthians 10:16: "The bread which we break, is it not a participation in the body of Christ?" In Acts 2:42, 46 St. Luke does not refer to any ordinary food and prayers, but rather to the sacred food of Christ's Eucharistic body promised in John 6 and delivered at the Last Supper with the special consecratory formula ("This is my body") – a rite our Lord commanded His Apostles to repeat "in remembrance" of Him. The context of 1 Corinthians 11:23-26 makes this clear, because in the immediately preceding passage (1 Corinthians 11:17-22) St. Paul reprimanded the Corinthians for their reprehensible behavior "when [they] assemble as a church" (verse 18). Their previous distractions hindered them from devoting full attention to the subsequent Eucharistic feast (see especially verses 20-22, along with verses 33-34).

Furthermore, it was transparent to the early Church (or at least to their leaders) that this "breaking of bread" was not simply the occasion for a gathering to consume earthly food; otherwise, St. Paul would not have issued such a stern warning about sacrilege in 1 Corinthians 11:28-29.

Now, given St. Paul's numerous references (throughout his letters) to his apostolic ministry, it would be incongruous and disorderly for anyone other than those specially delegated to officiate at the "breaking of bread and prayers" in the Eucharistic celebration, which by this time seems to have moved away from just any private homes into specially designated church buildings. The Apostles must have appointed (or "ordained") particular Christians to conduct this holy service. This conclusion can be verified in several places.

First, Acts 13:2-3 informs us that, during a worship gathering marked by prayer and fasting, the Holy Spirit consecrated Barnabas and Saul for missionary work through a laying on of hands. This passage is illuminating when we learn that the verb "worshiping" is the *RSV* translation of the Greek verb derived from the root *leitourgia* (rather than the more customary and expected *latreia* or *proskuneisis*). Another rare translation of the Greek noun *leitourgia* as "worship" occurs in Hebrews 9:21 in connection with Moses sprinkling blood over the sacred "vessels used in worship (*leitourgia*)". This Mosaic act is a *type* foreshadowing the blood of Christ made present through the consecration and transubstantiation of wine in the chalice at the Last Supper (see Matthew 26:27-29; Mark 14:23-25; Luke 22:17-18, 20; 1 Corinthians 11:25-29). Therefore, in other words, these Christians were engaged in a solemn ceremony that required fasting from mundane food, and they were acting in an official ecclesiastical capacity in their liturgy and subsequent missionary ordination.

Secondly, Acts 14:23 tells us that Paul and Barnabas "appointed elders ... in every church", and "with prayer and fasting, they committed them to the Lord". Again, we witness these disciples fasting at prayer, suggesting a formal liturgical setting that demanded abstention from normal food – followed by an ordination rite. Moreover, in Titus 1:5 St. Paul directed St. Titus to "appoint elders in every town". What would be the purpose of appointing elders "in every church" and "in every town", unless to officiate at the Eucharistic "breaking of bread and the prayers"? Indeed, these "elders" are no mere preachers. St. Paul warned St. Timothy in 1 Timothy 5:22: "Do not be hasty in the laying on of hands." If ordination simply bestowed the right to preach about Christ, such a stringent admonition would not be necessary, because Christ Himself did not prevent others from proclaiming Him and even casting out demons in His name (see Mark 9:38-39; Luke 9:49-50).

No, the privilege of performing a far more sacred task must be conferred through the imposition of hands. But someone may protest: perhaps it is an administrative duty. After all, St. Paul instructed St. Timothy in 1 Timothy 5:17-18, "Let the elders who rule well be considered worthy of double honor; especially those who labor in preaching and teaching; for the scripture says, 'You shall not muzzle an ox when it is treading out the grain,' and, 'The laborer deserves his wages.'" According to this passage, it seems that not all the "elders" labored at preaching; some kind of governance was involved in the official capacity of all of them, since those who *also* taught were to be esteemed for a two-fold reason. But let us not forget (from Romans 15:15-16) that St. Paul regarded his service as a priestly one unto sanctification. If the appointed "elders" were to serve as surrogates or vicars for him and the other Apostles, their governing office must have encompassed a sanctifying role. This is confirmed by the remarkable metaphors St. Paul used in comparing the "elders" with oxen treading out grain and with laborers – perhaps, therefore, agricultural harvesters (see Matthew 9:37-38; Luke 10:2). This image of harvested grain is a striking sacramental symbol for the body of Christ, distributed at the Last Supper under the outward form of wheat bread (see John 12:24; Luke 22:19; 24:30, 35; 1 Corinthians 11:23-24; Acts 27:35, 38). Hence, the "elders" who figuratively work to make the grain available are in reality sacred officials who feed the faithful with the body of Christ through Holy Communion. After all, a legitimate *episkopos* (overseer, bishop, guardian, or custodian) of the flock must ensure that the sheep are adequately fed (see John 21:15-17; Acts 20:17, 28). In other words, the "presbyters" are actually priests who confect the Blessed Eucharist at the Holy Sacrifice of the Mass, under the supervision of the "overseers" (*episkopoi*) or bishops.

Again, since these priests are partakers in the high priesthood of Jesus, who offered Himself "once for all" in the bloody sacrifice of the cross, their sacerdotal actions cannot be bloody (see, e.g., Hebrews 7:27; 9:25-26; 10:4). Indeed, Christ is a priest "after the order of Melchizedek" (Hebrews 5:6, 10; 6:20; 7:3, 11, 15, 17) – the "priest of the Most High God" (Hebrews 7:1) who employed "bread and wine" for his sacrificial offerings (Genesis 14:18). Hence, it is most fitting that the priests subordinate to the New Melchizedek in the New Covenant should likewise offer to the heavenly Father, in union with the Son, the "pure", "unblemished", "perfect" oblation of Christ's body (Malachi 1:11; 1 Peter 1:19; Hebrews 7:28) under the external forms of wheat bread (see Luke 22:31-32) and grape wine (see John 15:1-5).

It makes sense, then, that St. Peter and St. John should have called themselves "elders" (see 1 Peter 1:5; 2 John 1:1; 3 John 1:1). They, along with the other Apostles, were the first priests to be ordained in the New Covenant by and under the high priest Jesus Christ. Furthermore, St. Paul reminded St. Timothy (in 2 Timothy 1:6) about "the gift of God" that Timothy received "through the laying on of my [Paul's] hands". But St. Paul (in 1 Timothy 4:14) also stated that this gift "was given you [Timothy] by prophetic utterance when the elders laid their hands upon you". It follows that Paul implied his presence as one of the "elders" at Timothy's ordination marked by the enunciation of a special formula. Thus, once again, the "elders" who performed these ordinations were priests who held an even higher rank and degree of power: i.e., they were "overseers" (*episkopoi*) or bishops. Judging from Paul's detailed instruction to Timothy in 1 Timothy 3:1-7 about appointments to "the office of bishop", we can deduce that Timothy himself must have eventually been consecrated a bishop with the authority to ordain deacons and priests. An amazing thing is that this whole business of ordination through "the laying on of hands" is counted among "the elementary doctrines of Christ" (see Hebrews 6:1-2), which ought not be disputed.

We recall from the first section of this chapter that "remembrance" and "sacrificial offering" are scripturally linked. In particular, when we read in Philippians 1:1-4 that Paul (along with Timothy) tacitly considered himself a colleague of the "bishops and deacons" (*episkopos, diakonos*) addressed, of whom Paul makes "remembrance" during "every prayer", we can reasonably surmise that these prayers were (at least sometimes) being offered during the memorial celebration of the Last Supper at St. Paul's daily Mass.

Analogy between the Old and New Testaments

In this section we investigate the relationship between, on the one hand, the Aaronic priests and the Levites of the Old Covenant, and, on the other hand, the bishops, presbyters, and deacons of the New Covenant.

Some pertinent passages from the Old Testament in this regard cast light on what at first glance seems perplexing in the New Testament. Numbers 3:5-10 is an important text, in which God commands Moses to have the tribe of Levi serve the priests (Aaron and his sons). A similar text is Numbers 18:1-7. Likewise, 2 Chronicles 13:10 repeats: "We have priests ministering to the Lord who are sons of Aaron, and Levites for their service." More specifically, Numbers 3:31 elaborates: "And their [the Levites'] charge was to be the ark, the table, the lampstand, the altars, the vessels of the sanctuary with which the priests minister, and the screen; all the service pertaining to these."

Let us relate these passages to what is evidently a hierarchy established in the early Church. Acts 6:1-6 reports the famous episode wherein the Apostles determined to select men for the role of serving the poor. Their decision was a solemn one, because it involved an official assembly together with a rite of prayer accompanied by imposition of hands. Since these men were delegated to perform tasks at a subordinate level to the Apostles, it seems that the Holy Spirit was inspiring the Twelve to establish a clerical rank higher than the laity but lower than the bishops and presbyters. In fact, the traditional interpretation that these men were ordained *deacons* (in a very specific sense of the term) seems to find support in this text.

Numbers 3:5-10, 31 and 2 Chronicles 13:10, all cited above, corroborate this interpretation. Indeed, the ministry of Levites subservient to priests, as explained in these passages, adumbrates the ministry of the New Testament deacons relative to the bishops and presbyters. We can set up an analogy that seems valid to a high degree of approximation: as the Levites were to the priests of the Old Covenant, so are the deacons to the bishops and priests of the New Covenant.

Further relevant material for scriptural typology appears in the book of Nehemiah, which records how the chastened post-exilic Israelites committed themselves anew to the Lord, vowing: "We make a firm covenant and write it, and our princes, our Levites, and our priests set their seal to it" (Nehemiah 9:38). The key passage, though, is Nehemiah 10:32-39. Although it is too lengthy to quote verbatim here, the gist of it concerns the people's pledge to provide material support (wood, grain, fruit, wine, oil, animals taken from herds and flocks) for the Levites and the priests in their divine service in God's house. This passage contains rich symbolism prefiguring the sacramental order of the New Covenant Church. We ought to ponder its ramifications.

As St. Paul tells us in 1 Corinthians 15:20, echoing our Lord in John 12:24 about the "grain of wheat" falling into the earth, dying, and rising, Christ is the "first fruits" among all those who will have been raised from the dead. Thus, in the above passage from Nehemiah 10, the "first fruits of all fruit", the "first-born of our sons", and the "continual cereal offering" all signify the Eucharistic body of the risen Christ. This "continual burnt offering" is made on the "sabbath" (and even daily), with the transubstantiation of wheat bread, on altars of the Catholic Church ("the house of God") throughout the world (see Malachi 1:11). This oblation is a mystical, non-bloody re-enactment or re-presentation of Christ's once-for-all self-holocaust on the "wood" atop Mount Calvary, carried out in the Holy Sacrifice of the Mass "to make atonement for" the sins of mankind. The "showbread" symbolically foreshadows the Blessed Sacrament reserved in the tabernacles of "the house of our God".

Now, although deacons (like the Levites) may be instrumentally involved in certain roles of service at the altar, functioning as intermediaries between the laity and the priests, Nehemiah 10 implicitly prophesies that "the first of our coarse meal" (i.e., wheat flour) and "the wine" will be brought "to the priests who minister in the house of our God", specifically "to the chambers of the house of our God" ("where are the vessels of the sanctuary"). For it is the priests, not the deacons, who confect the body and blood of the Lamb of God ("the firstling of our herds and of our flocks") out of the materials of wheat bread and grape wine.

Nehemiah 10:39 tacitly admonishes us "not [to] neglect the house of our God". We fall into danger of this neglect if we downplay the Sacraments and the key role that the priests play in administering them. So precious is the sacred rank of the ordained priesthood for the good of the Church that Ezra 8:24-30 associates priests with gold. This costly metal, purchased with the blood of Christ the day after He ordained His first priests, must never be devalued.

(II) The Ordained Priesthood Is Restricted to Men

Introduction

The Catholic Church teaches that the Sacrament of Holy Orders is reserved exclusively to men. Many people seem not to grasp any solid rationale for the allegedly anachronistic, arbitrary, and unjust "discrimination". We often hear the tiresome and superficial refrain: "I don't see why the Church does not ordain women priests, because they can do just as good a job as men." In our egalitarian age infected by feminist influences, there is evidently a deeply entrenched reluctance to admit that the differences between the two sexes carry any theological relevance. Hence, it is our duty to advance some scriptural demonstrations sustaining the Catholic position. We do so under three main subheadings, each containing its own line of argumentation.[1]

Sacrificing-Priesthood and Victim Argument

We maintain that the all-male priesthood of the Old Testament is an authentic *type* of the New Testament priesthood. This proposition is certainly true for the mysterious priesthood of King Melchizedek (see Genesis 14:18-20), which was perfectly and everlastingly fulfilled in Christ, as Psalm 110:4 suggests and Hebrews 5:5-6; 6:19-20; 7:1-28 explains at length. But the claim is true, as well, for the Levitical priesthood of Aaron that was (*as such*) eventually abolished. Indeed, despite the formal abrogation of the Aaronic priesthood, Isaiah 66:21 uses Levitical language to prophesy about the remotely adumbrated New Covenant priesthood: "And some of them also I will take for priests and for Levites, says the Lord." Observe that Leviticus 6-8 forever restricts hierarchical participation in the sacred rites (which were commanded Moses by God) to males: specifically, "to Aaron the priest and to his sons, as a perpetual due from the people of Israel ... throughout their generations" (Leviticus 7:34, 36; see also Numbers 18). Now if it were merely a mutable Hebrew custom that males alone could serve as priests, Christ would undoubtedly have annulled the practice upon the institution of His new priesthood – just as the early Church changed the official day of community worship from Saturday to Sunday.

In particular, the divine decree that the Passover lamb be a "male without blemish" (see Exodus 12:1-28, especially verse 5, and Leviticus

1:10-11), whose expiatory blood would rescue from wrath those submissive to God's ritual law, is an allegory for the heavenly mission of the "Lamb of God" (see Isaiah 53:7; John 1:29, 36; Acts 8:32; 1 Peter 1:18-19; Revelation 5:6-8, 12-13; 7:9-10, 13-17; 21:9, 14, 22-23; 22:1, 3), whose bloody death redeemed mankind from the clutches of the evil Serpent (see Genesis 3:15). The mandate that the Paschal lamb be male cannot be ignored or relegated to insignificance. It has weighty repercussions for the Sacrament of Holy Orders, whose very purpose is a sacrificing priesthood – prolonging through the ages the Lamb's unique atonement to God for humanity's sins under the non-bloody appearances of bread and wine (offered according to the order of Melchizedek). The priests of the New Covenant, like the priests of the Old Testament (whether Melchizedek or the descendants of Aaron), must be male, for they act in the name and power of the Victim-Person of the male Lamb of God, who is the eternal high priest of the everlasting dispensation under the law of grace.

Here is a subsidiary argument that we place under this heading, because it also involves the notion of sacrifice.[2] A priest officiating at the altar is engaged in offering a sacrifice of self through identification or assimilation with the person of Christ – the groom who delivered Himself over for His bride, the Church (see Matthew 9:15; Mark 2:19-20; Luke 5:34-35; John 3:27-30; 2 Corinthians 11:2; Ephesians 6:21-33; Revelation 19:7; 21:2, 9; 22:17). Now, a female possesses a nature already inherently directed to sacrifice through the offering of her body to the presence of a baby. Even if she never actually bears a child, the essential biological significance of her femininity still holds. One might say that a woman is constantly, by virtue of her very being, in a state open to sacrifice. After all, since she may become pregnant even against her will, an orientation to self-oblation is deeply embedded within her. The same is not true for a male, whose sacrificial aspect is more superficial and dependent on a freely willed choice. Thus, if a woman were to serve in the priestly capacity, she would in effect be offering *two* disparate sacrifices: an involuntary one on the natural level and a voluntary one on the supernatural level. But God demands only *one* basic sacrifice of a person's life unto salvation (see Hebrews 9:27, along with 1 Timothy 2:12, 15).

The Catholic Church takes the reality of the body very seriously. For this reason, it would be unfitting for a woman to utter the words of consecration "This is my body" during the Mass, just as it would make a farce of natural symbolism were a man to play the part of Mary in a re-enactment of the first Christmas Day. Someone may object that the institution narrative recalled by the priest merely reports what Christ said at the Last Supper, and therefore the gender of the celebrant is irrelevant. But, in offering the Holy Sacrifice, the priest acts in the very *person* of Christ – not as a mere reporter or commentator or "presider" over the assembly. Hence, it would be sacramentally suitable only for a man to serve in this sacerdotal role.

Priest-Father Argument

Abraham is called "father" in many verses of Sacred Scripture (e.g., Genesis 17:4-5, Isaiah 51:2, Matthew 3:9, Luke 16:24, John 8:56, Acts 7:2, Romans 4:16-18, James 2:21). But God made him "the father of a multitude of nations" (Genesis 17:4-5) only because he obeyed, with a heroic act of faith, the divine command to sacrifice his son Isaac, through whom God's covenant would be established (see Genesis 17:19,21). Now the promised child Isaac is a *type* of Christ (as shown by Genesis 22:1-10 and Hebrews 11:17-19). Thus, Abraham, in his willingness to physically immolate Isaac on a pile of wood carried up the mount by Isaac himself, made a mystical oblation of Jesus Christ on the Cross on Mount Calvary. In spiritually offering up his sole son of the covenant, Abraham represented God the Father, thereby acting symbolically as a supreme high priest himself. Consequently, there is a strong (even coextensive) relationship between priesthood and fatherhood.

Another Old Testament account lending much credence to an all-male priesthood is the tale of Micah and the Levite in Judges 17:7-13. This text narrates the search of a young Levitical tribesman from Bethlehem (literally meaning "the house of bread") for another residence. During his journey, he met a layman named Micah who offered to take him into his home like a son, providing him with food, clothing, and a stipend – all in exchange for spiritual service. Micah implored the young man (in Judges 17:10): "Stay with me, and be to me a father and a priest." The paradoxical thing here is that the foster father pleaded that his adopted son also be *his* "father"! The hermeneutical clue to comprehending this seemingly odd reversal of relationships resides in the role of *priest*. Micah realized that the Levite's religious function elevated him to the rank of spiritual fatherhood, notwithstanding the disparity in the chronological ages between the two men. A later episode centering on this young Levite is recorded, in which he finally agrees (under pressure from a delegation of intruders) to leave Micah's house and function as "father and priest" for "a tribe and family in Israel" at a different locale (see Judges 18:1-27, especially verse 19). The main lesson here is that the priesthood is being intimately linked with fatherhood and hence masculinity.

Nevertheless, we may consider some auxiliary points. The young man, though descended from the tribe of Levi, had been staying in a town of the tribe of Judah: namely Bethlehem, "the city of David" (Luke 2:4,11; see also 1 Samuel 16:1,4). Yet, he emigrated from there, only to receive an invitation to priestly service elsewhere for other tribes of Israel. His departure and later spiritual exaltation can be construed as an allegory of Christ's global redemptive mission, since these events recall the prophecy in Micah 5:2 about Bethlehem as the earthly origin of the Messiah whose reign would be universal. (See also 2 Samuel 5:2; Isaiah 49:6; Matthew 2:4-6; John 7:42.) This young man appears to be a sort of transitional *type*-figure. While still a descendant of the Levitical line of priests, he mystically shares in and foreshadows to some extent the Eucharistic priesthood of Jesus Christ, the "Son of David", born in Bethlehem (see Matthew 1:1; Mark 11:10; Luke 20:41-44), which is thus the original terrestrial dwelling of the "Heavenly Bread of Life" (see John 6:35, 51, 58).

Another element to emphasize within the Micah-Levite story is the very title "father" accorded a priest. This term has been Catholic tradition for all priests – especially the pope ("Papa"), who is fondly addressed as the "Holy Father".

On this score, it is appropriate to correct a misinterpretation of Christ's words in Matthew 23:9, where He warns against addressing an earthly man as "father". Christ must intend this prohibition in a supernatural way, as meaning that we are not to view our spiritual lineage in a worldly manner, thereby inverting the proper order of priority, since our ultimate inheritance derives from heaven (see Matthew 8:21-22; 10:34-37; 19:29; 25:34; Mark 1:20; 10:17-19, 29-30; Luke 9:59-62; 10:25-28; 12:51-53; 14:26; 18:18-30; 1 Corinthians 6:9-10; Ephesians 1:13-14, 18; 5:5; Colossians 1:11-12; 3:23-24; Hebrews 6:11-12; 9:15; 1 Peter 1:3-5). We are not to put our trust in mere "flesh and blood" for our everlasting welfare (see John 1:13; 1 Corinthians 15:50), but rather in God's paternal mercy (see, for example, Luke 15:11-32). In historical context, Christ in Matthew

23:9 was tacitly admonishing certain scribes and Pharisees, who thought that their mere genetic descent from "Father Abraham" (see Matthew 3:9; Luke 3:8; 16:24; John 8:39, 53, 56) sufficed for their salvation. If Christ had meant that no man should ever be addressed as "father" in any sense, then He Himself would not have referred to "Father Abraham" at all and He would not have alluded to earthly fathers numerous times. Both St. Paul and St. James also call Abraham our "father" (see Romans 4:16-18; James 2:21), as did St. Stephen (see Acts 7:2). Moreover, St. Paul, who surely did not misunderstand Christ's words in this matter, explicitly called *himself* a "father" several times (see 1 Corinthians 4:15; Philippians 2:22; 1 Thessalonians 2:11). Implicitly, as well, he designated himself a father (see 1 Timothy 1:2, 18; 2 Timothy 1:2; Titus 1:4), as did St. Peter (see 1 Peter 5:13). In addition, St. Paul teaches that the head of every family on earth takes his name from God the Father (see Ephesians 3:14-15). Lastly, St. John practices what St. Paul preaches, by addressing an unspecified number of men as "fathers" (see 1 John 2:13-14). Therefore, the objection that it constitutes disobedience for Catholics to address priests as "fathers" is biblically unfounded.

Continuing our discussion after this digression, we find in Isaiah 22:20-24 that a kind of priestly authority is invested in Eliakim, who is designated as a "father". This passage foreshadows the reign of Jesus in Revelation 3:7. Both texts suggest the papal office of Vicar of Christ instituted by our Lord in Matthew 16:19. At any rate, once again the priesthood is intimately entwined with the symbolism of fatherhood, which can be sacramentally represented only via maleness.

In 1 Corinthians 4:15, St. Paul refers to his *paternal* role exercised by virtue of the apostolic ministry through which he personally brought people into the Church: "For though you have countless guides in Christ, you do not have many fathers. For I became your father in Christ Jesus through the gospel." Whereas the *RSV* translates the Greek "εγω υμας εγέννησα" as "I became your father", the *KJV* similarly renders the phrase as "I have begotten you", using the masculine term "beget" for generation rather than the feminine term "conceive".

Finally, in his instruction on the appointment (or "ordination", according to the *KJV* translation) of "elders" ("presbyters" in the Greek), St. Paul insists that an individual of this class be a "man [who] is blameless, the husband of one wife", with "children [who] are believers" (see Titus

1:5-6). Since he does not demand marriage (see 1 Corinthians 7:25-40), his logic here is hypothetical: *If* a priest is married with children, *then* that priest is a father, hence a man. So, St. Paul essentially rules out women as priests. In light of this passage, as well as 1 Corinthians 14:33-35 and 1 Timothy 2:11-12), it is impossible to entertain the idea that the early Church permitted female priests.

The Feet-Washing Argument

This is an intriguing and sophisticated argument. On account of its complicated subtlety, though, some background is needed. The reader's patience is implored with what might seem at the outset an aimless digression. Loose strings will be tied up at the end.

1 Samuel 11 recounts how King David contrived a scheme (encompassing a second plot after his first plan failed) to cover up his adulterous guilt for the pregnancy of Bathsheba. Unfortunately for David, her husband Uriah had been at battle away from his wife. David could not afford to let more time pass out of fear lest his deed be discovered. Upon learning that Bathsheba was with child, he hastened to recall Uriah home. Desperately scrambling to escape blame in the hope that Bathsheba's condition would be attributed to her husband, he told Uriah: "Go down to your house, and wash your feet" (1 Samuel 11:8). Now this was a Hebraic circumlocution, which Uriah well understood. For in later explaining to the King why he could not accede to David's request, Uriah replied that he did not think it right to indulge in the relaxation and luxury of dining and sleeping with his wife (see 1 Samuel 11:11). Hence, "wash your feet" (spoken to a man, at least) was a euphemism for advising engagement in conjugal intercourse. We may speculate that this decorous phrase probably arose as a synecdoche, intended to include purifying the remainder of the legs in preparation for marital coitus.

This episode is hardly the only place in the Bible where feet-washing is linked with masculine procreative activity. Another instance occurs in Genesis 18:1-10, where the Lord appeared to Abraham in the form of three male guests (perhaps, therefore, a Trinitarian theophany). In verse 4 Abraham offered them water to wash their feet. In verse 10 the triumvirate predicted that Abraham's wife Sarah would bear a son within a year. Thus, God performed a miracle by causing an evidently sterile couple to beget and conceive. Consequently, this famous passage associates divine power to create human life with washing of the feet – in this case the metaphorical "feet" of the Lord (visibly represented by the three men).

A few other passages exemplify this theme revolving around male generation of offspring in relation to feet-washing. Two of these feet-washing incidents concern this theme in a negative way: namely, Genesis 19:2 (in the context of an angelic visitation to punish the citizens for perversion of the male procreative faculty) and Judges 19:21 (also connected with a gruesome sequel to the corruption of male sexuality).

But the remaining stories are positive. For instance, the feet-washing in Genesis 24:32 occurs in the context of procuring a wife for Isaac.

Particularly interesting is Genesis 43:24, a feet-washing verse that appears in the context of the poignant reunion of Joseph and his brother Benjamin. In order to bargain further with Joseph for relief from the famine gripping the Middle East, his half-brothers had to bow to Joseph's demand that they leave Simeon behind as a hostage and return with Benjamin – a kind of offering to Joseph in exchange for grain. Jacob was understandably disconsolate over the threat of the loss of his youngest son, after (so he thought) irretrievably losing his son Joseph. But in order to redeem Simeon and save his family from starvation, Jacob felt compelled to sacrifice Benjamin, the last male offspring of his union with his wife Rachel. Yet, in the end, everyone benefited from the gift of a renewed lease on life through Joseph's generous deeds as "lord" and "father" (Genesis 45:8).

Other texts explicitly connect feet-washing with priestly service – a ministry of spiritual regeneration. A notable passage wherein the Lord prescribes this washing for Aaron and his descendants before they could officiate at worship ceremonies is Exodus 30:17-21 (see also Exodus 40:30-32 and Leviticus 8:6). In Joshua 3:13-17; 4:3,9,18, we read that the ark-bearing Levitical priests, whose feet merely step into the Jordan River, are endowed with divine power to divert the flow of the water – thereby ensuring both the immediate physical safety and ultimately the spiritual life of the Israelites in their promised land. In addition, this narrative prefigures the dominion over the supernaturally vitalizing waters of Baptism exercised by the New Testament priesthood.

Two Old Testament passages, while not referring to foot lavation, nevertheless associate the feet with spiritual generation or fruitfulness: in fact, these texts contain prophecies of the coming Redeemer. In Genesis

49:10, Jacob (on his deathbed) foretells the advent of the sovereign ruler who will inherit the "scepter" or the "staff" that will not depart "from between the feet" of Judah. The use of "feet" here undoubtedly constitutes a euphemistic transference from the center of the procreative faculty; indeed, the *Douay-Rheims-Challoner* translation renders "feet" as "thigh". (Exodus 4:25 also has some pertinence here.) Lastly, Isaiah 52:7 portrays the expected Savior arriving "upon the mountains" with "beautiful feet", because He brings glad tidings announcing the reign of God and the way to salvation.

Let us keep firmly in mind the entire Old Testament backdrop delineated above. The diverse texts examined are united in a pervasive motif that irrefutably juxtaposes feet-washing with male generative power. In light of these historical precedents, we can understand the culminating, profound significance of our Lord's washing of the Apostles' feet during the Last Supper – a scene depicted in John 13:2-15. Since at this Passover meal Jesus first authorized His Apostles to confect the Sacrament of His Body and Blood, telling them to "do this in remembrance" of Him (Luke 22:19 and 1 Corinthians 11:24-25), we conclude that the washing of their feet was a fulfillment of Old Testament symbolism relating this cleansing ritual to masculine begetting of life in marriage. Of course, in this case it is a spiritual (rather than a biological) fecundity that supernaturally channels the life-giving grace of Christ into souls through the Holy Sacrifice of the Mass (see Matthew 19:10-12). The washing of their feet by the Head of the Church was thus a preparatory purification for their assimilation into His eternal priesthood – a protracted ordination ceremony that began on Holy Thursday night and ended on the evening of Easter Sunday, when our Lord empowered His Apostles to forgive sins (see John 20:21-23). His washing of their feet can, by the same token, be viewed as a pre-nuptial purification for their wedding to the Church, the Bride of Christ (see Revelation 21:2 and Ephesians 5:22-33) – consecrating each of them as a groom acting in the Person of Christ. A woman could not, of course, play this role without conjuring up baneful lesbian symbolism. The upshot of Christ's handling of the crucial Old Testament typology is that His hierarchical priesthood is restricted to men.

Conclusion

The foregoing three arguments have aimed to establish that, according to the divine economy of salvation, the ordained priesthood is restricted to men. This precept does not imply that women are inferior to men, for the issue at hand concerns merely the *role of service* played by the two genders in God's plan.[3] There is no question of "worthiness" at stake here. If that were the overriding factor, then Christ would have ordained His most holy Mother Mary to the hierarchical priesthood. Concerning the question whether anyone at all has a right to receive Holy Orders, we simply quote Hebrews 5:4, which admonishes that "one does not take the honor upon himself, but he is called by God, just as Aaron was."

(III) The Discipline of Celibacy

Introduction

All those reading these pages would probably recognize what "WWJD" stands for. In popular Christian culture, this acronym can be found on bumper stickers, key straps, bracelets, and anywhere else that the disciple of the Lord may want to pose the question, "What Would Jesus Do?" – in order to help him or her to walk more closely the way of Jesus. Don't all Christians wish to use the Lord's life as the guide for our own? This is why "WWJD" is so popular; it succinctly directs our attention to the comparison of what we do and what Jesus' life shows us should be done. Could there be anything that the Lord did that we may not want to emulate?

One of the most curious things that I observe in the lives of many non-Catholic evangelizers is that they are married. Why is that curious? Well, Jesus was not married. Why, then, is it the case among so many who proclaim His gospel as the guide for Christian life that they don't apply this important part of the Lord's life to their own? Except for the Latin Rite Catholic Church, and as a rule, the bishops of the various Orthodox churches, it seems to be rare amongst Christians to see celibacy or evangelical continence practiced.

Let us first define our terms. "Chastity" is the living out of our lives using sexuality according to the law of God and our state in life. "Virginity" is the absence of bodily sexual experience. "Consecrated virginity" is the state of life acquired when one freely vows to God to remain in the virginal state in order to be a sign of the life to come. "Continence" is the putting aside of bodily sexual actions, whether one is a virgin or not, or whether or not one is married. "Evangelical continence" is the choice not to enjoy the marital embrace so as to celebrate the holy mysteries (Sacraments) of God in a way that points to the superiority of the next world. "Celibacy", as the term is used in the Catholic Church, is the state of the deacon, priest, or bishop who promises his bishop that he will not marry so as to point to the Kingdom by the way in which he lives his life and the sacrifice that he has made; it assumes the living of a chaste life. Now all of these conditions in life have a spiritual aspect; indeed, without that aspect one is not likely to remain chaste, continent, virginal, or celibate for long. The power to live our sexual lives in a God fearing way only comes from a vibrant spiritual life with our Lord, especially with the aid of the Sacraments.

Pointing toward Heavenly Marriage

Of course, no knowledgeable Christian contends that Jesus was married after the way of men and women in this world or that He had anything other than the most correct relationship with any woman that He encountered.[4] No one is ever mentioned as a wife of Jesus, nor does He have any children of the flesh according to Christian tradition.[5] (You can be sure that if He did, they would have been of great stature in the Christian community.) Jesus was so proper with women – but at the same time very natural and kind – that, although His disciples marveled when they found Him speaking with the woman at the well, they dared not question Him nor make any negative remarks to Him (see John 4:27). That Jesus' relationship with women was in no way touched by any sort of disdain can be seen clearly in reading the entire conversation He had with the woman of Samaria whom He met at the well on that very hot day (see John 4:1-30).

So why did Jesus *not* marry after the manner of men and women in this world? It cannot be held that this was because such sensual things as the marital embrace and the procreation of children were too worldly for Jesus. Didn't He take on our flesh in order to redeem our entire lives? Isn't marriage a central reality to most of those seeking salvation? And how could it be below His dignity to fulfill the first command of the Father to man and woman, "Be fruitful and multiply" (Genesis 1:28)? I suppose one could argue that the state of marriage had fallen with the sin of Adam and Eve, which was after God's command, and hence had become too corrupt for Him. But that would prove too much. It would be a reason for there to be no Incarnation at all, since all that is human – indeed all of creation – was in some way corrupted by the Fall. Could not the Redeemer save and lift up marriage by His own participation in it?

Indeed, it would have been most logical for Jesus to marry and have a progeny – a dynasty! Yet, that would have obscured the spiritual progeny that is the goal of Christian life. This goal of having many spiritual children was hinted at when God promised that He would bless Abraham, making of him a great nation (see Genesis 12:2-3). St.

Paul explains in Romans 4:16 that the great blessing of Abraham is his example of faith: "That is why it depends on faith, in order that the promise may rest on grace and be guaranteed to all his descendants – not only to the adherents of the law but also to those who share the faith of Abraham, for he is the father of us all." The fatherhood to which St. Paul refers is a spiritual fatherhood that does not depend on descent from the flesh. As Jesus came to inaugurate the Kingdom, He showed that God did not need earthly marriage in order to fulfill His promises. God did truly give Abraham earthly progeny, but He even more generously gave him spiritual children. Such children are the result of a heavenly marriage.

Jesus did not marry after the manner of men and women on earth because He would thus become a *bigamist*. (I know that this is a startling word – but I did get your attention!) You see, He was already married in the Kingdom. And His spouse was and is us. St. Paul tells us about His love for His bride in Ephesians 5:25-32. The comparison in this passage is obvious. Paul can teach about marriage through the example of Jesus, who is married to the Catholic Church. His whole life was a nuptial union with the people of God. The celebration of that eternal marriage is featured in the vision of St. John in Revelation 19:7-9:

> Let us rejoice and exult and give him the glory, for the marriage
> of the Lamb has come; and his Bride has made herself ready; it
> was granted her to be clothed with fine linen, bright and pure"
> – for the fine linen is the righteous deeds of the saints. And the
> angel said to me, "Write this: Blessed are those who are invited
> to the marriage supper of the Lamb."

Later on, the New Jerusalem is described as "a bride adorned for her husband" (Revelation 21:2). Writing to the Corinthians, Paul even claims his own part in the presentation of the bride: "I betrothed you to Christ to present you as a pure bride to her one husband" (2 Corinthians 11:2).

This nuptial relationship between God and His people is taught in the Hebrew Scriptures in many places. For example, Yahweh tells the prophet Hosea that on the day of Israel's restoration she would call God "my husband" (see Hosea 2:16). Then Yahweh explains, as He directly addresses Israel through the prophet: "I will betroth you to me for ever;

I will betroth you to me in righteousness and in justice, in steadfast love, and in mercy. I will betroth you to me in faithfulness; and you shall know the Lord" (Hosea 2:19-20).

There are many other references that could be made if we had the space (see Isaiah 54:5ff; Ezekiel 16:6-14). Jesus referred to these eternal nuptials when He gave the reason for the Apostles' lack of fasting in the presence of the Bridegroom (see Matthew 9:15). For the same reason, Jesus began His public life at the Wedding of Cana (see John 2:1-11), told the story of the Ten Bridesmaids (see Matthew 25:1-13), and compared the Kingdom of Heaven to a wedding banquet (see Matthew 22:1-13) – so that all His followers would know that He was the Bridegroom coming to fulfill the Old Testament prophecies.

St. John the Baptist denied he was the Messiah, knowing that the Lord Jesus was the Bridegroom. This is why he said (in John 3:29): "He who has the bride is the bridegroom; the friend of the bridegroom, who stands and hears him, rejoices greatly at the bridegroom's voice; therefore this joy of mine is now full." John the Baptist's joy was that he was in the presence of the Bridegroom coming to bring about the espousal of the people of God, according to the words of Hosea, and that he had heard His voice. For the Kingdom of Heaven, which Jesus inaugurated as He walked the earth, is the nuptial banquet of the Lamb of God, who is the Bridegroom – the banquet to which we are all invited, because, as members of the Catholic Church, we are the "bride". The Lord's entire life on earth pointed to the consummation of the marital love that God has planned for His people. His not taking an earthly wife was a particularly stark sign that there was something greater than earthly marriage in Heaven.

We must understand that this heavenly marriage is real. In fact, earthly marriage is a mere shadow in comparison. Yet, it has a real purpose, which is to point to the heavenly reality. When God made man and woman "in his own image" (Genesis 1:27), He made them husband and wife. How do we know this? God calls Eve Adam's "wife" (Genesis 3:17) and Adam Eve's "husband" (Genesis 3:16). In addition, when teaching about marriage Jesus refers back to "the beginning" (Matthew 19:4; Mark 10:6), thus confirming that Adam and Eve were created as a married couple. Earthly (and originally un-fallen) marriage was put in our nature in order to prepare the "language" of marital experience that God would use in order to explain His eternal nuptial love for us.[6]

God's children are destined for this marriage to the Lamb in Heaven, which is why there is no "marriage" (after an earthly understanding) in Heaven. So He explained to the Sadducees who tried to trip Him up with the question about the seven men who had married one woman: Who would be her husband in Heaven?

> And Jesus said to them, "The sons of this age marry and are given in marriage; but those who are accounted worthy to attain to that age and to the resurrection from the dead neither marry nor are given in marriage, for they cannot die any more, because they are equal to the angels and are sons of God, being sons of the resurrection." (Luke 20:34-36)

Perhaps we have the problem of the Sadducees: we cannot imagine what Heaven is like. This is why we must open our hearts to see what sort of marriage Jesus is pointing to in Heaven. It surpasses the kind on earth, and indeed is its fulfillment. This is so true that in Heaven earthly marriage has no more use. Like a set of directions, earthly marriage points to the heavenly reality. Once we have reached eternal marriage with the Lamb, what is earthly is dispensed with, since it has achieved its purpose.

Jesus wanted His disciples to focus on this heavenly marriage in the conduct of their lives, just as He did. This is why they gave up living with their wives. We know that this is true, because in Luke 18:28 St. Peter reminded our Lord that the Apostles had left everything behind to be His followers. To this declaration, Jesus responded that all those who leave their families in pursuit of God's kingdom would receive numerous blessings on earth and everlasting life in the next world (see Luke 18:29-30, along with Matthew 4:18-22; 19:27-30, and Mark 10:28-31). We might see a sort of pride in the words of Peter, basically meaning: "See how dedicated we are – we have given up so much!". But could Peter have said what he did if they had *not* left their wives and families? Jesus' words in response affirm the truth of Peter's statement, and point to the reward that will come from their sacrifices. Yet, these words were not just for the generation of the Apostles; they are for the disciples of every age and time.

A Taste of Continence in the Face of God's Presence

One is able to understand God's mind regarding sexual continence by scrutinizing the Old Testament. Although the original command was to be fertile and multiply (Genesis 1:28), thus making the sexual embrace a good thing, we need to keep in mind that marriage is only a foretaste of what is to come in eternity (the nuptial unity of God's people with God).

In this light, we can understand Exodus 19:9-17. In this passage, God commanded Moses to forbid the people from even touching the holy mountain (Mount Sinai) when they approached its foot. But prior to this awesome meeting with God to receive His commandments, Moses consecrated the people, who washed their clothes and abstained from sexual relations. How shall we interpret all this? We avoid some things because they are evil in themselves, but other things only because they are not appropriate at the time. The married avoid the marital embrace when they have guests over to their house. No one would dream of thinking that this meant the husband and wife disdained that sign of love. When the people of Israel were called to the mountain, they had a great Guest! Actually, they were *His* guests. Thus, they dispensed with nuptial intercourse for a time. This tradition of sexual abstinence would be continued by the priests when they served in His presence at the Temple in Jerusalem. This was not because sex is bad, but rather because God is a higher good; and we are more completely His when we put aside all earthly distractions while in His presence. The more we empty ourselves of the good and noble things of this world, the more we are able to receive the maximum benefits of His Grace. Throughout her history, the Church has preserved an ancient tradition by maintaining the practice of evangelical continence and celibacy for her priests.

Eunuchs for the Sake of the Kingdom

We now must consider the primary text that deals with evangelical continence (or celibacy). In the midst of teaching about marriage, and in response to the Apostles' concern about the difficulty of permanent marriage, Jesus says:

> "Not all men can receive this saying, but only those to whom
> it is given. For there are eunuchs who have been so from birth,

and there are eunuchs who have been made eunuchs by men, and there are eunuchs who have made themselves eunuchs for the sake of the kingdom of heaven. He who is able to receive this, let him receive it." (Matthew 19:11-12)

By these words, Jesus brought the discussion to an entirely new level, explaining both His own life without an earthly wife, as well as the lives of His Apostles who had given up the noble earthly joys of marriage "for the sake of the kingdom".

We should keep in mind that a eunuch is a man who is incapable of marriage because a deformity (from birth or acquired) prevents him from the full expression of the marital embrace. Such a man's condition is presumably against his will. So how could becoming a "eunuch" be "for the sake of the kingdom"? It is easy to see how marriage can be "for the sake of the kingdom". Who would deny that marriage, creating a Christian family that is sometimes referred to as the "domestic Church", is one of the best ways to spread the Faith? Both the mutual help that husband and wife can give to one another along the Lord's path, and the instruction and example given to their children, are primary examples of spiritual life and growth in the Faith. So how can being a "eunuch", dispensing with these good things, be "for the sake of the kingdom"?

Those who practice continence, consecrated virginity, or celibacy are, by the very way they live their lives, signs of the nuptial union with the Lord that is beyond this world. Indeed, in a certain way they *constitute* the presence of that nuptial union by reason of their spiritual choice. Jesus told the Sadducees that there was no marriage in Heaven – according to their earthly understanding (see Luke 20:34-36) – because there is eternally celebrated in Heaven *the* marriage of the Bride of Christ with the Lamb.

A spiritual eunuch, called to be such by God, is one who *chooses* to put aside marriage, or, as in the case of the Apostles who were already married, to not experience the marital embrace "for the sake of the kingdom." To do anything "for the sake of the kingdom" is to transcend this world and profess by our actions that the here and now is not our final end. The kingdom of Heaven is beyond the earthly plane, and we must live our lives so as to attain it. We do this by using the world as a means of giving glory to God. Yet, to dispense with the good and noble things of this world is an even greater way of living "for the sake of the kingdom". As Jesus says, the ability to do so is a gift, and such a gift must be freely received.

From what is cited above, it is evident that the Apostles received this gift. St. Paul (in 1 Corinthians 7:7) also attested to practicing evangelical continence during his ministry: "I wish that all were as I myself am. But each has his own special gift from God, one of one kind and one of another." This verse is proof that he was celibate. In 1 Corinthians 7:25-35, St. Paul teaches that the celibate life has a greater excellence than the married life. He argues that marriage has many cares, but, most importantly, he says that "the form of this world is passing away" (verse 31). Then he writes: "I say this for your own benefit, not to lay any restraint upon you, but to promote good order and to secure your undivided devotion to the Lord" (verse 35).

These verses show that celibacy (or evangelical continence) is related to the next world, so that we can be ready for it and give due attention to its advent in this world. We cannot spend time on the teachings of St. Paul regarding marriage, but in them we see the enduring value of the Sacrament of creation that has been restored by Christ in being made a Sacrament of the New Dispensation. Christ restored the understanding of marriage as it was in the will of the Father "from the beginning" (see Matthew 19:3-9), so that both it and celibacy point to the marriage of the Lamb to His Bride, the Church.

There is evidence in the early history of the Church that as a rule bishops and priests practiced evangelical continence, which means that they lived with their wives but did not share the marital embrace with them. Assuming that this is the case (we have no room here for an involved historical investigation), why would this be? And why does the Latin Rite of the Catholic Church demand celibacy of her priests today? One significant reason, as has been indicated above, is that such evangelical continence and celibacy point to the kingdom of Heaven. The other reason concerns the holy things that are approached by those who are ordained.

What do we mean by "holy things"? The Catholic Church lives by the Sacraments given by our Blessed Lord. We have many presences of the Lord in the Church: her faithful people, Sacred Scripture, and the Sacraments. All of the Seven Sacraments in some way are the presence of the Lord, just as surely as He was present on Mount Sinai (see Exodus 19:12-17). Yet the Blessed Sacrament constitutes a more excellent presence than ever could have been imagined before. The Catholic Church teaches the ancient orthodox belief that Jesus Christ is truly present, Body and Blood, Soul and Divinity, in the consecrated Host and in the Precious Blood of the chalice. (See John 6:22-71 for the very words of Jesus regarding the gift of Himself that He intended us to receive; read also how many rejected that gift and hence Him, especially Judas.) Now, the priest at the altar touches His very Body. Is there any doubt as to why the Old Testament tradition of temporary continence was made permanent in the face of such a Presence of God?

The theology of the priesthood gives another reason: the priest in the celebration of the sacred mysteries (the Sacraments) is Christ Himself. This does not mean that the priest's own personhood is annihilated. But when the priest is in the actual celebration of the Sacraments he is acting "in the person" of Christ; he is "another Christ". Since Christ was celibate, so must His priests be. It is also interesting that, according to the theology of Marriage, the spouses give the Sacrament to one another (the priest is just the required canonical witness). This implies that in a certain analogous way the husband and wife are acting in the person of Christ when they pronounce their vows. This is one among many reasons why they should be virginal as they approach their marriage, as was Christ.

Yet, is this gift too great to bear? As the Lord said, "He who is able to receive this, let him receive it" (Matthew 19:12). The gift is offered to many, but it must be *received*. In other words, one cannot receive the gift and live it well if one has the mindset of this pagan lust-filled world. We have recently seen the results in the lives of a small number of priests in the Catholic Church who tried to live celibacy without struggling against the modern mindset that sees sex as primarily a thing for pleasure. And if you add on top of it homosexual inversion, you end up with an almost impossible situation in the life of the one ordained to serve God.[7]

The gifts of evangelical continence, consecrated virginity, and celibacy necessarily involve a conversion of the self and a grace-inspired ability to see members of the opposite sex as brothers and sisters in Christ and not as objects of pleasure. One who has this gift, and indeed all Christians, are called to compare with the gospel of Christ all sexual influences so that they can be purified and lifted up to the meaning that God has always meant them to have. When this is done, then the devil, who has claimed sexuality as a weapon to which he has no right, will be overthrown and his attempt to pervert the eternal significance of marriage will be defeated. The gifts of evangelical continence, consecrated virginity, and celibacy, when lived out fully in the lives of those given such graces, are living signs of the biblical truth that Christ the Bridegroom has truly come to call us to the heavenly wedding banquet.

CHAPTER EIGHT
The Sacraments of Penance and Anointing of the Sick

(I) Penance

The Need for Repentance

Beyond the deprivation of sanctifying grace inherited by virtually the entire human race as a result of Adam's Original Sin,[1] the majority of rationally competent adults in mankind's history have also been guilty of committing actual personal sins. We know this from common observation, and Scripture ratifies our conclusion. God's verdict about our plight is recorded in Romans 3:23, Ephesians 2:1-3, and 1 John 1:8, 10.

The Second Person of the Blessed Trinity became man to atone for humanity's transgressions against God's commands (both Original Sin and subsequent offenses), to make it possible for mankind to enter heaven, and to establish a kingdom of righteousness on earth, wherein the reign of sin would be ended. Jesus Christ Himself stated that this was the purpose of His redemptive act. He declared that His blood inaugurating the new covenant would be "poured out for many for the forgiveness of sins" (Matthew 26:28). An integral part of the "Great Commission" to His Church was "that repentance and forgiveness of sins should be preached in his name to all nations, beginning from Jerusalem" (Luke 24:47). St. Peter repeated these words to the Jewish officials who had arrested the Apostles: "God exalted him at his right hand as Leader and Savior, to give repentance to Israel and forgiveness of sins" (Acts 5:31). Moreover, in His personal apparition to Saul of Tarsus, Jesus told the former persecutor of the early Church that He was appointing him "to open their [the Gentiles'] eyes, that they may turn from darkness to light and from the power of Satan to God, that they may receive forgiveness of sins and a place among those who are sanctified by faith in me" (Acts 26:18).

So, according to Christ's own words, His vicarious atonement does not relieve us from the responsibility of repenting for our sins, seeking divine absolution, and amending our lives. Hence, we must be wary of misinterpreting such verses about "belief" as Acts 10:43 and John 6:40. Our "belief" cannot be a stagnant, slothful, empty, merely intellectual assent to the fact that Jesus Christ is our personal Lord and Savior. As He teaches in the parable of the two sons (see Matthew 21:28-31), those who act on their convictions and persevere in their commitment to follow Him are the ones who have a living faith. He identifies true belief with repentance and righteous deeds in His reprimand of the Jewish elders: "John came to you in the way of righteousness, and you did not believe him, but the tax collectors and the harlots believed him; and even when you saw it, you did not afterward **repent** and believe him" (Matthew 28:32, boldface emphasis added). St. Paul also speaks of "the obedience of faith" in Romans 1:5 and 16:26. Other scriptural passages that should prevent a misunderstanding of texts such as Acts 10:43 and John 6:40 include Matthew 7:21, John 3:36, John 14:15, and 1 John 2:1-3). These verses all stress conforming to God's will by obedience to His commandments.

In short, there is a practically universal need for repentance on account of our lapses in abiding by Christ's commandments.

Who Can Forgive Sin?

Now, there is no question about the power of Jesus Christ to forgive sin. As God, whom sin offends, He holds the primary authority to pardon sin. He gave a stunning public demonstration of this divine prerogative in the course of His cure of the paralytic (see Matthew 9:2-6; Mark 2:5-10; Luke 5:20-24).

The objection raised by many people (not only non-Christians and Protestants, but even some nominal Catholics), though, concerns the ability of certain men to forgive sins in the name of God. When confronted with the Catholic doctrine of the forgiveness of sins through auricular confession to a priest, they respond with the standard line: "Why should I confess my sins to a mere man, when I can go directly to God and feel forgiven?" This rejoinder attempts to bypass the entire sacramental system of the Church — the economy of salvation whereby God uses human beings as channels of grace.

But, lest this counter-response be dismissed as unbiblical question-begging on the part of apologists for a so-called "man-made" (or "Romanish") institution designed to oppress humanity, let us turn to the very words of the Church's Founder related to us in the Gospels:

> Jesus said to them again, "Peace be with you. As the Father has sent me, even so I send you." And when he had said this, he breathed on them, and said to them, "Receive the Holy Spirit. If you forgive the sins of any, they are forgiven; if you retain the sins of any, they are retained." (John 20:21-23)

In this passage, we behold our Lord delegating to His Apostles the authority to pardon or refuse to pardon sins. Since Christ did not necessarily endow them with the ability to read minds, the task with which he charged them tacitly assumes that a prospective penitent would tell them what his or her sins are. Thus, the Founder of the Church Himself instituted the practice of auricular confession of sins: it is not the invention of an allegedly corrupt, apostate church.

Christ's astonishing transfer of divine power to mortal men cannot be ignored; unfortunately, it is often downplayed or even dismissed. But it ought not be; indeed, it was already implicit in Christ's earlier promises to St. Peter (and, by extension, the other Apostles and their successors):

> "I will give you the keys of the kingdom of heaven, and whatever you bind on earth shall be bound in heaven, and whatever you loose on earth shall be loosed in heaven." (Matthew 16:19)
> "Truly, I say to you, whatever you bind on earth shall be bound in heaven, and whatever you loose on earth shall be loosed in heaven." (Matthew 18:18)

This control over entrance into heaven itself, which Christ said He would grant to His Apostles (and, by extension, their successors), implies jurisdiction over the route to heaven. Since a key condition of the heavenward journey is "repentance for the forgiveness of sins" (Mark 1:5; Luke 3:3), it is logical that Christ would later explicitly include in this generic "binding and loosing" the specific power to remit sins in His name.

Do Christians in general possess this all-encompassing power? Well, we are told to forgive others who have wronged us – indefinitely, so long as they continually and sincerely repent (see Matthew 18:21-22 and Luke 17:3-4). St. James even advises us to "confess your sins to one another" (James 5:16). And we know how the loving father of the prodigal son forgave his wayward child immediately upon the young man's return home (see Luke 15:17-24). Yet, beyond the forgiveness of our fellow human beings, we yearn for the assurance that God Himself has pardoned us. How can we verify that this has happened in the objective order of things, aside from a subjective inner sense of confidence (which may be elusive)?

It does not follow that an ordinary Christian has the authority to absolve sins *in the name of God*. Such power presupposes that the individual has been commissioned to act in the very person of Christ: in other words, that the individual has been ordained to a sacred office within the Church. Thus, the Sacrament of Penance is intimately associated with the hierarchical priesthood, whose primary function (as we saw in the previous chapter) is to offer *in persona Christi* the perfect sacrifice to God consisting in the non-bloody re-presentation or prolongation through time of our Lord's unique self-oblation on Calvary. Hence, the Sacrament of Penance looks toward the Holy Eucharist as a preparatory purification for partaking in Holy Communion:

> Whoever, therefore, eats the bread or drinks the cup of the Lord in an unworthy manner will be guilty of profaning the body and blood of the Lord. Let a man examine himself, and so eat of the bread and drink of the cup. For any one who eats and drinks without discerning the body eats and drinks judgment upon himself. (1 Corinthians 11:27-29)

Just as a priest alone can confect the Blessed Sacrament in the Holy Sacrifice of the Mass, so also only a priest can forgive sins in the name of the Lord: the two functions are inextricably linked. Two of the other Sacraments can be administered by laypeople: namely, Baptism and Matrimony. Although the ordinary minister of Baptism is a priest (or deacon), in an emergency a layperson can validly baptize. As for marriage, it is Catholic teaching that each Christian spouse confers the Sacrament of Matrimony on the other; however, the Catholic form of marriage requires adherence to the precept that a priest (or deacon) witness the ceremony. But the remaining five Sacraments (Confirmation, Holy Eucharist, Penance, Holy Orders, and Anointing of the Sick, as we shall see in the second section of this chapter) demand a priest for their performance (actually, Holy Orders necessitates a bishop).

We can discover in 2 Corinthians further scriptural evidence for the intrinsic connection between the hierarchical priesthood and the Sacrament of Penance. St. Paul says: "Any one whom you forgive, I also forgive. What I have forgiven, if I have forgiven anything, has been for your sake in the presence of Christ" (2 Corinthians 2:10). The *Revised Standard Version* translates the Greek "prosopon" (πρόσωπον) as "presence", as indicated here. But the *King James Version* renders the Greek term as "person". For the sake of consistency, the *RSV* should have done the same, because it translates "prosopon" as "person" in 1 Thessalonians 2:17. It is inexplicable that the *RSV* should have rendered the same word used by St. Paul in different ways in these two verses. At any rate, St. Paul refers to his act of forgiveness as being accomplished in place (whether the "presence" or the "person") of Christ — in the manner of a deputy or viceroy or vicar, we might say. Since St. Paul was a priest (indeed a bishop, as we saw in the previous chapter), this verse shows at least some superficial correlation between the priesthood and the Sacrament of Penance.

But we can establish a much stronger link by moving forward three chapters in the same Pauline letter:

If any one is in Christ, he is a new creation; the old has passed away, behold, the new has come. All this is from God, who through Christ reconciled us to himself and **gave us the ministry of reconciliation**; that is, in Christ God was reconciling the world to himself, not counting their trespasses against them, and entrusting to us the message of reconciliation. So we are ambassadors for Christ, God making his appeal through us. We beseech you on behalf of Christ, be reconciled to God. For our sake he made him to be sin who knew no sin, so that in him

we might become the righteousness of God. Working together
with him, then, we entreat you not to accept the grace of God
in vain.... We put **no obstacle** in any one's way, so that no **fault**
may be found with our **ministry**. (2 Corinthians 5:17-21; 6:1, 3,
boldface emphasis added)

We observe in this profound passage that St. Paul repeatedly associates
the notions of forgiving sin ("reconciliation") with the apostolic office
("our ministry"), in which he and his fellow priests "work together with"
Christ, serving as deputies ("ambassadors") for Him. Yes, God reconciles
the world to himself through Christ, but Christ works through His
ordained ministers to forgive sins. Moreover, the urgency of repentance
comes across in this vehement appeal: salvation can be lost if this grace
of God, which arrives through the Sacrament of Penance, is rejected.
This is the gracious "help" that God wills to give mankind: sacramental
medicine operating via other men.

St. Paul insists that he (and, by extension, every other faithful priest)
puts "no obstacle in any one's way" (6:3) for receiving the Sacrament of
Penance. Perhaps some people are reluctant to confess their sins to a priest
on account of shame or embarrassment. If a priest were to treat their
contrite acknowledgment of failings with anything other than mercy,
his unpastoral conduct would indeed be imputed to him as a "fault"
in his ministry. Since no priest wants to incur such guilt, it is virtually
assured that penitents will find no "obstacle" in priests for hearing their
confessions in peace. No trauma should accompany the reception of this
Sacrament.

A more serious danger is pride within the sinner. Perhaps that is
precisely why God has so disposed this sacramental arrangement. Pride
needs the spiritual antidote of humility to cure a basic sickness of the
soul – a sickness so deep that, absent this remedy, it blocks the very
possibility of salvation. Confessing one's sins interiorly to God is less of a
humiliation than confessing exteriorly (though still privately) to another
specifically designated human being who is also a sinner. By hearing
the priest's words of absolution pronounced over us, accompanied by his
sign of the cross over us, we experience with our bodily senses reliable
signs of the profound transformation that this Sacrament works in our
souls – whether restoring the lost state of sanctifying grace or increasing

grace through the removal of spiritual blotches. Thus, in His compassion for us creatures composed of soul and flesh, Christ has thereby granted us the means to know with moral certitude that He has pardoned our sins (see 1 John 1:9). But the channel of this special merciful grace is an ordained priest. Being the beneficiaries of this divine dispensation is infinitely better than relying solely on our own subjective feelings of trust that God has forgiven us.

Kinds and Degrees of Sin

We have so far been speaking of "sin" in general. But we must not get the idea that all sin is on the same plane. Just as the virtues can vary widely in kind and in intensity, so also can sins. In fact, St. John tells us:

> If any one sees his brother committing what is not a mortal sin, he will ask, and God will give him life for those whose sin is not mortal. There is sin which is mortal; I do not say that one is to pray for that. All wrongdoing is sin, but there is sin which is not mortal. (1 John 5:16-17)

What St. John says is logical and evident to common sense. Obviously, there is a vast difference – an essential difference in kind – between, for example, murder and stealing a candy bar from a store.

Murder is an example of a mortal sin. By usurping the divine prerogative over human life and death, the murderer has placed himself in radical opposition to God. No longer on friendly terms with God, he has driven the divine life of sanctifying grace from his soul. Unless this state of spiritual death is repented before physical death, it will cast the perpetrator into hell.[2]

This fundamental rupture between God and the human person does not occur in a lesser kind of wrongdoing, which the Catholic Church traditionally calls "venial" sin. When a venial sin is committed, the divine image in the soul is tarnished, but the person retains the state of friendship with God characterized by the presence of sanctifying grace.

Even within the domain of each broad category of sin, there can be large differences of degree along a spectrum of objective evil (see John 19:11, for example). Although adultery is a mortal sin, constituting a terrible betrayal of the integrity of marriage, it is far less grave and abhorrent than murder; indeed, "sins of the flesh" usually proceed from weakness rather than utter malice. On the other hand, although stealing a baseball cap from a store is a venial sin, it is more serious than taking a candy bar.

The upshot is that sin is not homogeneous in nature. A further complication is culpability. Not only must the objective matter of an act be discerned, but also the extent of the doer's knowledge and free consent of the will must be taken into account in assessing subjective guilt.

Because of the variability of sin, each kind of sin requires its own remedy. In the passage quoted above, St. John indicates the possibility that prayer for someone who has committed a venial sin may be immediately efficacious in maintaining that person's life of grace. God may accord the sinner the gift of remaining on the path to eternal life despite this sin. Although they do not bring about spiritual wreckage in themselves, there is always the danger that an accumulation of venial sins can so weaken the sinner's will that he eventually succumbs to a mortal sin. Hence, such prayer for pardon and the preservation of a strong spiritual life is not idle or superfluous. Furthermore, it follows from their very nature that venial sins do not have to be confessed in the Sacrament of Penance; yet, on account of their debilitating tendency, it is prudent to pursue this spiritual medicine, along with receiving our Lord in Holy Communion and engaging in works of charity, which "cover a multitude of sins" (James 5:20).

By contrast, intercessory prayer for the direct repair of mortal sin entails something impossible. Since the sinner has voluntarily severed his relationship with God, he himself must turn to God and plead for the grace of contrition, leading to confession of his serious sin in the tribunal of the Sacrament of Penance, where he will find assurance of pardon. Of course, the prayers of others can be offered that God will grant the mortal sinner the actual graces to cooperate by seeking pardon, conversion of heart, and amendment of life, but such prayers in and of themselves cannot restore the lost state of righteousness.

Can any sin whatsoever be forgiven? Christ told the Pharisees: "Every sin and blasphemy will be forgiven men, but the blasphemy against the Spirit will not be forgiven" (Matthew 12:31). What is the character of this blasphemy? Since the Holy Spirit is the "Spirit of truth" (John 14:17; 16:13), the unforgivable sin must consist in implicitly accusing the Holy

Spirit of lying. In consequence, the blasphemer obstinately resists the actual truth, self-deceptively pursuing the path of falsehood as though it were the right course. How does this work out in practice? One way is to invert the order between good and evil – calling good evil and evil good. Christ's declaration in Matthew 12:31 occurs precisely in this context: Jesus, who is wholly good, is accused of acting with the power of the Devil. If someone persists in this mentality of treating what is evil as good (and vice versa), he has blinded himself to both truth and goodness, and thus cannot be saved: "Woe to those who draw iniquity with cords of falsehood.... Woe to those who call evil good and good evil" (Isaiah 5:18, 20). Sin is, in practice, a falsification or denial of the true relation that ought to obtain between a rational creature and God. And someone who refuses to repent of a serious breach in this relationship, because he thinks that what is evil is actually good (or the reverse), is so far advanced in his hardness of heart that he does not possess the disposition to seek and receive forgiveness.

Catholic doctrine on the nature of sin, its kinds and degrees, as well as their manner of forgiveness, displays a brilliant logic that is firmly grounded in the Bible.

(II) Anointing of the Sick

Unlike the situation for the other six Sacraments, there is not a large quantity of scriptural evidence for the existence of the Anointing of the Sick as a distinct Sacrament. Nevertheless, there is one remarkable text that is decisive:

> Is any among you sick? Let him call for the elders of the church, and let them pray over him, anointing him with oil in the name of the Lord; and the prayer of faith will save the sick man, and the Lord will raise him up; and if he has committed sins, he will be forgiven. (James 5:14-16)

Here St. James explicitly links healing of sickness with prayer and anointing by "the elders (πρεσβυτέρους) of the church" using "oil" (ἐλαίῳ). The fact that the ministry of the presbyters (or priests) must be procured in order to secure the beneficial effects of this prayer and anointing proves that this service is an official rite of the Church – one probably present from the beginning. St. James would not have fabricated it, but must have received it directly from the Lord. Indeed, the precedent basis for this Sacrament in the apostolic ministry is evidently Mark 6:13: "They cast out many demons, and anointed with oil many that were sick and healed them." Thus, the Anointing of the Sick was established by Christ for the purpose of imparting grace in a time of dire illness. Since it employs outward signs (prayers and anointing), it satisfies the Catholic criteria for being a true Sacrament.

Some additional comments are relevant.

In the Old Testament, the priests had custody of the oil of anointing. This is explicit, for instance, in Numbers 4:16, but Nehemiah 10:37 also suggests this idea. Therefore, the oil of this Sacrament is not any common oil, but rather one specially blessed for this purpose and used only by priests.[3]

St. James mentions two kinds of healing: the physical cure of illness and the spiritual healing consisting in forgiveness of sins. The bodily healing, if it should occur according to God's will, seems to be foreshadowed in Psalm 23:5: "Thou anointest my head with oil, my cup overflows." This verse was fulfilled, at least partially, in Mark 6:13.

Regarding spiritual healing, we saw in the previous section of this chapter that only priests, as "other Christs", can pardon sins in the name of God. Hence, the Sacrament of Penance is intimately connected with the Sacrament of the Anointing of the Sick. This aspect of the Sacrament was probably not realized in Mark 6:13, because Jesus had not yet given His Apostles the power to forgive sins (as He would on the evening of Easter Sunday, as recorded in John 20:19-23). If someone is unconscious or otherwise unable to confess his sins, however, St. James seems to imply that the person will be forgiven even mortal sins, provided he is contrite. Of course, the obligation would remain to confess them later, if the penitent should sufficiently recover.

Perhaps in no other sacrament do we perceive the unfathomable mercy and compassion of God, manifested through the Church toward us sick sinners, as clearly as in the Anointing of the Sick. As Jesus advises us, "I counsel you to buy from me ... salve to anoint your eyes, that you may see" (Revelation 3:18; see also Tobit 11:7-15, where the fish prefigures Christ's sacramental healing unction). At the time(s) of our lives when perhaps we are most in need, we receive from Him, through the priests of His Church, this anointing that illuminates our souls with grace, enlightens our minds with truth, and may even cure our physical ailments.

CHAPTER NINE
The Sacrament of Matrimony

(I) Matrimony is a Sacrament

The Catholic Church holds that "[the marital] covenant between baptized persons has been raised by Christ the Lord to the dignity of a sacrament" (*Catechism of the Catholic Church*, n. 1601). Although this teaching is undoubtedly a part of that Sacred Tradition constituting one of the sources of God's revelation to mankind,[1] it does not appear explicitly in the words of Sacred Scripture.

The absence of an obvious proof-text enabled at least two of the founders of Protestantism to deny the sacramentality of Christian marriage. For example, in *The Babylonian Captivity*, Martin Luther wrote: "Not only is the sacramental character of matrimony without foundation in Scripture; but the very traditions, which claim such sacredness for it, are a mere jest.... Marriage may therefore be a figure of Christ and the Church; it is, however, no divinely instituted sacrament, but the invention of men in the Church, arising from ignorance of the subject." Similarly, John Calvin rejected the sacramental nature of marriage, asserting in his *Institutes of the Christian Religion* that "all admit [matrimony] was instituted by God, though no one before the time of Gregory regarded it as a sacrament. What man in his sober senses could so regard it? God's ordinance is good and holy; so also are agriculture, architecture, shoemaking, hair-cutting legitimate ordinances of God, but they are not sacraments."[2] It might seem a futile enterprise to attempt a biblical defense of Matrimony as a Sacrament truly established by Jesus Christ, when two leading luminaries of Protestant thinking scoffed at the notion as a "mere jest" grounded in "ignorance" and nonsense devoid of sobriety. Nevertheless, it is quite feasible to furnish an *indirect* scriptural proof that Christ willed His Church to celebrate marriage between His followers as a Sacrament. How? At least one way of doing so is by examining the context of the sacramental economy at work down through the history of God's covenants with man. Not only can we establish the *fittingness* of Matrimony as one of the seven Sacraments instituted by our Lord and Savior, but we can even demonstrate a greater biblical warrant for the sacramental status of Matrimony than for the opposing Protestant thesis – thus warding off the dismissive claims of Luther and Calvin.

The Sacraments and Covenantal Theology

There would seem to be a remarkable relation between the Sacraments and what might be referred to as "covenant moments" in salvation history.[3]

First, the Sacrament of Baptism is foreshadowed in the Abrahamic covenant recorded in Genesis 17:9-14. Indeed, St. Paul specifically connects this Abrahamic/Mosaic rite with Baptism in Colossians 2:11-12. Hence, God works in the human soul the elevation to the divine life of grace through circumcision (under the Old Law) and through Baptism (in the New Law) – the latter commanded by Jesus Himself in John 3:5 and Matthew 28:19.[4]

Second, our Lord instituted both the Sacraments of the Eucharist and Orders at the Last Supper, when He changed bread and wine into His own body and blood and then commanded His Apostles (including their successors) to enact the same rite (see Matthew 26:26-28; Mark 14:22-24; Luke 22:19-20; 1 Corinthians 11:23-26). Notice that the establishment of these two Sacraments occurred in a covenantal setting. In fact, every single institution narrative for the Lord's Supper (Matthew, Mark, Luke, Paul) employs the key words "my blood of the covenant" – with the last two emphasizing that this "covenant" (*diathekei*) is "new" (*kainei*). Indeed, the shedding of Christ's blood inaugurated a new covenant between God and mankind, a covenant to be remembered via an efficacious re-presentation in His Church through the action of His priests by their offering the Sacrifice of the Mass.[5]

Third, Christ instituted the Sacrament of Confirmation through His guarantee to send the Holy Spirit (see John 14:16-17, 26; 15:26; 16:7; Luke 24:49; Acts 1:4-5) – a promise that was fulfilled for the first time on Pentecost Sunday (see Acts 2:1-42). Although Scripture does not employ the term "covenant" (*diathekei*) at this point, the word "promise" (*epaggelia*) used in Luke 24:49; Acts 1:4; 2:33, 39 has unmistakable covenantal undertones and implications. Indeed, the Holy Spirit, who is called the "Counselor" (*Parakletos*) in John 14-16, is termed the "**promise of the Father**" in Luke 24:49 and Acts 1:4 (boldface emphasis added). In other words, the Holy Spirit is the *seal* of the New Covenant etched in Christ's blood, as St. Paul indicates in Ephesians 1:13 (boldface emphasis added): "In him [Christ] you also, who have heard the word of truth, the gospel of your salvation, and have believed in him, were **sealed** with the promised Holy Spirit". This explains why anointing with oil is the appropriate material sign for Confirmation – since oil, from the Bible's perspective, connotes sealing.[6]

Fourth, Christ instituted the Sacrament of Penance on the evening of Easter Sunday with a repeated greeting of peace, as reported in John 20:19, 21-23. This doubly reassuring proclamation of peace through the forgiveness of sins harks back to the Noahic covenant recorded in Genesis 8:20-9:17. Although the Flood itself foreshadows the cleansing from Original Sin that transpires only in Baptism (as St. Peter teaches in 1 Peter 3:20-21), the covenant of *peace* affirmed in its aftermath signifies the peace with God that reigns in the soul of anyone whose sins have been forgiven.[7]

Similarly, the purification of the earth after its watery deliverance from all wickedness can be viewed as prefiguring the healing of the soul (and perhaps the body, too) that takes place through the Sacrament of the Sick. It is interesting to note that, after St. James brings up this Sacrament in James 5:14-15, he immediately illustrates the power of healing prayer by the story of Elijah, who exhibited control over rainfall. The anointing oil used in this Sacrament has associations with both the dove and the olive leaf of Genesis 8:8-12 – two symbols of covenantal peace intimately linked with the Holy Spirit (see, for example, Mathew 3:16; Mark 1:10; Luke 3:22; John 1:32; 2 Maccabees 14:4).[8]

The Marital Covenant

After the above review matching important "covenant moments" in salvation history with six of the Sacraments in the Catholic Church, it would be surprising and evidently unfitting if Christ did *not* elevate marriage between a Christian man and woman to the level of a Sacrament. Truly, we can boldly venture further: if *any* of the "divine ordinances" mentioned above by John Calvin has the right to be considered a grace-giving Sacrament, it should be Matrimony! For in fact (unlike, for example, shoemaking) the Bible begins and ends its pages with the "divine ordinance" of marriage! Let us review the key passages.

In Genesis 1:27-28, upon the creation of mankind in the divine image, God Himself "performs" (as it were) a marriage ceremony between the first two members of their respective genders, blessing their fertility and charging them with dominion over the entire earth. In Genesis 2:18-25, we read the famous account of the primeval union between man and woman as husband and wife. Thus, Scripture most certainly begins with a human marriage somehow reflecting the vital unity of the three divine Persons (note the phrases "our image" and "our likeness").

We may also note that the theme of a marital covenant between God and His people occurs at several points in the Old Testament – especially in Isaiah 61-62, Jeremiah 2-3, and Hosea 4.

But it is in Revelation 19:7, 9; 21:2 where we witness the Church depicted as a Bride adorned for everlasting life with her Groom – our Lord Jesus, the Second Adam. This is the eschatological *Wedding* Feast that concludes Sacred Scripture.

It is well known that Christ's first public miracle took place at a wedding feast (see John 2:1-11). St. John tells us that our Lord's transformation of water into wine was "the first of his **signs** (*semeion*)" (John 2:11, boldface emphasis added). Moreover, St. Paul calls the bond between Christ and His Church a "mystery" that is mirrored in the human marital relationship (see Ephesians 5:32).

Let us now connect the dots. Six Sacraments, each of which imparts grace in its own particular way, correspond to "covenant moments" in salvation history. But the Bible features *marital* covenants at the beginning, the middle, and the end. Therefore, to say the very least, it is only fitting that marriage (the "covenant moment" *par excellence*) should likewise correspond to a Sacrament that bestows grace in its own unique manner.

It is precisely through the Sacraments that God delegates to mere human beings the authority and power to do what only He can do by right and in virtue of His omnipotence, thereby making men intermediaries for the communication of His grace in various ways. Christ commissioned the Church to baptize (Matthew 28:19), imitating what *He* did (John 3:22). He commanded His priests to offer the Eucharistic sacrifice, just as *He* did (Luke 22:19-20; 1 Corinthians 11:23-26). He authorized His priests to forgive sins (John 20:21-23), just as *He* did (Matthew 9:2-6; Mark 2:5-10; Luke 5:20-24; 7:48-49). Just as *He* sent His Church the promised Holy Spirit (John 14:16-17, 26; 15:26; 16:7; Luke 24:49; Acts 1:4-5), so likewise His ordained disciples later served as channels for conferring the gift of the Spirit in Confirmation (Acts 8:14-17; 9:17). Further, we can infer from James 5:14-15 the very same thing about the Anointing of the Sick – namely, that it was an obedient reenactment of what our Lord Himself did.

Note that in the six aforementioned Sacraments, material substances and physical actions (water, wheat bread, grape wine, olive oil, visible gestures, audible words) function as channels for the bestowal of grace. Yet God joined man and woman as husband and wife at the dawn of human history, decreeing that the two should become one *flesh* (see Genesis 2:24; Matthew 19:4-6) – a carnal bond so sacred that it can signify the union between Christ and the Church (Ephesians 5:32). Hence, by analogy, it is more than fitting that He should likewise empower His Church to ratify the "fleshly" conjugal union as a means of grace for the spouses involved.

At this point, someone may object that, contrary to Christ's enactment of the six aforementioned Sacraments, He never once "performed" a marriage ceremony. This, though probably true, is irrelevant. For Matrimony differs from the other Sacraments in a crucial way: unlike them, it is administered by the contracting parties themselves. Indeed, the priest or deacon officiating at a wedding does *not* "administer" the Sacrament but is simply a witness who *blesses* the union. And Christ undoubtedly *did* bless marriages whenever He was present – just as the three divine Persons blessed the marriage of our first parents in Genesis 1:28. It would be inconceivable to think that, in His infinite generosity, Jesus would refuse His blessing upon such a sacred sign (provided, of course, a wedding ceremony did not incur any invalidating impediments).

Jesus accorded inestimable prominence to marriage by working His very first public **sign** at a wedding (John 2:1-11). This miraculous event happened long before the equally wondrous multiplication of the loaves, which in turn prefigured the Sacrament of the Eucharist. Just as the eucharistic bread is a visible **sign** of Christ's *physical* Presence, which grants eternal life to those who partake worthily of it (see John 6:33,

35, 48, 50-51, 53-58), so also is Matrimony an external **sign** pledging Christ's *spiritual* presence in the lives of the marriage partners, endowing them with the grace to bear witness to His love for the Church by their love for each other and for any children they may procreate. Again, since marriage is a **sign** of the union between the Church and Jesus Christ, who is the source of all grace, it is only logical to deduce that He must have regarded marriage as a suitable **sign** for the transmission of grace according to the divine purpose in creating human family life.

All of the foregoing points to one immense fact. Matrimony really does satisfy the definition of a Sacrament: it is an outward sign instituted by Christ to give grace. However indirectly, the Holy Bible appears to teach that very truth.

(II) The Attributes of Marriage

Marriage, as a conjugal society relating man and woman, must be a monogamous and indissoluble union open to the procreation of children. Therefore, in this essay marriage will be discussed under the headings of conjugal society, monogamy, indissolubility, and procreation for the sake of family life.

Marriage as a Conjugal Society

There is a bumper-sticker that reads: "A woman without a man is like a fish without a bicycle." Now the author (presumably a woman) probably does see a natural connection between men and women, but is obviously angry (no doubt with reason), and so she denies that men and women have anything to do with each other. As Garrison Kiellor once said on his radio show, sometimes you have to look reality in the face and deny it. Still, the truth she opposes, that man and woman complete each other, is so beautiful and profound that it is hard to imagine she has seen beyond its surface. To borrow from her analogy, it is as if she noticed that fish are wet without ever appreciating that they are alive. Her statement, moreover, is especially jarring because it rejects a truth of the first magnitude and substitutes its opposite. It is like the Pharisees claiming that Jesus was not God but an evil man in league with the devil.

Most of us have small appreciation for marriage. We marry and our marriages bring us a measure of joy, but we don't understand what marriage is or why it is so good. Because we don't understand it, we don't know how to live a marriage when we are called to make decisions, and because we don't know how good it is, we talk about things like our divorces and contraceptive methods or even our inherently sterile sexual acts as if they were matters of light social conversation suitable for almost complete strangers. (In fact, the next time I'm working a concession stand at a little league game and someone tells me about the contraceptives they use, I'm going to ask about their hemorrhoids.) We don't know what is shameful anymore because we don't know what is good. A society that does not understand the goodness of its traditional ways or the goodness of God's ways will lose these blessings and be condemned to live without them. Unfortunately, today we find ourselves having to argue that stuff like same sex "marriage" is nonsense, like pairing a bicycle with a bicycle.

Let us turn from this babble back to the word of God, which has much to say about the true nature of the relationship between woman and man, and let us begin with the creation of Adam and Eve.

In Genesis 2:18, the Lord God says: "It is not good that the man should be alone; I will make him a helper fit for him." It is strange to hear God say that "it is not good" about something before sin enters the world, but He does say this in the passage above, right after He makes Adam from the dust of the ground. The world is clean of sin, with nothing messed up, yet God says that the man should not be alone. The man, of course, is not defective, but he *is* incomplete. Like any creature, he has needs. (If God had made fish but no food or water, the situation would be similar.) Specifically, Adam needs a companion, "a helper fit for him". So, God brings Adam some candidates: cats, dogs, birds. Maybe fish? God may as well have brought him a bicycle, because none of the animals He brings can be a true companion to the man. Perhaps this was simply God's way of teaching the man that he was indeed alone, because once Adam sees that nothing in the garden is like him, then his solitude can hit home. It is like being marooned on a deserted island; you are in fact alone the whole time, but you feel the true weight of your solitude only when you have explored the island and found no one.

So, after showing Adam his problem, God fixes it by making Eve, and she is a true companion. But God does not make Eve in the way He made Adam. Instead, He takes one of Adam's ribs and makes the woman out of that (see Genesis 2:21-22). The fact that Eve is not made independently out of clay as Adam was, but out of Adam himself, means of course that she is a natural part of him. And this is exactly Adam's conclusion (note the relief in his voice when he sees her): "This at last is bone of my bones and flesh of my flesh" (Genesis 2:23). She is part of him, and so he is no longer alone. But notice that God has completed Adam in a paradoxical way by making him less complete in himself, for Adam is now missing a rib. If the message was not clear before that Adam is incomplete, it is now. The man can only be complete by turning to the woman who has a part of him, or better, who *is* a part of him. The message is that man and woman are not whole, and in some ways they are not even wholes; they are parts of each other. Acknowledging one's incompleteness is a blow to pride, and pride is the prince of evil. Now, while it is not revealed to us why Satan rejected God, certainly pride played a part. One can imagine that the humility of being a creature, of not being God, of being incomplete, would be hard for Satan to accept. Similarly, Adam might well have stood on his pride and had a real problem with what God had done (completing him by making him less complete in himself). In his anger and to his own despair he might have refused God's gift by insisting that he needs the woman about as much as a fish needs a vasectomy. Happily, though, Adam received Eve with great joy and relief as the complement and companion that she was.

Scripture punctuates the lesson of this account of the creation of man and woman with an exclamation point by concluding that their relationship is so natural as to trump its closest rival: the relationship between a parent and child. Genesis 2:24 states: "Therefore a man leaves his father and his mother and cleaves to his wife." Father and mother give a man life, but they do not complete him. Only his wife can do this. The two unite into "one flesh". In marriage they become what they were meant to be: a complete human being.

The first creation account has something else to say about man and woman, but, before considering it, let us consider the very first words of the Bible and what they imply about the nature of God: "In the beginning God created" (Genesis 1:1). In the Hebrew the word for "God" (*Elohim*) has a plural form, but the word for "created" (*bara*) is singular in form, meaning "he created". There are different ways to explain this odd combination, but with Christian hindsight it is not hard to see how the grammar of the passage suggests that God must be a plurality of some kind united into a single being.

Now compare the verse: "So God created man in his own image, in the image of God he created him; male and female he created them" (Genesis 1:27). This sentence about man functions in a way similar to Genesis 1:1 in the Hebrew, and suggests the very same thing: "in the image of God he created *him* [singular]; male and female he created *them* [plural]" (emphasis added). The juxtaposition of this wording in the two passages suggests that a human being is a single thing, and that this thing is male and female by nature. Of course, individuals are one or the other, but man is both. Male and female is man. Each gender represents only one form, one incomplete expression of humanity and one that needs the other to be whole. It is perhaps the first case of the whole being more than the sum of its parts. Actually it is the second, the first being God himself; for, as we said, He is a single being (one God) who is at the same time a community of distinct Persons (Father, Son, and Spirit).

Now, it is hardly a coincidence that the focus or apex of the first creation account is precisely the revelation that God made man in His own image. God has made many wonderful things, but man is special; only he and she are in the very image of God. Does this mean that man has a soul, intellect, and free will, and is in God's image in those ways? Well, yes, but much more than this. It means that just as God can only be who He is by being a unity of persons, so a woman and man can only mirror the nature of God when they are a unity of persons. The union of man and woman is meant to be an earthly or creaturely expression of the inner life of God. That's what marriage is: an image of the inner life of God.

But what sort of union are we talking about in marriage? Physical? Spiritual? The answer is: all sorts of union, or all sorts applicable to human nature. This means physical (but not physical without affection and love), as well as spiritual (but not spiritual without the physical union of the two). For human beings are neither animals nor some sort of second-rate angels; they are not just bodies, nor are they souls in a body, but beings of both a physical and spiritual kind. Therefore, the union of man and woman is multifaceted: two minds that are of one mind, two bodies in physical union functioning as one complete body, two lovers with the same love of goodness, soul-mates and body-mates. Of course, they do not have to have the same favorite color, and one can say "po-tay-to", the other "po-tah-to". But those things are neutral.

Forms or aspects of union apply only to things that are genuinely good. Now "union" is a poorly understood concept. People argue sometimes that a condom, for example, thwarts the union of a couple because it prevents contact between them, as if contact were identical to union or sufficient for it. But suppose I try to poke my neighbor in the eye (because he has started to tell me about the condoms he likes) and he bites down on my finger and won't let go. There would be plenty of contact in this case, but no union of persons, no more than there would be if I had succeeded in getting my finger stuck in his eye (and didn't have these nasty scars). There is no coordination of functions here, no complement of parts into a whole. There is merely the incoherent sticking together of unrelated things. So it is with sodomy, and other kinds of inherently sterile sexual acts. The unity of incomplete natures into a whole often involves the coordination of function, as with a light bulb and its socket. These things are oriented toward each other by their natures, and so they are whole only when they are together. In fact, only together do they each function in accordance with what they are individually.

Friendship (i.e., a non-sexual relationship between two men or two women) is open to many dimensions of unity and is therefore a source of real joy. But it is an incomplete form of human relationship. Adding sex into this relationship (much like adding finger-biting) would not make it any more complete or unitive, but rather introduce an incoherent, destructive element. Even the relationship between a man and woman is damaged by sexual activity when the relationship is only a friendship.

Of course, the center-piece of the union of woman and man is love: that combination of affection and desire to be with a person for the rest of one's life which is the impetus behind a person's committing himself totally to an other. St. John tells us that God Himself, a mysterious union of Persons, "is love, and he who abides in love abides in God, and God abides in him" (1 John 4:16). When man and woman unite in love, they become a union of persons themselves and live the image of God. In some way we all understand that there is no union of persons without mutual love. Sex between a man and woman outside the context of love, in the absence of a desire for commitment, has a superficial coherence about it because of the physical aspect, but without love it is no more coherent or unitive than sex with a device, for without love the two are simply using each other as things, as biosex toys. If you treat a person like a thing, then you are related to him as a thing rather than a person.

Monogamy

Since the beginning, God has made covenants with man. Think of Noah (Genesis 6:18), Abraham (Genesis 15:17-18), Moses (Exodus 19:3-8), and the new and eternal covenant in Christ (Matthew 26:28; Hebrews 8:6-10; 9:15; 12:24; 13:20). Even Adam and Eve seem to be under an implicit covenant in the garden. You can't escape the impression that there is something very important about covenants. Unlike a contract, which is an agreement made with someone you may or may not care much about, except for the purpose of benefiting yourself, a covenant is a personal exchange whose purpose is to unite yourself to someone you unconditionally care about. It is an exchange of selves, not a deal for goods.

Marriage, of course, is a type of covenant, even the archetypical earthly covenant, and because it is so much more than a contract, infidelity to it is so much more grave and devastating. While certainly wrong, there is nothing appalling about cheating a customer, because there is no pretense or expectation of love. But to cheat on your spouse to whom you have pledged your life out of unconditional love is mind-boggling.

Scripture, fittingly, often uses marriage as an image for God's covenant with His people (take the book of Hosea, for example) and for Christ's relationship to the Church (see Matthew 9:15; Ephesians 5:23-33; Revelation 21:2). Like any lover, God tolerates no rivals. He expects fidelity and demands an exclusive relationship with the beloved. Ignorance could excuse the pagans from religious polygamy, but the Jews would not be excused. For much of their history they no doubt believed that there were other gods, but they understood "I am the Lord your God... You shall have no other gods before me" (Exodus 20:2-3) and why this was the first commandment of the law. But unlike God, who is faithful even when He is not legally bound to be, man is prone to infidelity, and Israel throughout her history readily broke the covenant by turning to other gods. The tablets of the covenant were practically just cooling down when Aaron was putting the finishing touches on the golden calf (see Exodus 32). In keeping with the similarity between marriage and God's covenant, the prophets commonly characterized the idolatry of Israel as adultery or prostitution (see Jeremiah 2:20; 23:10; Ezekiel 16:15; 23:35), and it provoked the strongest reaction from God. Israel had not just worshipped another god, but she had broken a covenant. Israel had "played the harlot" (Hosea 2:5).

Interestingly, God not only insists that His people have one God, but that He have one bride, one people, one Church. Of course there are distinct individuals within the Church, just as there are distinct communities of Christians: one at Corinth, one at Rome, some in Galatia, but St. Paul commonly calls them simply "the church of God" (1 Corinthians 1:2, 10:32; 11:16, 22; 2 Corinthians 1:1; Galatians 1:13; 1 Thessalonians 2:14; 2 Thessalonians 1:1; 1 Timothy 3:5, 15; Acts 20:28).

Just as Christ has only one Church for His bride (see Revelation 21:2), so also can each marriage partner have only one spouse.

There is a kind of "already, not yet" dynamic regarding the oneness of the Church, for in some ways the people of God already *are* one (see 1 Corinthians 12:27). But man is no less prone to schism and faction than he is to infidelity; and just as the Jews almost immediately broke the covenant at Sinai, the early Christians almost immediately split into factions (see Acts 15 and 1 Corinthians 1:10-16). Christ prayed at the Last Supper that His disciples would manifest the same oneness that exists between the Father and Him (see John 17:21). God will no more engage in polygamy Himself than He will tolerate it from us. That requires not only that we love Him alone, but that we (husband and wife) be one as He is. Marriage is therefore an exclusive covenantal relationship between one man and one woman.

Indissolubility

So how does divorce fit into all of this? In much the same way that death does – as a direct opposite to the nature of God. God is a unity of distinct persons. A divorce in God (were it possible) would be His utter destruction and with it the destruction of all things, of all goodness, of all joy. Of course, God's nature is not subject to divorce because there is no failure of love in Him. His nature as it exists in Him is unassailable, but His nature exists in us as well, and here it is vulnerable. Divorce is nothing less than an attack on the image of God in man. We know that death is a consequence of evil (see Genesis 2:17; 3:19; Romans 5:12-14). Coming from the God of life, we were not meant to die, but to have life and have it to the full (see John 10:10; Wisdom 2:23-24).

Likewise, we are not meant to form a union in the very image of God and then break it. Divorce is no less a consequence of evil than death, and it has no place in God's plan:

> And Pharisees came up and in order to test him asked, "Is it lawful for a man to divorce his wife?" He answered them, "What did Moses command you?" They said, "Moses allowed a man to write a certificate of divorce, and to put her away." But Jesus said to them, "For your hardness of heart he wrote you this commandment. But from the beginning of creation, 'God made them male and female.' 'For this reason a man shall

leave his father and mother and be joined to his wife, and the two shall become one flesh.' So they are no longer two but one flesh. What therefore God has joined together, let not man put asunder." (Mark 10:2-9)

"Every one who divorces his wife and marries another commits adultery, and he who marries a woman divorced from her husband commits adultery." (Luke 16:18)

Moreover, as St. Paul teaches us in Ephesians 5:21-33, the union between a husband and wife is like the union between Christ and His Church (see also Revelation 21:2). In other words, marital love is sacramental, since this human relationship signifies the christological-ecclesial wedlock. Just as the Lord Jesus will always remain faithfully espoused to His Church, so is a married couple indissolubly wed, each to the other. A failed marriage, then, is a tragedy of the first magnitude. And just as people die because of sin (the curse of original sin), so marriages fail because of sin.

Of course, no one has to or should live with an abusive person. Separating oneself from such a person to whom one is married is as legitimate as killing someone in self-defense. But in a true union where the two have exchanged a solemn vow out of love "for better or worse" and thus crossed over the interpersonal space separating them, there is no divorce. There is no way to delete the vow because things have gotten worse. And if the two made the *conditional* vow of "for better, but not worse", then they did not cross this space separating them, but kept each other at arm's length out or fear or some lack of love. There is no true union, no marriage to break here. Their relationship did not mirror the inner life of God anymore than if they had made a five-year commitment with the option to renew.

Procreation and Family

God is the source of new life, and this in two ways. In Genesis we see life pouring out of Him in the form of fish and birds and cattle and plants of every kind. We see that God is fertile, almost uncontainably so. And because He is love, it is easy to see how appropriate it is for new life to flow from Him. But somehow God is fertile within Himself too, for God is not just first, second, and third Persons of the Trinity; these Persons are specifically revealed as "Father" and "Son" and "Spirit of truth who proceeds from the Father" (John 15:26). Obviously, we are way over our heads in mystery here, but there is no mistaking the consistent, deliberate familial language God uses to reveal the relationships within the Trinity. The first Person is specifically "Father", and He is father of the "Son", who testifies that He too "proceeded and came forth from God" (John 8:42). Now, just as we tend to think of the Trinity as three gods (because it is much easier to understand), we tend to think of the three persons of the Trinity as siblings, much like the three fates in Greek mythology. We can imagine that they are distinct and related, but in a kind of horizontal way so that one does not come from another. They are all just there together. This does make the theology of the Trinity simpler, but it's simply not true. God uses the language of "father" and "son", and this language expresses a relationship of one person coming forth from another: "The living Father sent me, and I live because of the Father" (John 6:57). As the Christians at Nicea put it, Jesus is the "only begotten Son of the Father, God from God, light from light, true God from true God." This is what I mean by saying that somehow God is fertile even within Himself.

The fact that God has given us the power to bring new life into the world is not a mere necessity of the organism (like the ability to make or shed heat); rather, it is a further image of God in us. Just as life comes forth from Him because of His love and freedom and joy, so it can be with us. He has given us the power to beget new life, to bring forth our own kind, human beings from human beings. How fitting is the wonder in Eve's voice as she says, "I have gotten a man with the help of the Lord" (Genesis 4:1). And this new life is meant to come forth when woman and man out of joy freely unite into one as an expression of love, when they become a living image of God.

Now imagine tying one's tubes, or putting on a condom, or taking a pill, or putting in a barrier, or getting a shot every few months, or using a cream to kill sperm, or cutting off the flow of sperm. Imagine sterilizing ourselves so that we could not bring forth new life. In other words, imagine remaking ourselves, temporarily or permanently, so that life could not come forth from us. Imagine that life was fundamentally unwelcome. That would surely be a fallen world, a world in which God, God's image within us, was rejected. As in Eden, man would be making himself his own god by refashioning himself to better suit his desires.

These desires are obvious and easy to understand. It is almost too conspicuous to point out how sexual fantasy dominates our culture, our fashions, our entertainment, and our advertising. My favorite is the one about supercharging yourself to give you the sexual appetite and stamina of a tyrannosaurus. We look to maximize pleasure, which means minimizing or eliminating our ability to bring forth new life. And where is love in all this? We want, not the joy of God, but the lust of a beast. I can't help thinking of Romans 1:22-23: "Claiming to be wise, they became fools, and exchanged the glory of the immortal God for images resembling mortal man or birds or animals or reptiles." It is small wonder, then, that Christ could pray for us from the cross, "Father, forgive them, for they know not what they do" (Luke 23:34). We don't realize what we are doing. How could we and still do it? It is as if we only knew that sex is wet, without ever suspecting that it is sacred. When God blessed us in the beginning and said, "Be fruitful and multiply, and fill the earth and subdue it" (Genesis 1:28), He was telling us to be the living image of God on earth. We might paraphrase His command as: "Bring forth life, and bring it forth in abundance and with great joy. Be what I, your God, am and what I have made you to be."

God has given us an image of His own life through the union of man and woman, but it cannot be forgotten that this is an earthly image, and therefore something that falls short of the reality of God. We already saw that the earthly image is vulnerable to corruption when a marriage fails and it is necessary to separate, but God's image in man is also limited by the inherent limits of man and woman as creatures, and this in two main ways.

First of all, when we are young we can live out certain human potentials with ease because we have so much energy. As children we never think about budgeting our energy to get through all the running around we are going to end up doing in a day, because we don't have to. We are free, free to play basketball in the morning and tennis in the afternoon if we want. But as we get older, we run and do grow weary. We get to the point where we can't even go grocery shopping and to the library on the same day, because it's just too tiring. We are creatures, and our nature eventually shows its limitations.

A married couple is in a similar situation when it comes to children. As a young couple, we can simply live fertile lives if we want, bringing new people into the world without reckoning the costs, because we have the resources to take on whatever comes. It is a blessed time, more closely resembling the boundless joy and strength of God than any other. But since we are not God, this time cannot last. What is unchanging for Him is for us a season of our lives, a summer that gives way to autumn and finally winter. Gradually we become less capable of living God's image in a full earthly way because we are simply wearing out. Eventually the day comes when, for one reason or another, we are not well suited for giving life. We may still be capable of dragging ourselves up and down the court, but the joy has gone out of the game. It is then time for us to quit (see Ecclesiastes 3:1).

Now under normal circumstances, a couple's fertility wanes as their strength does. At thirty-five a woman's fertility drops sharply, so that, while she can still conceive and carry a child to term, she is less likely to. A couple in this situation may not ever have to make the heavy decision of whether to have any more children. They are like people who begin to tire as the sun is setting. The game ends when they can no longer play it. But there are circumstances that warrant the couple's quitting before the sun goes down. To take just one instance, suppose one or both of the spouses is sick or spent. How do they live at such times when they have a grave reason not to bring a new person into the world? Maybe now it is time to tie and cut tubes, to kill and block sperm, to take drugs to make the woman's body think she is pregnant when she isn't, or to irritate the womb so that life can begin but not survive.

Before addressing this directly, take a similar case. Suppose someone needs to lose weight for some serious reason. Should he look for some way to eat as much as he wants but without consequences? He could, for example, chew but not swallow, or vomit after eating, or eat a lot of stuff his body can't use, or take one of those carb-blockers to prevent his body from using most of the stuff he eats. He could also just eat less. In other words, instead of making the activity of eating senseless by perverting it, he could preserve its integrity and place in his life by controlling himself instead.

When it comes to sex the case is no different. If a couple shouldn't have a child for some serious reason, they should not have sex during those times of the month when they could have a child. Sex is holy ground. Instead of tampering with it so that they can engage in it whenever they want without consequences, they should modify their behavior in recognition of their respect for it. Sexual relations can still have a place in their lives, but simply not during fertile times. Even in the prime of life, fertility comes in cycles, and most days of the month a couple is not fertile. There is nothing inappropriate about having relations during those times even when the couple knows they are infertile. They did not remake themselves to be sterile or tamper with the act to avoid its natural consequences, but simply found themselves periodically incapable of giving life. The couple could forego sex altogether, but if they should not conceive a child, then they are called only to periodic abstinence, to not having sex when they can conceive a child.

Periodic abstinence, though legitimate for serious reasons, should not be seen as a kind of Catholic contraception, a loophole that allows Catholics who just don't want children to reject the life-giving dimension of their marriage. It is a little like killing in self-defense: legitimate under serious circumstances, but profoundly regrettable. It is something that a couple resorts to with a sense that the game has ended for them, a reminder that their world is broken, that their joy is incomplete.

Limits of Earthly Vocations

But human limitation goes in another direction also; for while man and woman do complement each other as human beings, only God can complete them as created beings. Man and woman are not just complementary forms of humanity, but also creatures who, coming forth from God, are radically dependent upon Him for their ultimate fulfillment. God is our lover and our beloved. And although many, but not all, are called to marriage on earth, everyone is called to union with God in heaven. Even those who are called to marriage are reminded by Christ that these unions pass away: "The sons of this age marry and are given in marriage; but those who are accounted worthy to attain to that age and to the resurrection from the dead neither marry nor are given in marriage" (Luke 20:34-35).

The fact that all are called to union with God helps put some of the harder realities of life into perspective. To take just a few cases, suppose a person is not called to marriage, is infertile, or suffers from same-sex attraction. It would be true to say that not all dimensions of earthly fulfillment are open to that person. It would be true to say that others have been given gifts that he or she has not. And at some point in wrestling with God, the person for whom these are real issues should probably confront God about this. Of course, there are countless other inequalities of life. Why, for example, are some people more musically or mathematically or aesthetically or culturally or athletically gifted than others? These are good questions, to which God will have to give each of us a measured, personal answer. But the point here is that these questions have to be seen in light of the gift He has given to all of us, that we are designed and made for eternal union with Him: "As a hart longs for flowing streams, so longs my soul for ... God" (Psalm 42:1).

Since we have this gift, it is hard to see ourselves as less loved by God because we were unmusical or infertile or not called to union in marriage with someone on earth. This is not to retract anything said earlier about how marital union on earth is a foretaste of the inner life of God. But just as man is made in God's image but is not God Himself, so marriage gives us merely an image of God's life, not that life itself. And the union we experience in marriage, holy as it is, is not ultimately the union we were meant for: "For in the resurrection they neither marry nor are given in marriage, but are like angels in heaven" (Matthew 22:30).

Still, nothing that was good or holy in marriage is lost in God, but rather perfected. Marriage gave us union with someone who completed us in a way; heaven is union with our Creator who completes us in all ways. Marriage gave us an image of God's life; God gives us this life itself. Marriage gave us a measure of joy; God's joy is measureless. Marriage was a union of love; heaven is a union with Love Himself.

The same sort of thing could be said about life. Human life on earth is a great good, but it is imperfect and ends because it is the life of a creature separated from God. But when it ends, it does not end completely; rather, it becomes a new form of life – life in God. They are both genuine forms of life. When a person dies he loses only what was imperfect about the life he had apart from God, but keeps whatever was the same. It is similar with marriage. Human union in marriage ends, but only to give way to union in God. The images of God give way to the realities in God. Whatever was imperfect, making these earthly unions less than their reality in God, passes away; but whatever was the same, making them images rather than counterfeits, remains.

It is easy to see that forms of union, love, and joy remain, but what of fertility? For a time (and like their Maker), men and women can bring forth new life, but does this pass away utterly? Surely, it does not pass away in God, whose life is not subject to seasons. In fact, in light of His love and joy, it is hard to imagine anything but a perpetual gift of creation pouring forth from Him. Could we participate in this life-giving aspect of God? There is an earthly precedent, one that stands at the very center of the Christian Faith. For God Himself was brought into the world through a mere human being, Mary. By the almighty power of the Lord, she participated in the coming forth of the God-man (see Luke 1:31, 35). Overwhelmed with this gift, she exulted, breaking forth in her joyous acclamation of divine praise called the *"Magnificat"* (see Luke 1:46-47, 49). If the Blessed Virgin could be taken up into the fecundity within the Trinity itself on earth, then perhaps we too can be taken up into it when we are taken up into Him.

CHAPTER TEN
The Intercession of Saints and Angels

(I) Catholic Devotion to the Saints in the Light of Jewish Scripture and Tradition

As a Jew who has gratefully entered the Catholic Church (which is really nothing other than the continuation of Judaism after the coming of the Messiah), I find it curious to see the objections that some non-Catholic Christians have to the Catholic devotion to the saints. For this, too, seems an organic continuation of Judaism, well supported by the Jewish scriptures as well as tradition. If Catholic devotion to the saints truly constituted a veiled form of idolatry, as is sometimes mistakenly suggested, than it should be more offensive to Biblical Judaism than to any other religious system, since it was the Jews who were given the honor of introducing to all of mankind the worship of the one true God, to the exclusion of all other gods or "idols", for the very first time in history. The rejection of idolatry is at the very heart of God's revelation to the Jews. There are over one hundred vehement prohibitions against idolatry in the Jewish scriptures, including, of course, the very first of the Ten Commandments (see Exodus 20:2-3). Jesus Himself names this as the most important – the "first and greatest" – of the commandments in Matthew 22:38. Other stringent prohibitions against idolatry also appear in Leviticus 26, Deuteronomy 29 and 32, Psalms 31, 97, 106, 115, and 135, and throughout the prophets Jeremiah, Ezekiel, and Hosea, and elsewhere as well.

So obviously if anyone should object to the veneration of the saints as a form of idolatry, it would be the Jews. Yet, profound veneration for saints permeates the very same scriptures in which one finds the prohibitions against idolatry. God even identifies Himself in reference to the greatest of the Jewish saints, the three Patriarchs Abraham, Isaac and Jacob (later renamed Israel). When asked by Moses who He is, He replies: "I am ... the God of Abraham, the God of Isaac, and the God of Jacob" (Exodus 3:6).

Abraham is considered the first and greatest of the Jewish saints, rightly held by the Jews in the highest veneration, because all of the blessings that God promised for all eternity for the Jews came to the Jews solely because they were the offspring of Abraham.[1] God swore to reward Abraham for his fidelity by showering blessings on his posterity. Pledging to reward Abraham's willingness to sacrifice his dearly beloved son Isaac, God also promised that through Abraham's descendants all nations on earth would be blessed (see Genesis 22:16-18). How could the Jews not hold Abraham in the highest veneration, since he was the sole source of the extraordinary blessings that they have received ever since? Not to do so would be the rankest ingratitude, as well as being a violation of the Fourth Commandment, "Honor your father and your mother" (Exodus 20:12), since the Jews are the "seed of Abraham". From a Christian perspective, there is a striking symmetry between Abraham's willingness to sacrifice his only legitimate, dearly beloved son on the top of Mount Moriah (Genesis 22:2) out of obedience to God, with God's later willingness to sacrifice *His* dearly beloved, only-begotten Son two thousand years later on the very same mountain top, then known as Calvary. The implication is inescapable that somehow, on a deep mystical/theological level, it was Abraham's fidelity to God that was reciprocated two thousand years later in the ultimate blessing that brought about the redemption of all mankind, giving Christians their own reason to be grateful to Abraham.

The same principles can be applied in understanding the Catholic veneration of the Saints. Let us take, as an example, the "greatest" (and most controversial) of the saints, the Blessed Virgin Mary. As the Jews owe Abraham veneration as the source of all of their blessings, certainly no less do all Christians owe Mary veneration as the source of all of *theirs*. For as it was Abraham's pleasingness to God that brought about the Jewish blessing, so it was Mary's pleasingness to God that enabled the greatest blessing known to mankind – the birth of God as Man, Jesus – to come about. Let us consider the moment when the Incarnation took place – the moment when Jesus was conceived in the virginal womb of Mary (see Luke 1:28-33). Clearly, according to the angel's words in this passage, the Incarnation of Jesus in the womb of Mary was not unrelated to her virtue, to her having found favor with God. As the blessings of the Jews were the result of the favor that Abraham found with God, the blessings of Christianity flow from the favor that Mary found with God. And as God's gift to the Jews came about because of Abraham's willingness to say "yes" to the sacrifice of Isaac (see Genesis 22:16), so did God's gift of *His* Son come about because of Mary's willingness to say "yes" to the Incarnation (see Luke 1:38). Mere common decency would demand that the Jews venerate Abraham, and the Christians Mary, if only out of gratitude for the blessings that they enjoy as a result of these saints' virtue.

In prayer, it is typical for Jews to refer to God as the "God of Abraham, of Isaac, and of Israel" (Jacob's name was changed to Israel in Genesis 22:38), much as God had named himself to Moses. This formula was used by the prophet Elijah (in 1 Kings 18:36), by King David (in 1 Chronicles 29:18), and by the prophet Hezekiah (in 2 Chronicles 30:6). It reappears constantly in the Jewish liturgy. Such a formula serves to indirectly remind God of how pleasing the Patriarchs were to Him, and asks Him to bestow blessings on those making the prayer as their descendants. This technique is sometimes explicit, as in the liturgy of the Jewish weekday Morning Prayer: "We are Your people, the sons of Your covenant, children of Your beloved Abraham, with whom You made a pledge on Mount Moriah. We are the seed of Isaac, Abraham's only son, who was bound upon the altar. We are Your firstborn people, the congregation of Jacob, whom You named Israel and Jeshurun because You loved him and delighted in him." (*Weekday Prayer Book*, Rabbinical Assembly of America, 1961, p.13.)

In a similar way, when Catholics name and honor Jesus as the son of Mary (e.g., "blessed is the fruit of thy womb, Jesus" in the "Hail Mary" prayer), they are reminding Jesus of the love and filial devotion that He had for His mother Mary, and laying claim to some of that special favor as her adoptive children. For Jesus gave Mary as adoptive mother to all of His "beloved disciples" from the Cross (see John 19:25-27). The Catholic who embellishes his prayers to Jesus with references to Mary is thus doing the same thing as the Jew who makes repeated reference to Abraham – reminding God of His special love for the named person, and laying claim to some of that love as his/her descendant. And since Abraham is the father of the Jews, and Mary the adoptive mother of every disciple of

Jesus, the respect shown to them is no more than the fulfillment of the fourth commandment: "Honor your father and your mother" (Exodus 20:12).

It also undoubtedly grates on some non-Catholics when they hear of Mary referred to as the "Queen of Heaven", as in the well-known Easter prayer the *Regina Coeli*: "Rejoice, Queen of Heaven, Alleluia! For He whom thou didst merit to bear for us, Alleluia! Has arisen, as He promised, Alleluia! Offer now our prayers to God, Alleluia!" (The Blessed Virgin Mary's stature as Queen of Heaven was formally defined by Pope Pius XII in the 1954 encyclical *Ad Coeli Reginam*.) Yet here, too, the role of Abraham in Judaism provides a parallel which can shed some light. At the time of Jesus, the Jews called their "heaven" the "bosom of Abraham" (this was, in fact, not heaven proper – which was inaccessible to mankind until Jesus descended to the dead after dying on the Cross – but a place of lesser happiness, bereft of the full blessedness which consists in the vision of God, and known in Catholic theology as the "Limbo of the Fathers"). It was to this "bosom of Abraham" that Jesus made reference in His parable about Lazarus and the rich man in Luke 16. If the blessedness of the "Jewish heaven" flowed from intimacy with the greatest of the Patriarchs, Abraham, how logical that the joys of the ultimate Heaven should flow, in part, from intimacy with the most perfect human being ever created, the Blessed Virgin Mary.

There is also another, more mysterious, way in which it is natural for me as a Jew to see the Blessed Virgin Mary as the "Queen of Heaven". In Judaism, the Sabbath is the summit of pre-Messianic life on earth, a kind of antechamber of Heaven, a foretaste of the life to come. And the Sabbath itself is seen, mystically, as a Virgin (i.e., bride) Queen – the Sabbath Queen. Each Friday evening the oncoming Sabbath is greeted with the following song/prayer:

> "Come, my Beloved.
> Let us welcome Sabbath the Bride, Queen of our days.
> Come, let us all greet Sabbath, Queen sublime,
> Fountain of blessings in every clime.
> Anointed and regal since earliest time,
> In thought she preceded Creation's six days.
> Arise and shake off the dust of the earth.
> Wear glorious garments reflecting your worth.

Messiah will lead us all soon to rebirth.
My soul now senses redemption's warm rays.
Awake and arise to greet the new light
For in your radiance the world will be bright.
Sing out, for darkness is hidden from sight.
The Lord through you His glory displays.
Then your destroyers will themselves be destroyed;
Ravagers, at great distance, will live in a void.
Your God then will celebrate you, overjoyed,
As a groom with his bride when his eyes meet her gaze.
Come in peace, soul mate, sweet gift of the Lord,
Greeted with joy and in song so adored
Amidst God's people, in faith in accord.
Come, Bride Sabbath; come, crown of the days.
Come, my Beloved.
Let us welcome Sabbath the Bride, Queen of our days."

Repeatedly throughout this prayer, there are parallels between the images of the Sabbath Queen and the Catholic understanding of the Blessed Virgin Mary as the Queen of Heaven. It is Mary who is the "fountain of blessings" – that is, the channel though which all of the graces won by Christ flow (as their ultimate divine Source). In thought, she preceded Creation, which is the justification for the Catholic identification of Mary with the personification of Wisdom in the deutero-canonical Book of Wisdom and in Sirach. Through her the Lord's glory of God is displayed, as sunlight through a flawless crystal. The destruction of her enemies was foretold in Genesis 3:15, a passage known as the "protoevangelium" precisely because in it Eve foreshadows the Blessed Virgin Mary. And so forth, throughout the prayer. And just as the Sabbath is the precursor and foretaste of the Kingdom of Heaven on earth for Jews, so is the purity of the Blessed Virgin Mary a precursor and foretaste of the perfection of virtue of the God-Man.

Another aspect of Catholic devotion to the saints that sometimes draws criticism is the typical attention Catholics pay to the bodies of "dead" saints. Yet, this form of devotion is also familiar to Jews and to the Jewish scriptures. Jews have continually venerated the burial site of the three Patriarchs, Abraham, Isaac, and Jacob, since their deaths about four thousand years ago. As Catholics make pilgrimages to the tombs of "dead" saints (sometimes enclosed in churches) to pray, so do Jews, both in Biblical times and still today. Today it is sometimes at the risk of their very lives, as a number have been killed praying there in recent years, yet they continue. Other tombs of Old Testament saints to which Jews go to pray include those of Joseph, Rachel, King David, and of the prophets Haggai, Malachi, and Samuel, all of whom have been venerated for millenia. We know that the tombs were held in great respect at the time of Jesus, for He Himself mentioned that the Jews "build the tombs of the prophets and adorn the monuments of the righteous" (Matthew 23:29).

Jews make also pilgrimage to, and pray at, the tombs of many post-Biblical Jewish "saints", too. These are typically the great Jewish rabbis of the past two thousand years, such as Rabbi Shimon Bar Yohai (credited with composing the great Jewish mystical work the Zohar in the 2nd century A.D.), Rabbi Yonatan ben Uziel (who, dying young and unmarried in the first century A.D., promised that whoever would pray on his tomb for a match would marry within the year), Rabbi Akiva (killed in the Bar Kochba rebellion of 132 A.D.), the great medieval Jewish scholar and rabbi Maimonides (d. 1205 A.D.), and on and on. Thousands of Jews from around the world visit these sites, year after year, to pray, make petitions, and pay their respects. No, although there were many new aspects that I had to get used to when I embraced the Catholic faith, praying at the tombs of saints was not one of them!

The Catholic use of relics, too, is sometimes accused of being "idolatrous" and "non-Biblical", but again it is well substantiated in the Old as well as the New Testament. How can one accuse a Catholic of being superstitious when he applies a relic of a saint to a sick person in the hopes of obtaining, with prayer, a healing, when in the Old Testament mere contact with the bones of the great prophet Elisha – *without* any prayer – brought a dead man back to life? Read 2 Kings 13:20-21:

> So Elisha died, and they buried him. Now bands of Moabites used to invade the land in the spring of the year. And as a man was being buried, lo, a marauding band was seen and the man was cast into the grave of Elisha; and as soon as the man touched the bones of Elisha, he revived, and stood on his feet.

Catholics are also sometimes criticized for praying to "dead" saints for their intercession; that is, praying for them to ask God for some special favor, relying on their relationship with God to obtain something that He might not grant the petitioner without such intercession. Yet the Old Testament is full of cases in which God granted special favors through the intercession of saints – favors that He would not have granted the petitioner directly. Well known examples include Abraham petitioning for God to spare Sodom if just ten righteous men could be found (see Genesis 18), Moses interceding with God not to destroy the Jews for their worship of the Golden Calf (see Exodus 32), and Elijah praying to bring a dead child back to life (see 1 Kings 17:17-24 and Sirach 48:1-6). In fact, Elijah is a particularly interesting example, because, according to the Scriptures, he never died, but went up to heaven alive (see 2 Kings 2 and Sirach 48:9), from whence he will return just before the end of the world (see Malachi 4:5-6 and Sirach 48:10). So the question is: If Elijah was willing to intercede on behalf of a petitioner before he was taken up to heaven, and his prayer was particularly effective, would he not be equally willing, and even more able, to intercede now that he is in heaven in the presence of God? He is not even dead! And it cannot be that he no longer has any interest in affairs on earth, because we know that he will return in the last days to "turn the hearts of fathers to their children and the hearts of children to their fathers, lest [God] come and smite the land with a curse" (Malachi 4:5). Of course, there is no reason why being dead should prevent any other saint from being able to do the same thing. After all, the human soul is spiritual and immortal.

We know that the Blessed Virgin Mary is both interested in, and effective in, asking her Son for special favors for others. Remember that, at the wedding at Cana, it was she who got Jesus to turn water into wine for the wedding feast, even though (apparently) He was initially unwilling to perform any miracle, since He had not yet begun His public ministry (see John 2:1-11). As we began with the Blessed Virgin Mary, so it is with her that we conclude. As she led others to Jesus at Cana when she pointed to him and said: "Do whatever he tells you", so it was she who led me to her Son Jesus, even before I had any interest in, or sympathy with, the claims of Christianity. Although the story of my conversion is too long to go into here, the conversion began with an unintended visit to a Marian shrine, and culminated with Mary's appearance in a dream.

Thus it would be the rankest ingratitude for me not to acknowledge the role she played, to thank her for her intercession, and to pray, in the spirit of the Old Testament reliance on the intercession of the special friends of God, the saints, that she, the greatest of all the saints, make use of her unique relationship with God and the resultant intercessory power to bring us all – Catholic and Protestant, Christian and Jew – closer to her Son, our Lord Jesus Christ.

(II) Why Do Catholics Pray to Saints? An Explanation from the New Testament

Introduction

Catholics look strange! At least I think so, and I've been one since I was two weeks old. We kiss relics, talk to the dead, and bow down and burn incense before images. When you grow up with these practices, they seem perfectly natural. It isn't until you exhibit Catholic behavior in front of the politely raised eyebrow of a non-Catholic friend that you realize you have some explaining to do. According to St. Peter, this is not a bad thing; it is a challenge (see 1 Peter 3:15).

Catholic practices are not only strange to outsiders; they are scandalous. Such notables as John Calvin, Martin Luther, and Dr. Ian Paisley speak for evangelicals when they accuse the Church of making things up – or worse, practicing things expressly forbidden in the Bible. To these learned men, Catholic devotion to the saints, with its accompanying bits of bone and blood, is hard evidence of pagan deviancy. To Catholics, it is part of the immense spiritual treasury of authentic Christianity. In this essay I will attempt to show evidence that the Bible supports these Catholic practices.

This section of the chapter is supposed to focus on the New Testament, but I can't resist mentioning 2 Kings 13:20-21, which tells a favorite story from the Old. No doubt, the man who was restored to life upon contact with the bones of Elisha had some explaining to do when he got home that night. Strange, indeed! Then again, God's ways are strange to us, as Isaiah 55:9 states. The Bible is full of such things as these, which are unfit for polite society – some might say, scandalous. The brutal life-giving Cross is the crown of them all.

Controversy about prayer to Saints

Early in the history of Christianity, various sects condemned seeking the intercession of saints. The Catholic Church, in her turn, rose to defend the practice. Later, the foremost Protestant founders made it a key issue.

Luther's teachings were summed up in 1530 in the Confession of Augsburg, which still serves as the doctrinal summary in many Protestant denominations: "But the Scripture teaches not the invocation of saints or to ask help of saints, since it sets before us the one Christ as the Mediator, Propitiation, High Priest, and Intercessor." (Article 21, *Of the Worship of the Saints*)

Due to his differences with Luther on the nature of the Eucharist, John Calvin signed a modified version of the Confession of Augsburg later. In his own work, the *Institutes of the Christian Religion*, he treats the subject of praying to saints extensively and with fire:

> Moreover, we have shown that this is ignorantly transferred to the dead, of whom we nowhere read that they were commanded to pray for us. The Scripture often exhorts us to offer up mutual prayers; but says not one syllable concerning the dead. (*Institutes*, Vol. 3, Part 23)

And still today, Dr. Paisley continues this mode of thought:

> It is a pure invention of man or rather of Satan and wholly unwarranted in Scripture. It ignores the precious truth that Christ has come in the flesh and that in Him we have a High Priest who can be touched with the feelings of our infirmities; it is fitted to lead sinners away from Christ the only Mediator; and it is gross idolatry. (*A Concise Guide to Bible Christianity and Romanism*)

To sum up these objections, the idea of the intercession of saints is not found in Scripture, it offends against the unique mediatorship of Christ, and diverts prayer from God to creatures. If this is what Catholics are doing, I too say it is condemnable. To find out, let us get into the Catholic mind.

Just what do we think we're doing?

My religious education started as I lay in my cradle. As soon as my eyes could focus, they took in a portrait of a saint hanging on the wall. It was St. Thérèse of Lisieux, a French Carmelite nun who died in 1897. Her expression was mild; she had a bit of a Mona Lisa smile about her lips. She held a crucifix and a bouquet of roses.

As I grew, I learned a little about St. Thérèse. She had a secure middle class childhood, a two parent home, a bunch of siblings, and a dog – she was like me. Later, when I read her autobiography, I found out she had been an irksome crybaby. Hmmm, me too.

At age fifteen, she entered a Carmelite monastery and became a contemplative. This meant that she would give up the world and give herself to Jesus completely: "O Divine Word! You are the Adored Eagle whom I love and who alone attracts me!" (*Story of a Soul, the Autobiography of St. Thérèse of Lisieux*) From inside the enclosure she spent the rest of her short life in prayer and sacrifice. (My husband could tell you what it is like trying to get along with a bunch of women – we have five daughters.) She gave back to God in an offering of love all the sufferings that God sent her. It is a way of taking up the Cross and following Him. The Church calls it "the Little Way".

Through union with Jesus, she wished to pray for the salvation of others. This desire stayed with her at her death when she said she wished to "spend heaven doing good on earth". That is the meaning of the roses – they are spiritual favors (graces) she would send those who asked her help, or, to put it in Catholic phraseology, "prayed to her".

Christ is in the picture of St. Thérèse. He is depicted on His cross at the moment of the Redemption. She is holding Him close to her in an embrace. The Church holds her up as someone for today's generation to imitate. What does the Bible say about that? Well, St. Paul calls his fellow Christians to imitate *him* (see 1 Corinthians 4:16-17). A true Christian is one who not only *believes in* Christ but also *imitates* Christ. Most of us understand that we are not called to live in the Middle East, sleep out of doors, and preach from town to town – as Jesus did. It is, rather, the meaning of His life that we are to imitate: His humility, obedience, charity, and so on. All of us do this according to our state in life. This is where the saints come in. They are Christians who have gone before us and set the example. The idea is that St. Thérèse, as a middle-class girl, imitated Christ in her Little Way. If I imitate *her*, I imitate *Christ*.

Who are these Saints?

The key question is: who are these "saints"? The word "saint" ("*hagios*" in Greek) literally means "sanctified" or "holy". Nowadays, in Catholic jargon, the term "saint" usually refers to the blessed in heaven. Sometimes we use it to describe a living person who strikes us as particularly holy, as in: "Your grandma is such a saint!" Dr. Paisley says, "All who believe savingly on the Lord Jesus Christ are saints." Well, I do and I'm Catholic. Am I in? If not, then does he care to change his statement?

St. Paul uses the term "saints" in many places to address his fellow earthbound Christians. (In particular, see Acts 26:10; Romans 1:7; 8:27; 12:13; 15:25, 26, 31; 16:2, 15; 1 Corinthians 1:2; 6:2; 14:33; 16:1, 15; 2 Corinthians 1:1; 8:4; 9:1, 12; 13:13; Ephesians 1:1, 15, 18; 2:19; 3:8, 18; 4:12; 5:3; 6:18; Philippians 1:1; 4:21-22; Colossians 1:2, 4, 12, 26; 1 Thessalonians 3:13; 2 Thessalonians 1:10; 1 Timothy 5:10; and Philemon 1:5, 7.) Moreover, he asks these "saints" to pray to God for him. He also pledges his prayers for them (see 2 Corinthians 13:9). The Gospels are full of instances of divine favors (graces) obtained through the pleading of others. Jairus pleaded for his daughter's life (see Mark 5:22-23 and Luke 8:41-42); the centurion asked for healing for his servant (see Matthew 8:5-7 and Luke 7:2-3); the Mother of Jesus petitioned her Son to help the hosts of the wedding feast at Cana (see John 2:1-11).

Dead people need not apply?

As seen at the beginning of this essay, Luther and Calvin agree that there is biblical precedent for Christians to pray for one another *while living*, but they claim to find nothing in Scripture that supports the intercession of "dead" saints. To their objection, I respond, with Christ, that the saints are *not* dead! Jesus testifies that the three patriarchs are not dead at all, but are living:

> "And as for the resurrection of the dead, have you not read what was said to you by God, 'I am the God of Abraham, and the God of Isaac, and the God of Jacob'? **He is not God of the dead, but of the living.**" (Matthew 22:31-32, boldface emphasis added)

It was the faithless Jews who claimed that the saints were dead (see John 8:52).

In addition, God granted the disciples a vision of two of the greatest prophets with Christ in His glory (see Matthew 17:1-8, Mark 9:2-8, Luke 9:28-36). If God thought that attention given to saints would detract from His act of Redemption, He would not have featured Moses and

Elijah in the Transfiguration. And I dare say He would not have made the following astonishing event happen:

> The tombs also were opened, and many bodies of the saints who had fallen asleep were raised, and coming out of the tombs after his resurrection they went into the holy city and appeared to many. (Matthew 27:52-53)

In the book of Revelation, it is clear that the blessed in heaven pay regard to the things of earth. For example, see Revelation 18:20.

Thus, from Scripture it is evident that the blessed are alive in heaven. Catholics believe that their prayers are much more effective than the prayers of those who are still on earth, since they see God in the face. If "the prayer of a righteous man has great power in its effects" (James 5:16), this must be true of the saints to the highest degree.

The Saints are witnesses to Christ and share His power

Just as Jesus was unjustly sentenced to death by the testimony of false witnesses, so, in the opposite direction, the saints testify to the truth about Him (see Acts 1:8). St. Stephen was the first blood witness after the Redemption. Since his time, countless others have followed.

Furthermore, the saints (those who live lives of faith in Christ) have a large share in His power (see John 14:12). In Matthew 11:11, Jesus attests to the greatness of St. John the Baptist during the prophet's lifetime. St. John is now in heaven. Reflecting on the parables of the faithful servant, we can only imagine how great is his power now (see Matthew 24:46-47).

It is Catholic teaching that all that the saints do and all the power that they have comes through Christ's name (see Luke 10:16). For instance, Christ cures through Peter in Acts 3:7-8. This commission to act in accordance with His name is given to us, as well as to the first disciples, in Matthew 5:16.

Christ's work through the saints is mighty – so great that, as Christ testifies, certain of the blessed are destined to take part in the final judgment (see Matthew 19:28; 12:41-42). Likewise, St. Paul and St. Jude declare that the just will take part in judgment.

Do you not know that the saints will judge the world? And if the world is to be judged by you, are you incompetent to try trivial cases? Do you not know that we are to judge angels? How much more, matters pertaining to this life! (1 Corinthians 6:2-3)

It was of these also that Enoch in the seventh generation from Adam prophesied, saying, "Behold, the Lord came with his holy myriads, to execute judgment on all, and to convict all the ungodly of all their deeds of ungodliness which they have committed." (Jude 14-15)

This does not contradict the scriptural doctrine that all judgment of souls is reserved for Christ. It simply means that the blessed will witness and approve His judgment over corrupt flesh and wicked spirits.

Jesus Himself testifies to the greatness of His followers. Their fidelity is an important part of the gospel. For instance, He praises aloud the faith of the centurion and the guilelessness of Nathaniel (see Luke 7:9 and John 1:47). There is also the passage in which he grants everlasting fame to the repentant woman: "Truly, I say to you, wherever this gospel is preached in the whole world, what she has done will be told in memory of her" (Matthew 26:13; see also John 12:26).

The Church has granted immortal fame to many saints since then. Why? First, for the glorification of God; second, for an example to the faithful; and third, in remembrance of them.

Why not just pray to God directly?

We can and we do pray directly to God. But then again, one might inquire, why did St. Paul ask his fellow Christians for prayers, instead of just praying to God directly for himself? Why get others in on it? After all, God knows what we suffer.

Here is why. It is a supreme act of charity to pray for another person. It is also the supreme act of community. When we pray for one another, we are knit together spiritually. This is God's intention for mankind. The root of this practice is the "Communion of the Saints". This phrase is found in the Apostles' Creed, which Catholics recite and which is used in many Protestant denominations as well. In the Catholic understanding, the communion of saints spans the generations. It includes the souls of the faithful on earth, in heaven, and in purgatory.[2]

Christ founded a Church. Much as Catholics believe in and nurture a personal relationship with Jesus Christ (especially through the Eucharist), we believe we are saved together within the Church. Christ is the Head, and we are the members of His mystical body. In Hebrews 11:39-40, St. Paul testifies to God's plan that the Church be communal. He is referring in this passage to the heroes of the Old Testament, who waited until the Redemption to be perfected with those who chronologically came after Jesus. For the same reason, we believe that the whole of mankind will be judged collectively at the end of time. Why does God insist on the communal aspect of His Church? God Himself is a community – the Holy Trinity. Jesus, in the mystical Gospel of St. John, proclaims unity with the Father and asks for the same unity for us (see John 17:20-22).

Consider again the book of Revelation:

> And when he had taken the scroll, the four living creatures and the twenty-four elders fell down before the Lamb, each holding a harp, and with golden bowls full of incense, which are the prayers of the saints. (Revelation 5:8)
> And another angel came and stood at the altar with a golden censer; and he was given much incense to mingle with the prayers of all the saints upon the golden altar before the throne; and the smoke of the incense rose with the prayers of the saints from the hand of the angel before God. (Revelation 8:3-4)

Calvin claims that the saints referred to in the two previous passages are not the blessed in heaven, but the faithful on earth. To show the strong probability that, in fact, the blessed are indicated, note the following verse that comes between these cited passages:

> When he opened the fifth seal, I saw under the altar the souls of those who had been slain for the word of God and for the witness they had borne; they cried out with a loud voice, "O Sovereign Lord, holy and true, how long before thou wilt judge and avenge our blood on those who dwell upon the earth?" (Revelation 6:9)

Therefore, these saints who pray about earthly matters have experienced bodily death, although they are spiritually alive in heaven.

But Calvin maintains that, although the "dead saints" may well pray for the coming of God's Kingdom, they are in no wise distracted with the particular cares of men:

> They, with one fixed and immovable will, long for the kingdom of God, which consists not less in the destruction of the ungodly than in the salvation of believers. But though I grant that in this way they pray for us, they do not, however, lose their quiescence so as to be distracted with earthly cares: far less are they, therefore, to be invoked by us. (*Institutes*)

Catholics don't believe, either, that the blessed "lose their quiescence". God sees our sins and these offend Him, yet He is mysteriously happy at all times. The blessed share in this happiness, despite the fact that they observe us closely (with all our joys and sorrows): "We are surrounded by a great cloud of witnesses" (Hebrews 12:1). *In a sense, therefore, the blessed are in our midst.* So Calvin's conclusion does not follow. Instead, the aforementioned passages from Revelation show that the saints' work continues in Paradise.

But didn't St. Paul condemn the idea of using any other mediator than Christ? We read: "For there is one God, and there is one mediator between God and men, the man Christ Jesus, who gave himself as a ransom for all" (1 Timothy 2:5). St. John supports the same idea: "But if any one does sin, we have an advocate with the Father, Jesus Christ the righteous" (1 John 2:1). These passages, however, refer to the Redemption itself: note the words "ransom" and "sin". If they condemned intercessory prayer, no one would be permitted to pray for anyone.

Look at 1 Timothy 2:5 once more. For Jehovah's Witnesses, couldn't this same verse be said to support their claim that Christ is a creature and not truly God? It indeed seems to make a distinction between God and Jesus − one of many scriptural passages leading them to deny His divinity. But Catholics revere the Book too much to risk muddling up God's doctrines by our own misinterpretations.[3] We must agree with the cautious warnings that St. Peter issues in 2 Peter 1:20 and 2 Peter 3:15-16.

Calvin states that we Catholics "are filled with anxiety, as if ... Christ were insufficient or too rigorous" to approach directly. He also states that, without mentioning the saints, "Papists think there is no prayer." Not so. We pray to Him directly again and again at Mass, our central and highest act of worship: "Lord have mercy on us and save us. Protect us, O God, by your grace" (from the Byzantine Rite Mass). Before even discussing the Catholic attitude, it is necessary to listen to the facts about what we really believe.

The Saints do not detract from Christ

Calvin claims that giving honor to saints detracts from Christ. I find it interesting that, for partial proof, he quotes St. Augustine:

> *Contra Parmenian, Lib. ii. cap. 8*: Likewise in another passage Augustine says, "If thou requirest a priest, he is above the heavens, where he intercedes for those who on earth died for thee." (*Institutes*)

But Augustine is also on the record as saying:

> A Christian people celebrates together in religious solemnity the memorials of the martyrs, both to encourage their being imitated and so that it can share in their merits and be aided by their prayers. (*Against Faustus the Manichean*)

Is Augustine contradicting himself? No. His thinking is in accordance with the Church: namely, that the Mediator of Redemption is Jesus alone (he mentions His death), but the mediators of intercession are many. It is Catholic doctrine that Christ's Redemption is the only thing that establishes the New Covenant between God and man. It alone expiates sin and gives grace. Anyone who prefers the saints to Christ offends against the First Commandment and breaks with Catholic teaching.

Once I was challenged to point out the faith of old ladies who kneel in front of Mary statues, mumbling and weeping over their beads. The challenge was an echo of Calvin:

> I say nothing of the more monstrous specimens of impiety

in which, though detestable to God, angels, and men, they themselves feel no pain or shame. Prostrated at a statue or picture of Barbara or Catherine, and the like, they mutter a Pater Noster. (*Institutes*)

I can only say that all the old ladies I've ever known who have made themselves look like fools this way have done it for Christ. To them it is no contradiction to love Christ's mother or His friends. *He* certainly loved them.

Whenever we see Christ with His disciples, we see Him conferring power on them for His sake. He wants their glorification. It adds to *His* glory! St. Thérèse's spiritual writings are centered on a deep affection for Christ. See her and forget *Him*? Impossible.

Statues and pictures of saints

How about statues and other pictures representing saints? How does this Catholic practice square with Exodus 20:4-5? In this passage, the Lord forbids making graven images. It is true that Catholics actually bend over and kiss images – and, yes, even burn incense in front of them. Paganism rehashed?

Pagans had the illogical notion that they were actually kissing a real deity – even though moments before it had been in the back of a delivery truck, hot off the smithy's cast. Catholics have no such notion. Idol worship is against the First Commandment. The use of images to worship the true God, however, is not. Actually, God Himself commanded that "cherubim of hammered gold" be engraved as adornments on the Ark of the Covenant (see Exodus 25:18-22; 37:7-9).

Early Christians left images of Christ and symbols of the Redemption (such as Jonah's whale) on the walls of the catacombs. These taught the basics of the faith back when most of the world was illiterate. They also lifted the heart to holy things. Let's face it: the setting the first Christians worshipped in was more likely to remind them of the netherworld than of heaven. Catacombs are dark, dank, narrow mazes of tombs. The early Christians would have been the first to distance themselves from anything that reeked of paganism, and so it is important to note that they did use images.

Today, images are used across the denominations. We erect nativity scenes in our homes, outside of churches, and, in fewer instances, in public squares. Many times, I have even seen images of the Reformers in Protestant churches. A rosetta window with Luther's visage in the center is in a church in downtown Allentown where I live. Years ago I came upon a relief of Luther, Calvin, and Zwingli on the exterior of a pink stucco church in Buchs, Switzerland. These examples are reminiscent of the Catholic urge to depict our beloved patron saints. It is perfectly natural and good.

A gentleman once complained to me about a statue of the Madonna and Child with the statement: "She's so big and he's so small." My response, after a pregnant pause, was well thought out and highly intellectual: "Huh?" I was momentarily stumped. Finally, I understood he was saying that we pay more attention to her than to Him. That's not the point at all! The point is there was a time in Christ's life when He was so small that His mom could pick Him up – and we think it a rather endearing image.

Catholics plant kisses on images of saints as tokens of spiritual devotion. Call us sentimental – but don't call us pagan. In our house, St. Thérèse's picture was a lot like the photo of my grandmother that my mom hung in the hallway. Grandma was about four hundred miles away and we didn't want to forget her. St. Thérèse was a century before my time. What did it matter? Both were part of the Catholic family, which we call the "Communion of the Saints".

Relics

Now we come to the strangest of all Catholic practices regarding the saints – relics. For the most part, Catholics keep them as precious objects that once belonged (some of them intimately) to a holy person. It's a very human trait: that of keeping things that belonged to our loved ones.

According to Acts 19:11-12, objects were used when the sick could not travel to see St. Paul in person: "God did extraordinary miracles by the hands of Paul, so that handkerchiefs or aprons were carried away from his body to the sick, and diseases left them and the evil spirits came out of them." In Acts 5:15-16, even such a non-substantial entity as St. Peter's mere *shadow* (never mind cloth items such as kerchiefs or aprons) sufficed to cure the sick. The Chananite woman was likewise sure that she would receive a miraculous healing upon contact with a physical article associated with Christ: "If I touch even his garments, I shall be made well" (Mark 5:28; see also John 20:5-7 in light of the long history concerning the burial cloths of Christ). So there is scriptural precedent for Catholic veneration of relics.

Admittedly, Catholics have been known to go overboard on the practice. An overly zealous noble woman once bit off the toe of St. Francis Xavier, since no one would give her a piece of him and she was used to getting her own way. At least that's one I've heard and, unfortunately, believe. (They say madness runs in those families.) We do not, however, as Dr. Paisley claims, possess "the tail of Baalim's ass" or "the feather of St. Michael". Nor do we give relics "formal and public worship" as to the Sacred Host or altar. We do celebrate Mass on an altar stone that contains the relics of saints. This practice has a sensible origin, dating back to the catacombs, where the first Christians offered Mass on the tombs of their beloved martyrs.

That said, Catholics have made and continue to report plenty of downright dubious cases of signs and wonders attributed to saints and their stuff. The Church herself has never sanctioned these, and, after investigating, has declared some of them false. For the Church to keep track of all instances of blood reportedly oozing from plastic statuettes is unreasonable. Church membership is rather huge. So, it is the job of the faithful to use common sense. When the Church does authenticate any miracle, such as the cures at the shrine of Lourdes, she does so after every doubt has been scientifically removed.

Catholics continue the traditions of the first Christians. We are body as well as soul. When a person is a saint, we believe his body is as holy as his soul — so much so that he will receive it back again, glorified, at the end of time.[4] The early Christians brought this reverence for the body to western civilization. Rather than burn their dead as the pagans did, they buried their dead. In the catacombs, they wrote beautiful epitaphs, which may still be read, for example: "To Cartilius Ciriacus, most sweet son, that you may live in the Holy Spirit."

The Angels

The angels are also alive in heaven and have much to do with us. In Scripture, God manifests Himself through these creatures in the earthly lives of men. He sends Gabriel to the Blessed Virgin and to Zechariah. An angel stirs the waters of the healing pool of Bethsaida. Angels are players in man's eternal destiny: "And he will send out his angels with a loud trumpet call, and they will gather his elect from the four winds, from one end of heaven to the other" (Matthew 24:31). We also read about guardian angels: "See that you do not despise one of these little ones; for I tell you that in heaven their angels always behold the face of my Father who is in heaven" (Matthew 18:10-11). After his conversion, St. Paul calls himself a Pharisee in that he believes in both resurrected spirits and pure spirits (see Acts 23:6, 8).

Why does God give angels such a prominent place in the lives of men? It certainly isn't because He can't gather us up from the four winds Himself. It isn't because He can't protect His own children. It is because He willed it, plain and simple. I believe King Lear said it best. Every King has his court. *O, reason not the need!*

St. Paul clearly condemns the adoration of angels, however. Colossians 2:18 is often used against the Catholic position. In fact, the angels themselves condemn it, for instance in Revelation 19:10; 22:8-9 when St. John tries to give the angel worship. Likewise do Catholics condemn the adoration of any creature.

What we do believe, as evidenced in the Bible, is that the angels are active in our spiritual lives. Why should not the saints in heaven be? Christ says they are! While on earth St. Paul labored ceaselessly for the conversion of the nations – to the point that he poured out his own blood as witness to Christ. What happened to him when he went to live with the Redeemer? Here is what our Lord says (in Matthew 25:23) happens to the faithful servant: "Well done, good and faithful servant; you have been faithful over a little, I will set you over much; enter into the joy of your master."

This verse is about the death of the holy. The day of reckoning has come. Certainly there is no unfinished business in heaven, but there is plenty on earth – and the saints maintain active interest in human affairs:

> He who conquers and who keeps my works until the end, I will give him power over the nations, and he shall rule them with a rod of iron, as when earthen pots are broken in pieces, even as I myself have received power from my Father. (Revelation 2:26-28)
> Also I saw the souls of those who had been beheaded for their testimony to Jesus and for the word of God.... They came to life, and reigned with Christ a thousand years.... They shall be

priests of God and of Christ, and they shall reign with him a thousand years. (Revelation 20:4-6)

God is Love

God, in His infinite generosity, creates and redeems us. He does not need us. In countless instances, however, He wills his creatures, whether angels or men, to be His instruments. He has chosen to bind us to one another in the spiritual community that is His Church. Why? For love's sake. He gives us a connection with our fellow Christians, including those who see His face in heaven. When we pray to saints, it is to unite ourselves to these holy ones in prayer to God. It is an act of spiritual community.

As a sojourner in a sinful world that continually tempts me away from God, I rejoice as a Catholic with St. Thérèse: "I believed, I felt there was a heaven and that this heaven is peopled with souls who actually love me, who consider me their child." (*Story of a Soul, the Autobiography of St. Thérèse of Lisieux*)

CHAPTER ELEVEN
Marian Dogmas

A ll that Catholics believe of Mary of Nazareth has some basis in Holy Scripture, and hence can be defended by invoking the Bible. This chapter will attempt to present the most accurate picture possible of Mary, the Mother of our Lord Jesus Christ, in the hope that the reader may discover this brave, humble, and holy woman for who she really is and open his heart to welcome her into his life. After all, in giving her as a mother to the beloved disciple, St. John, who already had his own biological mother, Christ also made her our spiritual mother (see John 19:26-27).

If the reader allows the light of Scripture to guide his faith, very soon his heart will be speaking as well. For what child is not grateful and loving towards his mother (as Jesus would have expected nothing less from the beloved disciple)? What soul would not erupt in joyful praise before the beauty and glory of such a creature (as the angel in his praise of Mary, which was indeed the praise of God Himself)? What follower of Christ would not take her into his own heart?

Mary, the Mother of God

Mother of Christ, Mother of God

From all eternity, God had in mind the unique role of Mary in salvation history. Speaking to the Serpent, God said: "I will put enmity between you and the woman, between your seed and her seed; he shall bruise your head, and you shall bruise his heel" (Genesis 3:15). Since Jesus Christ is the one who would crush the head of the Serpent and conquer the kingdom of Satan (see Colossians 2:15), He (the principal protagonist in the drama of mankind's salvation) is the woman's "seed". The Lord God foretells here the advent of a "woman" who, in having this divinely given enmity with the Serpent, would be the mother of the promised Redeemer, the serpent-head-crusher. Since Eve had just sinned by listening to the Serpent, it is not she to whom the passage refers; rather, this "woman" is Mary, the mother of Jesus.

The use of the word "seed" when referring to a woman is unique, for "seed" (rendered *"spermatos"* in the Greek) is obviously applicable only to the male gender. But "seed of woman" is used here to indicate that the Redeemer would have no earthly biological father; in other words, He would be the Son of God Himself. Hence, the "woman" would be the Mother of God.

Of course, it does not necessarily follow that the serpent-crusher *must* be of divine nature, since divine justice would demand that a creature (the Serpent) should most fittingly be crushed by another creature. This creature would be Mary. In fact, many would argue that, in the curse uttered by God against the Serpent, there are two creatures being addressed – the Serpent and the "woman". Thus, it is conceivable that the actual serpent-crusher is the "woman" who is empowered by her divine Son to crush. This line of thinking is seen in the Douay-Rheims Bible, which follows the Latin Vulgate, which in turn follows the Septuagint.

Next, let us contemplate the angelic annunciation to Mary of the conception and birth of Christ in Luke 1:31-33, 35. In this passage, the angel Gabriel informs Mary that the very same individual who will become her real son is already the Son of God. Upon hearing the angel's words, Mary must have immediately associated them with the great promise given by God to King David when he was informed that it would be his son who would build the temple in Jerusalem (2 Samuel 7:13-14): "He shall build a house for my name, and I will establish the throne of his kingdom for ever. I will be his father, and he shall be my son. When he commits iniquity, I will chasten him with the rod of men, with the stripes of the sons of men." Clearly, the immediate promise was for the building of the temple via Solomon, but the true fulfillment of the promise was realized in Christ, who was "chastened" with "stripes", having shouldered *our* "iniquity" (see Isaiah 53:4-12; 2 Corinthians 5:21). The fact that the Messiah's throne would be everlasting indicates a divine characteristic, and one can already see that Mary was singled out to be the mother of this Messiah with the divine characteristic of eternal kingship.

But to conclude with complete certainty that Mary is indeed the mother of God, we need to review the next passage, taken from the infancy narrative in St. Luke's Gospel:

> When Elizabeth heard the greeting of Mary, the babe leaped
> in her womb; and Elizabeth was filled with the Holy Spirit
> and she exclaimed with a loud cry, "Blessed are you among
> women, and blessed is the fruit of your womb! And why is this
> granted me, that the mother of my Lord should come to me?"
> For behold, when the voice of your greeting came to my ears,
> the babe in my womb leaped for joy. And blessed is she who
> believed that there would be a fulfilment of what was spoken
> to her from the Lord." (Luke 1:41-45)

The phrase "blessed are you among women" can be understood to mean
"you are most blessed of all women". Why is Mary "most blessed"? St.
Elizabeth, inspired by the Holy Spirit, states the reason: Mary is "the
mother of my Lord". Just in case we may think that the "Lord" referred
to in verse 43 is just some high dignitary, we are informed in verse 45
that the Lord referred to is in fact *God*. Now, we can safely conclude that
Mary is indeed the Mother of God.

Note that in Matthew 2:11 the wise men "saw the child with Mary
his mother, and they fell down and worshiped him." In recognizing
His divinity (symbolized by gold, one of their gifts), they implicitly
acknowledged Mary's divine maternity.

Finally, St. Paul tells us: "When the time had fully come, God sent
forth his Son, born of woman, born under the law, to redeem those who
were under the law, so that we might receive adoption as sons" (Galatians
4:4-5). The Apostle implies that Mary, the mother of the Redeemer, is
the Mother of God. She is the one through whom "the Word became
flesh and dwelt among us" (John 1:14).

Thus, the title "Mother of God" derives from Catholic teaching on
the Incarnation of the Word, with these passages as the scriptural basis
for this teaching. Mary conceives and brings forth, in His human nature,
the Second Person of the Holy Trinity, one who is God from all eternity.
Jesus is not God by the fact that he is conceived or born of Mary – this
would not be a mystery but an absurdity, because it would make Mary
mother of the divine nature. Mary is Mother of God because from her
own flesh she gave to the Word a human nature like hers. And just as in
ordinary human generation the terminus of the parents' generative action
is not the human nature produced but the person subsisting in this

nature, so in the case of Mary: her maternal action reaches to the Person of the Word, who by this very fact is truly her son. Mary is *"Theotokos"* (the "God-bearer", as pronounced at the Council of Ephesus in 431 A.D.), because "the Word was made flesh" (John 1:14) in her and through her. The formula is simple: Jesus is a divine Person, and this Person is God. Mary is Jesus' mother, so Mary is the Mother of God. (Mary is not just the Mother of Jesus' human nature – mothers are mothers of persons, not natures.)

Mary is Mother of the Savior in a sense much deeper than when we say of a woman that she is the mother of a priest or a president of a nation. The fact of being a priest or president of a nation does not result from the generative action of the parents but from a call, a consecration, or an election, which affects a subject already "humanly" constituted. The same is true of a "hereditary" title, bestowed in virtue of juridical determinations that are completely extrinsic to generation as such. This is not the case here. The engendering to which Mary was called, with all the spiritual and physical resources of her being, could not but produce the Mediator *par excellence*, whom she for her part was instrumental in constituting as such (by her consent, according to Luke 1:38). This also indicates the depth of the association that exists here between Mary and the Holy Spirit, who alone was capable of realizing in her such a wonder.

The reality of the Divine Motherhood explains the human and supernatural perfection of Mary. It is the only case in which a son was able to "fashion" his mother as he wanted her to be. This Son is all-powerful. He could not but prepare for Himself a mother worthy of Him, a "worthy Mother of God", totally devoted to her exceptional vocation.

When the Blessed Virgin freely said "yes" to the plans revealed to her by the Creator, the divine Word assumed a human nature (with a rational soul and a body) that was formed in her most pure womb. The divine nature and the human nature were united in a single Person: Jesus Christ, true God and, thenceforth, true man – the only-begotten and eternal Son of the Father and, from that moment on, the true Son of Mary. This is why Mary is the Mother of the Incarnate Word, the Second Person of the Blessed Trinity, who has united our human nature to Himself forever, without any confusion of the two natures. The greatest praise we can give to Blessed Mary is to address her loudly and clearly by the name that expresses her very highest dignity, upon which rests all her other attributes: "Mother of God".

Mary is also our Mother

In John 19:26, as Jesus died on the cross, He made Mary the Mother of us all, by saying: "Behold, your mother." Jesus did not say: "John, behold your mother", because He gave Mary to all of us, His beloved disciples. All the words that Jesus spoke on the cross had a divine purpose. Jesus was not merely telling John to take care of His mother; this would make Jesus a negligent son who had not made provisions for His own mother, thereby violating the fourth commandment. But since Jesus could not sin, the explanation of providing for His own mother is not available in His case. We must go more deeply to see the significance of this utterance.

From Genesis 3:15 and Revelation 12:1-6, we observe that the Scriptures begin and end with the "woman" battling Satan (the "serpent" or the "dragon"). But in John 2:4 and John 19:26, Jesus called Mary "woman," signifying that she is the "woman" of Genesis 3:15 (and consequently Revelation 12). His terminology of address teaches us that Jesus and Mary are the new Adam and the new Eve, and hence our new "parents" in the spiritual order. Just as Eve was the mother of the old creation, so Mary is the mother of the new creation. Since *this* woman's "seed" would crush the Serpent and *his* "seed" (the Devil is the "father of lies" according to John 8:44), those who are "of the truth" and "hear the voice" of Christ (John 18:37) are subordinately included under the woman's "seed". In other words, Mary is the Mother of all the disciples of Christ.

Indeed, Revelation 12:17 proves the meaning of John 19:26. The "woman's" (Mary's) "offspring", who are assailed by the dragon, are those who follow Jesus (i.e., "who keep the commandments of God and bear testimony to Jesus"). We are her offspring in Jesus Christ, and she is our Mother. The master plan of God's covenant love for us is the family. But we cannot be a complete family with the Fatherhood of God and the Brotherhood of Christ without the Motherhood of Mary.

In John 2:3, Mary, acting as our mother, tells all of us to do whatever Jesus tells us. Furthermore, Mary's intercession at the marriage feast in Cana triggered Jesus' ministry, because He granted her request. This marriage feast is a foreshadowing of the Eucharistic celebration of the Lamb – a celebration uniting all believers into one family through the marriage of divinity and humanity.

When we call Mary "our Mother", we grasp instinctively the essential meaning of the title, since it evokes memories of a human experience that is universal and runs deep. But when it comes to explaining clearly and precisely the content of the title, the matter requires further elaboration. Here are some fundamental characteristics of Mary's motherhood.

It is in and through service to her Son that Mary, during her life on earth, first exercised her maternal activity toward us. Mary's spiritual motherhood is coextensive with her service to Jesus the Savior. Everything she did for Him and with Him concerns us in our life as children of God.[1]

Mary continues to live today her spiritual motherhood. This motherhood of Mary in the order of grace, which began with the consent she gave at the Annunciation and which she sustained without wavering beneath the cross, will last until the eternal fulfillment of all the elect. Taken up to heaven, she did not lay aside this salvific duty, but by her constant intercession continues to bring us the gifts of eternal salvation. The purpose of Mary's maternal activity is to unite us with Christ so completely that each may say: "It is no longer I who live, but Christ who lives in me" (Galatians 2:20), so that Christ may be "all in all" (Colossians 3:11)

Mary's maternal function toward us is entirely the fruit of Christ's saving action; it flows from it and depends on it in everything. In other words, it does not diminish the unique mediation of Christ, but rather shows its power.

Mary conceived the Word of God in her heart and flesh by the power of the Holy Spirit who overshadowed her (see Luke 1:35). It is by the same power of the Spirit, soul of her soul and life of her life, that she attains the spiritual fecundity that makes her our Mother. We can't forget that Mary spent nearly every day of her life just like millions of other women who look after their families, bring up their children, and take care of their houses. Mary sanctifies the ordinary, everyday things – what some people wrongly regard as unimportant and insignificant (everyday work, looking after those closest to us, visits to friends and relatives, etc.). What a blessed ordinariness, that can be so full of love of God!

Mary, Conceived without Original Sin

Full of Grace

In Luke 1:28, the angel Gabriel delivered a message from God to Mary, greeting her with the words: "Hail, O favored one (*kecharitomene*), the Lord is with you." The *KJV* translates the Greek *"kecharitomene"* as "highly favored", whereas the *RSVCE* renders the term as "full of grace". The literal Greek phrase "full of grace" (*pleires charitos*) is used in John 1:14 and Acts 6:8 to refer to Jesus and to St. Stephen, respectively, but the only place in Scripture where the term *"kecharitomene"* is employed is Luke 1:28, referring to Mary. The connotation is that Mary is so thoroughly engraced that *"kecharitomene"* is her primary title of address, designated by God through Gabriel – as opposed to a mere factual description. It is true that Christ is called "full of grace", but this means in His case that He is actually the *Source* of all grace: "From his fulness have we all received, grace upon grace" (John 1:16) [see also John 1:1-4, 12; 14:6]. The crucial distinction lies in the fact that Mary is the *recipient* of grace, having had the fullness of grace *bestowed* on her, whereas Christ, even in His human nature, was *not* a recipient of grace. At any rate, such a unique and noble title for Mary, implying a perfection of grace from a past event, suggests that she had no share in contracting the defect of Original Sin.

This conclusion is corroborated by Luke 1:46, wherein Mary claims that her "soul magnifies the Lord". This is a bold statement from a young Jewish girl from Nazareth. Yet, since it is inspired scripture, it is a trustworthy testimony to her uniqueness. But what soul could "magnify" (*megaluno*) the Lord in the deepest sense except one unsullied by the taint of sin?

At both the beginning and the end of the Bible (Genesis 3:15 and Revelation 12), we encounter the "woman" and the Serpent-Dragon engaged in spiritual combat. From John 2:4 and John 19:26, we know that the "woman" is the Mother of the Redeemer. The profound hostility between this Mother and Satan proves that he never had any dominion over her; in other words, Mary was preserved from any enslavement to his power via the sin infecting the rest of the human race. The verses of Revelation 12:13-16 show that the Devil still seeks to destroy the woman even after the Savior is born. This proves that Mary is a danger to Satan, even after the birth of Christ: "Who is this that looks forth like the dawn, fair as the moon, bright as the sun, terrible as an army with banners?" (Song of Solomon 6:10)

The Immaculate Ark of the New Covenant

There is a remarkable parallel between certain narratives about the ark of the covenant in the Old Testament and narratives about Mary in the New Testament. Let us consider some excerpts from 2 Samuel 6:

> David arose and went with all the people who were with him from Baale-judah, to bring up from there the ark of God, which is called by the name of the Lord of hosts who sits enthroned on the cherubim. And they carried the ark of God upon a new cart, and brought it out of the house of Abinadab which was on the hill; and Uzzah and Ahio, the sons of Abinadab, were driving the new cart with the ark of God; and Ahio went before the ark. And David and all the house of Israel were making merry before the Lord with all their might, with songs and lyres and harps and tambourines and castanets and cymbals. And when they came to the threshing floor of Nacon, Uzzah put out his hand to the ark of God and took hold of it, for the oxen stumbled. And the anger of the Lord was kindled against Uzzah; and God smote him there because he put forth his hand to the ark; and he died there beside the ark of God. (2 Samuel 6:2-7)
> And David was afraid of the Lord that day; and he said, "How can the ark of the Lord come to me?" (2 Samuel 6:9)
> And the ark of the Lord remained in the house of Obed-edom the Gittite three months; and the Lord blessed Obed-edom and all his household. And it was told King David, "The Lord has blessed the household of Obed-edom and all that belongs to him, because of the ark of God." So David went and brought up the ark of God from the house of Obed-edom to the city of David with rejoicing; and when those who bore the ark of the Lord had gone six paces, he sacrificed an ox and a fatling. And David danced before the Lord with all his might. (2 Samuel 6:11-14)

As the ark of the Lord came upon the city of David, Michal ... saw King David leaping and dancing before the Lord. (2 Samuel 6:16)

(The chapters 1 Chronicles 13, 15-16 give another account of the same story.)

St. Luke makes conspicuous comparisons between the ark and Mary. In Luke 1:39, "Mary arose and went with haste into the hill country, to a city of Judah." Similarly, in 2 Samuel 6:2, "David arose and went ... to bring up ... the ark of God." In Luke 1:41, 44, John the Baptist "leaped for joy" in the womb of his mother Elizabeth when he heard the arrival of Mary. Similarly, in 2 Samuel 6:5, 14, 16, David was "leaping and dancing" before the ark of the Lord. In Luke 1:43, St. Elizabeth asks: "And why is this granted me, that the mother of my Lord should come to me?" This echoes a corresponding question that David asked about the ark of the Lord in 2 Samuel 6:9. Finally, Luke 1:56 states: "Mary remained with her [St. Elizabeth] about three months" – a time of great blessing for Zechariah and Elizabeth. In like manner, 2 Samuel 6:11 (as well as 1 Chronicles 13:14) reports a three month stay for the ark, during which the hospitable household was blessed.

When these parallel verses are lined up and compared, the conclusion is convincing and undeniable: Mary is the Ark of the New Covenant. Moreover, just as the ark of the Old Covenant bore earthly manna (see Exodus 16:32-33; Hebrews 4:9), so also did Mary give birth to the Heavenly Manna or Bread of Life (see John 6:33, 35, 41, 48, 50, 51, 58) in Bethlehem, the City of David and House of Bread (see Luke 2:4-7). And just as the ark of the Old Testament also contained the tablets of the Mosaic Law (see Exodus 40:20; Hebrews 4:9), so also did Mary carry in her womb the New Moses, giver of the New Law (see Matthew 5-7).

But what does this Marian title have to do with the Catholic dogma of the Immaculate Conception? Everything. In 2 Samuel 6:3-7, the ark is so holy and pure that when Uzzah simply touched it, the Lord slew him. By this event, God intended to impress upon the Israelites that the ark was untouchable. By analogy, Mary, the Ark of the New Covenant, is spiritually undefiled, spared by God from the touch of all sin, and in particular from the stain of Original Sin. In order for Christ to dwell within Mary the Ark, Mary *had* to be conceived without sin. To argue otherwise would be to say that God would let the finger of Satan touch His Son made flesh. This is incomprehensible.

Here are some further elaborations. In Exodus 25:11-22, the ark of the Old Covenant was made of the purest gold for the word of God's Law. Now gold is a symbol of God (see Job 22:25). Since Mary is the Ark of the New Covenant, she must have been the purest vessel for the Word of God made flesh. It follows that she must have been unblemished by sin. According to Song of Solomon 4:7, which in a spiritual sense applies to Mary, "You are all fair, my love; there is **no flaw** in you" (boldface emphasis added).

Let's look at Revelation 11:19. At this point in history, the ark of the Old Covenant has not been seen for six centuries (see 2 Maccabees 2:4-7), and now it is finally seen in heaven. The Jewish people would have been absolutely amazed at this. However, St. John immediately passes over this fact and describes the "woman clothed with the sun" in Revelation 12:1. (Remember that Revelation 11:19 and Revelation 12:1 are tied together, because there was no chapter-verse subdivision of the Bible at the time when these texts were written.) John is emphasizing that Mary is the Ark of the New Covenant, who reflects the glory of the Sun of Justice, Jesus Christ. She is therefore clothed with His righteousness: i.e., immune from the darkness of sin.

The Curse of Eve?

An objection might arise about Revelation 12:2 in connection with Genesis 3:16. Some Protestants argue that, because the "woman" had "birth pangs" (Revelation 12:2), she was a woman with sin, like the fallen Eve (see Genesis 3:16). First of all, it does not necessarily follow that, if Mary had felt pain in childbirth, she must have been tainted with Original Sin. It is theoretically possible that God, with the consent of Mary, could have allowed her to suffer what other women endure. But this does not seem to be what actually happened, as will be explained below.

Now, with regard to Eve, the fact that God said He would "greatly multiply your pain in childbearing" (Genesis 3:16) does not necessarily prove she would have undergone any pain had she not sinned. The word "multiply" comes from the Latin *multum* ("many" or "much"), and can mean "to make many"; here, it may simply indicate that henceforth Eve would suffer a manifold variety of pains with "great" intensity. Thus, the phrase "greatly multiply" may simply be designed to emphasize the extent of the foretold punishment – a locution that is neutral relative to what might have happened in childbirth *before* Eve's sin. Indeed, the next clause of Genesis 3:16 asserts that "in pain you shall bring forth children" – which seems to suggest that she would *not* have undergone any pain if she had not sinned.

But whatever may have been true about Eve (along with her female descendants), the case of Mary must be handled with greater caution. The Book of Revelation is apocalyptic literature of the first century, containing varied symbolism and imagery that shifts and melds. Therefore, there can be multiple meanings and fulfillments of the "woman" of Revelation 12 (Mary, Israel of the Old Covenant, Christ's Church of the New Covenant).

For example, since Revelation 12:1 depicts the "woman" as wearing "on her head a crown of twelve stars", there could be a possible reference to the twelve tribes of Israel. The "birth pangs" may then signify the birth of the Church from the Old Israel upon the tumultuous accomplishment of the Messiah's mission, symbolized by the upheaval of an earthquake and the tearing of the curtain in the temple (see Matthew 27:51, 54; Luke 23:45).

On the other hand, since Revelation 11:19 introduces the ark of God's covenant, whose ultimate fulfillment is the Blessed Mother, Revelation 12:2 does seem to involve Mary in some way. Mary *did* consent to "deliver" over her Son in His self-offering on the cross – the sacrificial act whereby His birth as mankind's Redeemer was completed. The "birth pangs" may also denote the arduous process whereby Mary's offspring are formed in Christ. After all, Mary remained on earth for some years after Christ's Ascension, and must have suffered from the martyrdom of early Christians such as St. Stephen and St. James (see Acts 7:58-60; 12:1-2). At this point, however, the symbolism of the "woman" appears to blend Mary with the Church, which remains on earth susceptible to diabolical persecution (see Revelation 12:13-17).

Furthermore, note that, in Galatians 4:19, St. Paul also describes his pain in forming disciples of Christ as "travail" (*"odino"*, the same Greek term for "pangs of birth" found in Revelation 12:2). Again, in Romans 8:22, Paul says that "the whole creation has been groaning in travail together" before the coming of Christ, and he uses a term with the same

Greek root. We are all undergoing "birth pangs" (so to speak), because we are being reborn into Jesus Christ. In all these contexts, "birth pangs" describe formation in Christ, and not the acute physical pain that most women feel in literally giving birth. For other metaphorical uses of "birth pangs" in the Scriptures, see Jeremiah 13:21; Hosea 13:12-13; Micah 4:9-10. Even Micah 5:3, which mentions the "travail" of the mother of the Messiah, probably refers to Mary's role in subordinately helping give birth to the children of the Church along with her Son at Calvary, as well as her eschatological role in the conversion of the Jews near the end of the world (see Matthew 21:43; Luke 21:24; Romans 11:1-31).

At the very least, it is a solid and sound theological position for Catholics to hold that, in point of fact, Mary had no birth pangs in delivering her only Son.[2] Since Jesus is the Source of all joy and delight (see Song of Solomon 5:16), His *presence* with His mother would never have *directly* caused her physical or emotional pain. It is true, however, that the Mother of Sorrows experienced anguish of soul at His *absence* (note, for example, her grief at the three day disappearance of the Child Jesus in the temple, recounted in Luke 2:41-49 and foreshadowed in Song of Solomon 3:1-3).

The thesis at issue can be scripturally defended by pondering Isaiah 66:7, which prophesies: "Before she [Mary] was in labor she gave birth; before her pain came upon her she was delivered of a son [Jesus]." This is a remarkable verse showing that Mary gave birth without the pains of labor that normally culminate a pregnancy. Mary's actual affliction consisted in the fulfillment of Simeon's prophecy (Luke 2:34-35), coming about by both anticipation and final realization at the foot of the cross, when she compassionately suffered with her Son in His epoch-shattering act of giving "birth" to the Church from His pierced side (see Matthew 27:51 together with John 19:34). According to Song of Solomon 8:5, applied to Jesus and Mary, "There [under the "tree"] your mother was in travail with you, there she who bore you was in travail." But Mary's pain at the foot of the cross was only *indirectly* due to her Son – that is, she suffered by what was done *to* Him rather than from anything that He did to her. In short, it would have been unfitting for Mary to have physically suffered in giving birth to Christ at Bethlehem; the New Eve was not in any way under the curse of the original Eve.

Misunderstanding about "all have sinned"

Some Protestants use Romans 3:23 ("All have sinned and fall short of the glory of God") in an attempt to prove that Mary was also with sin. This objection can be answered in several ways.

Note that the Greek word for "all" is *"pantes"*. But *"pantes"* does not necessarily mean "every single one". For example, in Romans 5:12 St. Paul says that "death spread to all men," and in 1 Corinthians 15:22 he says that "in Adam all die". But "all" in these two verses does not mean literally everyone, because in 1 Corinthians 15:51 he says that "we shall not all sleep" (see also 1 Thessalonians 4:15-17, which implies that those who are alive at the Second Coming of Christ will *not* die). Thus, "all have sinned" does not exclude exceptions. In fact, Jesus must be an exception to this general rule. But there can be other exceptions, as well. First, "all have sinned" refers only to those able to commit sin. This is not everyone; for example, children who die before reaching the age of reason and the severely mentally retarded cannot sin. Second, "all have sinned " only means that all human persons are *subject* to Original Sin. It does *not* mean that God could not exempt someone, such as Mary, from actually contracting the stain of Original Sin. In fact, Mary was spared from Original Sin by God – not by herself. The popular analogy is that God let us fall into the mud puddle, and then cleaned us up afterward through Baptism, whereas in Mary's case God did not let her hit the mud puddle in the first place.

As a further counterweight to Romans 3:23, consider Romans 5:19. Here Paul says that "many were made sinners", using "many" (the Greek *"polloi"*) rather than "all" (*"pantes"*). Is Paul contradicting what he said in Romans 3:23? Of course not. Paul simply means that all are *subject* to Original Sin (Romans 3:23), but it does not follow that all actually experience sin, whether by contracting Original Sin or by rejecting God through personal sin (Romans 5:19).

Protestants also use Romans 3:9-12 to prove that all human beings are sinful: "All men ... are under the power of sin, as it is written: 'None is righteous, no, not one; no one understands, no one seeks for God. All have turned aside, together they have gone wrong; no one does good, not even one.'" They conclude that Mary must be sinful. Now, the basis of this passage is Psalm 14:1-4 and Psalm 53:1-4. But these psalms do not teach that all human beings are sinful. In context, they are talking about "fools" who in practice deny God's existence and "evildoers" who oppress God's people with their "corrupt" and "abominable" deeds. In these psalms, the righteous continue to seek God (see Psalm 14:5-7; Psalm 53:6). Obviously, then, there are those (the righteous) who are not included in the apparently sweeping statement of "None is righteous, no, not one" – and neither does Mary fall under this indictment.

What about Luke 18:19, where Jesus says: "No one is good but God alone"? But in Matthew 12:35, He also says: "The good man out of his good treasure brings forth good." (See also Matthew 13:43; 25:46 about the eternal reward of the "righteous".) The verse from Luke must mean that God alone is the source of all good; creatures can be good only by sharing in God's essential goodness.

In Romans 9:10-13, St. Paul says that God distinguished between Jacob and Esau in the womb, before they sinned. Mary was also distinguished from the rest of humanity in the womb by being spared by God from Original Sin. Is this an "injustice on God's part" (Romans 9:14)? St. Paul answers in Romans 9:15-16 that God's sovereignty determines how divine mercy is displayed or applied. Mary appreciated that all her blessings were unmerited and entirely dependent on God's mercy, when she prayed her Magnificat (Luke 1:46-55).

With regard to this song of praise, some Protestants use Luke 1:47, where Mary calls God her "Savior", to denigrate her. Why? Of course, God is Mary's Savior! But that truth does not entail a denial of the Immaculate Conception. In Mary's case, it simply implies that she was freed from Original Sin at the outset in the womb – unlike the rest of us who are freed from sin later, outside the womb.

Some people may object that in Luke 1:48 Mary calls herself "lowly" – as though such a state would contradict her freedom from sin. But any creature, including an angel who never sinned, is lowly compared to God. For example, in Matthew 11:29, even Jesus says He is "lowly in heart". Lowliness is a sign of humility, which expresses the truth about our situation with respect to God. For us creatures subject to sin, it is the greatest virtue marking holiness, because it allows us to empty ourselves and receive the grace of God to change our imperfect lives.

Misunderstandings about Jesus "rebuking" Mary

Jesus asks (in Matthew 12:48, Mark 3:33, Luke 8:21): "Who are my mother and my brothers?" Some Protestants argue that Jesus is here rebuking Mary in order to belittle her. To the contrary, when Jesus' comments are read in light of the parable of the sower (Luke 8:5-15), which Jesus taught right before the context of His question, Jesus is actually implying that Mary has already received the word as good ground and is bearing fruit. Jesus is teaching that others must, like Mary, also receive the word and obey it.

Jesus' question about the identity of his mother and brothers was also made in reference to Psalm 69:8-9. Jesus the Prophet was answering the psalmist's prophecy that those closest to Him would betray Him at His Passion. Jesus is emphasizing the spiritual family's importance over the biological family, and the importance of being faithful to Him. While many were unfaithful to Jesus, Mary did remain faithful to Him, even to the point of standing at the foot of the cross.

Lastly, to argue that Jesus rebuked Mary is to claim that Jesus violated the Torah, in particular the fourth commandment. This idea is blasphemous, because it essentially says that God committed sin by dishonoring His Mother.

In Luke 11:27, we read: "A woman in the crowd raised her voice and said to him, 'Blessed is the womb that bore you.'" When Jesus replies in verse 28, "Blessed rather are those who hear the word of God and keep it," some Protestants also call this a rebuke of Mary. Again, to the contrary, Jesus is actually exalting Mary by emphasizing that her obedience to God's word is more critical than her biological role of mother. This affirms Luke 1:48: "All generations will call me blessed."

Another important point about Luke 11:28 is that the Greek word for "rather" is *"menoun"*. But *"menoun"* really means "yes, but in addition" or "further". Thus, Jesus is saying, yes my mother is blessed indeed, but further blessed are those who hear the word of God and keep it. Jesus is encouraging others to follow Mary's example in order to build up His kingdom.

A final aspect about Luke 11:27-28 is that Jesus is actually the one being complimented, not Mary. Therefore, Jesus is refocusing the attention from Him to others who obey the word of God. If He is refocusing the attention away from Him to others, His comment cannot constitute a reproach of His mother.

John 2:4 contains another example that Protestants use to diminish Mary's significance. Jesus' question to Mary ("What have you to do with me?") does no such thing. To the contrary, Jesus' question can be interpreted in an ironic sense, with the implication that Mary has *everything* to do with Jesus' mission. It thereby illustrates the importance of Mary's role in the kingdom. Jesus' question is in reality an invitation to His mother to intercede on behalf of all believers and begin His ministry, and His Mother understands this. Mary thus immediately intercedes, and Jesus then obeys her by performing the miracle that commenced His public ministry of redemption.

Note that, in Luke 8:28, the demon asks Jesus the same thing ("What have you to do with me?"). The demons are not rebuking Jesus, for God would not allow it. Instead, the demons are acknowledging the power of Jesus by their question to Him: He has *much* to do with them.

On a similar note, when Jesus addresses His mother using the title "woman" ("*gynai*") in John 2:4; 19:26, it does not connote an aloof dismissal. Instead, it is a title of dignity and respect. It is the equivalent of "Lady" or "Madam". Moreover, it indicates Christ's avowal that Mary is the "woman" of Genesis 3:15 who would be the nemesis of the demons.

A Worthy Mother

The ark of the Old Covenant was worthy of veneration and praise. 1 Chronicles 15 and 16 display the awesome reverence the Jews had for the ark – involving vestments, songs, harps, lyres, cymbals, trumpets. We should have an even greater reverence for Mary.

How would we have acted, if we could have chosen our own mother? Undoubtedly, we would have chosen the one we have, adorning her with every possible grace. That is what Christ did. Since Christ is all-powerful, all-wise, and Love itself, His power carried out his Will. This is the clearest reason why our Lord granted his mother, from the very moment of her Immaculate Conception, all possible privileges. She was free from the power of Satan. Therefore, she is beautiful, spotless, and pure in soul and body – worthy to bear the Eternal Word in her womb.

Chosen by the Father to be the Mother of His Son, and accepting this mission by characterizing herself as the "handmaid of the Lord" (Luke 1:38), Mary could never have consented to an offense against God.

The Church sees in Mary one who never denied God the least sign of love.

Mary was the object of special attention on the part of God, who prepared her to become the Mother of His Son. From birth she was filled with the Holy Spirit. Mary was indeed "full of grace", as Gabriel said in greeting her.[3] All holy, Mary obviously was exempt from sin, because sin always means denial that leads away from God, as in the case of the prodigal son who strayed from the father's house. Mary was never away from God. Like the servant of Psalm 123, she kept her eyes on her Lord to do His will at the least sign of it.

The dogma of the Immaculate Conception proclaims the total immunity from sin in the soul of the Virgin Mary and, consequently, the exceptional grace bestowed on her. To say that this grace goes back to the moment when Mary began to exist is to prove, as it were, her perfect impeccability, demanded by the holiness that the Church acclaims in the Mother of God. Indeed, if at sixteen this humble maid of Nazareth could declare herself "handmaid of the Lord" with such apparent confidence, it was because no sin ever touched her from the beginning of her life. In other words, God had filled her with grace in view of what He would one day ask of her.

The question in the minds of many people is this: Was Mary absolutely preserved from all sin, including Original Sin? Or was she touched by this contagion and then cured by the grace of her Son, even before birth? Preserving Mary from all sin, even Original Sin, would represent the most glorious result of Christ's work. I will answer with the words of a modern theologian (Le Bachelet):

> There are two kinds of ransom: one is ransom paid for an individual already prisoner, redemption by liberation; the other is ransom paid even before the acquired right of servitude is exercised, redemption by preservation. In making to His Mother an anticipated application of His merits to preserve her from the taint of original sin, which as a daughter of Adam she had naturally to incur, Jesus Christ became more fully her Redeemer. Far from being diminished, the excellence of Redemption is enhanced by Mary's privilege.

Mary's holiness should encourage us to seek her help and protection in our continual effort to overcome sin and sanctify our lives. Like her, we ought to respond generously to the suggestions of the Spirit in order to live as our Baptism requires. Mary is indeed an incomparable model, but also a Mother attentive to the needs of her sinful children. The devotion of the saints to the Immaculate Conception teaches us to entrust our own striving for holiness to the all-holy Virgin, Ark of the New Covenant.

Mary, Ever Virgin

In calling Mary "ever virgin", we are saying that after conceiving Jesus in virginity Mary always remained a virgin, abstaining from all conjugal relations. We also mean that the birth of Jesus left unimpaired or intact the integrity of His mother's flesh.

Isaiah 7:14 had prophesied the virgin birth of the Messiah, a prophecy cited in Matthew 1:23: "Behold, a virgin shall conceive and bear a son, and his name shall be called Emmanuel (which means, God with us)." The Greek term used is *"parthenos"* (actually, with the Greek feminine definite article), which should be rendered *"the* virgin". The prophecy thus points to a unique Virgin – Mary, the Mother of God.

Another remarkable prophecy is found in Ezekiel 44:1-3:

Then he brought me back to the outer gate of the sanctuary, which faces east; and it was shut. And he said to me, "This gate shall remain shut; it shall not be opened, and no one shall enter by it; for the Lord, the God of Israel, has entered by it; therefore it shall remain shut. Only the prince may sit in it to eat bread before the Lord; he shall enter by way of the vestibule of the gate, and shall go out by the same way."

This passage contains a mystical reference to Mary, the New Ark of the Covenant – here described as "the outer gate of the sanctuary that faces east". Since the east is the direction from which the sun rises, this "gate" is open to receiving the "sun of righteousness" (see Malachi 4:2; Luke 1:35, 38, 78-79). Mary is therefore the "Gate of Heaven". Ezekiel prophesies that no man shall pass through "this gate" by which our Lord entered the world as Mary's Son. He alone is the "prince" (Son of the King, according to Psalm 2 and Psalm 110) whose "bread" is to do the will of His Father (see Matthew 4:4; Luke 4:4; John 4:34; Hebrews 10:5-7). Mary bore only one Son (the "prince"), and His conception occurred miraculously, without the intervention of any human agency. Moreover, since the "gate" *remained* "shut", Mary must have retained her virginity completely — before, during, and after the birth of Jesus. It would seem to follow that Christ emerged from her womb in a mysterious manner, analogous to the way in which He entered the inner sanctuary of His mother (and perhaps passed through the walls of the tomb, as well as the upper room, on Easter Sunday — see John 20:19, 26). At any rate, this is truly a prophecy of Mary's perpetual virginity.

We discover another prefiguring of Mary's complete virginity in Song of Solomon 4:12: "A garden locked is my sister, my bride, a garden locked, a fountain sealed." Here the Holy Spirit, the principal Author of Sacred Scripture and Divine Spouse of Mary (see Luke 1:35), is asserting that no one has access to His bride (see also Song of Solomon 8:9). Let us juxtapose this passage with the previous one from Ezekiel. The New Eve, who bore the Tree of Life in her womb, is like the Garden of Eden, which was *closed on the eastern side* after mankind's Original Sin and subsequent banishment therefrom (see Genesis 3:23-24).[4]

Let's consider the New Testament in more detail. In Luke 1:31, the angel tells Mary that you "will" conceive (using the future tense). Mary responds in verse 34 by asking, "How shall this be?" If we consult the original Greek, Mary's response demonstrates that she had taken a vow of lifelong virginity, having no intention to engage in relations with a man. If Mary did not take such a vow of lifelong virginity, her question would make no sense at all (for we can assume that she knew how a child is conceived). According to tradition, she was a consecrated Temple virgin, as was an acceptable custom of the times.

The Gospels furnish no argument against the doctrine of Mary's perpetual virginity. In Mark 6:3, Jesus is referred to as "the son" of Mary, *not* "a son" of Mary. In the search of the Blessed Mother and St. Joseph for Jesus and their subsequent finding of Him in the temple (see Luke 2:41-51), there is never any mention of other siblings. Furthermore, it would have been utterly unthinkable for Jesus to commit the care of His mother to a friend in John 19:26-27 if He had any brothers at all.

Misunderstanding about "not until"

Matthew 1:25 declares that Joseph "knew her [Mary] not until she had borne a son". Some Protestants argue that this proves Joseph had relations with Mary *after* she bore a son. This is an erroneous reading of the text, because "not until" does not mean "did not ... until after." *"Heos"*, the Greek for the English "until", refers to the past, never to the future. Instead, "not until" she bore a son merely means "not up to the point that" she bore a son. This confirms that Mary was a virgin when she bore Jesus, but does *not* imply that she was *not* a virgin later.

The following are other scriptural texts proving that "until" simply means "up to the point that". First, we list some New Testament verses and then some verses from the Old Testament.

In Luke 1:80, John the Baptist "was in the wilderness till the day of his manifestation to Israel." The verse is silent about whether he may also have lived in the desert even *after* his first public appearance. In Luke 2:37, the prophetess Anna lived "as a widow till she was eighty-four". This simply means "up to the point of being eighty-four years old". We cannot infer that she got married later – that she was *not* a widow *after* eighty-four years of age. In Luke 20:43, Christ quotes Psalm 110: " 'The Lord said to my Lord, Sit at my right hand, till I make thy enemies a stool for thy feet.'" Obviously, the Son of God will *not* be deposed from sitting at the right hand of the Father *after* the defeat of His enemies. In Matthew 28:20, Jesus promises to be with the Church until the end of the world, but this does *not* mean He will vanish from the midst of His people *after* the end of the world. In 1 Timothy 4:13, St. Paul charges St. Timothy: "Till I come, attend to the public reading of scripture, to preaching, to teaching." This exhortation does *not* mean that Timothy should cease these tasks *after* Paul arrives.

The Semitic locution "until" is neutral, making no judgment about the future. For example, in Genesis 8:7 the raven "went to and fro until the waters were dried up from the earth". The raven did *not* necessarily stop flying around *after* the waters dried. Again, in Genesis 28:15 the Lord promises Jacob: "I will not leave you until I have done that of which I have spoken to you." This does *not* in the least imply that God will abandon Jacob *after* the fulfillment of His pledge. Deuteronomy 34:6 states that no one knows Moses' burial place to this day. This does *not* mean that his burial location was discovered later. Moreover, when Scripture says that David's wife Michal was childless up to the day of her death (see 2 Samuel 6:23), it does *not* imply that she had children after she died – which would be absurd. Furthermore, Psalm 71:18 beseeches: "So even to old age and gray hairs, O God, do not forsake me, till I proclaim thy might to all the generations to come." Obviously, the psalmist does not mean to insinuate that God might forsake him *after* he has proclaimed the divine power to future generations. Lastly, 1 Maccabees 5:54 reports that "not one of them had fallen before they returned to safety". Clearly, the victorious men were *not* slain *after* they returned to safety.

The Issue of Jesus' "Brothers"

But, someone may object, Luke 2:7 says that Mary "gave birth to her first-born son". Doesn't it follow that Mary subsequently gave birth to other sons? The term "first-born" alludes to the legal prescriptions concerning the first male child of a family, even if there were no other children. As indicated in Exodus 13:2, 12, "first-born" is a common Jewish expression meaning the first child to open the womb. It has nothing to do with the mother having future children. According to Exodus 34:20, under the Mosaic Law the "first-born" son had to be sanctified. But "first-born" status does not require a "second-born". Therefore, the term "first-born" does not imply that Mary later had other children.

The Gospels on several occasions speak of "brothers" (*"adelphoi"*) of Jesus: namely, James, Joseph (or Joses), Simon, and Judas Thaddaeus (see Matthew 13:55 and Mark 6:3, along with Matthew 10:3 and Mark 3:18). How do we resolve this apparent difficulty? Well, in the Semitic world, the name "brothers" was often applied to relatives or kinsmen.

Let us first consider examples from the Old Testament. From Genesis 11:27, we learn that Lot was actually Abraham's nephew (*"anepsios"*), yet, in Genesis 13:8; 14:14, 16, Lot is nevertheless called Abraham's "kinsman" (*"adelphos"*, usually translated from the Greek as "brother", as indeed the *KJV* renders it). This proves that, although a Greek word for "cousin" is *"anepsios,"* Scripture also uses *"adelphos"* to describe a nephew or other male relative. In Genesis 29:15, Laban calls Jacob his "kinsman" (or "brother", according to the *KJV*), even though he is more specifically Jacob's uncle. In 1 Chronicles 15:5-18 and Nehemiah 4:14; 5:10, 14, the word "brethren" means "kinsmen". In 1 Chronicles 23:21-22, Eleazar's daughters married their "brethren" who were really their **cousins**. David calls Jonathan his "brother" in 2 Samuel 1:26, when they were merely best friends. In Nehemiah 5:1, 5, 7, 8 and Jeremiah 34:9, a fellow Jew is called a "brother". In Deuteronomy 23:7 and Amos 1: 9, "brotherhood" signifies an ally, where no bloodline is involved. In Tobit 5:10-11, Tobit asks Azarias (the angel Raphael in disguise) to identify himself and his people, but still immediately calls him "brother" before getting a reply to his question. Thus, "brothers" can refer even to those who are unrelated by blood, such as countrymen, friends, or allies. Hebrew and Aramaic have no specific word for "cousin".

Now we look at some New Testament examples. In Luke 22:32, Jesus tells Peter to strengthen his "brethren" ("*adelphoi*") – the same Greek word that is applied to Jesus' "brothers" in Matthew 13:55 and Mark 6:3. In this case, we clearly see that Jesus uses "brethren" to refer to the other Apostles, *not* Peter's biological brothers. In John 7:3-4 and Mark 3:21, we see certain "brothers" advising Jesus. But if they were really blood brothers, they must have been younger than Jesus, since *He* was Mary's "first-born"; however, this situation would have been extremely disrespectful for devout Jews, who deferentially honored the priority of chronological age. So, they could not have been biological brothers.

In Acts 1:15-16, Peter addresses "the brethren" ("*adelphoi*"), who number "about a hundred and twenty". That is a lot of "brothers" to have! But "brothers" here clearly means companions in community – not even blood relatives, much less familial siblings. Some of many other instances where "brethren" does not mean blood relations include Acts 7:26; 11:1; 13:15, 38; 15:1, 3, 23, 32; 28:17, 21. In Romans 9:3, Paul uses "brethren" and "kinsmen" interchangeably with reference to the Jewish people.

In fact, we maintain that the "brothers of Jesus" in Matthew 13:55 and Mark 6:3 are cousins (or other kin) of Jesus, but not biological brothers or half-brothers. The following argument proves it. First, they are sons of another Mary, who is expressly called "the mother of James and Joseph" (see Matthew 27:56 and Mark 15:40, 47) and who can be identified neither with the Mother of Jesus nor with Mary Magdalene (since this "other Mary" is named after Mary Magdalene in Matthew 27:56, 61; 28:1 and Mark 15:40, 47, but before Mary Magdalene in John 19:25). Next, in John 19:25, the "other Mary" (of Matthew 27:61; 28:1) is called "the wife of Clopas" and the "sister" of Jesus' mother. Now, in Matthew 10:3 James is called "the son of Alphaeus". This does not disprove that James is the son of Clopas. The name Alphaeus may be Aramaic for Clopas or perhaps the "other Mary" remarried a man named

Alphaeus. On the other hand, perhaps this "other Mary" is actually the *sister-in-law* of the Virgin Mary (who, according to tradition, was an only child) – having married one of Joseph's brothers (Clopas or Alphaeus). It would then follow that the "brothers" of Jesus were His mother's legal nephews and thus His legal cousins.

Of course, certain "brothers" of the Lord could theoretically have been Joseph's children from a former marriage that was dissolved by death, and so they would have been legal stepbrothers rather than blood brothers of Jesus. Nonetheless, the fact remains that the "brothers" mentioned by name in the Gospels were sons of the "other Mary", who was still living. Moreover, just as Jesus and Mary were virgins, it is most likely (perhaps certainly) true that Joseph was a virgin. As such, they embodied the true Holy Family, fully consecrated to God. At any rate, the bottom line is that the phrase "brothers of Jesus" does not prove Mary (or even Joseph) had other children.

Mary, Queen of the New Davidic Kingdom

We see in 1 Kings 2:17-20, for example, that, in the Old Testament Davidic kingdom, the King does not refuse his mother. She intercedes on behalf of the King's subjects in her role as the Queen Mother (or *"Gebirah"*). Since Jesus is the new Davidic King (see Psalm 45:6; Luke 1:32-33; Revelation 1:5; 17:14), He does not refuse the requests of His mother Mary (see John 2:1-11), who must therefore be the Queen. Under the New Covenant, Mary is our heavenly *Gebirah*. In the Old Testament Davidic kingdom, the King bows down to his mother and she sits at his right hand. We, as children of the New Covenant, should imitate our King and pay the same homage to Mary our Mother. By honoring Mary as Queen, we honor our King, Jesus Christ.

In 1 Kings 15:13 and 2 Chronicles 22:10, the Queen Mother had a powerful position and played a significant role in Israel's royal monarchy. In 1 Kings 15:13, the Queen was removed from office. But now, in the Davidic kingdom perfected by Jesus, our Mother Mary is forever at His right hand. Indeed, in Nehemiah 2:6 the Queen Mother sits beside the King. She is the primary intercessor before the King. In Psalm 45:9, 12, the psalmist teaches that the Queen stands at the right hand of God dressed in gold. This contains a mystical prefiguring of Mary, the New Ark of the Covenant (recall that the old ark was gilded) and thus the

House of Gold. Mary is the Queen of heaven and earth, seated at the right hand of the Son of God. (See also Song of Solomon 7:1, 5.)

According to Wisdom 5:15-16, "the righteous live for ever" and "receive a glorious crown and a beautiful diadem from the hand of the Lord". In 2 Timothy 4:8, Paul foresees that there is laid up for him "the crown of righteousness". In James 1:12, James writes that those who endure "will receive the crown of life which God has promised to those who love him". In 1 Peter 5:4, Peter says that "when the chief Shepherd is manifested" we "will obtain the unfading crown of glory". According to Revelation 2:10, Jesus will give "the crown of life" to those who are "faithful unto death". In light of these verses, we know that all the saints are crowned in heaven. But Mary is the greatest saint of all. Hence, Mary is with Jesus forever, crowned in His glory. Mary has received the crown of life by bringing Eternal Life into the world (see John 14:6). Indeed, Revelation 12:1 portrays Mary, the "woman", as "clothed with the sun " and "on her head a crown of twelve stars". She is thus arrayed with the golden light that basks the earth and is crowned in the glorious splendor of the heavens. In short, she is Queen of heaven and earth.

Mary is Queen because she is the mother of the Word Incarnate. She gave birth to a Son who at the very moment of conception was "King of kings and Lord of lords" (1 Timothy 6:15; Revelation 17:14). It was in this Incarnate Word that "all things were created, in heaven and on earth, visible and invisible, whether thrones or dominations or principalities" (Colossians 1:16). She is Queen because she was associated wholeheartedly with Christ the Redeemer. By an eternal plan of God, the Blessed Virgin is the new Eve, who plays a great part in the work of salvation by which Christ Jesus, the new Adam, redeemed us and purchased us for Himself and made us into a "kingdom" for our God (see Revelation 5:10). Mary consented to the Divine plan and advanced in the journey of faith. She heard and kept the Word of God (see Luke 1:45; 2:51) and faithfully preserved her union with the Son even to the cross (John 19:25). She then persevered in prayer together with the Church, awaiting the Holy Spirit (Acts 1:14).

Mary is Queen because she was the perfectly faithful disciple of Christ, from the beginning of her earthly life until its end: "Be faithful unto death, and I will give you the crown of life" (Revelation 2:10). Mary is Queen because She is the most excellent member of the Church. She is "blessed among women" (Luke 1:42), and holds a preeminent place in the Communion of Saints for a twofold reason: her mission and her holiness. Mary truly stands out in the "chosen race, royal priesthood, and holy nation" (1 Peter 2:9) which is the Church, on account of the singular mission given her with regard to Christ and all members of His Mystical Body, and because of her copious virtues and fullness of grace (Luke 1:28). She is the outstanding victor, to whom her Son would necessarily grant the right to sit with Him on the throne, as He Himself conquered and sat with the Father on His throne (Revelation 3:21). Therefore, she deserves to be called "Queen of all Saints".

Mary, Assumed into Heaven

Mary's glorification in body and soul resulted from the divine munificence. But it also came, so to speak, as the logical conclusion of her vocation on earth and the way in which she lived it. Her Divine Maternity is in utter harmony with her bodily Assumption into heaven — just as her Immaculate Conception and her Perpetual Virginity are. Her unique motherhood called for these additional favors of the Lord. How could the body of her in whom "the Word was made flesh" have known the corruption of the grave? Or the body of her who totally escaped the power of sin? Or the body of her who, by her virginal consecration, belonged to her Son and His mission in a perfect and exclusive way?

Let's consider some scriptural evidence for Mary's Assumption. Certain Old Testament events foreshadow the Assumption of Mary. We learn from Genesis 5:24 (and Hebrews 11:5) that Enoch was assumed bodily into paradise without dying. According to 2 Kings 2:11-12 and 1 Maccabees 2:58, Elijah was assumed into heaven in a fiery chariot. Would God do any less for His own Blessed Mother? We read in Matthew 27:52-53 that, when Jesus died and rose, the bodies of some saints were raised. Hence, nothing in Scripture precludes Mary's bodily assumption into heaven. To the contrary, in Revelation 6:9 we see only the souls of the martyrs in heaven, while in Revelation 12:1 we see Mary (the "woman"), *both* body and soul, in heavenly glory ("clothed with the sun").

Certain Old Testament passages foretell the Assumption of Mary. Psalm 16:9-10 says: "Therefore my heart is glad, and my soul rejoices; my body also dwells secure. For thou dost not give me up to Sheol, or let thy godly one see the Pit." Since Mary is "full of grace", she qualifies as "godly", and thus her "body dwells secure" from the "pit" of the grave. In Psalm 132:8, the psalmist prays: "Arise, O Lord, and go to thy resting place, thou and the ark of thy might." This is a direct prophecy. Since Jesus ascended to His eternal resting place in heaven, so also His Ark (Mary) would be taken up there. (See also Song of Solomon 2:10, 13.)

In 2 Thessalonians 2:15, Paul instructs us to hold fast to oral (not just written) tradition. Apostolic tradition says that Mary was assumed into heaven. Although claiming the bones of the saints was a common practice during those early Christian times (and it would have been especially important to obtain Mary's bones, since she was the Mother of Christ), Mary's bones were never claimed. This can only be because they were not available. Mary was therefore taken up body and soul into heaven. Luke 1:45 says: "Blessed is she who believed that there would be a fulfillment of what was spoken to her from the Lord." The promises of the Lord were fulfilled for Mary, and, as always, beyond all expectation.

Mary is now in eternal life. For her, on the personal level, this means the joy and blessedness that comes from loving and beholding the God who is Light, Life, and Love. It also means fullness of communion with all who love God, with all whom God loves – and God loves everything He has made, creation being the effect of His love. But though the blessedness of eternal life is true of all elect in heaven, it is true of Mary in a very special way – not only by reason of the perfection of her glory, but also because her Assumption enables her even now to live her blessedness in the fullness of her glorified humanity. And it does not mark the end of her 'service'. On the contrary, her service could now assume its universal dimensions: "Taken up to heaven, she did not lay aside her salvific duty.... By her maternal love she cares for the brethren of her Son who still journey on earth."[5]

Yes, Mary is now in a position to exercise fully her "Motherhood in order of grace", without interruption until the eternal fulfillment of all the elect. It is not immaterial that Mary's maternal love for us engages not only her soul, but also all the powers of her human nature lifted up to glory. Anything that happens to Mary concerns the Church, of which she is a member, a type, and Mother. What the Lord did for Mary in her Assumption is for us (the Church) a sign and promise of the total glory that awaits us (see Romans 8:18-23). Yes, we are still pilgrims, but our

Mother has gone on ahead, where she points to the reward of our efforts. She tells us that we can make it. If we are faithful, we will reach home. Not only is the Blessed Virgin our model, but she is also the Help of Christians. And as we beseech her with our petitions ("Show that you are our Mother"), she cannot help but watch over her children with motherly care.

Our Lady, a full participant in the work of our salvation, follows in the footsteps of her Son: the poverty of Bethlehem, the everyday work of a hidden life in Nazareth, the manifestation of His divinity in Cana of Galilee, the tortures of his Passion, the atoning sacrifice on the cross, the eternal blessedness of Paradise, reigning with the King in her bodily splendor as Queen. All of this affects us directly, because this supernatural itinerary is the way we are to follow. Mary shows us that we can walk this path with confidence. She has preceded us on the way of imitating Christ; her glorification is the firm hope of our own salvation. For these reasons we call her "our hope, cause of our joy".

She lives now and is protecting us. She is there as the Queen of heaven and earth, present in both body and soul, with the Father and the Son and the Holy Spirit. She is the same person who was born in Palestine, who gave herself to God while still a child, who received the message from St. Gabriel the Archangel, who gave birth to our Savior, and who stood beside him at the foot to the Cross. In her, all ideals become a reality. But we should never think that this sublime greatness of hers makes her inaccessible to us. Yes, she is truly a Queen, but she is also our Mother.

The Significance of Mary

In Luke 2:35, Simeon prophesied that a sword would pierce Mary's soul. Mary thus played a very important role in our redemption. While Jesus' suffering was all that we needed for redemption, God desired Mary to participate on a subordinate level in her Son's atoning suffering, just as He allows us to participate through our own sufferings. According to Galatians 4:4, God sent His Son, born of a woman, to redeem us. Mary is this woman – "the woman with the Redeemer" (note also the Emmanuel prophecy in Isaiah 7:14). When Catholics call Mary "co-redemptrix", we are simply affirming this truth. This is because "co" is from the Latin word "*cum*", which means "with". Mary was "with" Jesus, not only throughout

His childhood (see Luke 1:51), but, perhaps even more crucially, during His passion and death. Mary had a unique but totally subordinate role to Jesus in our redemption.

Mary is our powerful intercessor – so powerful that her mere voice would cause the great prophet and precursor John the Baptist to leap for joy in the womb of his mother, Elizabeth (see Luke 1:44). Catholics seek her intercession especially through the "Hail Mary" prayer, containing the words of the angel Gabriel and of St. Elizabeth (Luke 1:28, 41-43).

If you seek Mary, you will find Jesus. And you will learn a bit more about what is in the heart of God, who humbles Himself, discarding all manifestations of His power and majesty to take the form of a servant. Speaking in human terms, we could say that God outdoes Himself, because He goes much further than He needs to go in order to save us. The only way to measure what He does is to say that it cannot be measured; it comes from a madness of love that leads Him to take on our flesh and bear the weight of our sins.

The mystery of Mary helps us to see that in order to approach God, we must become little. Christ said to his disciples: "Truly, I say to you, unless you turn and become like children, you will never enter the kingdom of heaven" (Matthew 18:3). To become children, we must renounce our pride and self-sufficiency, recognizing that we can do nothing by ourselves. We must realize that we need grace and the help of God our Father to find our way and keep it.

Mary does the immense favor of bringing to the cross, of placing face to face with the example of the Son of God, those who come close to her and contemplate her life. It is in this confrontation that Christian life is decided. And Mary intercedes for us so that our behavior may lead to a reconciliation of the younger brother – you and me – with the firstborn Son of the Father (see Luke 15).

Sometimes, I like to go back in my imagination to the years Jesus spent close to His mother, years that span almost the whole of His life on earth. I like to picture Him as a little child, cared for by Mary, who kisses Him and plays with Him. I like to see Him growing up before the loving eyes of His mother and of Joseph, His foster-father on earth. What tenderness and care Mary and the holy Patriarch must have shown toward Jesus, as they looked after Him during His childhood – all the while, silently, adoring Him and learning so much from Him. Their souls would become more and more like the soul of that Son, who was both man and God. This is why His mother, and after her St. Joseph, understand better than anyone the feelings of the heart of Christ; and the two of these heavenly patrons are thus the best way to reach the Savior.

Born and raised in Mexico, my first recollections of an initial seed of faith have a great deal to do with the amazing story of the miraculous apparitions of Our Lady of Guadalupe in my country. It is safe to assume that 98% of my country's men and women are "Guadalupanos". Her apparitions, back in 1531, originated the faith of millions and transformed an entire culture. These apparitions brought a pagan society into the Catholic Church and ended a gruesome era marked by human sacrifice under the reign of the Aztec Empire. They continue to sustain the faith of my people to this day. As a little boy, I accepted that I had two mothers: one on earth and one in heaven. Now both are in heaven and I can't wait to see them one day. I could spend an entire book and more sharing how Mary has truly blessed my life; and although that will remain as a project for the future, I wanted to state that Mary has been a Mother, a mediatrix of many blessings, an inspiration, a helper, a role model of discipleship, and much more to me.

Many conversions, many decisions to give oneself to the service of God have been preceded by an encounter with Mary. Our Lady has encouraged us to look for God, to desire a change, to lead to new life. I certainly hope that this chapter helps you to have such an encounter, for I am convinced that if we seek Mary, we will find Jesus.

In 1978, when Archbishop Karol Wojtyla of Krakow was elected Pope, he took the name John Paul II and dedicated his pontificate to Mary, taking the motto *"Totus Tuus"* ("I am all yours, O Mary"). Some of our readers may find this expression in reference to the Blessed Mother overwhelming and, most likely, exaggerated; but for those who have discovered Mary truly as a Mother, mediatrix of all graces,[6] and role model for our faith, it makes perfect sense – and that is the case I have argued in this essay.[7]

CHAPTER TWELVE
The Last Things

Introduction

The first thing we should say as we take up the topic of the Last Things is that we should joyously look forward to the end time. After all, Jesus brings us the good news – that we have been saved from our sins by the mercy of God and given a share in the divine life. Of course, this does not mean that we can think about the final judgment without some concern, for we have all sinned and sin deserves punishment. Still, we should always keep in mind the example of the repentant thief. He was certainly a sinner, and unlike Jesus was justly put to death according to the law. But his plea for mercy was met, even amidst the intense suffering of our Lord on the cross, with the assurance of eternal life with Christ in heaven.

Indeed, the First Things were clearly good (see Genesis 1:1, 31). It is a good creation, created by a loving God, who cares for each sparrow and every hair of every head (see Luke 12:6-7). We are told to have confidence even regarding divine judgment; for God is love and there is no fear in love (see 1 John 4:17-18). When His disciples were deep in sorrow because Jesus had said He must go away and they could not follow Him at that time, He comforted them with the assurance that His love is everlasting. Just as He would never abandon them, neither will He abandon us:

> In my Father's house are many rooms; if it were not so, would I have told you that I go to prepare a place for you? And when I go and prepare a place for you, I will come again and will take you to myself, that where I am you may be also. (John 14:2-3)

Jesus has promised to take care of us, and we should believe and be comforted.

There is still, of course, the problem of the fall from grace. Somehow we find ourselves separated from God, with a tendency toward sin and a kind of aversion to God. Add to this the many actual sins we have committed, and doubt about the possibility of our salvation creeps in. But through His profound sacrifice of love, Jesus has more than made up for any human failings (see Roman 5:17).

So our first thought about the Last Things should be positive – the hope and faith in God's promise of everlasting life. The free creation, however, remains free. We can turn away from God. We can say no to the gift of divine mercy. We can sin and persist in sin. And if we do, there must be consequences. Justice demands it. Thus, Sacred Scripture makes it clear that there will be a particular judgment of each person's behavior (see, for example, Revelation 22:12). Heaven is the free gift of God, not something to which we have a right. There are the well-known parables of the talents and of the sheep and the goats in the gospel of St. Matthew. We shall be judged by how well we use what we have been given. Jesus embraces those who use their talents well: "Enter into the joy of your master" (Matthew 25:21). But those who do not are rejected: "Cast the worthless servant into the outer darkness; there men will weep and gnash their teeth" (Matthew 25:30). And we shall ultimately be judged by how we have treated others:

> Before him will be gathered all the nations, and he will separate them one from another as a shepherd separates the sheep from the goats, and he will place the sheep at his right hand, but the goats at the left…. And they [the goats] will go away into eternal punishment, but the righteous into eternal life. (Matthew 25:32-33, 46)

We cannot presume on the mercy of God, while neglecting to amend our lives. To do so would be to ignore our own understanding of justice and fairness. Even though grace can overcome sin, we should never be content with sin. To help us overcome sin, Jesus offers us love. And love is, most assuredly, the best reason for repenting. But for those who do not care, Jesus also provides in His mercy the fear of eternal punishment. So great is His love that He does not give up on those who refuse to accept this love: He pursues them through justice, appealing to their knowledge of their own moral negligence and sin and of how such behavior ought to be punished.

As we pursue our meditation on the Last Things, we shall consider five topics: heaven, purgatory, hell, the resurrection of the body, and the meaning the resurrection has for the whole of creation. But we should emphasize that there is a crucial difference between heaven and hell on the one hand, and purgatory on the other hand. This difference is tied up with the distinction between the general judgment at the end of the world and the particular judgment of each individual at death, as outlined in Hebrews 9:27-28: "And just as it is appointed for men to die once, and after that comes judgment, so Christ, having been offered once to bear the sins of many, will appear a second time, not to deal with sin but to save those who are eagerly waiting for him." This eschatological event will include a universal manifestation of the ultimate state of every human being who has ever lived, as described in Revelation 20:12: "And I saw the dead, great and small, standing before the throne, and books were opened. Also another book was opened, which is the book of life. And the dead were judged by what was written in the books, by what they had done." (See Daniel 7:9-10 and 1 Corinthians 4:5, as well.) It will become clear below that purgatory is merely a temporary condition after death, whereas heaven and hell are everlasting. The latter two states are final abodes of man after the general resurrection from the dead.

Let us begin with heaven.

Heaven

The reality of heaven is abundantly clear from the words of Christ. The whole Gospel is centered around the coming of the kingdom of heaven. John the Baptist first announces it in Matthew 3:2. And after John is arrested and put into prison, Jesus proclaims the same message (see Mark 1:15). Many of Jesus' parables speak of the kingdom of heaven. For two instructive examples, read Matthew 13:44-45. According to these two parables, heaven is the most precious of all things, the one thing to which we should devote our lives. As we know so well, Jesus teaches us to pray in the "Lord's Prayer" for the coming of God's kingdom (see Matthew 6:10).

The fullness of the kingdom of heaven awaits a future state where God will bring all things to perfection. Thus, Jesus explicitly assures the good thief, who is suffering horribly on his cross, of a place with Him in paradise (see Luke 23:42-43)

In heaven, all suffering and sorrow will be wiped away. St. Paul says that the trials of this life are trifling when viewed in light of our future glory (see Romans 8:18). Heaven is beyond anything we have experienced or can even imagine: "No eye has seen, nor ear heard, nor the heart of man conceived, what God has prepared for those who love him" (1 Corinthians 2:9).

Heaven, in short, will be perfect life with God. There will be no sin, no ignorance, and no fear to distort our vision of God: "For now we see in a mirror dimly, but then face to face. Now I know in part; then I shall understand fully, even as I am fully understood" (1 Corinthians 13:12). If we think of St. Paul's analogy in terms of today's mirrors, we'll miss the point. In St. Paul's day, mirrors were made of metal, and the best mirror only provided a dim and somewhat distorted reflection. St. John implies that the happiness of heaven is beyond anything we are capable of describing in earthly terms: "Beloved, we are God's children now; it does not yet appear what we shall be, but we know that when he appears we shall be like him, for we shall see him as he is" (1 John 3:2).

Although the fullness of heaven will come only in the beatific vision of the *Eschaton*, even in this life, as hard as it is, the heavenly life begins. In John 14:1-3, Jesus comforts His disciples by promising that He is going to prepare a place for them. Not only this, but He assures them that they *do* know the way. When Thomas complains that they cannot know the way since they do not know where Jesus is going, Jesus declares that *He* is the true way to everlasting life (see John 14:6, along with Simon Peter's profession in John 6:68). Most essentially, heaven is life with God. This means, for the disciples and for us, life with Christ (see John 14:6-7). Such communion with God actually begins in this life (see John 14:23 and Revelation 3:20).

St. Paul tells us in Romans 13:14 that we must put on the Lord in this life. How is it that we should live? We should carry out the commandments of God. We should be perfect, as our heavenly Father is perfect (see Matthew 5:48). But how do we do this? None of us is always good; we all make mistakes. The only way to overcome our evil inclinations is to live in Christ. Then we shall live by the Spirit of God. However, not only do we face our own evil inclinations, but we are also battling supernatural enemies – the wicked angels who are much smarter and more powerful than we. The only hope we have for victory lies in the help we get from God (see Ephesians 6:11-13).

This sounds like a difficult and frightening enterprise. And it is, particularly if we try to undertake the fight on our own. But Jesus promises his help. It is not that we shall have no difficulties in life. We certainly shall, just as our Lord did. But we shall also receive the grace to persevere, if yoked to Him (see Matthew 11:28-30). The light burden to which Christ refers in this passage is the burden of love, wherein our souls find repose. For if we love, we are in God, since God is love (see 1 John 4:16). In Christ, we too can overcome the world, with its temptations and persecutions (see John 16:33). The love of God is always offered to us; according to Romans 8:38-39, nothing (except, of course, our own refusal) can keep it from us.

The Old Testament witness to heaven is mixed. Certainly the idea of heaven as life with God in this life is everywhere in the Old Testament. God enters history to help His chosen people, and the prophets, the psalms, and the wisdom literature all aim at letting God live in our hearts. But the idea of a future life in which there is a final judgment and in which those who love God are brought to perfection in Him is less clear in the Old Testament. An outstanding exception would be Wisdom 3:1-9; 4:7-17; 5:1-5, 15-16.

At the time of Christ, there were two major parties in the religious establishment – the Pharisees and the Sadducees. Of these two groups, the Pharisees believed in the resurrection, and therefore in final judgment; the Sadducees did not. We will speak about this issue at further length when we discuss the Christian belief in the resurrection of the body. The Psalms make references to life beyond this life, and in Job, Isaiah, and Daniel there are passages indicating a future life and ultimate judgment.

Purgatory

Purgatory should be treated along with heaven because it winds up on the same side in the final judgment. That is, those in purgatory are on their way to heaven. They have accepted the grace of God but have need of purification, the purging of their sins. Unlike the many references to heaven, purgatory is not mentioned by name in the Scriptures, though it can be cogently inferred.

Purgatory is not a logical requirement, absolutely speaking. Given the omnipotence of God and the fact that all grace comes from God, it is certainly metaphysically possible that God could bring people immediately to heaven. Nevertheless, given the divine wisdom in establishing the economy of salvation, it *would* seem to be a logical requirement relatively speaking – that is, according to the ordained will of God. Moreover, there are a number of scriptural passages that make sense only in the context of the reality of purgatory, and there are also theological and philosophical reasons for accepting this third (and transitory) state.

An important scriptural passage suggesting a third state of existence after death (along with heaven and hell) is 1 Peter 3:19-20: "He [Christ] went and preached to the spirits in prison, who formerly did not obey, when God's patience waited in the days of Noah." St. Peter here implies the existence of a place of imprisonment or penalizing detention for those who committed sins of disobedience. It could not have been the "Limbo of the Fathers", the waiting place for those righteous people of the Old Covenant who, on account of their virtuous obedience, did not merit any punishment (for example, Noah and Abraham). Evidently, though, their sins of disobedience were not grave enough to deserve hell, and so they were punished (at least initially) in a temporary confinement. This penal center seems to correspond with what we call "purgatory". After they had made spiritual "restitution" (so to speak) for their sins, they may have entered a different state (the "bosom of Abraham") of simply awaiting the Messiah's triumphal arrival to liberate them and lead them to heaven upon the completion of His redemptive suffering and death.

In a couple of Gospel passages, Christ implies the reality of a temporary imprisonment in the afterlife. We quote the first below.

> Make friends quickly with your accuser, while you are going with him to court, lest your accuser hand you over to the judge, and the judge to the guard, and you be put in prison; truly, I say to you, you will never get out till you have paid the last penny. (Matthew 5:25-26)

The "accuser" in this passage may represent our own conscience. If we have not made peace with ourselves by perfectly cleansing our state of soul in this life ("quickly, on the way to court"), then we will be our own instrument for handing ourselves over at death's tribunal to the divine judge, who will consign us to a punitive spiritual condition from which we will be released only after making complete restitution for our earthly offenses. This possibility lends deep significance to Christ's admonition in the last verse of the same chapter of Matthew: "You, therefore, must be perfect, as your heavenly Father is perfect." In other words, any shadow of stain or blemish excludes us from heavenly beatitude (see Revelation 21:1-2, 27).

Another pertinent verse in the Gospel of Matthew: "And whoever says a word against the Son of man will be forgiven; but whoever speaks against the Holy Spirit will not be forgiven, either in this age or in the age to come" (Matthew 12:32). The Greek word for "age" is αἰών (from which we get the English "eon"), suggesting an entirely different period of human existence: in this case, the afterlife. Since sins can be forgiven neither in heaven (where all is perfection) nor in hell (due to a definitive rejection of God), Christ's assertion indicates the reality of a third "place" where sins can be pardoned and atoned for.

In his first letter to the Corinthians, St. Paul speaks of the practice of being baptized for the sake of the dead. This is in the context of St. Paul's discussion of the last judgment and the resurrection of the dead. St. Paul asks: "What do people mean by being baptized on behalf of the dead? If the dead are not raised at all, why are people baptized on their behalf?" (1 Corinthians 15:29). We might ask, how is such a practice to be reconciled with the dichotomy of heaven and hell? If the dead are without doubt in heaven, they do not need our prayers and sacrifices. And if the dead are in hell, they are beyond our help, as revealed in the parable of Lazarus. As Abraham says, speaking to the rich man in Hades who refused to help Lazarus, "Between us and you a great chasm has been fixed, in order that those who would pass from here to you may not be able, and none may pass from there to us" (Luke 16.26). Such a practice only makes sense if baptisms can be of help, if our actions can somehow help those who have died to reach beatitude. This suggests a third state in which communion with God is possible but not completely actual.

In addition to this passage on intercessions for the dead, there are numerous passages on the need for purification. Let us first consider 1 Corinthians 3:11-15. Here the Apostle Paul tells us that we must all build on the foundation that is Christ. When the day of judgment comes, our works will be tested by fire. As long as the foundation is Christ, we will be saved, though perhaps seared by the flames. Why? The quality of our work varies due to the irreducible reality of human free will. Not all of us welcome the grace that is offered to us by God as fully as we might. St. Paul speaks of a cleansing fire of purification that will cause suffering but will not cut us off from life with God. This is neither heaven nor hell, for heaven is complete unity with God where there will be no suffering, and hell is suffering the worst of all losses – separation from God.

Just as we can participate in heaven in this life, so we can participate in a purgative process of purification in this life. St. Peter suggests our current need for purification when speaking of the final judgment to come (see 1 Peter 1:17). God is merciful, but God is also just. If we have done evil, we should expect to be punished for it, if not in this life then at the final judgment. That is why it is so critical to live lives as holy as possible (see 1 Peter 1:22). Since we must work to purify our souls, it is reasonable to think that, if we fall short of such purification in this life, it will be completed in the next. As it is written in Revelation 21:27 about heaven, "nothing unclean shall enter it". Indeed, only those who are purified of all flaws may partake of the Beatific Vision: "Blessed are the pure in heart, for they shall see God" (Matthew 5:8).

Of course, all purification comes from the hand of God. That is, purification, even if painful, is grace. All good comes from God (see James 1:17), and this is true of the good that is punishment. Whether the purification comes in this life or after death, it is a gift from God. After all, there is no need to purify something or somebody that is to be destroyed. When St. John speaks of the need for purification, he says we must turn to God and hope in his promises: "And every one who thus hopes in him purifies himself as he is pure" (1 John 3.3).

There are some Old Testament texts that witness to the worthiness of interceding for the dead (as well as for the living) because of their need for purification. The clearest reference to the goodness of interceding for the dead is found in 2 Maccabees. (Although Protestants in general regard this book of the Bible as apocryphal, it at least bears witness to

Jewish beliefs about the afterlife, and the Catholic Church deems the book inspired.) When Judas Maccabeus discovers that those who died in battle had been wearing tokens dedicated to idols, he prays for them to be forgiven:

> And they turned to prayer, beseeching that the sin which had been committed might be wholly blotted out.... Therefore, he made atonement for the dead, that they might be delivered from their sin. (2 Maccabees 12:42, 45)

This prayer, of course, entails the possibility of deliverance from sin in a state of the afterlife that is neither heaven nor hell.

In addition to this explicit text on interceding for the dead, we find in Job an example of praying for the living. Just as texts referring to the importance of purification in this life support the notion of purgatory, so too do texts that refer to prayers for others in this life. The point is that we can affect the lives of other people for the good by interceding for them. Job worries about the sins incurred by his sons when they feast, and so he sacrifices for their sakes, interceding with God for them (see Job 1:5). Thus, it is not useless for us to sacrifice and pray for others, whether they be alive or dead.

The purification theme is central in the Book of Daniel. Daniel has a vision of what is to come, a vision in which there is the call for purification (see Daniel 12:10). Although it is unclear in this passage whether the purification is at the end of time or in this life, what *is* clear is the need for purification, that is, the saving of the person through suffering of some kind. This is the basic insight behind the Catholic Church's teaching on purgatory.

These texts on sacrificing or praying for the dead and on purification (especially those that refer to the final judgment) make sense only if there is the possibility of a state of grace that involves suffering – what the Church means by purgatory. Beyond these texts, there are some fundamental theological and philosophical reasons for including purgatory along with heaven and hell.

Theologically, our faith is a faith in the covenant made between God and human beings. Although it is a mystery why God should deign to let us share freely in the plan of salvation, He has done so. This means that our free actions do make a difference. Just as our free actions turning us away from God in sin deserve punishment, so our free actions to do good deserve reward. If this is so, then the free action to intercede for our neighbor deserves the reward of having such mercy make a difference. After all, it is our Lord's intercession for us that is the heart of our faith. He surely would not condemn our efforts to intercede for each other, to wish to mitigate the suffering of others and to take their punishments upon ourselves (see John 15:13).

There are also moral issues involved here. We mentioned in the first section that, although we should have confidence in the love of God, we should not presume on His grace. After all, sin should be punished. We know this theologically and philosophically. To assume that our faith in Christ and our efforts to be good Christians guarantee us immediate entrance into heaven is to be presumptuous or to ignore the importance of justice. After all, as St. Peter says, God judges us impartially according to our deeds (see Acts 10:34-35). We must guard against the idea that we are exceptions. And to think that all sins should be forgiven without some kind of punishment is to ask that God be unjust. This we should obviously not do. As St. Paul states in his letter to the Romans:

> For he will render to every man according to his works: to those who by patience in well-doing seek for glory and honor and immortality, he will give eternal life; but for those who are factious and do not obey the truth, but obey wickedness, there will be wrath and fury. (Romans 2:6-8)

Finally, we can speak of the mysterious grace of suffering. When we face the prospect of purgatory ourselves (it is likely that few of us will be perfectly purified in this life), we should take comfort in the example of the holy suffering of Jesus Himself. Although He did not seek the suffering, He accepted it (see, for example, Matthew 26:39). It was His suffering, death, and resurrection that worked our salvation – not solely His dying and rising. If Christ, who knew no sin and no need for purification, accepted suffering patiently, how much more should we accept suffering, we who have sinned and whose sins were the cause of His suffering.

Beyond the fittingness that we should suffer, it is – in a mysterious way – a privilege to suffer. Would we participate fully in the grace of Christ, we must suffer. It is not something we seek or should seek. But freely accepted, suffering is grace: Christ's suffering first, but also, through His mercy, ours (see Colossians 1:24).

It is a great mystery that we should be permitted through suffering to participate in Christ's act of salvation. Hence, the suffering of purgatory, although clearly ordained for the punishment of our sins, is also a participation in the salvific suffering of Christ.

Hell

At the final judgment, besides the promise of heaven and heaven's antechamber purgatory, there is the possibility of hell. This possibility is clearly stated by our Lord on many occasions, and indeed it must be a possibility if there is any such thing as freedom of choice. It is possible to turn away from God; it is possible to sin and not repent. But just as we are guarded against presumption by the knowledge that heaven and purgatory are given us by grace beyond our deserts, so we are guarded against despair by the knowledge that hell is our choice. We only get to heaven through God's power; we only go to hell by our own choice. Heaven is deeply communal; hell is isolation. The only thing that we do completely on our own, without God's help, is sin. It is true that God wants all of us to be saved (see 1 Timothy 2:4 and 2 Peter 3:9), but He will not force us into heaven. If we choose to separate ourselves from God, we will be separated from God. And just as heaven is life with God, so hell is life separated from God. In this section we shall, first of all, examine the texts of our Lord on the last judgment and the reality of hell. Then, as we did with the notion of heaven, we shall consider how hell is a reality in this life. Finally, we shall deal with the issue of the difficulty of getting into heaven and avoiding hell, and the possibility of salvation available to all.

In the opening section, we discussed the parable of the sheep and the goats; let us begin with that passage here:

> Then he will say to those on his left hand, "Depart from me, you cursed, into the fire prepared for the devil and his angels."

... And they will go away into eternal punishment, but the righteous into eternal life. (Matthew 25:41, 46)

Now of course this passage is predicated on the contingency that we do not help our brethren in this life. Thus, it is not a prediction so much as a warning. And again, the best way to avoid hell is to love God and live in His Spirit. But, as we said above, Jesus is so concerned about our salvation that He provides us with another reason to turn away from sin and love each other — the fear of hell. The possibility of eternal damnation is real; and if it does not frighten us, it should.

This passage about hell as final punishment is no isolated passage in the Gospels. Jesus repeats the real possibility of eternal damnation over and over again. In the same passage in Matthew, in the parable of the talents, Jesus condemns the servant who has not invested his talent and brought forth more: "Cast the worthless servant into the outer darkness; there men will weep and gnash their teeth" (Matthew 25:30). The grace we are given must be welcomed and nurtured. In Mark 9:42-48, Jesus teaches our great responsibility not to lead others into sin. The cost of scandalous conduct is high indeed. In this passage, Christ uses graphic language to emphasize the reality of hell, "where their worm does not die, and the fire is not quenched" (Mark 9:48).

It matters what we freely choose to do. If we sin and persist in sin, we shall reap our reward — endless misery, including the "worm" of gnawing remorse (see Isaiah 66:24, to which Christ's metaphor seems to allude). In the parable of the weeds in the field, Christ repeats the same point about the final judgment: "The Son of man will send his angels, and they will gather out of his kingdom all causes of sin and all evildoers, and throw them into the furnace of fire; there men will weep and gnash their teeth" (Matthew 13:41-42). As we live our lives, we should fear sin much more than suffering: "Do not fear those who kill the body but cannot kill the soul; rather fear him who can destroy both soul and body in hell" (Matthew 10:28). Although suffering appears to be more painful in the short run, in the long run sin is much worse for us. Indeed, we have some experience of this in the devastating pain of the mental anguish of a guilty conscience as compared with physical pain.

Hell is mentioned elsewhere in the New Testament, as well. When discussing the judgment against those who do not know God and do not follow the gospel, St. Paul speaks of eternal punishment: "They shall suffer the punishment of eternal destruction and exclusion from the presence of the Lord and from the glory of his might" (2 Thessalonians 1:9). St. Peter reiterates the power of God to reward and punish:

> For if God did not spare the angels when they sinned, but cast them into hell and committed them to pits of nether gloom to be kept until the judgment..., then the Lord knows how to rescue the godly from trial, and to keep the unrighteous under punishment until the day of judgment. (2 Peter 2:4, 9)

The proclamation of hell is made for the last time in the New Testament in several passages near the end of the Book of Revelation, of which we quote two (see also Revelation 21:27; 22:15):

> This is the second death, the lake of fire; and if any one's name was not found written in the book of life, he was thrown into the lake of fire. (Revelation 20:14-15)
> But as for the cowardly, the faithless, the polluted, as for murderers, fornicators, sorcerers, idolaters, and all liars, their lot shall be in the lake that burns with fire and sulphur, which is the second death. (Revelation 21:8)

Even the Old Testament contains similar references; along with Isaiah 66:24, see Malachi 4:1.

Since hell is most essentially separation from God, it is possible to participate in hell even in this life. Just as we can begin to live in heaven insofar as we live in the Spirit of God in this life, so we can begin to die in hell insofar as we reject that Spirit in this life. Every time we sin, we put an obstacle between ourselves and God. The most frightening thing about sin is that the more we sin, the less we see ourselves as sinners. The more we cut ourselves off from God, the less we see ourselves as isolated from God. The worst thing that could happen to us is that we should grow comfortable in sin. To the extent that we love and do good, we participate in heaven, which is life with God; to the extent that we hate and do evil, we participate in hell, which is life without God (see John 3:36; 1 John 3.14-15).

Having established the clear presence of the doctrine of hell in the Scriptures, we can turn to the question of how many will be saved. From the words of our Lord, it does not look too promising (see Matthew 7:13-14; 22:14; Luke 13:23-24). That it is hard to be good comes as no surprise to us. It is easy to go wrong, but difficult to be perfect. And when we consider ourselves and those around us, it seems obvious that all of us sin. If the condition for salvation is freedom from sin, it does not look very promising for us. Still, we are taken aback when we read such passages. After all, God is all-powerful, and God is good; so why doesn't God just save us all? We have to admit that God could do this, for it is no contradiction for God by His grace to move our free will to faith and good action. But we also have to allow for the reality of free will and the integrity of the Covenant. We can choose to turn our backs on God. And it seems that we have a natural tendency to do this.

Alongside some rather pessimistic texts, however, we have texts that support a more optimistic assessment. After all, Christ came to redeem the world, not to reject it (see John 3:17; 1 John 4:14). St. Paul says in his letter to Timothy that God "desires all men to be saved and to come to the knowledge of the truth" (1 Timothy 2:4). And St. Peter echoes the same thought: "The Lord is not slow about his promise as some count slowness, but is forbearing toward you, not wishing that any should perish, but that all should reach repentance" (2 Peter 3:9).

Here is a key idea. Christ wants all to be saved, but we are saved through repentance. This makes sense of the harsh assessments of Christ, in which He encourages us by all means to repent. For it is only through free repentance that we can be saved. Moreover, St. Paul declares faith in the mystery of God's grace that brings good out of evil (see Romans 5.20-21). Of course, Paul also says (in Romans 3:8) that we must in no case sin so that grace may abound. That would be absurd. The moral demand is absolute: never do evil, even for the sake of good.

And it is because of this moral absolute and our ability to violate it freely that there must be the possibility of condemnation. But we should remember that hell is our choice. Nothing can separate us from the love of God — except our own will. The only act that we can, in some mysterious way, do all on our own is saying "No" to God. But our saying "No" to God does not make God love us less. It is not as though God loves us because we deserve to be loved and so might stop loving us when we are unlovable; for it was when we were sinners that God came to save us (see Romans 5.6-8). His love is not conditional on our acceptance, which is why we should never despair. Yet, although God's love is always offered us, it is also true that His love honors the integrity of our freedom of choice. The good news is that love is stronger than death (see Song of Solomon 8:6). Nevertheless, love is a relationship. God loves us first, but we must love, too, if we would live in God's love (see 1 John 4:10, 19).

The Resurrection of the Body

All our talk about heaven, purgatory, and hell presupposes that there is life after death. Jesus Himself draws witness to this fact from God's words in Exodus 3:6:

> "And as for the dead being raised, have you not read in the book of Moses, in the passage about the bush, how God said to him, 'I am the God of Abraham, and the God of Isaac, and the God of Jacob'? He is not the God of the dead, but of the living." (Mark 12:26-27)

God is the God of the living, and so Abraham, Isaac, and Jacob are alive in God. But to be alive as a human being is to have bodily existence. The final judgment at the end of the world will be the judgment of the whole person – body, soul, and spirit (see Matthew 13:40-43; 16:27; 24:31). Of course, we know that the resurrection is possible, because Jesus rose from the dead. And the resurrection is fitting, because it is the whole human being who sins or who does what is good.

But more than just revealing the possibility of the final resurrection, Jesus Himself *is* the resurrection:

> Jesus said to her, "Your brother will rise again." Martha said to him, "I know that he will rise again in the resurrection at the last day." Jesus said to her, "I am the resurrection and the life; he who believes in me, though he die, yet shall he live, and whoever lives and believes in me shall never die." (John 11:23-26)

All talk about the resurrection, indeed all talk of creation, is centered in Christ. All things were created in Christ (see Colossians 1:16), and all things will be redeemed in him (see Romans 8:19-21). Jesus, like His Father, has power over sin and death: "For as the Father raises the dead and gives them life, so also the Son gives life to whom he will" (John 5:21; see also Luke 14:14). Jesus proves His statement by raising Martha's brother Lazarus from the dead (see John 11:38-44). He also raises Jairus' daughter (see Mark 5:21-43) and the son of the widow of Nain (see Luke 7:11-17).

The resurrection to life (the gift of heaven) requires an act on our part – we must believe. To Jairus, when he is told that his daughter is dead, Jesus says: "Do not fear, only believe" (Mark 5:36). And to His disciples on His way to visit Martha and Mary, He says: "Lazarus is dead; and for your sake I am glad that I was not there, so that you may believe" (John 11:14-15). Within the Bread-of-Life discourse, He declares: "For this is the will of my Father, that every one who sees the Son and believes in him should have eternal life; and I will raise him up at the last day" (John 6:40). The context of this passage shows a connection between the Holy Eucharist and bodily resurrection unto heavenly glory.

Indeed, not only was Christ the resurrection to Lazarus and the people of His day, but He remains so to us in the real presence of the Holy Eucharist and the Sacrifice of the Mass. And closely tied to the willing assent of the mind in faith is the action of participating in the Eucharist, for "he who eats my flesh and drinks my blood has eternal life, and I will raise him up at the last day" (John 6:54). Just as Jesus claims that the God of Abraham, Isaac, and Jacob, is the God of the living and not of the dead, so the Christ who is "the resurrection and the life" continues to be with us in faith and in the Blessed Sacrament. Hence, just as we participate in heaven or hell during this life, so also we participate in the resurrection during this life through the liturgy of the Church, especially in the Eucharistic celebration.

This continuing participation is made evident in the power of Jesus' disciples to carry on His work. While Jesus is with them in the flesh, the disciples are able to cure the sick and drive out demons (see Mark 6:13). And after Jesus' resurrection and ascension, and the gift of the Holy Spirit at Pentecost, the disciples are even given the power to raise the dead. For instance, St. Peter calls upon the name of the Lord to bring Tabitha back to life (see Acts 9:40-41). As reported in Acts 20:9-12, St. Paul exercises the same power over death by raising a dead young man (Eutychus) to life. This passage links the celebration of the life-giving Eucharist ("had broken bread") with restoration to physical life.

The letters of St. Paul are filled with references to the resurrection. He makes the direct connection between Jesus' Resurrection and the general resurrection: "God raised the Lord and will also raise us up by his power" (1 Corinthians 6:14). And again, "For since we believe that Jesus died and rose again, even so, through Jesus, God will bring with him those who have fallen asleep" (1 Thessalonians 4:14). Paul elaborates on this theme in 1 Thessalonians 4:16-17:

> The Lord himself will descend from heaven with a cry of command, with the archangel's call, and with the sound of the trumpet of God. And the dead in Christ will rise first; then we who are alive, who are left, shall be caught up together with them in the clouds to meet the Lord in the air; and so we shall always be with the Lord.

This passage describes the so-called "Rapture", which St. Paul indicates will occur at the time of the general resurrection from the dead at the end of the world.

The key passage in St. Paul's letters, though, is 1 Corinthians 15: 12-19. Here he debates with those who deny the resurrection. Many Christians today either assume that when we go to heaven we are disembodied angels or they do not give much thought to the resurrection of the body. Against this, Paul insists that the resurrection of the body is not tangential to life after death, but at its very center. There are a number of important points in this text. The first is the connection between Christ's Resurrection and the general resurrection. The difference in this passage is that the implication runs the other way. Instead of arguing that the general resurrection would be impossible without Christ's Resurrection, Paul reverses the order and says that Christ's Resurrection is impossible if there is no general resurrection. Why would this be so? Why couldn't Christ's case just be a special one with no implications for us? The whole center of the gospel is at stake. The good news is that Christ has suffered and died for the forgiveness of sins and has given us, through His Resurrection, a share in the divine life. But sharing in God's life is sharing in Christ's life – incarnated life in God. This is impossible if we are not resurrected. If we deny the resurrection, there is no life in God; we are still in our sins; and we are without a hope of life forever with God (heaven). If there is no resurrection, we who have believed are the most miserable of human beings, since we have given up the pleasures, honors, and advantages of the world for nothing.

One can surely ask (and those with Paul evidently did) how the dead are raised and what could be meant by a resurrected body. To the first question, the answer is the power of God. God, who has created all things out of nothing, can create a suitable kind of body: "God gives it a body as he has chosen, and to each kind of seed its own body" (1 Corinthians 15:38). The living things in our world are given suitably distinctive bodies; God will do the same for each resurrected individual. To the second question, the answer must be a body such as Christ had after His Resurrection. This was a real body. It could be touched (Thomas put his hands into Jesus' wounds), and it could eat (Jesus ate a number of times with his disciples). But it could also walk through walls (see John 20:19) and vanish at will (see Luke 24:31). So, the resurrected body will be like and unlike the one we have now. One thing is clear: it will not be less of a body than the one that we have now, not some poor substitute or airy imitation. Rather, it will be more of a body. Just as Jesus is more human (in a perfective sense) than we are, so our resurrected bodily participation in Christ will be more human, not less, than the bodily existence we enjoy in this life. In fact, St. Paul calls the resurrected body a "spiritual body" (1 Corinthians 15:44) – a real body, as we said, but a spiritualized one sharing in the "power" and "imperishability" of the soul (1 Corinthians 15:42-43). One of its attributes is evidently brightness: "Then the righteous will shine like the sun in the kingdom of their Father" (Matthew 13:43). This brilliance, however, will vary from person to person: "Star differs from star in glory" (1 Corinthians 15:41; see also John 14:2; 2 Corinthians 3:18; Colossians 3:4). Finally, the resurrected body will be immune from suffering:

> For this perishable nature must put on the imperishable, and this mortal nature must put on immortality. When the perishable puts on the imperishable, and the mortal puts on immortality, then shall come to pass the saying that is written: "Death is swallowed up in victory." "O death, where is thy victory? O death, where is thy sting?" (1 Corinthians 15.53-55)

The witness from the Old Testament to the resurrection is actually quite strong. In Jesus' day, there was division among the authorities on this point. The Pharisees (the party to which St. Paul belonged) believed in the resurrection; the Sadducees did not. The victory over death, to which St. Paul alludes above, is taken from passages in Isaiah and Hosea, which promise the overcoming of death:

> And he will destroy on this mountain the covering that is cast over all peoples, the veil that is spread over all nations. He will swallow up death forever, and the Lord God will wipe away tears from all faces, and the reproach of his people he will take away from all the earth; for the Lord has spoken. (Isaiah 25:7-8)
> They shall not hurt or destroy in all my holy mountain. (Isaiah 11:9)

The apostle Paul seems to be echoing the prophet Hosea: "Shall I ransom them from the power of Sheol? Shall I redeem them from Death? O Death, where are your plagues? O Sheol, where is your destruction?" (Hosea 13:14)

Moreover, Job declares his faith in meeting God face to face in his body. With his own eyes he will see God:

> For I know that my Redeemer lives, and at last he will stand upon the earth; and after my skin has been thus destroyed, then from my flesh I shall see God, whom I shall see on my side, and my eyes shall behold, and not another. (Job 19:25-27)

And in the Psalms, the promise of bodily salvation is clearly stated: "Therefore my heart is glad, and my soul rejoices; my body also dwells secure. For thou dost not give me up to Sheol, or let thy godly one see the Pit" (Psalm 16:9-10).

Near the end of the Old Testament, there are overt references to the resurrection. The prophet Daniel affirms the raising of the dead to judgment:

> And many of those who sleep in the dust of the earth shall awake, some to everlasting life, and some to shame and

everlasting contempt. And those who are wise shall shine like the brightness of the firmament." (Daniel 12:2-3)

Again, as in Matthew 13:43, we see the gift of brilliance with which the glorified resurrected body will be endowed. Regarding the disparate conditions of resurrected bodies, the passage from Daniel recalls another verse (Isaiah 66:24): "Their worm shall not die, their fire shall not be quenched, and they shall be an abhorrence to all flesh."

The story of the seven valiant brothers and their courageous mother in 2 Maccabees is an explicit witness to faith in the resurrection. (Once again, Catholics regard this book as inspired Scripture; although Protestants may disagree with its inclusion in the canon, it does testify to Jewish belief in the resurrection. Likewise for the tantalizing hints in Wisdom 3:7-8.) The brothers are threatened with death unless they renounce the beliefs and traditions of their faith. As they go to their death under terrible tortures, the seven, along with their mother, profess their faith. Several of their testimonials express unshakable conviction in the ultimate resurrection of the dead (see 2 Maccabees 7:9, 11, 14, 23, 29). What a wonderful affirmation of a mother's love for her sons, tied to her hope and faith in God's power and will to give her and them the resurrection to life!

Resurrection and Redeemed Creation

Not only is the resurrection of the body (to eternal life for the good, to eternal death for the wicked) essential to the judgment of all humanity; but the resurrection to life affects all of creation as well. The fall not only affected human beings, but also in some mysterious way the rest of created things. We are not just fallen in our wills and minds, but also in our bodies. Through our bodies, we are in communion with the rest of material creation. But if the fall affected the rest of creation, so too does the redemption: (consider 2 Corinthians 6:17 in this light). We bring the rest of creation to Christ with us:

> For the creation waits with eager longing for the revealing of the sons of God; for the creation was subjected to futility, not of its own will but by the will of him who subjected it in hope; because the creation itself will be set free from its bondage to

decay and obtain the glorious liberty of the children of God.
(Romans 8:19-21)

Against the modern scientific tendency to reductionism (viewing higher
things in terms of lower), Scripture teaches just the opposite. Instead of the
freedom of human beings being reduced to matter in motion following
laws of physics, the rest of creation will participate in the freedom of
human beings. Of course, this is only possible because of the grace of
God. Ultimately, the freedom is the freedom of God, of Jesus Christ who
freely suffers and dies for us, who freely lays down His life and takes it
up again, sharing it with us. In the same passage, St. Paul speaks of our
waiting for the "redemption of our bodies" (Romans 8:23). But our bodies
come from the entirety of creation. The body is redeemed through and
through. Every level is perfected – from the moral and intellectual, to
the psychological, biological, chemical, and physical. All creation shares
in this perfection.

There will be new heavens and a new earth, transformed by the
love of God: "According to his promise we wait for new heavens and a
new earth in which righteousness dwells" (2 Peter 3:13). In the Book of
Revelation, St. John has a vision of the new creation: "Then I saw a new
heaven and a new earth; for the first heaven and the first earth had passed
away, and the sea was no more" (Revelation 21:1). The sea is a symbol of
chaos and imperfection (see Genesis 1:2); having given up its dead (see
Revelation 20:13), the sea will vanish in the new and perfect order of the
world. It is not that all will be heaven, or all will be angels and human
souls; rather, the earth as well as the heavens will be restored in grace,
the body as well as the soul. All creation will be made new in Christ:

> Then comes the end, when he delivers the kingdom to God
> the Father after destroying every rule and every authority and
> power. For he must reign until he has put all his enemies under
> his feet. The last enemy to be destroyed is death. "For God
> has put all things in subjection under his feet." (1 Corinthians
> 15.24-27)

Although this full transformation will occur in the *Eschaton*, even now
we, together with all of material creation, participate in the redemption.
We said above that we participate now in heaven or hell, depending on
how we act. The same can be said about the new creation. In the Old

Testament, the prophet Isaiah reveals that even now God offers us new heavens and a new earth, which we can await with joyful anticipation:

> For behold, I create new heavens and a new earth; and the former things shall not be remembered or come into mind. But be glad and rejoice for ever in that which I create; for behold I create Jerusalem a rejoicing, and her people a joy. (Isaiah 65:17-18)

Near the end of the New Testament, God's renewal of the heavens and the earth is repeated: "Behold, I make all things new" (Revelation 21:5). God is always present to His creation in every particular. Creation is always new.

And although our redemption is worked out in time, throughout the Old and New Covenants God's plan is timeless. This eternal plan has been made know to us (see Ephesians 1:9-10). It has always been God's plan to unite all things in Christ. All things are created in Christ and redeemed in Him. The grace of God leading to redemption and immortal life is given to us primordially in Christ Jesus, before the world was created (see 2 Timothy 1:9-10, along with John 3:16; 10:10; 17:3; 1 John 1:2; 4:9). In the mystery of God's plan, we too exist primordially, in some way prior to creation. God's purpose and grace involving us are given prior to creation and brought to light in the mission of the Son from the Father (see 1 Peter 1:20).

Conclusion

So, in some mysterious way, last things are first things. Although we may not share in the fullness of heaven in this life, we do share in the fullness of God's plan of redemption. Our free participation in this work is integral to it. Just as Christ would not have been born if Mary had not freely said "Yes", so our "Yes" is invaluable in the fulfillment of God's will. God has made His covenant with mankind. This does not make us divine, but it does mean that we freely figure in God's plan, through God's free act of creation and redemption. Final judgment awaits the *Eschaton*, but the *Eschaton* is not just related to the past and present in a linear relation of before and after, as if the future replaces both past and present. All things are freely created in Christ, who is the Lord of history. Although we must end up either in heaven or in hell, in this life we are free to accept the grace of God or to reject it and we are free to change our minds. All is under God's providence, but such providence does not take away our freedom. St. Paul says that from the beginning we are destined in love (see Ephesians 1:3-6), but there is no love where there is no freedom. Creation is free, first and last. The God of love draws us freely to Himself through the twin gifts of creation and redemption. If we go to Him, we do so freely; if we refuse, we do so freely. Only those, however, who *choose* to go to Him will have an everlasting *life* of freedom – for "where the Spirit of the Lord is, there is freedom" (2 Corinthians 3:17).

ENDNOTES

Chapter 3

1. This suggestion of the Trinity is mentioned by Dr. O. J. Graham, *The Six-Pointed Star* (Don Mills, Ontario: The Free Press 777, 4th Edition, 2000), p. 98.

2. *Polytheism* is the belief that there are many gods; *monotheism* is the belief that there is one God. Traditional and orthodox Christian doctrine explains that the Trinity is three *Persons* in *one God*. As long as you remember that there is an immense difference between the *uncreated divine nature* and the *created human nature*, and as long as you do not confuse *divine persons* with *human persons*, then you will not slip into polytheism. The ancient pagans, such as the Greeks and Romans, did not see the great difference. A cursory reading of their myths makes this abundantly clear.

3. **Nicea, the First Ecumenical Council** (325 A.D.), defined the divinity of Christ. Specifically the bishops described the Second Person of the Blessed Trinity, who is incarnate as Jesus Christ, to be "consubstantial with the Father". **The First Council of Constantinople** (381 A.D.) renewed the teaching of Nicea and produced a (now lost) document affirming the distinction of the three Persons of the Trinity. **The Council of Ephesus** (431 A.D.) proclaimed Mary, the mother of Jesus, to be the *"Theotokos"* ("God-bearer"), thus making clear that Jesus was always God and man from His conception and not "adopted" by the Father at some point in the midst of His earthly life. **The Council of Chalcedon** (451 A.D.) accepted the Tome of Pope St. Leo as the true teaching of the Church that Jesus had two natures, human and divine. **The Second Council of Constantinople** (553 A.D.) affirmed both Ephesus and Chalcedon, teaching that the Lord is one divine Person that unites a human and a divine nature (in what is called the "hypostatic union").

4. I know of no heresy denying the divinity of Christ that did not at the same time turn the Holy Spirit into a mere emanation of God.

5. In the Koran, the "Trinity" is thought to be God the Father, Our Lady, and Jesus!

6. The *"Incarnation"* of the Savior refers to the Second Person of the Blessed Trinity taking on a human nature, being born of the Virgin Mary, and henceforth known to us as Jesus Christ. In biblical terminology, "the Word became flesh and dwelt among us" (John. 1:14).

7. It was the theme of the Savior's life that He came to do the will of the Father. See, for example, John 17.

8. "Is" rather than "was", for the Incarnation is everlasting! Jesus Christ, the Second Person of the Blessed Trinity, God and Man, reigns forever with the Father and the Spirit in Heaven.

9. If this vow to virginity is not admitted, then Luke 1:34-37 is incomprehensible. To begin, the *RSV* translation is an incorrect rendering of the Greek *"ἄνδρα οὐ γινώσκω"*. Mary does not say, "I have no husband", but rather, "I do not know man". This is the biblical sense of "knowledge" between a man and woman, meaning the marital embrace. In Greek, the word is rendered in the present tense, implying an ongoing action. In effect, Mary is saying, "How is this to be, since I am in a state of life in which I do not and will not be knowing a man (in an intimate marital way)?" After all, she *did* have a husband, Joseph, to whom she was betrothed. Betrothal was not like an "engagement" in our own culture. It was, instead, a stage of marriage that preceded cohabitation of the couple during which the husband could work to fulfill the often onerous contractual obligations that he undertook in order to marry, and the young woman (or girl) could grow to full womanhood in her parents' home. Unless one is to assume that Mary had no knowledge of human reproduction, the angel's obvious response to her question about how the conception was to be achieved – if Mary *had not* taken a vow of virginity – would have been something like, "Your husband, Joseph, will know you and God will give this child". But of course, that was not to happen, and the angel responded as he did so that Mary would know that she did not have to break her vow in order to accept God's will – and thus the conception and birth would be miraculous.

10. It seems as though Peter's confession of faith includes the truth of Jesus' divinity, if for no other reason than that it was revealed by the Father: "[Jesus said] 'But who do you say that I am.?' Simon Peter replied, 'You are the Christ, the Son of the living God.' And Jesus answered him, 'Blessed are you, Simon Bar-Jona! For flesh and blood has not revealed this to you but my Father who is in Heaven'" (Matthew 16:15-17). In the acceptance of the doctrine on the Eucharist (see John 6:22-59), Peter again came to the conclusion that Jesus was more than man and was a special presence of God, which was why he could accept an otherwise impossible teaching (see John 6:68-69). This is another time in which Peter is speaking for all the Apostles, though not for Judas (see John 6:70-71). Yet, the actions of Peter during the Passion of Jesus, and indeed those of all the Apostles (except John), show that they had not understood the full meaning of the term "Son of God" – or at least were too weak to carry through with their beliefs. This was why they would deny or abandon Him.

11. It is interesting that in the *mishnah* the miracles of Jesus are not denied; rather, they are attributed to magic!

12. St. Paul calls Christ the "last Adam" in I Corinthians XV:45 and contrasts Him with "the first man Adam". To be the "last Adam" under the old creation, who brings man back to his proper relationship with God, is to be the New Adam of the New Creation saved by God's grace.

Chapter 4

1. While this chapter touches on glorification, the fullest treatment of this subject is better reserved for Chapter 12 dealing with "Last Things". Glorification is hardly a point of dispute between Catholics and Protestants. In both Catholic meanings of salvation, faith and living a moral life that includes acts of charity are conditions of salvation, but if the word is meant in the narrower sense, then faith and moral, loving conduct are prior conditions. The wider meaning of salvation is necessary in order to attribute to indulgences any appreciable degree of relevance to the subject. The lack of indulgences cannot cause someone to lose his

"eternal salvation". The Protestant reformation began as a controversy about indulgences. They are God's acts of pardon through the Church of some or all temporal punishment for sin. To the degree that a sin in some way involves an unhealthy attachment to anyone or anything but God, to that degree it results in temporal punishment. Some sins, mortal sins, also deserve eternal punishment, which has already been forgiven by the time that an indulgence has been granted. God remains completely free to pardon some or all temporal punishment even without the sinner ever receiving an indulgence.

2. Many who claim to follow John Calvin's teachings say that Jesus did not die to save absolutely everyone. But the Bible says, "He is the expiation for our sins, and not for ours only but also for the sins of the whole world" (1 John 2:2). Calvinists contend that Jesus died for the world only in the sense that He died for some special people ("the elect") from every race and nation throughout the world. If this were so, why then did the inspired author not simply write "the world" instead of "the whole world"? We need to make the effort to find out what he meant by this phrase. Fortunately, he makes one other reference to "the whole world". This is found near the end of this same relatively short letter. "We know that we are of God, and the whole world is in the power of the evil one" (1 John 5:19). Even Calvinists admit that "the whole world" in this last passage means absolutely everyone who is not a Christian, including babies. So we may safely conclude that Jesus Christ died to save all who are not Christians as well as all of us who are. Clearly, no one is excluded. Absolutely everyone needs to be transferred from the kingdom of darkness to the kingdom of God's beloved Son. Jesus has died so that all may see and enter God's kingdom. There are no exceptions.

3. Especially St. John's Gospel gives some readers the impression that believing is all that one needs to do to be saved. In a missionary context, belief in the Good News is normally the first step in becoming a Christian. Any document written to evangelize adults who are not yet Christians will emphasize this step. This is what the fourth Gospel does. Admittedly, John's language is a bit ambiguous. Stating in various ways that the person who will inherit eternal life is normatively a believer in Christ (see John 6:47) is quite different in intention, if not always in

actual wording, from stating that belief in Christ is the only requirement for salvation. Belief is the most basic requirement, but St. John teaches that a fearful refusal to confess this belief before others will cause God's disapproval and rejection on the Last Day (John 12:42-43, 47-48; see also Mark 8:38; Romans 10:9). Indeed, some physical healings in the Gospels took place because of faith alone (Matthew 9:22; Mark 10:52; Luke 17:19; see also Acts 3:16), but saving souls is an entirely different matter.

4. Without an appeal to "household" baptisms (Acts 16:15,33, 18:8, 1 Corinthians 1:16), a strong case can be made for the apostolic origins of infant baptism. The chain of proof is quite impressive. We can trace the practice from Augustine back to John the Apostle via Origen, St. Irenaeus, and St. Polycarp. In one of his many sermons, St. Augustine of Hippo said about infant baptism: "This the Church always had, always held. This she received from the faith of the ancients. This she preserves tenaciously to the end." Almost two hundred years before St. Augustine died, Origen, the great Christian theologian, wrote, "The Church received from the Apostles the tradition of baptizing infants, too" (from his *Commentary* on Romans, chapter six). About the time of Origen's birth, a staunch heresy-fighter named Irenaeus wrote of Jesus, "He came to save all by means of Himself – all, I say, who through Him are born again to God – infants, and children, and boys, and youths, and old men" (*Against Heresies*, Book 2, Chapter 22). Everywhere the early Church used the phrase "born again" to refer to Baptism. Christ had said that absolutely no one could get to heaven without being born again (John 3:3, 5). So babies were included. St. Irenaeus was a disciple of St. Polycarp, who was a disciple of St. John the Apostle. When Irenaeus was only a youth, Polycarp boldly confessed before his pagan persecutors, "Eighty-six years have I served Him [Christ], and He never did me any injury. How then can I blaspheme my King and my Savior?" (from *The Martyrdom of St. Polycarp*, chapter 9). When he spoke these words in 156 A.D., St. Polycarp was scarcely much older than eighty-six. Before his arrest, he stood praying for almost two hours straight (chapter 7), and he proceeded "speedily" on foot to the stadium, despite a bruised shin (chapter 8). Finally, he undressed himself for the torture stake (chapter 13). So Polycarp dates his Christian life from his infancy. Since he was baptized as a small child, he was baptized about 70 A.D., long before St.

John died. It seems John never taught him his infant baptism was wrong! Since the infant is not an adult, it cannot have a will to oppose God's justifying grace. A baby's cooperation with grace is guaranteed, because its mind and will are not fully developed to the level of reflective choice. Of course, it cannot make an act of faith before its justification. Indeed, a baby is justified without any act of its own. Infant salvation powerfully illustrates that eternal life is a gift from God, who loves us long before we love Him (1 John 4:10).

5. As concerns the issue of total immersion, it is true that Catholics today baptize far more babies by pouring than by immersion. It is not true that the only biblical form of baptism is total immersion. The Bible uses the Greek word for baptism in a broader sense. Since the "baptism with the Holy Spirit" (on Pentecost and at the house of Cornelius) is described in the Bible as a "pouring out" and a "falling upon" believers, the immersion-only view appears to be weak. The biblical phrase "baptized with the Holy Spirit" (Acts 1:5; 11:16-17) denotes something like a pouring (Acts 2:17-18, 33; 10:44-45; 11:15), not like an immersion. In addition, there are two or three other passages that seriously undermine this baptistic theory. The noun _baptismos_ is used in Hebrews 9:10 to describe Old Testament ceremonial sprinklings and pourings for purification, yet this very same author uses this very same Greek word also for Christian baptism (6:2). Also, in Luke 11:38, the original Greek tells us that Jesus was expected to be "baptized" before dinner, yet we know that this Jewish custom involved pouring less than a pint of water (a _hin_) over the hands. The washing of a part of the body by means of pouring is a "baptizing" of the whole person.

6. There is an old expression that goes, "the Devil is in the details." It means that the task at hand exceeds our human abilities to cope adequately with the complexities of its details. In the case of these far-reaching questions about micro-salvation, the Devil is not in the details. As Catholics, we know, because of Christ's promises to His people, that only the Holy Spirit is very much in the details, as He lives to guide the magisterium of the original Church to fathom these great mysteries with secure insights.

7. Despite this highly exaggerated and perhaps egotistical claim, many Lutheran theologians today are willing to affirm that the post-Tridentine Catholic Church has remained a part of the true Church of Jesus Christ. Martin Luther said the same of the pre-Tridentine Catholic Church. In 1528, eleven years after the start of the reformation, Luther wrote these words against those who rejected infant baptism: "We on our part confess that there is much that is Christian and good under the papacy; indeed everything that is Christian and good is to be found there and has come to us from this source.... The Christendom that now is under the papacy is truly the body of Christ and a member of it. If it is his body, then it has the true spirit, gospel, faith, baptism, sacrament, keys, the office of the ministry, prayer, holy Scripture, and everything that pertains to Christendom. So we are all still under the papacy and therefrom have received our Christian treasures." Martin Luther, "Concerning Rebaptism," translated by Conrad Bergendoff, *Luther's Works* (Muhlenberg Press, Philadelphia, Pennsylvania, 1958), volume 40, pp. 231-232.

8. Many groups of Protestants today do not share a belief in Original Sin with Lutherans, Calvinists, and Catholics. These other groups deny that Original Sin is real sin. All Christians agree that sin resulting from one's own free choice is real (Genesis 4:7; Ezekiel 18:20; John 5:29; Romans 4:15; 7:7-9; James 1:15; 1 John 3:4), but it is a mistake for these other groups to assume that only personally-committed sin is real. All Christian groups that teach the reality of Original Sin also stress the reality of personal sin and believe that most of the references to sin in Scripture are to personal sin. Therefore, the multiplication of such biblical verses as if they count against this Catholic dogma is really beside the point. Those non-Catholics who reject Original Sin are seriously mistaken. Their babies are born in Original Sin, though they deny it. They make or suggest a few seemingly strong arguments. They reason: (1) since, by definition, "sin is the transgression of the law" (1 John 3:4, *KJV*), all sin must be consciously and personally committed; (2) the Apostle Paul claims to have been spiritually "alive" before he committed his first sin instead of dead in Original Sin (Romans 7:9); (3) it is obviously unjust for God to punish anyone other than Adam for what Adam alone chose to do; and (4) biblical verses that prove that all humans inherit a weak nature inclined to sin are useless to prove the reality of universal, inherited guilt, which

is a Catholic dogma. How might a Catholic respond to these points? Let's take each of them in order. (1) The original Greek of 1 John 3:4 is more accurately translated as "sin is lawlessness", which means whatever does not conform to divine standards, either of action (personal sin) or of being (Original Sin); (2) as an Israelite born under the Old Covenant, Paul was spiritually "alive" in his early childhood because Original Sin was "dead", thanks to the rite of circumcision, or the providential remedy which was the prelude to the Christian Sacrament of Baptism under the New Covenant; we know that children under both dispensations could be filled with the Spirit (see Luke 1:15; Acts 2:38-39); (3) it would obviously be unjust for God to sentence a baby to spiritual death, unless he has been guilty of some sort of sin (Romans 6:23), and Original Sin is not only Adam's iniquity, but is also the baby's own, although he is bearing it precisely because Adam's first personal sin caused the baby's iniquity, the lack of holiness in its inherited human nature; and (4) Romans 5, which proves inherited sin must also prove inherited guilt, since every sin that is really sin must carry real guilt along with it. It is a fact that sometimes babies die as babies. Since the death of a human being always comes through sin (Romans 5:12), all who die before being born again are sinners (Romans 5:19), including babies, who die in Adam (1 Corinthians 15:22). They live under Satan's control (1 John 5:19) until they have been made alive in Christ. Jesus Christ died for all (2 Corinthians 5:15), even for dying babies, whether baptized or unbaptized (1 John 2:2). We are sure that this is true because He died for all who are sinners by nature (Psalms 51:5; 58:3; Ephesians 2:3-5), that is, all of us, even newborn babies. Their real need for justification and salvation, even while they are still infants, more than adequately vindicates the Catholic practice of infant baptism.

9. Lewis W. Spitz, *The Renaissance and Reformation Movements* (Rand McNally College Publishing Company, Chicago, 1971), p.488.

10. The fact that also St. Luke (18:18-23) includes this story in his Gospel should give serious pause to anyone finding salvation by faith alone in his writings. For example, salvation is made too easy by those who quote Acts 16:31 out of its context in order to prove that faith is all that is necessary. If St. Paul's response to the jailer has been stylized by St. Luke,

then the part (belief) obviously stands for the whole (baptism and a life of good works). To draw any other conclusion misses a crucial fact about human communication; this is an insight of David Currie: we almost always order a hotdog without mentioning a bun, yet hardly ever mean a bare hotdog without a bun. If this is a direct quotation, then it has the marks of an emergency response – St. Paul's knee-jerk reply to a fearful question provoked by a terrifying earthquake caused by God Almighty! The suicidal Philippian jailer asked: "What must I do to be saved?" St. Paul promised: "Believe in the Lord Jesus, and you will be saved, you and your household." St. Paul knew that he himself could do the baptizing if only the jailer and his family would do the believing, and so, in a truthful response as short as possible, one designed to encourage hope and faith in his despairing pagan hearer, he did not consider it necessary or wise to mention the Christian initiation rite of baptism, which requires a rejection of sin and a lifetime of devotion to the Lord Jesus. This could require too much explanation in this emergency situation. Further instruction on these matters is clearly implied in the statement that "they spoke the Word of the Lord" to them (v. 32) before they baptized them. For the writer of Luke and Acts, there is no genuine belief in Jesus as Lord and Savior without knowing and accepting the most important aspects of what He "began to do and teach" (Acts 1:1). For this reason, St. Luke does not assert that the jailer and his household "believed" until after they had been admitted to the cleansing waters of baptism (Acts 16:33-34).

11. "They [the scholastics] say that we must believe in Christ and that faith is the foundation of salvation, but they say that this faith does not justify unless it is 'formed by love.' This is not the truth of the Gospel; it is falsehood and pretense. The True Gospel, however, is this: Works or love are not the ornament or perfection of faith; but faith itself is a gift of God, a work of God in our hearts, which justifies us because it takes hold of Christ as the Savior. . . . Therefore, what the scholastics have taught about justifying faith 'formed by love' is an empty dream. For the faith that takes hold of Christ, the Son of God, and is adorned by Him is the faith that justifies, not a faith that includes love.... Just as our opponents refuse to concede to us the freedom that faith in Christ alone justifies, so we refuse to concede to them, in turn, that faith formed by love justifies.

Here we intend and are obliged to be rebellious and stubborn with them, for otherwise we would lose the truth of the Gospel." Martin Luther, "Lectures on Galatians 1535," translated by Jaroslav Pelikan, *Luther's Works* (Concordia Publishing House, St. Louis, Missouri, 1963), volume 26, pp. 88-90.

12. For John Calvin, love is not essential for faith to justify and does not in this way act as the foundation of justification. As an important part of the superstructure, a works-producing love necessarily follows on the foundation of true faith alone. "In vain do they lay hold of the frivolous subtilty, that the *faith alone*, by which we are justified, *'worketh by love,'* and that love, therefore, is the foundation of justification. We, indeed, acknowledge with Paul, that the only faith which justifies is that which works by love (Gal. v. 6); but love does not give it its justifying power. Nay, its [faith's] only means of justifying consists in its bringing us into communication with the righteousness of Christ." John Calvin, *Institutes of the Christian Religion*, Book III, chapter 11, section 20, translated by Henry Beveridge (Wm. B. Eerdmans Publishing Company, Grand Rapids, Michigan, 1957), volume 2, p. 56.

13. John Calvin, *Institutes of the Christian Religion*, Book III, Chapter 2, section 8, *Ibid.*, vol. 1, pp. 475-476. "It is no surprise that after 1518 there is a marked absence from Luther's writings regarding love and its place in the Christian faith." Robert A. Sungenis, *Not By Faith Alone: The Biblical Evidence for the Catholic Doctrine of Justification* (Queenship Publishing Company, Santa Barbara, California, 1997), p. 545.

14. Many sixteenth-century reformers insisted that sanctification, involving the performance of "good" actions, will, in every case, be present at our final salvation, though missing at the moment of justification, our initial salvation. These classical Protestants agreed with Catholics that moral deeds are in some way necessary for us to enter into heaven. Yet followers of John Calvin seek to maintain a respectable distance from Catholicism on this matter by promoting the clever slogan, "Faith alone saves, but the faith that saves is never alone." By this they mean that justification is apart from the merit of works but not apart from the existence of "good" works, which will inevitably follow on the heels of justification.

According to Calvin himself, sanctification is distinct from justification, yet "good" works flow automatically from the true faith that alone justifies, since spiritual regeneration immediately occurs within the soul of each and every justified believer. For him, justification *involves* a change in nature even though it does not *mean* one. Calvinists claim that re-birth can make one holier than he was, but not as holy as Catholics claim that baptismal regeneration can. In both belief systems, the resulting change in nature tends to improve the quality of our thoughts and actions. But Catholics believe in truly good deeds, whereas these Protestants believe in only so-called "good" deeds. They insist that even the best efforts of a true Christian are tainted by sin, and so fall abysmally short of God's full commendation. Some of them believe that God has promised to reward some of these imperfect works, and in this way even accept a very limited type of "meriting." Surprisingly, "orthodox" Calvinists, unlike "orthodox" Lutherans, place regeneration before justification in the logical order of God's saving activities. These Reformed Protestants therefore agree with Catholics that God, in every case of justification, justifies someone whom He views as already sanctified in a rudimentary way. There is a big difference, however. These Protestants claim that a justified person is only ever partially sanctified before death, whereas Catholics maintain that a person who has the proper disposition can be perfectly sanctified at his baptismal justification and/or anytime before death. It seems that, for all the Protestants' complaining about purgatory, their own various theologies require at least an instant of soul purification at the moment of death (instantaneous total sanctification). Catholic theologians are allowed to hold that an instant of purgatorial cleansing resulting in total sanctification may be the experience of at least some.

15. Many Protestant reformers were sixteenth-century humanists. They studied the Bible and other ancient classical documents in their original languages. They studied the Greek words that St. Paul used for "justification" and "justify". Melanchthon, a young protégé of Luther, concluded that these words always have a forensic meaning, that is, they always refer to a declaration of acquittal as in a courtroom. This conclusion was very quickly adopted by virtually all the major reformers, even though "the importance of this development lies in the fact that it marks a complete break with the teaching of the church up to that

point" (Alister E. McGrath, "Justification," *The Oxford Encyclopedia of the Reformation*, 4 vols., edited by Hans J. Hillerbrandt, Oxford University Press, Oxford, England, 1996, vol. 2, p. 367, col. 2). As humanists, these early reformers allowed these ancient words or metaphors about salvation to limit their understanding of the divine-human mystery to which they refer. This faulty methodology led them to restrict the reality of justification to the past moment of a declared acquittal of the believer within the divine courtroom of heaven. For them, it seemed, theological reality could not be any bigger than the biblical words used to describe it. So, for almost all of them (Luther is the chief exception), biblical justification had only a negative aspect (pardon from sin), not a positive one (sanctification). Martin Luther blurred justification and sanctification, despite his principles, not because of them. His most loyal followers, especially Melanchthon, clarified the distinction between the two on the basis of biblical word usages. This methodology ignores the limitations of language itself, even inspired language. Under the guidance of the Spirit, St. Paul had the daunting task of using old, common Greek words to symbolize and describe a newly revealed, unique mystery, one that the pagan Greeks and translators of the Septuagint had never imagined when they used the words. As humanists, the reformers tried mainly to use induction from biblical texts to craft essential doctrines about spiritual reality. In contrast, the bishops at Trent deduced their formulations from traditional spiritual reality. They faithfully represented justification and salvation as it occurred down through the ages within the Church of Christ, and as the Bible and the Church Fathers, especially St. Augustine, described it. Like a skillful tailor, the bishops used the right tools to craft beauty. They used spiritual reality to measure and cut biblical words rather than biblical words to measure and cut spiritual reality. A little careful reflection upon these two methodologies shows the Catholic approach to be far superior, because it honors God by stressing His activity in history as well as His words in the Bible. Also, because it is deductive rather than inductive, it can yield absolute certitude, while the Protestant approach can yield nothing greater than the highest probability. The Catholic Faith is grounded in unchanging and revealed certainties, not in highly plausible scholarly conclusions.

16. Alan Richardson, *An Introduction to the Theology of the New Testament* (New York: Harper & Row, 1958), p. 238, footnote 1.

17. "In the work of salvation God and man, grace and nature, sacrament and moral effort are united. We have therefore in justification a repetition of the fundamental mystery in Christianity, the incarnation of the divine in human form. The acts of a justified man are neither purely divine nor purely human, but a compound of divinity and humanity." Karl Adam, *The Spirit of Catholicism* (Sheed and Ward, London, England, 1929), p. 184.

18. The book of Acts teaches that the Church is the Mystical Body of Christ, which grows in wisdom and favor with God and man, and which continues the deeds and teachings of Christ. To persecute the Church is to cause suffering to Christ (see Acts 9:1-6). Christians who willingly bear this persecution in a state of grace increase the merits of the Mystical Body of Christ (see Colossians 1:24). The Catholic doctrine of indulgences assumes that God can use voluntary sufferings and other charitable deeds of some members of the Body of Christ for the benefit other members (see Galatians 6:2).

19. This chapter will not treat the topic of predestination. This is not because Catholics deny that it is a biblical teaching or that it is true. We believe that there is a predestination to grace as well as to glory. However, this is perhaps the most complex of all the complexities of God's plan of salvation. For an adequate theological treatment of this profound mystery, I highly recommend the work of Father Manuel Pinon, O.P., *Predestination and Salvation* (Dominican House of Studies, Quezon City, Philippines, 1977).

20. If the life of Jesus until His resurrection appearances (Luke's Gospel) is only what Jesus "began to do and teach" (Acts 1:1), the inspired writer clearly believes that Jesus Christ continues to act and teach through His Church under the leadership of His Apostles and their associates (the Book of Acts). As the Father sent the Son to act and teach for Him, so Jesus sends the Apostles to act and teach for Him, through the power of His Holy Spirit (John 20:21). All this helps us to understand better the

meaning of Jesus' statement on the cross, "It is finished" (John 19:30). It does not mean that all we need to do to be saved is to believe that Jesus on the cross did everything necessary for our salvation. We need to merit heaven. Even a careful evangelical Protestant will notice that Jesus spoke these words right BEFORE He died. In evangelical theology, the death of Jesus is an essential part of the work that He accomplished for our salvation. St. Paul goes further. He teaches that the resurrection of Jesus is required for our justification (Romans 4:25). Rising from the dead is one of the works of Jesus for the sake of our salvation (John 2:19-22). What, then, does Jesus mean by the statement, "It is finished"? He means quite simply that all the work that the Father has assigned to Him to do before His death has been accomplished. In His prayer right before His arrest, He states that this is already the case with the divinely assigned duties of His public ministry (see John 17:4). He then requests glorification for Himself, the glorification of the Passion that will return Him to His pre-incarnate glory. Now, finally, with the end of His sufferings, "it is finished." By these words on the cross, He is saying that each and every aspect of the Passion that the Father intended Him to endure before He died, including all the prophecies of Scripture, have now all been fulfilled as well. Thus, the proper understanding of these words neutralizes a common argument for salvation by faith alone.

21. For more on purgatory, see Chapter 12.

22. In addition to FIRST justification by faith, hope, and love, apart from the works of the unjustified, and FURTHER justification because of the good works of the already justified, there is the FINAL justification "according to works" of all who are justified and glorified at the Last Judgment. From the standpoint of a Christian living today in a state of grace, FIRST justification is in the past tense (1 Corinthians 6:11; Romans 5:1), FURTHER justification is in the present tense (James 2:24; Romans 8:33), and FINAL justification is in the future tense (Romans 2:13; Galatians 5:4-5). We believe that the Catholic teaching about justification is thoroughly apostolic and biblical. Its important aspects can be stated in one long sentence. *At first God in His sheer mercy justifies a repentant believer or an infant with Original Sin through the renewal in righteousness called "baptismal regeneration," which the Risen Christ through the*

Holy Spirit accomplishes within the person via sanctifying grace, which is infused into the believer's soul or the soul of the infant on account of Christ's merits in offering Himself on the Cross for our salvation; next, God in His justice toward the justified gives a greater degree of justification as a reward, that is, an increase of sanctifying grace won for us by the merits of Christ and infused into the soul of a Christian who remains in a state of grace and freely does one or more truly meritorious acts; and later, if the baptized person loses justification through his own most grievous fault, again and again, if necessary, God in His never-ending mercy justifies the believer who repents of post-baptismal mortal sins, because of the renewal in righteousness available in sacramental penance, that is, sanctifying grace won for us by the merits of Christ and infused into the soul of the penitent. Indeed, salvation is simple but it is also very complex.

23. I am indebted to Rev. Brian W. Harrison, O.S., for most of this analogy, which I have extended by likening sanctifying grace to food. It is, of course, true that food is a substance that modifies the body, but sanctifying grace, although it modifies the soul, is not a substance but a divine operation, a dynamic principle of supernatural life.

24. To the seeming detriment of God's goodness and fairness, these men emphasized God's greatness. In order to deny the possibility of all human merit in matters of salvation, these reformers denied freewill, or the power of contrary choice. According to them, we must will to do whatever we in fact do will. Our nature determines every decision we make. Without external compulsion, whenever we decided to do something, we could not have chosen to do something else or even nothing at all. Luther valued *Bondage of the Will* as perhaps his best theological work. This book teaches that God alone determines whether you and I will be saved or lost. We really have no free choice in this everlasting matter. John Calvin systematized this terrible teaching. According to these greatest Protestant leaders, from all eternity God has predestined only some to believe and go to heaven. The others most certainly will burn in hell forever, because they cannot do otherwise than what they will do, that is, perform outside of Christ deeds deserving of an eternal punishment. Their corrupted and unregenerated nature determines that they will perform only corrupt deeds deserving of everlasting hell. All this makes God appear to be a capricious and cruel tyrant. Most modern-day Protestants have departed

from these dreadful teachings of Luther and Calvin about salvation. The hearts of most Christians are convinced that God is totally good and fair as well as great, and so they are drawn more in the Catholic direction. Like Catholics today, most Protestants believe that we must freely choose to cooperate with God's grace in order to be saved.

25. "We are beggars. That is true" [*Wir sein Pettler. Hoc est verum*]. Jotted on a small piece of paper two days before his death, these are, as far as we know, the last words that Martin Luther ever wrote. Spitz, *Ibid.*, p. 355.

26. While there are some cases in which one cannot strictly merit for someone else, the Catholic practice of indulgences assumes the truth of our ability to do this for others in other cases. This chapter has mentioned all the building blocks of the Catholic doctrine of indulgences and has provided adequate support for them from the Holy Scriptures. (1) The Pope has binding-and-loosing power; (2) God can use voluntary sufferings and other charitable deeds of some members of the Body of Christ for the benefit other members; (3) God sometimes forgives the eternal consequences of a sin without remitting at least some temporal punishment for the same sin; (4) doing what Christ encourages but does not require, if done in a state of grace and out of love for God, is potentially beneficial for other members of the Mystical Body of Christ as well as being meritorious for the Christian who is doing this "work of supererogation", which is added to the treasury of merit; (5) a Christian in a state of grace, by free-will cooperation with grace, can truly merit for himself and, in many cases, even for others. An excellent, very readable and understandable explanation of indulgences for Protestants can be found in James Akin, *The Salvation Controversy* (Catholic Answers, San Diego, California, 2001), pp. 52-71. Many evangelical Protestants who strenuously object to the unbiblical nature of the phrase "the treasury of the merits of Christ and the saints" are inconsistent. They demand biblical phrases from Catholics, yet they have no objection to using similarly unbiblical bankers' images to present their own doctrine of justification by faith alone. Catholics draw upon a community chest while Protestants visualize a hidden, personal bank account, but the Scriptures nowhere present justification as a divine deposit of the infinite value of Christ's meritorious works, sufferings, and death "into the believer's account"

because of faith alone. In Revelation 21:6, Christ offers the sincere seeker the water of life "without payment". By these words, He is not denying that eternal life is the reward for meritorious deeds. He is not teaching that salvation by faith alone is a fact, "because Jesus paid it all" by His own merits. Rather, the point is more basic. A person cannot purchase salvation with money (see Acts 8:18-24). An informed Catholic knows that he does not buy indulgences. He may choose the type of good work to perform in conjunction with the gaining of an indulgence, and this might be giving alms to the poor (see Daniel 4:27; Luke 11:41), perhaps even by means of an alms box in church. An informed Catholic also knows that he does not buy Masses or the spiritual benefits of them. A Mass stipend, only a few dollars, merely covers the material costs for a Mass, which benefits many people. Jesus taught we cannot buy salvation, but what we do for our neighbor with our money most certainly affects our salvation (see Matthew 19:23-26).

27. One prominent scholar who did not overlook or totally misunderstand the incompatibility of divinization and Luther's doctrine of justification by faith alone is Ernst Kasemann, the German Lutheran biblical theologian. He considered divinization to be a wretched post-Pauline development that helped to displace St. Paul's central teaching within later Gentile Christianity. What he misses about divinization (Christ becomes man so that we can become as gods) is its truth as a legitimate development of biblical thought. With insight into its basic incompatibility with the Lutheran understanding on this point, he wrote: "It [the Pauline doctrine of justification by faith alone] calls the church, no less than the synagogue, in the name of Jesus, out of its pious dreams back to earth and to the humanity of the creature. The justification of the sinner is the only path on which God's creature remains before and under God and at the same time part of mankind, so that while he is in this world of ours he is also beneath the open heavens." Ernst Kasemann, *Perspectives on Paul*, translated by Margaret Kohl (Fortress Press, Philadelphia, Pennsylvania, 1971), pp. 73-74.

28. Ron Rhodes, an evangelical apologist who sometimes writes against Catholicism, is a good example of this misperception. He is quite pessimistic about justified humanity. He believes that trusting in one's

own personal efforts for attaining salvation is futile or delusional. He likens the earnest Catholic who expects to make great progress in his spiritual life because of his self-efforts to a sailor of a sailboat who finds himself stranded in the middle of the Atlantic Ocean because there has been no breeze for many days. The desperate man tries to get his boat moving once again by pushing against the mast with all his might. He gets nowhere fast, even though he deludes himself into thinking that he is making real progress, because he feels the rocking of the boat and sees a few small waves over the side of his boat. Ron Rhodes, *Reasoning from the Scriptures with Catholics* (Harvest House Publishers, Eugene, Oregon, 2000), p.139. This is an accurate enough description of the voyage of the Good Ship Natural but not of the Good Ship Supernatural. What Dr. Rhodes seems to overlook or misunderstand is that God has fully equipped Mr. Abel T. Christian with the Holy Spirit and with abundant graces as unmerited gifts for the purpose of his divinization. The life of grace has big challenges, but it is more like a wise sailor who, leaving homeport in his sailboat, takes along the gift of an outboard motor that can never fail or wear out, and an unlimited supply of free gasoline.

29. Fullness of grace does not mean that grace is a substance. It is a quality that allows for degrees. God so modifies the nature of the soul that it has new powers, including the ability do what is pleasing to God. In biblical terms, grace is the supernatural life that comes from God. It allows for degrees of intensity. Grace gives to our souls a resistible, inward force that is moving us ever closer to the Beatific Vision. This supernatural life has all that it needs to produce the fruit of supernatural actions. It also has everything it needs to maintain itself and to grow. Like all life, grace is a source of certain types of actions of the same order, supernatural deeds of love for God and mankind for His sake. Over time, a living plant becomes stronger, more and more like the plant that bore the seed that it once was. Similarly, a Christian living the supernatural life of grace becomes ever more like God, the Source of the seed of this life within the soul. Because this supernatural life bears fruit that glorifies God, it wins from Him a reward of the same order.

30. For the scriptural foundations of Marian dogmas, see Chapter 11.

31. For further reading on Catholic teaching about the saints, see Chapter 10.

32. St. Cyril of Alexandria, who died in 444, taught: "The Spirit is God by nature, since it is by participating in Him that we participate in the divine nature, that we can be called children of God and hence gods ourselves" (*In Joan. Comment.* P.G. 73; p. 157, I, I, 1-13). And in his book on the Blessed Trinity, he wrote: "The Spirit is God and transforms into God ... those who are worthy of it, by communicating the divine nature to them Himself." St. Athanasius, who lived from 295 to373, declared: "The Son is He through whom the Father deifies. Whence it follows that if He were God only by participation and not consubstantially, He could not deify others.... The true Son became man in order to make us gods" (*Epistula de Synodis.* P.G., 26; p. 784, 5,1). St. Basil the Great taught: "Souls that bear the Spirit within them (*animae quae spiritum ferunt*) attain a resemblance with God; and this results in the most sublime thing possible, your deification (*hinc est ut deus fias*)" (*De Spiritu Sancto*, 375; P.G., 32, p. 116; Ch. 19:23). St. Ambrose of Milan asked: "Who would dare maintain that the Holy Spirit is by nature different from the Father and Christ, since it is through Him that we receive the image and likeness of God and that we become partakers of the nature of God, according to the words of St. Peter?" (*De Spiritu Sancto*, P.L., 16, p. 723; 1.I, Ch. 6:80). Pseudo-Dionysius asserted: "Salvation is reserved for those who have been deified. This deification is, insofar as is possible, an assimilation to, an identification with God" (*De Ecci. hierarchia*, P.G., 3, p. 373, Ch. 1:3). St. Augustine of Hippo declared: "It is evident that since God calls men gods, He must deify them by His grace.... He alone deifies who is God of Himself and not by participation in another. It is He, too, who justifies, because in justifying men He makes them sons of God. If we become children of God, we become God" (*In Psalmum* 49:2, P.L., 36, p. 565). During the Protestant reformation, even some of the radical reformers, who were most committed to rejecting every type of non-biblical, traditional Catholic teaching, preferred to speak of salvation in terms of the image of divinization rather than justification (McGrath, *Ibid.*, vol. 2, p.366). This shows how deeply the teaching was embedded in Tradition.

33. "The love of God above all, and of men for His sake – that is the one indispensable work; and of itself, though all external works may be absent, it merits the kingdom of heaven. He who loves has passed from death to life; external good works can claim a reward so far, and so far only, as they spring from love, are the expression of love, serve to intensify love." William E. Addis and Thomas Arnold, "Merit," in *A Catholic Dictionary*, revised by T. B. Scannell (B. Herder, St. Louis, Missouri, 1917), p. 578. In Catholicism today, as was true almost a century ago when the above was written, the laws of the Church are meant to serve love and the salvation of souls. In the permissive post-Vatican II climate, very few contemporary Protestant critics, such as Tim Enloe, identify themselves with the major concerns of Luther and Calvin about Catholic legalism. Nevertheless, Mr. Enloe argues that Roman Catholicism, as a system of moralistic conformity, tends toward Pharisaism, with its alleged focus on "the most excruciating details and rigorous practice of external morality". In his view, Roman Catholicism obscures the Good News of Jesus Christ and His cross rather than promotes it, as evidenced in Church teaching on contraception and the rather irritating drumbeating of this issue by some former Protestants who have become Catholic apologists. He further cites as unbiblical the legalistic tenor of some confessional practices and nit-picking descriptions of the act of perfect contrition (Tim Enloe, "On Moral Issues as Grounds for Converting to Roman Catholicism," at http://graceunknown.com/Apologia/Romana/MoralGrounds.html). It is no doubt true that Mr. Enloe's own reformation version of the Good News makes a high degree of spiritual happiness a relatively easy matter for a guilt-ridden sinner to experience. By means of his unique, central doctrine on justification, Luther himself valued the great joy of a salvation that did not much depend upon real progress in personal holiness. But this is to make salvation too easy, according to Jesus: "For I tell you, unless your righteousness exceeds that of the scribes and Pharisees, you will never enter the kingdom of heaven" (Matthew 5:20). The supreme abiding lesson taught by all the saints is that an increase in true holiness is necessary for an increase in true happiness. You cannot have one without the other. Jesus did not come to oppose the Law. He proclaimed the Good News that God has made a way for all of us to fulfill the Law by the way of love (Mark 12:28-34; see also Romans 13:9-10; Galatians

5:14). This is the Law of Christ, and therefore of His Church. This was clearly a part of St. Paul's Good News as well (see Romans 8:3-4).

Chapter 5

1. For a fairly extensive study of the matter of six of the seven Sacraments, see David P. Lang, *Why Matter Matters: Philosophical and Scriptural Reflections on the Sacraments* (Huntington, IN: Our Sunday Visitor, 2002),

2. Refer back to Chapter 4 for an elaborate treatment of justification.

3. Regarding the issue of water as the only valid matter for confecting the Sacrament of Baptism, see *Why Matter Matters*, Chapter 1.

4. For many details not discussed here, see *Why Matter Matters*, Chapter 1.

5. For an abundance of detail on the matter of oil (especially olive oil) in connection with Confirmation, see *Why Matter Matters*, Chapter 4, Part I.

Chapter 7

1. I am indebted to David L. Vise for pointing out these three Scriptural arguments to me; the germ of the third one is essentially contained in *The Catechism of the Catholic Church*, n. 1337. In my article "Some scriptural arguments for the all-male priesthood", *Homiletic and Pastoral Review*, February 2003, I employed (on pp. 22-25) these three arguments, although earlier in that essay I also justified the all-male priesthood by a more philosophical argument connecting human biology with sacramental symbolism. For further reading, see also Chapter 5 of my book *Why Matter Matters*.

2. The basic idea of this argument is due to Francis B. Kelly.

3. See Chapter 5 of my book *Why Matter Matters* for more elaborate commentary on this point.

4. Such pestiferous books and films as *The Last Temptation Of Christ* notwithstanding....

5. Such preposterous books and films as *The Da Vinci Code* notwithstanding....

6. This important part that marriage on earth has in God's salvific plan makes clear how demonic is the present-day attempt to re-define marriage as a union of two of the same gender.

7. The idea that celibacy leads to child molestation is ridiculous. There are plenty of societies with no celibacy and children are still in danger. When heterosexuals don't live celibacy well, when they don't struggle against the lust-filled world, then their fall will be the common sins of heterosexuals. If homosexuals – against the continued cautions of the Holy See – are ordained priests and fail to struggle against this world, then their fall will be the unnatural sins of homosexuals. If the Catholic Church in the United States does not realize that the problem of the molestation of teenage boys is rooted in the fact that there are homosexual priests who have proven they are incapable of living celibately, then the scandal will not abate. (The "pedophile priest scandal" is a misnomer; most victims of the priests are post-pubescent. The victims of this small number of homosexual priests are the same as the targets of most homosexuals who fail to live chastely: young males.)

Chapter 8

1. For a discussion of the single exception, see Chapter 11 on the Marian dogma of the Immaculate Conception.

2. See Chapter 12 on the Last Things for further elaboration.

3. For more detail on the matter of oil (especially olive oil) in connection with the Anointing of the Sick, see *Why Matter Matters*, Chapter 4, Part II.

Chapter 9

1. See Chapter 1.

2. I am indebted to Dr. Arthur M. Hippler, weekly columnist for the *Wanderer*, for having located these two quotations from Luther and Calvin.

3. I am indebted to Jeremy J. Lancey for suggesting this line of argumentation.

4. See Chapter 5 for further details about Baptism.

5. See Chapters 6 and 7 for further details about the Holy Eucharist and Holy Orders.

6. See Chapter 5 for further details about Confirmation.

7. See Chapter 8 for further details about Penance.

8. See Chapter 8 for further details on the Anointing of the Sick.

Chapter 10

1. In this context, one should take note of John 8:31-59. In light of this lengthy exchange between Christ and certain Jewish elders, it seems that we must distinguish between the *true* spiritual children of Abraham and the merely carnal descendants of the great patriarch. [Editor]

2. See Chapter 12 on the Last Things for a discussion of purgatory.

3. See Chapter 2 on the Sources of Revelation.

4. See Chapter 12 for a discussion of the resurrection.

Chapter 11

1. "She presented Him to the Father in the temple, and was united with Him by compassion as He died on the cross. In this singular way she cooperated by her obedience, faith, hope, and burning charity in the work of the Savior in giving back supernatural life to souls. Wherefore she is our Mother in the order of grace." (*Lumen Gentium* 61)

2. We can actually go beyond this tentative statement by supplying conclusive evidence for the authentic Catholic teaching on this point. Indeed, the Preface for a Mass that can be offered on September 15, the Feast of Our Lady of Sorrows (a Mass titled "Mary at the Foot of the Cross II"), reads: "Father, all-powerful and ever-living God, we do well always and everywhere to give you thanks through Jesus Christ our Lord. In your divine wisdom you planned the redemption of the human race and decreed that the new Eve should stand by the cross of the new Adam: as she became his mother by the power of the Holy Spirit, so, by a new gift of your love, she was to be a partner in his passion, and **she who had given him birth without the pains of childbirth** was to endure the greatest of pains in bringing forth to new life the family of your Church (boldface emphasis added)." See **Collection of Masses of the Blessed Virgin Mary**, Volume I, **SACRAMENTARY** (Approved for Use in the Dioceses of the United States of America by the National Conference of Catholic Bishops and Confirmed by the Apostolic See), Catholic Book Publishing Co., New York, 1992, p. 12. The Vatican would never have approved this prayer for the Holy Sacrifice of the Mass if the thesis of Mary's freedom from birthpangs were not official Catholic teaching, in accordance with the precept *"Lex orandi, lex credendi"* ("As the Church prays, so she believes"). [Editor]

3. "From the first instant of her conception she was adorned with the radiance of an entirely unique holiness" (*Lumen Gentium* 56).

4. *The Catechism of the Council of Trent* (also called the *Roman Catechism*, published under the editorship of St. Charles Borromeo and promulgated under the authority of Pope St. Pius V) states in Article III, Part 2 (p. 45 of the 1982 TAN Books edition): "But as the Conception itself

transcends the order of nature, so also the birth of our Lord presents to our contemplation nothing but what is divine. Besides, what is admirable beyond the power of thoughts or words to express, He is born of His Mother without any diminution of her maternal virginity, just as He afterwards went forth from the sepulchre while it was closed and sealed, and entered the room in which His disciples were assembled, the doors being shut; or, not to depart from every-day examples, just as the rays of the sun penetrate without breaking or injuring in the least the solid substance of glass, so after a like but more exalted manner did Jesus Christ come forth from His mother's womb without injury to her maternal virginity. This immaculate and perpetual virginity forms, therefore, the just theme of our eulogy. Such was the work of the Holy Ghost, who at the Conception and birth of the Son so favored the Virgin Mother as to impart to her fecundity while preserving inviolate her perpetual virginity.... To Eve it was said: *In sorrow shalt thou bring forth children.* Mary was exempt from this law, for preserving her virginal integrity inviolate she brought forth Jesus the Son of God without experiencing, as we have already said, any sense of pain. The mysteries of this admirable Conception and Nativity being, therefore, so great and so numerous, it accorded with the plan of divine Providence to signify them by many types and prophecies. Hence the Holy Fathers understood many things which we meet in the Sacred Scriptures to refer to these mysteries, particularly that gate of the sanctuary which Ezechiel saw closed [Ezech. 44:2]; the stone cut out of the mountain without hands, which became a great mountain and filled the universe, of which we read in Daniel [Dan. 2:35]; the rod of Aaron, which alone budded of all the rods of the princes of Israel [Num. 17:8]; and the bush which Moses saw burn without being consumed [Exod. 3:2]." [Editor]

5. *Lumen Gentium* 62.

6. Even if this is not solemnly defined Catholic dogma, nevertheless Pope Leo XIII in his 1891 encyclical *Octobri mense* affirmed: "Nothing at all of the very great treasure of every grace, which the Lord confers, since 'grace and truth came by Jesus Christ' [John 1:17], nothing is imparted to us except through Mary, God so willing; so, just as no one can approach the highest Father except through the Son, so no one can approach Christ

except through His Mother." This was not a teaching that Leo XIII expounded only once. In his 1896 encyclical *Fidentem*, he wrote: "For, surely, no one person can be conceived who has ever made, or at any time will make an equal contribution as Mary to the reconciliation of men with God. Surely, she it was who brought the Savior to man as he was rushing into eternal destruction, at that very time when, with wonderful assent, she received 'in place of human nature' the message of the peace making sacrament brought to earth by the Angel; she it is 'of whom was born Jesus' [Matt. 1:16], namely, His true Mother, and for this reason she is worthy and quite acceptable as the *mediatrix to the Mediator.*" (Denziger's *The Sources of Catholic Dogma*, n. 1940a, emphasis in original) Teachings on Mary as "co-redemptress" and "mediatrix" were later reiterated by Popes Pius X, Benedict XV, and Pius XI (see Denziger, n. 1978a). [Editor]

7. "The Church's reflection on the mystery of Christ and on her own nature has led her to find at the root of the former and as a culmination of the latter the same figure of a Woman: the Virgin Mary, the Mother of Christ and Mother of the Church. And the increased knowledge of Mary's mission has become joyful veneration of her and adoring respect for the wise plan of God, who has placed within His family (the Church), as in every home, the figure of a Woman, who in a hidden manner and in a spirit of service watches over that family and carefully looks after it until the glorious day of the Lord. Anyone who with trust in God reflects upon present-day phenomena discovers that many tendencies of modern piety are meant to play their part in the development of devotion to the Blessed Virgin. Thus our own time, faithfully attentive to tradition and to the progress of theology and the sciences will make its contributions of praise to her whom, according to her own prophetic words, all generations will call blessed." (*Devotion to the Blessed Virgin*, Pope Paul VI)

Made in the USA
Columbia, SC
14 April 2018